Canadian Resource Policies

CONTRIBUTORS

Dr. Mary L. Barker, Associate Professor, Department of Geography, Simon Fraser University, Burnaby, B.C.

Dr. Dianne Draper, Assistant Professor, Department of Geography, Memorial University, St. John's, Nfld.

Dr. Harold D. Foster, Professor, Department of Geography, University of Victoria, Victoria, B.C.

Dr. Peter Harrison, former Associate Professor, Department of Geography, University of Ottawa. Now Assistant Director, Energy and Resources Policy, Department of Finance, Ottawa.

Felix A. Kwamena, Ph.D. candidate, Department of Geography, University of Ottawa, Ottawa, Ontario.

Dr. Alexander G. McLellan, Associate Professor, Department of Geography, University of Waterloo, Waterloo, Ontario.

Dr. Bruce Mitchell, Professor, Department of Geography, University of Waterloo, Waterloo, Ontario.

Dr. W.R. Derrick Sewell, Professor, Department of Geography, University of Victoria, Victoria, B.C.

Donald Tate, Water Planning and Management Branch, Inland Waters Directorate, Environment Canada, Ottawa, Ontario.

Dr. Geoffrey Wall, Associate Professor, Department of Geography, University of Waterloo, Waterloo, Ontario.

Dr. William C. Wonders, Professor, Department of Geography, University of Alberta, Edmonton, Alta.

CANADIAN RESOURCE POLICIES: PROBLEMS and PROSPECTS

Edited by
Bruce Mitchell, University of Waterloo
W.R. Derrick Sewell, University of Victoria

Methuen
Toronto New York London Sydney Auckland

Canadian Cataloguing in Publication Data
Main entry under title:
Canadian resource policies

Includes index.
ISBN 0-458-94970-1

1. Environmental policy—Canada.   2. Conservation
of natural resources—Canada. I. Mitchell, Bruce,
1944-   II. Sewell, W.R. Derrick, 1931-

HC120.E5C36   333.7′15′0971   C81-094648-3

51,404

Printed and bound in Canada

1 2 3 4 5   81   86 85 84 83 82

Contents

Preface

Events of the past decade have indicated clearly that resource development and environmental management will be among the most critical issues facing Canadian policy makers in the 1980s and 1990s. Problems concerning the exploitation of energy resources in the West and the North, conflicts over the use of oceans, and increasing pressures on recreational resources offer a few illustrations. Canadian researchers have done useful work in connection with some of these matters. Many of the problems, however, are not well understood. Even where the issues have been identified, the best course of action is not always evident. Alternative management responses offer strengths and weaknesses. None are perfect. Trade-offs and compromises usually are required to accommodate the multiple and often conflicting interests. Thus, as we move into the 1980s, it is an opportune time to assess some of the major issues, the strategies adopted and lines of research required.

This book is a collection of specially commissioned essays by geographers from across the country. The studies focus upon major issues to be faced over the next two decades, including energy, northern lands, coastal zones, fisheries, river basins, land rehabilitation, natural disasters and recreation. In addition, introductory and concluding chapters identify general constraints upon and opportunities for resource policy makers, as well as general patterns of resource management and development, research accomplishments and future research and personnel needs. The inevitable limitations of length made it necessary to be selective in commissioning the chapters. We are well aware that some important Canadian resources and management issues have not been covered. Nevertheless, we think that those covered are ones which are the most important.

Each author has drawn upon his or her own experience in preparing a chapter and has developed those aspects deemed to be most significant. While individuals had flexibility in preparing their chapters, they were asked to consider the following questions: (1) how serious are the management and development problems, and where is their incidence most severe in Canada? (2) what actions have been taken to deal with them? (3) to what extent have the strategies and actions succeeded and where have they failed? (4) what have been the characteristics of Canadian research effort relative to the problems? (5) what future research and actions are needed to resolve these problems? Not every author could treat each of these five questions in a balanced fashion, but these questions do provide a common thread and link between the chapters.

We would like to thank the authors who prepared the chapters for this book. Others also have provided valuable help which has been very much appreciated. Joan Mitchell obtained the necessary copyright permissions and assisted in preparation of the index. Ian Norie and his staff, Diane Brazier, Ken Josephson, and Ken Quan at the University of Victoria cartographic centre prepared all of the illustrations. Judith deBacker of Methuen was helpful and encouraging throughout.

Bruce Mitchell, Waterloo, Ontario
W.R. Derrick Sewell, Victoria, B.C.
April, 1981

1/The Emerging Scene

Bruce Mitchell and W.R. Derrick Sewell

Canada is viewed with envy by many nations which see a country endowed with a vast storehouse of natural resources. To many of these nations facing such problems as famine and poverty, Canada's resource "problems" are the ones they would like to have in place of their own dilemmas. Yet, within Canada, the question of how to allocate these resources is straining the fabric of the nation. Resource allocation has become symbolic of different interpretations as to the role of federal and provincial governments in governing the country, and the way to balance national and regional interests. Such fundamental concerns comprise the basic components of the emerging scene in resource management for Canada during the 1980s.

Other significant patterns also are appearing. The future offers the challenge of massive resource development projects, such as oil sands recovery plants and hydroelectric schemes, which will provide substantial challenges to the technological and financial skills of Canadians. Simultaneously, the emerging scene requires efforts to balance the benefits of such large-scale developments to the general population against the social and environmental impacts borne by a relatively small segment of it. The emerging scene also involves the appearance of the local or municipal level of government as an important participant in the resource allocation process through its involvement in mangement of environmentally sensitive areas and regulation of resource extraction activities.

Other aspects may be cited to suggest that the issues of the 1980s will not be identical to those of the 1970s: acid rain, disposal of toxic wastes, environmental health and safety, the conserver society. It is essential that Canadians become aware of the emerging scene so that policies address present and future needs rather than those which already are passing us by.

While the level of preparedness for emerging problems must be improved, future actions must be conceived, designed and implemented with awareness of current limitations. Thus, the purpose of this chapter is to explore the emerging scene associated with resource management. In this light, management policy and practice in Canada can evoke conflicting reactions from an observer. On one hand, major obstacles seem to frustrate or defeat management efforts. These obstacles arise in the form of incomplete information, divided and fragmented responsibilities, poorly integrated institutional arrangements, trade-offs and compromises, diffused and changing public interests, unresponsive educational structures, external events and decisions, foreign control of resource industries, and lack of political commitment. On the other hand, new problems and opportunities are identified, analyzed and tackled, more advanced concepts are developed and refined, new legislation is proclaimed, new organizational structures are developed, and innovative programs are implemented. In the remainder of this chapter, these barriers to and achievements in resource management are reviewed.

Barriers to Effective Resource Management
Incomplete Information
Whenever resource planners and managers get together, a frequently heard complaint is that there is too little data to reach decisions, that existing data are not in useful forms, and that the data are not available at appropriate scales.[1] However, it is naive or overly simplistic to hope that more information will resolve management problems. Difficult questions have to be addressed to ensure that information is of the right type. For what purpose is the information needed? At what scale and in which form should data be collected? Which resources should be inventoried? Which areas or regions should be surveyed? How frequently should the inventory be updated? Until these kinds of questions are resolved, there is little likelihood that collection of additional information will contribute to the solution of resource management problems.

Another aspect also deserves attention. While new information can be helpful, it is not assembled without expenditure of funds and the passage of time. A trade-off must be made between the cost and the value of acquiring more data. A point may be reached where the value of extra information is not proportional to the effort required to obtain it. In this context, it usually is recognized that managers can not collect data and study endlessly. A stage is reached where conflicts and issues demand action rather than further study and discussion.[2]

Many resource inventory systems have been established in Canada. Thus, basic data on water resources are collected at both the provincial and federal levels. Data are collected for lake and river levels, streamflow, sedimentation, groundwater, water quality and water use.[3] However, as Quinn and Spence note, no really accurate measurement is available for the extent, character or distribution of Canadian water resources. Many rivers are not gauged. Not all lakes have been counted. Uniform criteria for groundwater and water quality do not exist across the country.[4]

Other inventories and surveys exist for such aspects as vegetation, geology and fisheries at national and provincial scales. However, one of the most frequently used inventories in resource management is the Canada

Land Inventory. It is discussed in detail here to illustrate some of the opportunities and constraints of inventory systems.

One outcome of the Resources for Tomorrow Conference in 1961 was a recommendation for a comprehensive land capability survey in Canada. A need was seen for an inventory which incorporated a number of resources on a comparable basis at a national scale and which identified actual and potential use. These aspects became components of the Canada Land Inventory (CLI) which was developed during the early 1960s.[5] In addition to inventorying actual land use in the populated areas of Canada, the CLI incorporated capability inventories for agriculture, forestry, recreation, and wildlife. Seven capability classes ranging from very high (Class 1) to virtually zero capability (Class 7) were developed for each of the four resource sectors. The CLI program remains as the basic national resource inventory system in Canada, although during the mid 1970s work began on developing an ecological land classification system in which the biological and physical features of land resources are recorded without reference to any particular resource or land-use activity.[6]

The CLI information has proven valuable for reaching decisions regarding most appropriate uses of land, for planning to reduce regional economic disparities, and for resolving resource and land-use conflicts. However, it is essential to recognize that the CLI has real limitations which have always been recognized by the designers of the system, but often are overlooked by those using it in problem-solving situations.

The CLI was designed for use at the *regional* level of planning and management. The capability maps have been published on a national basis at a scale of 1:250,000, with special consideration for conditions in some provinces. Thus, due to the highly variable topography in British Columbia, the agriculture and forestry maps for that province were published at a scale of 1:125,000. When we recall that we can only delineate areas as small as just over 8 hectares (20 acres) at a scale of 1:63,360, it is apparent that the CLI maps should be used for regional rather than site planning. Unfortunately, users forget this limitation, try to use the maps for purposes for which they were never intended, and then complain about their "weaknesses" and "limitations."

Another problem is the basis of the capability classes. For agriculture, forestry and wildlife, the classes were established regarding the *degree of limitation* of the resource base for the productivity in that sector. Conversely, with recreation, the classes were based on the intensity of recreational activity which could be sustained. In other words, the different recreation classes reflect attributes of the resources which provide *opportunity* for recreational activity. This difference in the underlying rationale for the classes makes it difficult to draw direct comparisons between resource sectors. If resource planners do not understand the criteria for the classes, they are likely to conclude that an area mapped as

Class 2 forestry and Class 4 recreation would be best allocated to forestry. This type of comparison is not appropriate.

A related concern is that the capability rating is not explicitly related to production or yield measures except for the forest resource. For agriculture, Nowland and McKeague have shown that Class 1 and 2 lands in the Prairie Provinces have a much lower productive capacity than Class 1 and 2 land in Ontario.[7] Also, they can not be used for as many crops. On the other hand, the greater production per hectare in Ontario is achieved through higher consumption of energy in the form of fuel, equipment, fertilizer, and pesticides. Nowland and McKeague concluded that regional differences in productivity and energy consumption in lands rated in the same CLI class emphasize the need to ascertain the versatility of land for different uses, the investment required to overcome physical limitations, the significance of managment skills, and the nature of technology to be applied. Different levels of investment, managerial skills and technologies can result in substantially different productivity from one parcel of land, let alone two parcels ranked as similar under the CLI capability classification.

This abbreviated discussion of the CLI system suggests that the concern about "inadequate information" requires qualification. The CLI provides useful data for reconnaissance or regional level decisions for a variety of resources. However, not all resources are covered, and limitations most certainly exist. Many of the problems with CLI arise when users attempt to use the system for purposes for which it was never intended. Recognition of its original purpose and assumptions would help to alleviate many of the frustrations associated with it. At the same time, there are many functions that it can not satisfy, and there is no viable alternative.

A separate aspect relates to the role of the private and the public sectors in assembling information pertinent to resource management. For some resource sectors, such as energy, concern arises because the public regulatory agencies often are dependent on the private sector for information about potential recoverable reserves. When the National Energy Board decides whether Canada has surplus natural gas, its decision partially rests on data from the private sector concerning its estimates of available reserves. A regulatory agency having to rely on those being regulated for even some of the information on which regulatory decisions are made is clearly in an awkward position, especially when the implications of its decisions for such things as prices, anticipated reserves and export permits are so significant.

This dilemma is one which is likely to exist for many years, given the nature of the investment needed to collect the desired data. Awareness of the need for an independent source for such data was one of the reasons behind the establishment of Petrocan by the federal government. As Petrocan gains experience in the exploration for and development of energy-related resources, it should be able to provide a counterbalance to the information being produced by the private sector.

Our information about natural resources has shortcomings, and is likely always to be that way. The size of the country in itself presents a major barrier to the establishment and maintenance of a comprehensive resource inventory at a national level. Even if the funds were available for such information gathering, technical and measurement problems would result in an imperfect record of the resource base. This barrier must be recognized in approaching resource management in Canada. Key decisions hinge on the provision of better information, including whether to export oil, natural gas or water to the United States, the establishment of carrying capacity thresholds for use of recreational areas, and the use of pricing mechanisms to encourage conservation of resources.

Divided and Fragmented Responsibility

Jurisdictional control regarding natural resources and the environment is divided between the federal and provincial governments under the British North America Act, 1867. A distinction usually is made between proprietary rights and legislative authority (Table 1.1). Under Section 109, proprietary rights for natural resources were placed under the jurisdiction of the provinces. Even then, Alberta, Saskatchewan and Manitoba did not gain proprietary rights until 1930. On the federal level, proprietary rights are held for the Canadian North (91-Preamble).

The legislative authority is more mixed, and has been a source of considerable tension. The federal government's jurisdiction over trade and commerce gives it substantial control over both interprovincial and export trading of resource products (91-2). This has greatly frustrated provinces such as Alberta, Saskatchewan and British Columbia over sales of oil and natural gas. Their governments have regarded the setting of prices and selection of buyers for such resources as being related to their legislative authority over property and civil rights (92-13) and matters of local interest (92-16), and have resented the actions of the federal authority in regulating such prices and the negotiation of sales.

The federal government has the right to impose indirect as well as direct taxes (91-3), whereas the provinces are confined to direct taxes (92-2). This situation also has created debate between the resource-producing provinces, especially regarding oil and natural gas (Alberta, Saskatchewan, British Columbia) and potash (Saskatchewan) and the federal government.[8] Indeed, it has led to provincial demands for the federal government to withraw from regulation of interprovincial and export trade, as well as for the provinces to be given the right to levy indirect taxes.

The federal government also has used its legislative authority over navigation and shipping (91-10) to establish regulations for pollution. Similarly, responsibility for marine and inland fisheries (91-12) has been used both for fishery management and for pollution control regulation. The federal involvement in fisheries has generated a number of situations which illustrate the types of problems arising under divided jurisdiction.

Table 1.1
Jurisdictional Responsibility for Natural
Resources Under the British North America Act, 1867

Federal Government

Section 91 (Preamble) ... for the peace, order and good government of Canada, in relation to all matters not coming directly within the classes of subjects by this Act assigned exclusively to the Legislatures of the Provinces ....

91 (1) The public debt and property

91 (2) The regulation of trade and commerce

91(3) The raising of money by any mode or system of taxation

91 (10) Navigation and shipping

91 (12) Sea coast and inland fisheries

91 (24) Indians and lands reserved for Indians

91 (29) Such classes of subjects as are expressly excepted in the enumeration of the classes of subjects by this Act assigned exclusively to the Legislatures of the Provinces

Provincial Governments

Section 92 (2) Direct taxation within the Province in order to the raising of a revenue for Provincial purpose

92 (5) The management and sale of the public lands belonging to the Province, and of the timber and wood thereon

92 (8) Municipal institutions in the Province

92 (10a) Local works and undertakings other than such as are of the following classes: Lines of steam or other ships, railways, canals, telegraphs and other works and undertakings connecting the Province with any other or others of the Provinces, or extending beyond the limits of the Province ....

92 (13) Property and Civil rights in the Province.

92 (16) Generally all matters of merely local or private nature in the Province

Section 109 All lands, mines, minerals and royalties belonging to the several provinces of Canada. ...

Both Levels of Government

Section 95 In each province the Legislature may make laws in relation to agriculture in the province. . . .; and it is hereby declared that the Parliament of Canada may from time to time make laws in relation to agriculture in all or any of the provinces, . . .; and any law in the Legislature of a Province relative to agriculture ... shall have effect in and for the province as long and as far only as it is not repugnant to any Act of the Parliament of Canada.

During June 1980, the Supreme Court of Canada ruled parts of the federal Fisheries Act to be *ultra vires*, or going beyond the powers granted to the federal government. Jurisdiction over fisheries had facilitated federal involvement in pollution control, but the decision opened the way for only the provinces to regulate the dumping of debris and other forms of pollutants into provincial waterways used by fish. The case dealt with a B.C. logger charged in 1975 with dumping parts of trees and other debris into a small stream at Forbes Bay some 150 kilometres upcoast of Vancouver. Federal fisheries officers laid charges on the basis that the stream was used for spawning by salmon. However, the fisheries officers could not prove that the debris had actually harmed the salmon.

The Supreme Court judge rejected the charge on the grounds that a blanket prohibition of logging, an activity subject to provincial jurisdiction (Table 1.1, 92-5), was unacceptable if based on an unproven charge of damage to the fishery resource. To accept such a charge would be to acknowledge proprietary rights by the federal government over the fishery resource. The Court's view over a series of decisions consistently has been that the BNA Act does not give the federal government property rights to the rivers or fisheries, but rather jurisdiction to regulate for protection and preservation of stocks.

In the same month a different conflict arose when the federal Minister of Fisheries ordered Alcan Aluminum Ltd. to increase water levels in the Nechako River in north-central British Columbia to protect spawning salmon. The initial response of the company was to defy the order on the basis that it was unconsitutional for the federal government to intervene in fresh-water rivers and streams which fell under provincial jurisdiction. Alcan argued that it had signed an agreement with the B.C. government during 1950 which left it responsible only to the B.C. comptroller of water rights. After a B.C. Supreme Court justice validated the federal order in August 1980, Alcan accepted the order and raised the water levels.

This conflict illustrates the difficulties of resource management under divided jurisdiction. The B.C. forestry companies view the federal Fisheries Act as "single purpose" legislation since it was prepared with a view to protect and enhance the fishery. The Act does not consider the needs of other resource activities, such as logging, which is a provincial responsibility. Thus, a resource user could be caught between two jurisdictions, each one providing conflicting signals as to what constitutes appropriate behaviour.

The ambiguity and inconsistencies in jurisdiction over resources has been a major and continuing issue in Canada. During negotiations on constitutional reform between the federal and provincial governments, three of the twelve high-priority items were resource-oriented: (1) resource ownership and interprovincial trade, (2) offshore resources, (3) fisheries jurisdiction. However these issues are resolved, it is highly likely that in a federal system Canadians will continue to experience divided, fragmentary and inconsistent jurisdiction over resources. It is a reality within which resource management probably will always have to function. It also is likely that this situation will inhibit development of any truly national resource policies. There always will be federal and provincial policies which separately or in aggregate will not represent a comprehensive national policy.

Poorly Integrated Institutional Arrangements

If institutional arrangements are viewed as the mix of legislation and public agencies established to guide and implement resource management decisions, it is not surprising that difficulty is encountered in realizing integrated management of resources. At federal, provincial, regional and municipal levels there is a host of laws and agencies which often work at cross purposes to one another.

Referring to the federal level, Woodrow has described a variety of agencies involved in resource management.[9] During 1966 the Department of Indian and Northern Affairs was created to handle the social and economic development of Canada's North. This agency has struggled with a mandate that has required it to be concerned with both economic development and preservation of the environment and the cultural heritage of native peoples. In the same year, the Department of Energy, Mines and Resources was established. During the 1970s, energy became of increasing significance, and the Department sought to develop national energy policy. This task was complicated by the fact that the provinces have proprietary control over such key resources as coal, oil and natural gas. The outcome has been that the Energy, Mines and Resources "energy policy" has been a federal rather than a truly national policy.

Supported by the public interest in pollution and other environmental problems during the late 1960s and early 1970s, the federal government established a Department of the Environment in 1970. Given a mandate to protect air, water and land resources, this department has been described by Whittington as "a virtual patchwork of odds and ends and sundry organizational 'orphans.'"[10] An existing Department of Fisheries and Forestry was joined with units from the Department of Transport (meteorological service), Department of Health and Welfare (air pollution, public health), Department of Energy, Mines and Resources (water), Department of Regional Economic Expansion (land inventory), and Department of Indian and Northern Affairs (wildlife). Although the rationale was that this new department would provide a vehicle for an integrated approach to renewable resource management, the loose coalition has resulted in the different units tending to concentrate on their own areas of concern. In effect, while the units have been regrouped under a new name, they have continued to approach their respective functions just as they had when scattered among many separate departments. That the reorganizational process is a continuous one is demonstrated by the fact that in the late 1970s fisheries was allocated to a department of its own under the name of the Department of Fisheries and Oceans. This splitting of fisheries from other renewable resources suggests that a clearly thought out rationale for renewable resources management has yet to be developed.

While federal agencies have been used as examples here, the same patterns appear at the provincial level. Furthermore, when joint federal-provincial efforts become necessary due to the mix of legislative and proprietary interests, the complexity increases geometrically. In a study of coastal zone management in Atlantic Canada, Pross identified 8 agencies at the federal level and 34 at the provincial (shared among New Brunswick, Nova Scotia, Prince Edward Island, and Newfoundland) whose interests had to be accommodated.[11] Jessen, analyzing the approach to environmental and resources management associated with development of the Nanticoke industrial complex on the north shore of Lake Erie, discovered the potential involvement of eighteen agencies at three levels of government as well as 33 statutes and agreements.[12] A federal-provincial strategic planning exercise for Ontario fisheries recognized the potential role of 19 federal agencies, 13 provincial agencies, 54 federal statutes and 44 provincial statutes.[13] These complications are not confined to federal-provincial joint ventures. A review of regional government in one area of Ontario deplored the number of agencies (provincial, regional, municipal) involved in water management and made the extreme recommendation of disbanding the local Conservation Authority in the spirit of reducing the layers of government.[14]

Just as an inadequate information base and divided responsibility are part of the context for resource management in Canada, so is the proliferation of agencies and statutes. This pattern is unlikely to alter significantly during the 1980s and 1990s, as governments attempt to address the many needs of society. Reorganization of government structures will undoubtedly occur, but there will always remain the difficulty of achieving balance between specialist knowledge in selected areas and integrating expertise from disparate areas. No simple solution exists for this difficult problem. Super-ministries, coordinating agencies and decentralization all have strengths and weaknesses. Ultimately, the capability to achieve integration and cooperation depends upon the willingness of individuals working in specific policy fields or problem areas. Unless the individual inclination is present to share and to assist, it is unlikely that such activity can be attained through legislative or administrative means.

On a brighter note, the potential maze of agencies and red tape which emerges from a paper analysis of institutional arrangements does not always appear in reality. While theoretical arrangements frequently are formal and complicated, actual arrangements often are informal and simplified. Designation of lead agencies and acceptance of specified roles can result in workable systems. Nevertheless, the complex superstructure exists and can be invoked by anyone who wishes to delay or frustrate the management process.

Trade-offs and Compromises

The web of jurisdictional and institutional arrangements which often runs counter to attempts at realizing integrated resource management partially reflects the fact that resources are but one of society's concerns. Thus, in addition to posing potentially adverse environmental effects, an oil or natural gas pipeline offers the prospect of a stable and reliable energy supply for residential, commercial, industrial and transportation purposes. A factory or smelter which may cause air pollution offers the prospect of additional jobs. In brief, the environmental or resource consideration is but one of many which must be assessed by officials responsible for meeting society's often conflicting demands.

The existence of conflicting demands stresses that trade-offs and compromises are likely to be the order of the day. The individual who approaches resource management without recognizing this fact wears blinkers. Furthermore, we must recognize that trade-offs do not occur just within the resource sector. Resources may be traded-off to gain benefits in other policy areas. From the resource management viewpoint this may appear like an unsystematic and irrational way to allocate resources. However, the underlying question is whether these kinds of decisions in aggregate improve social conditions. If they do, we should be less quick to criticize such decisions.

In this context, resources may be traded-off to obtain other things, or used as mechanisms to achieve gains in other areas. Dosman has noted that the Arctic Waters Pollution Prevention Act, passed by Parliament in April 1970, can be criticized since it establishes rigorous standards for vessels, but does not regulate off-shore drilling for oil.[15] On this basis, many have viewed the legislation as inadequate for the problem of controlling pollution in Arctic waters. On the other hand, the Act may be viewed as an astute response to the direct U.S. challenge to Canadian sovereignty of Arctic waters resulting from the 1969 and 1970 voyages of the S.S. *Manhattan*. Although never explicitly stated as such, asserting Canadian sovereignty rather than regulating pollution may have been the primary motivation which led to the Act.

Other situations where trade-offs could occur can easily be imagined, especially at the international level. During the late 1970s and early 1980s the Canadian and American governments were involved in discussions over fisheries management on the Georges Bank, acid rain problems, Great Lakes water quality, the Garrison diversion, the sale of oil and natural gas, as well as with such apparently unrelated matters as auto trade pacts and defence agreements. In situations where such a mix of events is under consideration, "horse-trading" is to be expected. Thus, looked at in isolation, an apparently weak Canadian position on a specific resource issue may appear difficult to comprehend. However, viewing the larger package, it may well be that Canada consciously decided to "sacrifice" or compromise on a resource issue to realize a gain in another sector. The total net benefits of such decisions then must be appraised rather than those associated with any specific one.

The implication of this kind of situation is significant. It means that resource management decisions often are not going to be made by individuals whose main interest is in resource mangement. For example, at the federal level, individuals in the Department of External Affairs are likely to be as equally or even more influential in decisions affecting resources. These individuals also are likely to be more than willing to "sacrifice" resources for gains elsewhere. Elected officials with limited budgets are forced to seek compromises and trade-offs to accommodate the many demands placed on the public purse. Such decisions are made in all countries, so Canada certainly is not unique. Nevertheless, this pattern should be recognized by resource managers if they are to get the system to work in a way which gives fair attention to resource and environmental matters.

Diffused and Changing Public Interests

Those responsible for resource and environmental policy must accept that this policy field experiences varied and changing public interest. During the 1960s, Canadians generally became more aware of problems of pollution and environmental quality. This was reflected in conferences such as that organized by the Canadian Council of Resource Ministers on "Pollution and our Environment" in November 1966 and the one by the revised Canadian Council of Resource and Environment Ministers on "Man and Resources" in November 1973. During the early 1970s the federal and provincial governments established environmental ministries to wrestle with problems of air and water pollution, and spawned numerous statutes keyed to environmental problems. At the federal level, legislation such as the Canada Water Act, Clean Air Act, Arctic Waters Pollution Act and the Environmental Contaminants Act was passed.

During the 1960s a general atmosphere of affluence and economic well-being prevailed, allowing governments to allocate more funds and personnel to policies and programs designed to enhance the quality of life across the country. However, by the early 1970s, this pattern started to alter. The "energy crisis," initiated in 1973 by the price increases for oil by OPEC nations, served as a warning that resources were not infinite. Problems with increasing energy costs and other factors contributed to an unsettled and troubled world economy. As unemployment rates and inflation climbed, the general public and elected officials became less intrigued with environmental issues and became concerned with other issues such as job creation and economic growth. Environmental concerns often began to be viewed as placing unnecessary constraints upon economic development. As Whittington observed in 1980,

The "motherhood" issues of the sixties—the "sacred cows" such as water quality, clean air, forest conservation, and preservation of wildlife—look insignificant compared to issues such as unemployment, inflation and energy short-falls. It seems our sacred cows become expendable when the price of beef goes up![16]

This waning public interest in environmental issues closely fits the pattern sketched by Downs in his "issue-attention cycle."[17] Through this model, Downs suggested that issues or crises pass through five stages characterized by lack of public awareness, alarmed discovery and euphoric enthusiasm, realization of the costs for solution, gradual decline of intense public interest, and prolonged limbo (Figure 1.1).

While public and political interest shifted away from earlier pollution and environmental quality problems, other resource-based issues have arisen in their place. The emergence of acid rain on the public agenda in 1979 represented the continuance of pollution as an issue, even if in a new form. The disposal of toxic wastes, and the broad area of environmental health, attracted attention as society tried to find satisfactory ways in which to store chemicals and other hazardous wastes after their use. Indeed, such was the perceived urgency to find a site for disposal of liquid industrial wastes in Ontario that during late 1980 the government selected a site at South Cayuga, only five kilometres from the Lake Erie north shore, without conducting an environmental impact assessment. This prompted the opposition political parties to argue that the environmental review process was being abused, while the Minister of the Environment argued that he "made no apologies whatsoever for attacking what is one of the most serious social problems in this province and getting on with the job."[18]

Energy self-sufficiency became an important concept, as Canadians tried to reduce the impact of increasingly expensive imported oil. The concern over energy stimulated the concept of the *Conserver Society* as a response to apparently depleting natural resources. As described by the Science Council of Canada, a Conserver Society on principle seeks to avoid waste and pollution.[19] Such a society is also characterized by: (1) promoting economy of design in all systems (doing more with less), (2) favoring recycling and, wherever feasible, reduction of waste at the source, (3) questioning an ever-growing demand for consumer goods, and (4) seeking a diversity of solutions to gain economy, stability and resiliency. Pilot projects such as the ARK community on Prince Edward Island have been

Figure 1.1

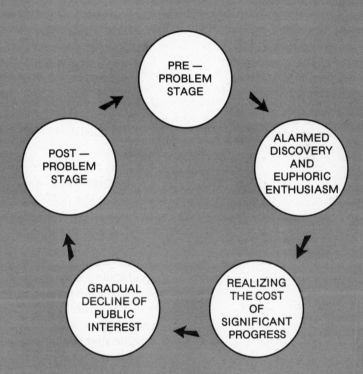

THE ISSUE-ATTENTION CYCLE

PRE —
PROBLEM
STAGE

ALARMED
DISCOVERY
AND
EUPHORIC
ENTHUSIASM

POST —
PROBLEM
STAGE

REALIZING
THE COST
OF
SIGNIFICANT
PROGRESS

GRADUAL
DECLINE OF
PUBLIC
INTEREST

SOURCE: after A. Downs

established to test the feasibility of different ideas emerging from the conserver society concept.

The social impact of resource development also drew attention. The lands claims by native peoples became a major issue in assessing resource projects such as pipelines in the Canadian North.[20] Provinces such as Newfoundland with prospects of oil development began to insist that its residents be given priority over other Canadians for much-wanted jobs. Eldorado Nuclear Ltd. had a proposal for a uranium refinery at Warman, Saskatchewan, rejected by a federal environmental assessment panel due to its potential negative impact on the largely Mennonite community in the area.[21]

There is little doubt that there is both a diffused and changing public interest regarding resource management issues. This situation creates difficulty for both the resource practitioner and researcher. Both usually require long time horizons either to see substantive results or to acquire indepth understanding relative to problems. As public interests shift from issue to issue, it often is difficult to obtain the sustained commitment of funds and personnel to see a task through to completion. This aspect provides another real constraint upon resource management in Canada.

Educational Structure

The postsecondary educational structure has been slow to respond to the need for individuals with an appreciation of resource policy and management issues as well as specific problem-solving skills. Individuals are required who have an understanding of the full range of basic resource management activities, from policy formulation and strategic planning through resource inventory, classification and evaluation, to implementation and monitoring. Unfortunately, organizational structures at universities which are based on disciplines provide little opportunity for students to be exposed to the necessary cross-section of concepts, methods and approaches.

On the positive side, new programs focussed upon resource management have appeared at the master's level. At Simon Fraser University, a two-year interdisciplinary resource management degree program started in the fall of 1979. The University of Manitoba has a master's program in natural resources with a regional economic development and project management focus. In Ontario, two programs are found. At the University of Guelph, a graduate program in resources was reorganized during 1980 to emphasize rural planning and resource development. At Queen's University, cooperation among the university, the private sector and government has led to a research centre for mineral resources. In the Maritimes, a program had been created through the Dalhousie Institute for Resource and Environmental Studies with special interest in fisheries, marine law and coastal zone management. Simultaneously, graduate programs in environmental studies have been created at such universities as Calgary, Toronto, York and Waterloo. Thus, across the nation, a number of programs have been developed, although the number of graduates being produced is relatively small.

Another concern about many educational institutions is their lack of concern about applied issues. Academics, and their students, when offering solutions to problems often ignore or neglect the practical constraints which limit the options of managers. Consequently, much academic research has little value for those struggling with the implementation and maintenance of resource policies. In addition to overlooking practical implications, Clark has noted that academics can be faulted for substantiating conventional wisdom at great length, getting over-concerned with methodology at the expense of problems, and assuming a level of refinement that goes beyond reasonable time and monetary constraints.[22]

One response to the concern about lack of practical orientation has been the development of cooperative education programs in which students systematically alternate study and work terms. A "co-op" degree takes longer to complete because of the work terms, but the student gains practical expererience along the way. Introduced into Canada at the University of Waterloo, cooperative education is now offered at a variety of Canadian universities. Cooperative programs in geography are available at Waterloo and the University of Victoria, while Ryerson Polytechnic Institute in Toronto has an applied geography degree program which requires practical work experience as a condition for graduation.

The cooperative approach offers one alternative to the regular academic programs. However, a cloud may be on the horizon. As more universities develop cooperative options, increasing competition will arise in obtaining work term positions for the students. A point will be reached when there might not be enough jobs to support all of the programs and all will be affected adversely. Hopefully this is a potential problem which can be resolved as the cooperative experience can be a rewarding one.

While educational institutions seem to be inherently conservative, there are some encouraging trends. Graduate programs specializing in resource management and undergraduate cooperative programs represent innovations which are relatively recent in Canadian postsecondary education. Counterbalancing these events is the academic inclination to ignore practical issues or to overlook real-world constraints when attempting to develop solutions to practical problems. These latter conditions are likely to exist as long as there are academics.

External Events and Decisions
Resource management in Canada is influenced by events and decisions outside the country which can have substantial implications upon resource allocation decisions in this country. Perhaps the most visible of these was

the Arab-Israeli war, the Arab embargo on oil shipments and then the OPEC decision to increase oil prices during 1973. Since that part of Canada east of the Ottawa River is dependent upon imported oil, pricing decisions by the exporting nations have a great impact on Canadian balance of payments. Such decisions also influence resource policy in Canada by serving as a stimulus to policies for energy self-sufficiency, and encouraging such concepts as the Conserver Society.

Investment decisions for resource exploration and development are also affected not only by policies within Canada, but by positions taken in other countries. Thus, if Canadian regulations become too restrictive relative to conditions elsewhere, multinational corporations will adjust their investment patterns accordingly. This situation creates tension for Canadian policy makers who often must juggle conflicting values and goals. Hence, in an effort to gain greater control of the national economy, the federal government implemented the Foreign Investment Review Act during 1974 to screen potential takeovers.[23] However, during the late 1970s, federal and provincial governments sough to attract foreign investment in order to stimulate economic growth and creation of jobs. One impediment to such investment was the Foreign Investment Review Agency which slowed investment by erecting another hurdle for investors.

External decisions, however, may sometimes work to Canada's advantage. In this country, our control on the health hazard of mercury is the use of a 0.5 parts per million (ppm) standard. If fish contain more mercury than that standard, they are banned from commercial sale and the fishery may be closed. Conversely, other countries such as the United States have a more lenient standard of 1.0 ppm. Thus, rather than closing a commercial fishery when the fish exceed 0.5 ppm mercury, the Canadian authorities could leave the fishery open, but restrict the fish to the export market. In this manner, the livelihood of the fishermen would not be damaged. Indeed, this procedure has been applied to catches of tuna in the East Coast fishery. The tuna have not been allowed into Canada, but are exported to the U.S. market.

The role of external events and decisions is likely to become more significant in the future. Multinational corporations are continuously diversifying and expanding, and scan the global economy to decide where the best returns on investment will be obtained. At the same time, decisions by other governments make Canada more or less attractive as a place to invest. This condition will be particularly important for energy-related investment, an area of great significance for the 1980s and 1990s.

Lack of Control
While external events and decisions partially take control of resource allocation decisions away from Canadian policy makers, investment within the country by foreign firms and individuals in resource-based activities

also reduces Canadian control over resources. However, this aspect is within the sphere of possible control if politicians decide that the benefits of such regulation outweight the costs.

The scope of foreign investment is broad. Recreation and agricultural land have been attractive to foreigners,and their purchase of property emerged as a public issue during the early 1970s. Unfortunately, as a federal-provincial study revealed in 1975, "generally comprehensive data on the nature and extent of foreign land ownership in Canada are not available."[24] Throughout the 1970s, numerous provincial governments initiated studies to determine the nature of foreign land ownership and began to design responses.[25]

Land ownership has not been the only concern. Foreign ownership or control of the Canadian oil industry has long been a point of discussion, and was one of the considerations which led to the creation of Petrocan by the federal government. Table 2.1 indicates that the Canadian oil industry continues to be dominated by foreign interests. These types of figures stress the difficulty in actually measuring foreign control and ownership. The data in Table 2.1 were based on a report from the federal Department of Energy, Mines and Resources. Industry spokesmen noted that this report used industry revenue as an index of foreign ownership levels. If the traditional index of total assets were used, they indicated that assets under foreign control had dropped 26 percent to 64 percent since 1971.[26]

The Institute for Research in Public Policy has stated that Japan intends to become the world's top economic power by the year 2000, and that Canada is viewed as a source of badly needed resources and a stable market for its manufactured goods.[27] The Institute cautioned that the Japanese can be expected to invest heavily in Canadian uranium, forest and fishing industries to the extent that they will get effective control. The Japanese already have gained a significant control of the fisheries industry in British Columbia, and are aggressively expanding their investments.[28]

Canada traditionally has played the role of "drawer of water and hewer of wood." In the past two decades, several initiatives have been taken to reduce foreign control of the economy. The Canada Development

Table 2.1
Foreign Control and Ownership of the Canadian
Petroleum Industry

	% of revenue under foreign control	% of revenue under foreign ownership
1971	94	80
1978	87	74
1979	82	72

Source: *Toronto Globe and Mail*, August 13, 1980, p. B1.

Corporation was established to nurture entrepreneurial skills in the business sector. The Foreign Investment Review Agency was created to examine proposed takeovers by foreign firms. Petrocan has been viewed as a means to increase Canadian participation in petroleum exploration, processing, distributing and marketing. Yet with these different initiatives, foreign ownership or control of Canadian resource industries is at best only declining gradually. Conversely, in some sectors such as fishing, it is on the increase. The issue of foreign ownership and control is thus an important one, especially as governments attempt to exert greater control in economic affairs and maintain the high standard of living which most Canadians enjoy.

Political Commitment

Political leaders and parties are often judged as having a low commitment to environmental issues.[29] This judgement is undoubtedly true, as witnessed by the exemptions of projects from environmental impact assessments, the relaxing or extension of pollution control orders, and the imposition of relatively minor fines for violations. In general, the need for economic development has been given greater priority than the need for environmental protection.

The reasons for this state of affairs are complex. Politicians properly are concerned about encouraging projects which create jobs. Thus, one of the main impetuses for the massive James Bay project was Premier Bourassa's campaign promise during 1970 to create 100,000 new jobs for a Quebec economy which had been suffering relative to those of other Canadian provinces. As a result, economic considerations overrode others to the extent that an environmental impact assessment was not conducted until after approval had been given to the project.

Jobs are not the only motive. Political considerations obviously are significant. People have votes. Moose, loons and sunsets do not have the franchise. Politicians are therefore likely to approve projects which have the greatest potential for gains at the polls. Unfortunately, the outcome is that most decisions are made with reference to a short time horizon.

Another aspect influencing the politicians and the public is the general social and economic climate. During the late 1960s and early 1970s, politicians responded to the public mood and prosperous economy by creating environmental departments and passing pollution control legislation. By the end of the 1970s, however, one observer could comment that the federal Department of the Environment was a mere shadow of what it was in 1970.[30] Budget and manpower cuts were pointed to as evidence for this claim.

As resource management issues arise during the 1980s and 1990s, it must be accepted that politicians and the political process will be intimately associated with environmental and resource management decisions. Politicians are in a position in which they must try to satisfy conflicting interests. The traditional response is to search for a compromise. In judging the adequacy of these compromise decisions, we must look beyond the resource issue itself to view it in a larger societal context.

Initiatives in Resource Management

The foregoing review examined some of the constraints on or barriers to resource management in Canada. Its conclusions emphasize that there are many difficulties to be faced, internally and externally. At the same time, there have been several policy areas in which accomplishments have been realized.

At the international level, Canada has been an active partner in the difficult and complicated Law of the Sea Conference which started during 1974 in Caracas, Venezuela. These deliberations have the potential to contribute to a redistribution of global resources through agreements on fish harvesting and offshore mineral and petroleum deposits. During 1972, Canada and the United States signed a Great Lakes Water Quality Agreement which was renegotiated in 1969. Although progress in rehabilitating the Great Lakes has been and will be gradual, it is begining to appear as if noticeable improvement is being realized.

Federal and provincial governments have introduced a raft of statutes to protect the environment and regulate resource development. With all of the legislation available, one wonders at the necessity for any more. A greater concern is with the willingness or otherwise to enforce it. There always will be inconsistent and conflicting legislation. But given that legislation usually allows considerable leeway for interpretation and judgement, mechanisms for action do exist. The key is to get administrators and the courts to use the existing tools in a more than perfunctory manner.

A variety of programs offer hope for improved resource management in the future. A traditional response to problems has been to engineer structural solutions. In this manner, answers are sought through manipulating and altering natural processes. During the 1970s, the structural approach came to be combined more and more with nonstructural approaches in which human behaviour is analyzed and modified. The National Flood Damage Reduction Program exemplifies this approach with a conscious effort to mix structural and nonstructural adjustments for flood control. Similar actions have been adopted by the provinces, especially in Ontario due to its Conservation authorities' long involvement in flood plain management. Progress has been made in several other provinces too. In British Columbia, for instance, an extensive floodplain mapping program is underway.

The introduction of formal requirements for environmental impact assessment was an innovation of the 1970s. Whether by statute or administrative decision, both federal and provincial levels of government developed assessment procedures to give environmental matters consideration comparable to technological and economic aspects.[31] While the concept has been introduced, there is scope for improvement.[32] Emphasis has been upon individual projects of substantial magnitude. The cumulative impact of many smaller projects also deserves attention. Provision for enforcement and monitoring of recommendations from environmental impact statements is not well developed. Furthermore, many projects have been exempted from the assessment process.

Public participation attracted considerable attention during the late 1960s and early 1970s, and has been institutionalized in many policy fields.[33] Major involvement exercises such as the Berger Commission have since evoked both admiration and skepticism. Those supporting participation viewed it as a detailed and sensitive attempt to determine the consequences of a proposal upon a given people and their way of life. Skeptics have pointed to the substantial amount of time and funds required for such an experience, and have questioned whether the returns have been proportional to the effort.[34] Another concern is whether public participation may increase public expectations to an unrealistic level to which the contemporary system can not respond. The questions of who gets to participate, at what stages, in what ways and with what power are thorny ones which have yet to be resolved completely.[35] Furthermore, these difficulties stress the need for improved means of monitoring and evaluating public participation programs.

While the future problems and opportunities faced by Canadian resource managers are numerous, we should recognize that our problems are of a different sort than those being faced in the developing countries. Some 300,000 people died in Ethiopia and the Sahel belt south of the Sahara during the 1972-74 drought in Africa. Even during the Great Depression of the 1930s, Canadians did not have to cope with such extreme hardship. Basic problems of population growth, food supply and disease control have not been primary Canadian concerns at a domestic level. Nevertheless, while the chapters in this book focus upon national resource management issues in Canada, we must recognize that Canada and Canadians are not isolated from the rest of the world. Just as we recognize that external events and decisions affect resource allocation in Canada, so we should appreciate that Canada has an obligation to the global community, especially that part in the developing nations. Our efforts at resource management will always be inadequate unless we commit some of our attention to these worldwide problems. This commitment constitutes one of the major challenges for Canadians during the 1980s.

Notes

[1] Roger Suffling, "Taking stock of forest resources in Ontario," *Geographical Inter-University Resource Management Seminars* 9 (Waterloo: Wilfrid Laurier University, Department of Geography, 1978-1979), p. 57.

2 Ralph R. Krueger and Bruce Mitchell, "Canadian resource management: an overview," in *Managing Canada's Renewable Resources*, eds. Ralph R. Krueger and Bruce Mitchell (Toronto: Methuen, 1977), p. 6.

3 Fisheries and Environment Canada, *Canadian Water Year Book 1977–1978* (Ottawa: Minister of Supply and Services, 1978), pp. 11–89.

4 Frank J. Quinn and Edward S. Spence, "Canada's surface water resources: inventory and management," in *Canada's Natural Environment*, eds. Geoffrey R. McBoyle and Edward Sommerville (Toronto: Methuen, 1976), p. 72.

5 William E. Rees, *The Canada Land Inventory in Perspective*, Report No. 12 (Ottawa: Fisheries and Environment Canada. Land Directorate, March 1977).

6 Jean Thie and G. Ironside, *Ecological (Biophysical) Land Classification in Canada*, Ecological Land Classification Series No. 1 (Ottawa: Environment Canada, Lands Directorate, 1976); Clay D.A. Rubec, *Applications of Ecological (Biophysical) Land Classification in Canada*, Ecological Land Classification Series No. 7 (Ottawa: Ministry of Supply and Services, March 1979).

7 J.L. Nowland and J.A. McKeague, "Canada's limited agricultural land resource," in *Managing Canada's Renewable Resources*, eds. Ralph R. Krueger and Bruce Mitchell (Toronto: Methuen, 1977), pp. 112–113.

8 Bruce Mitchell, "The provincial domain in environmental management and resource development," in *Resources and the Environment: Policy Perspectives for Canada*, ed. O.P. Dwivedi (Toronto: McClelland and Stewart, 1980), pp. 66–73. See also S.I. Bushnell, "The control of natural resources through the trade and commerce power and proprietary rights," *Canadian Public Policy* 6 (Spring 1980), pp. 313–324, and R. Simeon, "Natural resource revenues and Canadian federalism: a survey of the issues," *Canadian Public Policy* 6 (Supplement, 1980), pp. 182–191

9 R. Brian Woodrow, "Resources and environmental policy-making at the national level: the search for focus," in *Resources and the Environment: Policy Perspectives for Canada*, ed. O.P. Dwivedi (Toronto: McClelland and Stewart, 1980), pp. 33–37.

10 Michael S. Whittington, "Department of the Environment," in *Spending Tax Dollars: Federal Expenditures, 1980–1981*, ed. E. Bruce Doern (Ottawa: Carleton University, School of Public Administration, 1980), p. 99.

11 A. Paul Pross, "Atlantic Canada: conditions and prospects for coastal zone management," in *Institutional Arrangements for Water Management: Canadian Experiences*, ed. Bruce Mitchell, Publication Series No. 5 (Waterloo: University of Waterloo, Department of Geography, 1975), p. 219. Further details about mandates, legislation and agencies may be found in Canadian Council of Resource and Environment Ministers, *Proceedings, Shore Zone Management Symposium* (Toronto: Canadian Council of Resource and Environment Ministers, 1979).

12 Sabine Jessen, "An Assessment of Great Lakes Shore Management: Regulation of the Nanticoke Industrial Complex. Lake Erie, Ontario", Unpublished M.A. thesis (Waterloo: University of Waterloo, Department of Geography, 1980).

13 Environment Canada and Ontario Ministry of Natural Resources, *Federal-Provincial Strategic Planning of Ontario Fisheries—Second Report: Catalogue of Programs and Legislation* (March 1976), pp. vii–x.

14 William H. Palmer, *Report of the Waterloo Region Review Commission* (Toronto: Ontario Government Bookstore, March 1979), pp. 192–199.

[15] Edgar J. Dósman, "Arctic Seas: environmental policy and natural resource development," in Resources and the Environment: Policy Perspectives for Canada, ed. O.P. Dwivedi (Toronto: McClelland and Stewart, 1980) pp. 199–200.

[16] Michael S. Whittington, "Department of the Environment," p. 103.

[17] Anthony Downs, "Up and down with ecology—the 'issue-attention' cycle," Public Interest 28 (Summer 1972), pp. 38–50.

[18] "Parrott picks Cayuga for liquid waste dump," Globe and Mail (November 26, 1980), p. 2.

[19] Science Council of Canada, Canada as a Conserver Society: Resource Uncertainties and the Need for New Technologies, Report No. 27 (Ottawa: Minister of Supply and Services, 1978). Further discussion of this concept may be found in Lawrence Solomon, The Conserver Solution (Toronto: Doubleday Canada Ltd., 1978), and in Kimon Valaskakis, Peter S. Sindell, J. Graham Smith and Iris Fitzpatrick-Martin, The Conserver Society (New York: Harper and Row, 1979).

[20] Thomas R. Berger, Northern Frontier, Northern Homeland, Volumes 1 and 2 (Ottawa: Minister of Supply and Services Canada, 1977).

[21] "Environmental Assessment: Eldorado Refinery," Saskatoon Star-Phoenix (August 8, 1980), pp. 1–8.

[22] Cameron Clark, "Prescribing carrying capacity standards for wildland areas: bridging the gap between policy and management," Contact 10 (Spring 1978), pp. 65–66.

[23] Government of Canada, Foreign Direct Investment in Canada (Ottawa: Information Canada, 1972).

[24] Canadian Intergovernmental Conference Secretariat, Federal-Provincial Committee on Foreign Ownership of Land: Report to the First Ministers (Ottawa: Information Canada, 1975), p. 3.

[25] Bruce Mitchell, "The provincial domain in environmental management and resource development," pp. 58–66.

[26] "Company executives dispute report on petroleum industry," Globe and Mail (August 14, 1980), p. B10.

[27] Zavis Zeman, The Men with the Yen (Montreal: Institute for Research on Public Policy, 1980).

[28] C.R. Molson, Foreign Ownership in the Canadian Fishing Industry (Ottawa: Department of the Environment, January 1974); Trevor B. Proverbs, Foreign Investment in the British Columbia Fish Processing Industry (Vancouver: Fisheries and Environment Canada, July 1978).

[29] W.R. Derrick Sewell, "Environmental decision-making: the unevenness of commitment," in Environmental Health, ed. Norman Trieff (Ann Arbor: Ann Arbor Science, 1980), pp. 605–624.

[30] Michael S. Whittington, "Department of the Environment," p. 99.

[31] Bruce Mitchell and Richard Turkheim, "Environmental impact assessment: principles, practices, and Canadian experiences," in Managing Canada's Renewable Resources, eds. Ralph R. Krueger and Bruce Mitchell (Toronto: Methuen, 1977), pp. 47–66.

[32] W.R. Derrick Sewell and Timothy O'Riodran, Project Appraisal and Policy Review (Chichester: John Wiley, in press).

[33] W.R. Derrick Sewell and J. Terry Coppock, eds., Public Participation in Planning (London: John Wiley, 1977).

34 Richard F. Salisbury, "The Berger Report—But Is It Social Science?" *Social Sciences in Canada* 5 (3, 1977), pp. 14-15. J.C. Stabler, "The Report of the Mackenzie Valley Pipeline Inquiry, Volume 1: a Socio-Economic Critique," *The Musk-Ox*, 20 (1977), pp. 57-65; L.C. Bliss, "The Report of the Mackenzie Valley Pipeline Inquiry, Volume 2: An Environmental Critique," *The Musk-Ox*, 21 (1978), pp. 34-38, J.C. Stabler, "Gaslight Follies: the Political Economy of the Western Arctic," *Canadian Public Policy*, 6 (Spring 1980), pp. 374-388.

35 These difficult questions are addressed in Barry Sadler, ed., *Involvement and Environment* Volumes 1 and 2 (Edmonton: Environmental Council of Alberta, 1978), and in W.R. Derrick Sewell, L. Graham Smith and Audrey Fraggalosch, *Where Is Public Participation Going? An Annotated Bibliography Focussing on the Canadian Experience* (Edmonton: Environment Council of Alberta, 1979).

36 W.R. Derrick Sewell and Susan D. Phillips, "Models for the evaluation of public participation programs," *Natural Resources Journal* 19 (April 1979), pp. 337-358.

Bibliography

W. Donald Bennett *et. al.*, *Essays on Aspects of Resource Policy*, Science Council of Canada Special Study No. 27 (Ottawa: Information Canada, 1973).

Thomas R. Berger, *Northern Frontier, Northern Homeland* (Ottawa: Minister of Supply and Services, 1977).

Rorke Bryan, *Much is Taken, Much Remains* (North Scituate, Mass.: Duxbury, 1973).

Thomas L. Burton, *Natural Resource Policy in Canada* (Toronto: McClelland and Stewart, 1972).

Philippe Crabbé and Irene M. Spry, eds., *Natural Resource Development in Canada* (Ottawa: University of Ottawa Press, 1973).

Pierre Dansereau, *Harmony and Disorder in the Canadian Environment*, Canadian Environmental Advisory Council Occasional Paper No. 1 (Ottawa: Minister of Supply and Services, 1975).

O.P. Dwivedi, ed., *Protecting the Environment: Issues and Choices, Canadian Perspectives* (Vancouver: Copp Clark, 1974).

O.P. Dwivedi, ed., *Resources and the Environment: Policy Perspectives for Canada* (Toronto: McClelland and Stewart, 1980).

Janet Foster, *Working for Wildlife: the Beginning of Preservation in Canada* (Toronto: University of Toronto Press, 1978).

Robert F. Keith and Janet B. Wright, eds., *Northern Transitions*, Volume 2 (Ottawa: Canadian Arctic Resources Committee, 1978).

William Kilbourn, *Pipeline* (Toronto: Clarke, Irwin and Co., 1970).

Ralph R. Krueger *et. al.*, eds., *Regional and Resource Planning in Canada* (Toronto: Holt, Rinehart and Winston, 1970, revised).

Ralph R. Krueger and Bruce Mitchell, eds., *Managing Canada's Renewable Resources* (Toronto: Methuen, 1977).

Gerard V. LaForest, *Natural Resources and Public Property under the Canadian Constitution* (Toronto: University of Toronto Press, 1969).

Richard S. Lambert and Paul Pross, *Renewing Nature's Wealth* (Toronto: Ontario Department of Lands and Forests, 1967).

William Leiss, ed., *Ecology versus Politics in Canada* (Toronto: University of Toronto Press, 1979).

Philip Mathias, *Forced Growth* (Toronto: James Lewis and Samuel, 1971).

Geoffrey R. McBoyle and Edward Sommerville, eds., *Canada's Natural Environment: Essays in Applied Geography* (Toronto: Methuen, 1976).

J.W. MacNeill, *Environmental Management* (Ottawa: Information Canada, 1971).

Arthur H. Richardson, *Conservation by the People: the History of the Conservation Movement in Ontario to 1970* (Toronto: University of Toronto Press, 1974).

Science Council of Canada, *Natural Resource Policy Issues in Canada*, Report No. 19 (Ottawa: Information Canada, 1973).

Science Council of Canada, *Canada as a Conserver Society: Resource Uncertainties and the Need for New Technologies*, Report No. 27 (Ottawa: Minister of Supply and Services, 1978).

Philip Smith, *Brinco: the Story of Churchill Falls* (Toronto: McClelland and Stewart, 1975).

2/Energy, Planning and Policy Making
Mary L. Barker

Canada has been more fortunate than many industrialized nations in that her indigenous energy resources could serve as a buffer against the immediate and severe impacts of the international energy crisis brought about by the actions of the Organization of Petroleum Exporting Countries (OPEC). The existence of cheap and abundant fossil fuels and hydroelectric power has had a profound effect upon the industrial development, regional growth and export trade of Canada during this century. However, this legacy of abundance has resulted in Canada becoming the most energy-intensive nation in the world. Even before the oil embargoes and price hikes introduced in late 1973, a vocal minority of Canadians were questioning the assumption of continued historic growth in energy consumption, and the rationale for accepting the increasing capital, social and environmental costs of large-scale energy projects. Throughout the 1960s, the debate focussed upon how to deal with fossil fuel reserves which were apparently surplus to domestic needs, and upon the extent of foreign ownership of energy industries in Canada. As reserve estimates underwent radical revision and more massive energy projects were planned in resource hinterlands distant from centres of demand, the range of issues broadened to include the rights of northern native peoples, the environmental risks associated with offshore petroleum exploration, production, and transportation, the dislocations brought about by large-scale hydro projects, and the safety of nuclear power.

Now that governments, energy industries, and consumers must respond to higher prices, predicted shortfalls, and increased reliance upon eastern oil imports, crucial policy choices will have to be made in the increasingly complex and contentious forum of federal-provincial relations and diverse regional interests. As the provinces and federal government seek to alter their mutual relations, it seems clear that changes in energy policies will be bound inextricably to much broader constitutional issues. While adjustments to increasingly high-price energy will dominate in the near future, solutions to the longer-term problem of balancing supply and demand will involve not only the application of advanced technology, but significant institutional and social changes as well.

Setting the Stage—
Changing Patterns of Energy Supply

The energy supply scene in Canada has undergone a series of profound changes since the turn of the century, when coal and wood met more than 95 percent of the nation's fuel requirements. In the ensuing years, coal assumed an even greater importance, meeting 75 percent of the primary energy demand in 1920 (Table 1.2). Yet this pre-eminence was not to last, as the adoption of new exploration, energy transportation and conversion technologies during the 1950s permitted the widespread shift to cheap petroleum fuels throughout the industrialized world. By 1972, on the eve of rapid oil price increases and supply disruptions brought about by the actions of OPEC, almost 65 percent of Canada's energy needs were supplied by oil and natural gas.

The coal industry in Canada has responded to developments in production and conversion technologies, regional economic growth, and exports markets. Production began in Nova Scotia during the 1830s, and quickly expanded as domestic and export markets for steam coal grew in central Canada and northeastern United States. By 1850, export markets provided the impetus for coal mining on Vancouver Island, and Alberta production began in the 1880s. Domestic production, while protected by import tariffs introduced as early as 1879, fluctuated as interruptions to export trade during the first World War were superceded by the growth of industrial markets for eastern coal in central Canada.[1] After 1928, federal transport subventions enabled coal producers to offset the problems caused by distance from major centres of demand, and to increase their penetration of the Ontario market. Production peaked in the late 1940s, mainly as a result of the development of western coal mines. By this time, U.S. coal imports were able to capture an increasing share of the central Canadian market because of the types of coal required and lower transportation costs: imports represented 61 percent of the total domestic supply in 1950.

The successive displacement of coal by oil in the transportation, residential and commercial sectors during the 1950s resulted in stagnation and a continuous decline in production to a low point in 1961. Throughout the 1960s, the principal markets were for thermal coal used in electricity generation, and for metallurgical coal in the Ontario steel industry. However, underground coal mining in the Maritimes faced increasing technical difficulties, western producers were isolated from central Canada, and U.S. coal played a growing role in the Ontario market. During the late 1960s, coal production expanded in British Columbia and Alberta as long-term export contracts for metallurgical coal were secured from Japan. Output doubled between 1969 and 1972, reaching 12.6 million tons by 1977.[2]

While the structure of the industry changed with growth of western

Table 1.2

Primary Energy Consumption in Canada, 1900–1977 (percent)

	1900	1910	1920	1930	1940	1950	1960	1965	1970	1975[1]	1977[1]
Oil	0.8	2.0	6.8	15.0	20.0	28.2	44.6	45.3	44.0	45.7	44.7
Natural gas	–	0.2	0.4	2.1	2.7	2.8	10.2	15.3	19.4	18.6	18.8
Coal	56.6	70.3	75.0	63.1	57.6	41.9	14.9	13.2	11.0	8.5	8.9
Hydro	3.6	1.8	1.5	4.2	6.5	19.7	27.1	24.1	24.2	25.2	24.6
Wood	39.0	25.7	16.3	15.6	13.2	7.4	3.2	2.1	1.3	2.0	
Nuclear	–	–	–	–	–	–	–	–	0.1		3.0
Total (Btu 10[12])	477	961	1,142	1,414	1.593	2,493	3,671	4,814	6,328	7,826	8,267

[1] Information on wood-derived energy consumption not available.

Sources: John Davis, *Canadian Energy Prospects* (Ottawa, 1957), pp. 367–8; Department of Energy, Mines and Resources, *An Energy Policy for Canada* (Ottawa, 1973), p. 32; and *Energy Futures for Canadians* (Ottawa, 1978), p. 303.

coal exports, Canada remains a net importer largely because of the distance separating major producing areas from the central Canadian market. The future role of export-oriented production of metallurgical coals depends upon world trends in steel making and upon Canada's competitive position in relation to other countries, such as Australia, which possess substantial coal reserves. However, the rising price and predicted shortfalls of petroleum products has led to a renewed interest in thermal coal and coal gasification technology. Attention will most likely focus upon Alberta and British Columbia which possess 61 percent and 31 percent, respectively, of the total proven reserves in Canada. With a reserve-to-demand ratio of 310,[3] the Canadian coal industry has considerable potential, but the challenge will lie in overcoming problems of production costs and technology, long-distance transportation and environmental impacts.

As in the case of coal, the historical development of the petroleum industry has been characterized by a separation of producing areas from major markets. Oil already represented one-fifth of the primary energy needs by 1940, but Canada was reliant upon imported supplies to supplement the small production from Ontario fields. Ninety percent of the domestic requirements were imported in 1947, when a major light oil discovery at Leduc, Alberta and subsequent finds in Saskatchewan transformed the national energy picture. A drive began to develop Canadian and U.S. markets for western oil as proven reserves increased 45-fold between 1945 and 1955.[4] Local refining and consumption of Prairie oil gave way to regional transfers and exports with the construction of the Interprovincial Pipeline to the Great Lakes, and the Transmountain Pipeline which opened up markets in British Columbia and Washington State.

The threat of a production slump, brought about by a world oil surplus and the imposition of oil import quotas by the United States in 1959, provided a strong incentive for expanding into the eastern Canadian market, which was being supplied by international oil. The National Energy Board, which had been established by the federal government in 1959, introduced a National Oil Policy in 1961. The objectives were to encourage the use of domestic crude oil and the expansion of exports within the limits set by the protective U.S. import quotas. Canada was divided into two market regions, east and west of the newly created Ottawa Valley Line: areas west of the Line would be supplied by western oil, while consumers to the east would continue to use imported oil at the somewhat lower international price. (This price differential persisted until the Middle East crisis of October 1973 which resulted in a rapid quadrupling of the world oil price.)

Domestic production and demand for oil continued to grow during the 1960s, and exports equalled imports in late 1970 when the United States government relaxed its import quotas. Despite concerns voiced by energy critics, this was a time of official optimism regarding Canada's future fossil fuel supplies. On May 19, 1971 Joe Greene, then federal Energy Minister, announced that Canada had 923 years of oil and 292 years of gas left at current demand and production rates.[5] This overly optimistic assessment was based largely upon industry estimates of "probable" and "possible" reserves assumed to exist in the Arctic and offshore sedimentary basins. Exports approved under these assumptions tripled within three years, reaching 1.4 million barrels a day (or two-thirds of domestic production) in 1973. At this rate, it has been estimated that Canada was exporting 5 percent of her proven reserves each year, and that the ratio between remaining reserves and annual production was rapidly approaching the critical figure of ten.[6] This R/P ratio (which indicates a ten-year supply left at that production rate) is profoundly significant, given the low finding rate in the conventional producing-areas of southern Canada and in the Arctic and offshore frontiers, and the long lead times necessary for the development of frontier petroleum resources. Proven reserves have been falling steadily since 1969 and Canada became a net oil importer in late 1975, despite a major curtailment of exports in recent years. Throughout the 1970s, industry and government attention has focussed upon exploration in the Arctic and offshore areas, and the development of production technology for the exploitation of Alberta tar sands.

The history of Canadian oil has been matched by a similar, although delayed, development of natural gas production since the late 1950s. Before interprovincial pipelines were constructed, most of the natural gas sales took place in Alberta, close to producing areas. Although there was a dramatic expansion during the 1960s, further growth was inhibited by the distance from major markets, and by transportation costs which left natural gas only marginally competitive with imported oil in eastern Canada. In British Columbia, the second major producing province, the small regional market delayed development which eventually depended upon the securing of export markets in the Pacific Northwest. Canadian gas exports to the United States reached their highest point in 1970, within the limits established by the National Energy Board, and approximately 37 percent of the domestic production is exported at present.[7] Although natural gas producers were predicting a shortfall by 1980 during the mid-1970s, recent large discoveries in the traditional producing-areas of Alberta and British Columbia have resulted in shut-in capacity and renewed industry pressure to increase exports.[8]

While oil and natural gas assumed an increasingly dominant role in the domestic primary energy market, the relative contribution of primary electricity (i.e., hydro and nuclear power) remained unchanged between 1960 and 1978 (Figure 1.2). The availability of relatively cheap and readily accessible hydroelectric power has played a major role in industrial development and continues to exert a strong influence upon provincial

Figure 1.2

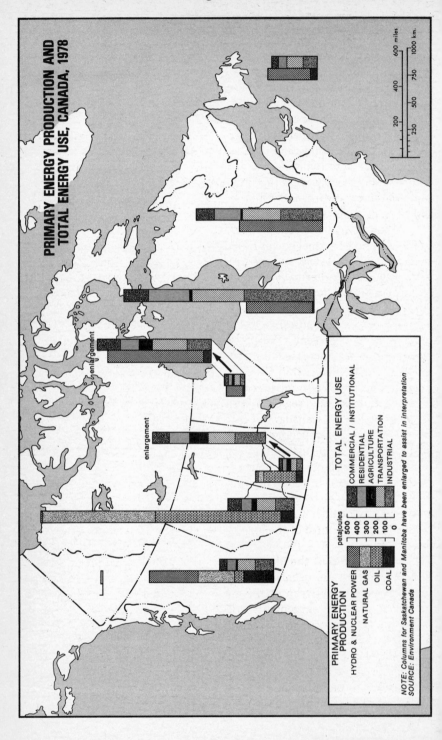

energy policies in eastern and western Canada. For 60 years since the late nineteenth century, almost the entire electricity supply was generated at hydroelectric power facilities close to centres of demand. While some energy-intensive mining, metallurgical and forest-products industries tended to generate their own power, this represented a small proportion of total Canadian production which was dominated by public utilities such as Ontario Hydro. These were able to provide a guaranteed service to the growing number of urban consumers, to capitalize upon economies of scale in future load planning, and to take advantage of inter-regional transfers. (For example, the hydroelectric generating and transmission systems of Ontario and Quebec were first interconnected more than fifty years ago, and Manitoba Hydro and Ontario Hydro's western system have been linked since 1956.[9])

Although hydroelectric generation continued to dominate, there was a gradual shift to thermal power facilities after the Second World War as the most readily accessible and inexpensive water-power sites became fully developed, as the thermal efficiency of coal- and petroleum-fired stations improved, and as demand increased in regions such as the Prairies which were well endowed with fossil fuel. Between 1945 and 1978, the contribution of hydroelectric power to the total generated electricity fell from 97.6 percent to 69.6 percent (Table 2.2)[10]. Over the same period, electricity consumption has increased at a faster rate (6.7 percent a year) than total energy use (4.3 percent) in Canada, although there has been a decline in average annual growth in recent years.[11]

There are marked regional differences in fuel sources used to generate thermal power in Canada. For example, the Maritime provinces have developed a strong dependence on imported oil to generate electricity, but coal is the dominant fuel source in Alberta. Ontario is the only province to have developed a large-scale nuclear generating capacity in response to load requirements which could not be met by hydroelectric sites close to demand centres, or by growing reliance upon increasingly expensive U.S. coal imports. British Columbia, Manitoba, Quebec and Newfoundland continue to fulfill most of their electricity requirements from hydroelectric sources.

Since the 1960s, the planning and construction of large-scale hydroelectric projects has been encouraged by the intensification of regional interconnections between provincial power utilities and the development of power transfer agreements with the United States, as well as by provincial demand growth. For example, Quebec, which has approximately 40 percent of installed hydro capacity in Canada, has a long-term contract to purchase most of the output from Churchill Falls, Labrador. While Quebec brought its first nuclear power station on-stream in 1971, the massive James Bay project, planned to have an installed capacity of 10.6 million kilowatts by 1985, shows a continuing commitment to hydroelec-

tric generation in the province. Federal interest in strengthening interconnections is evidenced by the Canada-Manitoba Nelson River Transmission Agreement, whereby the senior government provided support for
large-scale hydroelectric developments in the Churchill-Nelson basin,
scheduled for completion in the late 1990s. Such massive projects, which
involve long-distance transmission, and impose environmental and social
costs upon communities far removed from major centres of demand, have
been the source of much public debate. The experience gained from the
construction of the Bennett Dam in northern British Columbia, which
subsequently required mitigation of downstream impacts on the Peace-
Athabaska delta in Alberta,[12] and the controversy concerning the distribution of flood-control and power benefits derived from three Canadian
storage projects constructed under the terms of the Columbia River
Treaty,[13] raise serious questions which should be addressed if more large-
scale projects involving regional, interprovincial or international power
transfers are considered.

Proposals by provincial power utilities to increase nuclear generating
capacity have been the source of heated debate between industry and
government proponents, environmental groups and a concerned public.
While earlier disputes focussed upon the health risks and adequacy of
regulatory controls associated with uranium mining at Elliot Lake in
northern Ontario, more recent controversies have included concerns over
the local impacts of uranium exploration and mining (in Saskatchewan and
British Columbia), the proposal by the federal Crown corporation, Eldorado Nuclear Ltd., to build a uranium refinery in Saskatchewan, the
construction of the Point Lepreau nuclear power plant in New Brunswick,
Ontario Hydro's plans to undertake a large-scale expansion of its nuclear
generating program and Canada's role as an exporter of nuclear technology.

The debate over the capital requirements and the economic efficiency
of such advanced technology has been broadened to include questions
concerning its social, environmental and moral implications for this and
future generations. The economic costs of maintaining energy consumption at levels to which most Canadians have, until recently, taken for
granted are climbing. Capital expenditures on energy projects represented
16 percent of all capital investment in Canada until the mid-70s, but
reached 20 percent in 1978. One federal study estimated that 180 billion
dollars would have to be spent on energy-related developments between
1976 and 1990.[14] There has been growing recognition of the broader, total
costs of such investments as attention has focussed upon the social and
environmental impacts of large-scale technologies, whether they involved
Arctic pipelines, tar sands plants, massive hydroelectric projects or nuclear
generating facilities. Increasingly complex trade-offs will have to be made
as governments, energy suppliers and consumers respond to the new
reality of high-price, and high-cost, energy.

Electrical Energy Generation by Principal Fuel Type, 1978

gigawatt hours (10⁹ watt-hours)

Region	Conventional thermal				Total[1] thermal	Nuclear	Hydro	Total	% of total generation
	Coal	Oil	Natural gas	Wood					
Atlantic Provinces (percent)	1,497	10,787	—	17	12,301 (20.6)	—	47,348 (79.4)	59,649	17.7
Quebec (percent)	—	510	9	—	529 (0.6)	22 (0.03)	85,444 (99.4)	85,995	25.5
Ontario (percent)	27,000	2,075	4,388	91	33,598 (32.9)	29,435 (28.8)	39,168 (38.3)	102,201	30.4
Manitoba (percent)	361	133	6	—	500 (2.9)	—	16,983 (97.1)	17,483	5.2
Saskatchewan (percent)	5,421	20	842	—	6,317 (71.3)	—	2,548 (28.7)	8,865	2.6
Alberta (percent)	13,222	313	3,803	—	17,338 (90.4)	—	1,831 (9.6)	19,169	5.7
British Columbia (percent)	—	504	499	950	1,953 (4.6)	—	40,612 (95.4)	42,565	12.6
Yukon and N.W.T. (percent)	—	228	—	—	228 (27.6)	—	599 (72.4)	827	0.3
Canada (percent)	47,501	14,570	9,547	1,058	72,764 (21.6)	29,457 (8.8)	234,533 (69.6)	336,754	100.0

[1] Includes 88 gwh generated from other sources not shown in table.
Source: Statistics Canada, Catalogues 57-001 and 57-003.

The Energy Users

The pattern of Canadian energy demand reflects changes in the energy resources used, increasing energy efficiency, and shifts among major end-use sectors. A mix of socioeconomic factors, geographical characteristics and energy resource endowment has influenced the structure and intensity of Canadian energy use. Price differentials between various energy sources have affected consumption, lifestyles and climate have resulted in a considerable demand for space heating, and the sheer size of the country has affected the energy costs of increased mobility (including transmission losses as energy is transported from sources increasingly distant from centres of demand). The legacy of abundant, cheap and flexible energy resources such as petroleum fuels and electricity has contributed towards Canada becoming the most intensive energy-user in the world.[15] Canada consumes nearly three times as much energy per capita as Japan, and almost twice as much in relation to Gross Domestic Product as West Germany.

Between 1950 and 1975, total energy consumption increased at an average rate of 5.3 percent a year, although the growth rate has slowed in recent years as consumers and the economy respond to inflation and much higher energy prices. The relative share of industrial demand has grown steadily since the 1930s, as the wealth of indigenous resources encouraged the development of energy-intensive industries such as pulp and paper manufacture, metal refining and chemical processing. As secondary energy use quadrupled between 1930 and 1976, industry's share climbed from 21 percent to 33 percent of the total (Table 3.2). The transportation sector has consistently consumed a quarter of the total energy requirements. The boom in private automobiles and air travel has been matched by a relative decline in fuel consumption by rail transportation, as the substitution of diesel fuel for coal increased the thermal efficiency, and as commercial road haulage increased in importance. Private and commercial road transportation now account for 65 percent of the total energy consumption in this sector.

Commercial energy use grew rapidly over the last two decades as the service sector played an increasingly important role in Canada's economic structure. The relative decline in residential use over the same period has been attributed to lower rates of population growth, a general aging of the population, and shifts in housing mix in response to changes in family structure.

There are significant differences in the energy resources consumed by the various end-use sectors. Transportation is heavily dependent upon oil, representing over 40 percent of the total Canadian energy requirement.[16] Industry consumes almost 30 percent of the oil, approximately 60 percent of the natural gas and half the electricity. The commercial and residential sectors account for half the electricity consumed, but use a smaller share of the oil and natural gas.

Table 3.2
Secondary Energy Consumption in Canada, 1930–1976 (percent)

	1930	1940	1950	1960	1965	1970	1975	1976
Domestic and farm	36.2	34.3	29.0	24.4	22.9	20.8	19.8	19.7
Commercial	21.0	25.7	28.1	8.5	11.2	14.1	12.3	12.1
Industrial	25.7	27.3	30.1	34.3	33.1	32.2	33.0	32.9
Transportation	25.7	27.3	30.1	25.5	24.7	24.3	26.2	25.9
Energy supply industries	17.1[1]	12.7[1]	12.8[1]	7.3	8.1	8.6	8.7	9.4
Total (Btu 10^{12})	1,492	1,610	2,372	2,920	3,789	4,971	5,878	6,100

[1] Includes fuel losses and miscellaneous.

Sources: John Davis, *Canadian Energy Prospects* (Ottawa: 1957), p. 383; Canada, Department of Energy, Mines and Resources, *Energy Prospects Futures for Canadians* (Ottawa, 1978), p. 304.

The regional diversity of energy supply and demand, and therefore surpluses and deficits, is a striking feature in Canada (Figure 1.2). The oil and natural gas resources of Alberta enable this province to dominate as the leading primary energy producer, and as the highest per capita energy consumer, in the country. Ontario and Quebec, with their concentration of population and industrial activity, are the largest energy consumers (62 percent of the total). Both provinces suffer from an energy deficiency which is particularly serious in Ontario which accounts for 30 percent of Canadian oil demand. While the hydroelectric potential of Newfoundland has been developed, the Atlantic provinces are heavily dependent upon imported oil which meets approximately 75 percent of the regional requirements.

The sectoral differences in energy consumption and the strong regional diversity in energy production and demand are particularly significant as Canadians respond to major changes in energy pricing and availability. In response to projected increases in demand, the federal government and provincial power utilities have looked almost exclusively (at least until recently) to expanding the supply base. As fossil fuel surpluses transformed into shortfalls, and the price of imported oil escalated, the federal and provincial governments have had to reexamine their energy policies and programs within a context of fragmented jurisdictional responsibilities and conflicting regional interests.

Energy supply and demand forecasts underwent a series of major revisions as optimism regarding frontier petroleum discoveries proved to be unfounded, at least in the short term, and as Canada adjusted to the international oil crisis. Federal government projections of secondary energy demand to the year 2000 have undergone a marked downward shift from an assumed annual growth of 4.5 percent in a 1973 study to 2.4 percent in a 1978 review (Table 4.2). A more stringent energy conservation scenario outlined in 1977 postulated an annual growth of 1.2 percent to the year 2000. In fact, the rate of growth in national energy use has declined markedly in recent years, falling to 1.7 percent in 1977 and 2.5 percent in 1978.[17] However, these national averages mask significant regional differences. Energy use in Alberta increased by 8.2 percent during 1978, while regions beyond the Prairies experienced much lower growth: 3.3 percent in the Atlantic Provinces, 1.1 percent in Quebec, 1.9 percent in Ontario, and 0.9 percent in British Columbia. Although there is a clear distinction between energy-deficit and energy-surplus regions, such variations cannot be explained entirely in terms of energy resource endowment. (Note the wide variation between British Columbia and Alberta.) Industrial structure and performance, regional energy mix, consumer response to the increasing costs of different energy supplies, and government policies affecting demand should also be considered. Emerging differences in sectoral and regional responses to changes in energy supply and price are particularly significant as the federal and provincial governments revise their energy

Table 4.2
Changing Energy Demand Projections for the Year 2000

Year of Study	Scenario	Secondary energy demand in the year 2000 (quads)[1]	Annual growth rate, 1975–2000 (percent)	Source
1973	Energy balance	20.2	4.5	EMR, *An Energy Policy for Canada*
1976	High price	13.5	3.3	EMR, *An Energy Strategy for Canada*
1977	Energy conservation	7.2	1.2	EMR, *Energy Conservation in Canada*
1978	Reference demand	10.0	2.4	EMR, *Energy Futures for Canadians*

[1] 1 quad = 10^{15} Btu. Secondary energy is the amount available to end-users after conversion losses, waste and energy consumption by energy supply industries. In 1976, 6.1 quads of secondary energy were consumed.

policies and programs. It should not be overlooked, however, that the average annual growth in Canadian energy demand has approximately halved since 1973.

Energy Strategies in the 1970s
From Surplus to Shortfall: Energy Policy
Approaches Before the Oil Crisis

Although the provinces were granted ownership of all Crown lands and natural resources within their boundaries under the terms of the British North America Act,[18] and were thus able to exert a strong influence upon energy resource development in Canada, the federal government has played a considerable role via its exclusive proprietary rights north of 60°, its ownership (disputed) of seabed resources, it regulatory authority affecting provinical affairs (particularly interprovincial and international trade, and environmental protection), and its power to negotiate international agreements. The research capabilities and spending powers of the senior level of government have also enabled it to play an important part in what would otherwise appear to be matters of provincial jurisdiction.

The two key federal institutions concerning energy are the National Energy Board, which was established in 1959, and the Department of Energy, Mines and Resources which was created in November 1966 to replace its predecessor, the Department of Mines and Technical Surveys. The statutory functions of the National Energy Board, to advise on energy policy and to regulate the energy industry insofar as it lies within federal jurisdiction, gave it a major role in federal decision making. For example, one of its first actions was to produce the National Energy Policy in 1961, and it has continued to serve in an advisory capacity in energy planning. Its second responsibility has been to conduct hearings in response to applications for interprovincial pipelines and international petroleum transfers. (Successful applications are granted a certificate of public convenience and necessity which is referred to Cabinet for final approval.)

The Department of Energy, Mines and Resources has undergone a series of changes in its creation in 1966, when it acquired the responsibility for water resources inventory and planning, administration of offshore seabed minerals, and a newly created planning and coordination function for energy development. It was affiliated with the Atomic Energy Control Board (which had been created in 1946 to promote nuclear research and to regulate nuclear facilities) and has been responsible for a number of Crown corporations concerned with coal, uranium and nuclear technology.[19]

Within four years of the Department's creation, the federal government introduced a number of initiatives in response to the changing structure of the Canadian coal industry, and growing interest in the petroleum potential of the north.[20] In 1967, the Cape Breton Development

Corporation was established to rationalize an increasingly uneconomic Atlantic coal industry and to encourage diversification of the regional economy. Legislation was passed to dissolve the Dominion Coal Board, in preparation for the discontinuation of the 1962 coal transportation subventions to Alberta and B.C. producers by 1971. A departmental advisory committee on coal was established, and subsequent federal support focussed upon coal technology research and the provision of export-oriented harbour facilites such as Robert's Bank in British Columbia. During the same period, the Federal-Provincial Ministerial Committee on Long-Distance Transmission recommended the strengthening of regional electricity interconnections. Federal support of integrated electrical systems was further evidenced by the signing of an agreement with Quebec and Hydro Quebec to provide financial assistance for high-voltage and high-power transmission research at the Hydro Quebec Research Institute.

Meanwhile, industry and government interest in the oil and gas potential of the Arctic frontier had been revitalized by the announcement, in 1968, of a major oil discovery on the north slope of Alaska. The federal government acquired a 45 percent interest in Panarctic Oils Ltd. in order to secure an involvement in Arctic Island exploration, and a Task Force on Northern Oil Development was established to investigate the engineering and economic aspects of oil development north of 60°. By 1970, the Task Force had produced guidelines for northern pipeline construction and, in the following year, the Oil and Gas Production Act was amended to provide a legislative base for regulating the development of offshore petroleum resources.

Industry had already submitted proposals for a pipeline to be constructed along the Mackenzie Valley to carry Alaskan and Mackenzie Delta oil or gas south to U.S. markets, and it became clear that the Canadian government offered strong support to such an idea.[21] Both government policies and industry interests shifted in response to the U.S. decision to construct the Trans-Alaska Pipeline and to use tankers to carry oil to southern markets, and to the discovery of gas rather than oil in the Canadian Arctic. Despite rival industry proposals and uncertainty created by delays in final approval of the ALYESKA pipeline, the federal government appeared to endorse a Mackenzie Valley pipeline. Federal agencies were heavily involved in pipeline route planning, and several Cabinet Ministers, including Prime Minister Trudeau, made statements in support of a gas pipeline.[22] However, the rationale changed significantly in late 1972, when the National Energy Board announced its revised assessment of Canadian petroleum reserves. Assumed surpluses became predicted shortfalls, especially in the case of oil, and the objective of the proposed Mackenzie Valley pipeline changed to delivering Arctic gas to consumers in southern Canada rather than to the United States.

Earlier reliance upon industry reserve estimates, largely based upon the unproven potential of the northern frontier, left the federal government in a difficult position which was made even more vulnerable by the international oil crisis triggered by the Arab-Israeli conflict in October 1973. Decisions had to be made in a complex policy context which consisted of largely piecemeal federal and provincial measures directed at separate energy supply sectors, with minimal attention to demand management. While the National Oil Policy had been the keystone of petroleum development since 1961, it was not part of an integrated energy plan. Perceived supply surpluses, and the division of proprietary and regulatory authority between the federal and provincial governments, had not been conducive to the development of a comprehensive national policy.

Canadian Responses to the Energy Crisis

It is ironic that, just four months before the OPEC actions in late 1973, the federal government released the first comprehensive review of the Canadian energy situation since the Davis report to the Borden Commission in 1957. Although *An Energy Policy for Canada—Phase 1* drew attention to the security of Canadian oil supplies as it might be affected by Middle Eastern unrest, it did not foresee the rapid escalation in world oil prices. It concluded that Canada, during the 1980s, could develop abundant frontier oil and gas reserves from the Arctic, offshore areas, and the Alberta tar sands in order to meet a demand which would quadruple primary energy requirements by the year 2000. Subsequent events proved that the estimated volume of recoverable reserves and the high cost of developing frontier resources were miscalculated. The potential for energy conservation was noted, but key recommendations were based upon an assumption of "business as usual" with respect to demand growth (Table 4.2). Before energy critics had time to muster their arguments, external events were to provide a rude awakening.

The world of international petroleum was transformed in October 1973 when Middle Eastern oil became an increasingly expensive commodity of uncertain supply. Within two days of the outbreak of the Yom Kippur war, the Arab States agreed to use oil as a political weapon. Production levels were reduced and embargoes imposed on exports to the United States and other nations involved in the Arab-Israeli dispute. Within a few months, OPEC had quadrupled the official posted prices of oil, sending reverberations around a world which had become increasingly dependent upon cheap petroleum imports. By this time, oil and gas represented 65 percent of Canada's energy mix, and approximately one million barrels a day were being imported from OPEC members into eastern Canada. For consumers east of the Ottawa Valley Line, who had been enjoying cheaper oil than the rest of the population, the international oil crisis manifested itself in the form of the sudden shock of escalating prices. For the federal government, the immediate task was to adjust to the higher-priced imports and threatened balance-of-payments problem. The longer-term challenge was to devise policies and programs to provide protection against politically motivated supply uncertainties, and to achieve a balance between increasingly costly domestic and imported energy supplies and an unchecked growth in demand.

Some steps had already been taken in September 1973, when a voluntary price freeze on domestic oil and an export charge were introduced in response to higher international prices caused by the pressure of American demand on the world oil market. Following a policy announcement by Prime Minister Trudeau on 6 December, 1973 an Energy Supplies Allocation Board was established to allocate oil in times of shortage, and an Office of Energy Conservation was created within the Department of Energy, Mines and Resources. The planned extension of the oil pipeline from Sarnia to Montreal was announced on 16 January, 1974. This would abolish the Ottawa Valley Line and permit domestic oil supplies to extend further east into the Quebec market. The revised oil policy thus focussed upon emergency measures to offset dislocations in eastern Canada, and a stepped-up effort to secure frontier petroleum supplies. Key components included the provision of financial incentives for frontier exploration and development, intensification of research on oil sands technology, and a proposal to establish a national oil company to participate in development.

The principle of a single domestic price for oil was embodied in the Oil Import Compensation Program introduced in 1974 in order to counteract the reversal of traditional pricing relations east and west of the Ottawa Valley Line. The federal government, with agreement from the provinces, held the price to Canadian consumers down well below the OPEC prices. Eastern importers were compensated for the difference between costs of OPEC supply and the selling price with funds from the charge levied on exports of western oil to U.S. markets. However, these funds would not be limitless, as western oil exports were gradually reduced following a National Energy Board announcement in October 1974 that domestic supplies would not meet the Canadian market as far east as Montreal beyond 1982. In fact, Canada was to become a net importer by late 1975 and payments in the Oil Import Compensation Program climbed from 625 million dollars in the first year to 1.3 billion dollars in 1979,[23] when imported oil at Montreal cost 27 dollars a barrel. By this time exports had fallen to 200,000 barrels (18 percent of domestic production) and the costs of maintaining the single domestic price were being borne with only partial assistance from revenues from a federal excise tax on gasoline.

Predictions of a domestic oil shortfall coincided with warnings of looming natural gas shortages. In April 1975, the National Energy Board released its report which concluded that frontier gas would be needed very soon, thus adding weight to the arguments in favour of a northern pipeline. However, native groups and environmentalists were becoming increasingly vocal in their opposition to this proposal, and the minority Liberal government appointed B.C. Supreme Court Justice Thomas Berger on March 21, 1974 to conduct a public inquiry into the potential social, environmental and economic impacts of a Mackenzie Valley pipeline, and the terms and conditions that should be attached to the right-of-way permit required by the Department of Indian and Northern Affairs. When the Berger Inquiry hearings began the following March, two rival applications for a Mackenzie Valley gas pipeline had been submitted to the National Energy Board by Canadian Arctic Gas Study Ltd. and Foothills Pipeline Ltd. (which had broken away from the GAGSL consortium in September 1974).[24] The contrast in approaches between the Berger Inquiry hearings and the pipeline application hearings of the National Energy Board (begun in March 1976) has received considerable attention.[25] While the Berger Inquiry appeared to be constrained by its advisory role and potentially limiting terms of reference, its formal—and particularly its community—hearings received much greater public attention and more credibility than the more closed and structured proceedings of the NEB hearings which inhibited the effective participation of nongovernmental and non-oil-industry interests. The holistic approach adopted by Justice Berger in evaluating both the social and environmental implications of potential developments associated with pipeline construction marked a turning point in impact assessment in Canada. His highly readable report, *Northern Frontier, Northern Homeland*, tabled in the House of Commons on May 19, 1977, recommended rejection of the Mackenzie Valley route and a ten-year moratorium to allow time for native claims to be settled and appropriate institutions and programs to be developed.

By this time the rationale for northern pipeline construction had changed: discoveries in the Mackenzie Delta were insufficient to justify a pipeline to carry Canadian gas south. In late 1976, Foothills suddenly switched its proposals and submitted a new application to construct a pipeline along the Alaska Highway to carry Alaska's gas south to U.S. markets (Figure 2.2). A few months after the release of the Berger findings, the National Energy Board recommended rejection of the Arctic Gas application to construct a Mackenzie Valley Pipeline and acceptance of the Foothills proposal, despite incomplete documentation of its potential impacts.[26] In February 1978, the federal government introduced the Northern Pipeline Bill (Bill C-25), awarding Foothills a certificate of convenience and necessity. However, the issue was not fully resolved for, in light of subsequent events, it became clear that the U.S. government was not fully committed to the Canadian route, and attempts to secure private U.S. financing met with considerable difficulties.

Following the north slope oil discovery and approval of the Trans-Alaska Pipeline on May 11, 1972, sudden changes in policy context have

Figure 2.2

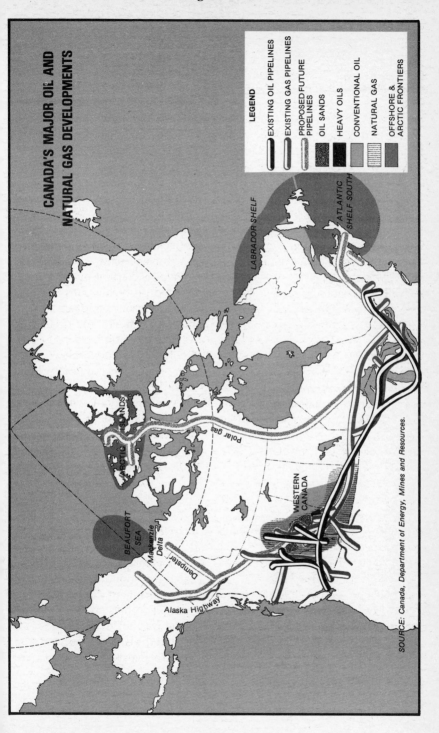

CANADA'S MAJOR OIL AND NATURAL GAS DEVELOPMENTS

LEGEND

EXISTING OIL PIPELINES
EXISTING GAS PIPELINES
PROPOSED FUTURE PIPELINES
OIL SANDS
HEAVY OILS
CONVENTIONAL OIL
NATURAL GAS
OFFSHORE & ARCTIC FRONTIERS

LABRADOR SHELF

ATLANTIC SHELF SOUTH

ARCTIC ISLANDS

Polar gas

WESTERN CANADA

BEAUFORT SEA

Mackenzie Delta

Dempster

Alaska Highway

SOURCE: Canada, Department of Energy, Mines and Resources.

been a characteristic feature as Canadian decision makers responded to a welter of petroleum industry proposals and U.S. government positions regarding the transportation of Alaskan oil and gas to southern markets. The U.S. government faced the problem of resolving the imbalance caused by the limited demand for Alaskan oil on the west coast with a deficit in central and eastern markets. The decision to develop a tanker route to transport oil from Valdez to west coast ports was inevitably complicated by a series of proposals and counter proposals to construct major oil terminals in Puget Sound, Juan de Fuca Strait, or at Kitimat with pipeline connections to the existing continental distribution system. In December 1976, Kitimat Pipeline Ltd. submitted an application to the National Energy Board to construct a pipeline from a proposed oil terminal at Kitimat to Edmonton. The growing public concern over the west coast oil pollution threat found an outlet when the federal government appointed Dr. Andrew Thompson to examine the social and environmental impacts of the proposal. However, the West Coast Oil Ports Inquiry was foreclosed fourteen months later when the federal Cabinet vetoed the Kitimat Project on February 23, 1978. Sewell has analyzed the sequence of events in terms of an issue-attention cycle, wherein the increasing complexity and breadth of economic, social, political and jurisdictional dimensions calls for new institutional approaches.[27]

This is particularly clear in the broader national context of the mid-1970s, when the federal government introduced a number of new policies and programs amid public ambivalence about the so-called "energy crisis."[28] During this period, two major federal policy studies were released: *An Energy Strategy for Canada: Policies for Self-Reliance* (April 1976) and *Energy Futures for Canadians* (June 1978). Brooks has characterized the policy adjustments made between the 1973 and 1976 reports as a shift from acceptance of historic growth in demand to a laissez-faire approach, which assumed that Canadian energy prices would reach world levels but that there would be no major structural changes in the economy.[29] The cornerstones of the econometric analysis and self-sufficiency policy were a target demand growth of 3.5 percent and the assumed economic viability of frontier petroleum.[30] Towards this end, the key elements of the strategy were to move oil prices towards international levels, to reduce net oil imports to one-third of the 1985 demand, and to double the frontier exploration effort within three years. The reduction in energy demand growth was to be achieved via higher prices and conservation measures which would not, however, require Canadian consumers to alter their lifestyles. This reinforced the approach embodied in the national policy on energy conservation, presented to the House of Commons on February 6, 1975, which emphasized the development of a public information and advertising campaign. In February 1976, the federal government announced a number of steps to improve the energy efficiency of automobiles, buildings and major appliances, followed by a series of incentive measures for home insulation. Wellhead oil prices were raised to 9.75 dollars in order to narrow the gap between the international price which was approaching 14 dollars a barrel. From June 1977 onwards, the domestic price was to be raised one dollar every six months until a policy review planned for 1980.[31]

On the supply side, the completion of the pipeline extension to Montreal enabled more domestic oil to reach Quebec, and the federal government announced two investment decisions affecting the frontier effort. Three hundred million dollars were to be invested in Syncrude of Canada Ltd., and a national oil company, Petro-Canada, was established to play a leading role in Arctic and offshore exploration.

Until this stage, the federal approach showed a strong commitment to what Amory Lovins has termed a "hard energy path," which emphasizes oil and gas, central-source electricity generation and nuclear power.[32] However, a series of initiatives in 1977 were directed towards renewable energy technologies. A Renewable Energy Resources Branch was established within EMR to develop policies, programs and public information focussing on solar, biomass and wind sources. Solar demonstration homes were financed through federal funding, and a grant for renewable energy research was awarded to the Institute of Man and Resources on Prince Edward Island. A number of energy-conservation measures were also piloted in the Atlantic Provinces, which were hard-hit by the escalating cost of imported oil.[33]

The difficult nature of energy transitions to be made in a time of rapidly changing domestic and international circumstances was underlined in *Energy Futures for Canadians*, the most recent comprehensive federal review of energy supply and demand options. In order to meet an energy demand growth target of 2.7 percent a year by the year 2000, and 1.3 percent by 2025, the report proposed a broad range of actions aimed at facilitating conservation, increased efficiency of energy use, and provision of alternative energy supplies. The proposed National Energy Policy offered a refinement rather than a significant departure from the 1976 strategy. In recognition of the regional distribution of supply deficits, it was proposed that at least a third of the energy requirements of central and eastern Canada be met by indigenous resources. Key targets included a reduction in the share of oil (especially imports) to 30 percent of the primary energy supply by the year 2000, an increase of electricity's share to 50 percent, and an expansion of oil sands, heavy oils, natural gas and coal development. These objectives, it was postulated, could entail fifteen oil sands and heavy oil plants in the next twenty years, large-scale tidal and hydroelectric projects,[34] and increased investment in coal-fired and nuclear generating facilities. Renewable sources, other than conventional hydro, were to provide at least 5 percent of the energy supply. The report assumed that, while domestic prices should rise towards the world level, the production costs per unit of these large-scale energy projects would be lower than international oil prices.

Federal government initiatives of the last three years have tended to reflect acceptance of the basic tenets of *Energy Futures for Canadians*. For example, within a month of the report's release, Royal Assent was given to the Energy Supplies Emergency Act which provided authority to allocate supplies during emergencies. Joint research funds were established by Canada, Alberta and Saskatchewan for heavy oil research and oil sands technology. Provisions for international prices for Syncrude oil were incorporated into the Petroleum Administration Act, and a number of expansion proposals were announced by the energy industry. Discussions were initiated between the federal government and Alberta regarding an incentive pricing system for natural gas in eastern markets. The Lower Churchill Development Corporation was established by the federal government and Newfoundland with an initial mandate to investigate the potential for further hydroelectric development in Labrador for the energy-short Atlantic region. In June 1978, Ontario and the federal government reached an agreement concerning radioactive waste management and investigation of deep underground disposal sites.[35] Coal evaluation programs were underway in western Canada and the Maritimes, and upgrading of the coal transportation system from the western provinces to eastern markets initiated.

Meanwhile, efforts to pursue soft energy technologies and to encourage conservation have intensified. The Renewable Resources Branch and Office of Energy Conservation were amalgamated in 1978, and new conservation and renewable energy programs costing 380 million dollars over five years were announced. These ranged from FIRE (Forest Industry Renewable Energy Program), which was designed to provide financial incentives for the forest products industry to convert to wood residues as an energy source, to LEBDA (Low Energy Building Design Awards) and PUSH (Purchase and Use of Solar Heating Program), which were intended to stimulate passive solar systems research and development in Canada.[36] A number of federal-provincial cost-sharing agreements concerning conservation and renewable energy demonstration projects are also under negotiation.

The central focus of the federal solar energy program has been to offer incentives to encourage the development of a viable solar home heating technology by Canadian manufacturers in order to eventually reduce residential energy requirements. In this respect, both Sewell and Berkowitz have noted that it differs significantly from the much larger U.S. program, which offers a wide range of incentives for the adoption of prototypes by homeowners, as well as research and development.[37] Sewell, in particular, argues that the Canadian emphasis upon design and demonstration projects alone is unlikely to result in rapid adoption of solar heating technology, and that a broader program is necessary to overcome barriers which include costs, the problem of retrofitting older housing stock, public apathy, lack of information and lack of support from financial and other institutions. The question of legal rights to sunlight must also be addressed if passive solar heating is to be more widely adopted in Canada.

The federal govenment and, to a lesser extent, the provinces have employed a somewhat wider range of incentives, disincentives and regulations aimed at promoting improved energy efficiency in specific end-use sectors but they have not introduced measures that would alter Canadian economic structure or lifestyles to any substantial degree. The key targets have been space heating savings and increased fuel efficiency in transportation, combined with an information and incentives approach for industry.

The residential and commercial sectors have been emphasized because space heating represents a considerable proportion of the total energy requirements. Federal programs have focussed upon providing information, via a number of publications including *100 Ways to Save Energy and Money in the Home*, demonstration projects such as the energy audit programs which began in Newfoundland and Prince Edward Island and later expanded to other provinces, and the incentive approach of the Canadian Home Insulation Program which offered direct grants to homeowners. A number of provincial authorities such as B.C. Hydro have introduced loan programs for reinsulation of houses. However, the provinces have been reluctant to adopt the draft energy conservation provisions prepared by the federal government in 1977 for incorporation into the National Building Code.

While some provincial governments have reduced speed limits and introduced other measures that affect the fuel efficiency of automobiles, there has been considerable foot dragging with respect to the funding of urban rapid transit systems by the two senior levels of government. The federal government embarked upon a very visible conservation information and advertising campaign, but met with less success in persuading car dealers to accept its voluntary fuel economy labelling scheme. A federal excise tax was placed on heavy cars and new automobile air conditioners, and in 1975 a gasoline excise tax was introduced with the aim of generating income for the oil import compensation program, and with the hope that it would promote conservation.

While some provinces, including Ontario, Nova Scotia and Prince Edward Island, have introduced some industrial energy conservation measures, the federal approach has been to provide information on improving energy efficiency and tax incentives for the use of energy-saving equipment, and to suggest the adoption of voluntary conservation goals. Although a number of alternative strategies were suggested in

Energy Conservation in Canada: Programs and Perspectives (1977), few steps have been made to address inherent energy inefficiencies within a broader societal context. Cogeneration (or the combined production of electricity and district heating) has received some attention, but the more fundamental issues of end-use matching, energy efficiency in land-use planning and agricultural production, resource recovery and waste reduction have only recently been explored.[38]

The assumptions underlying Canada's move towards an increasingly electrical society are now under question. While proponents argue that electricity is a highly versatile form of energy which can be derived from a variety of sources to meet a wide range of uses, Lovins and other advocates of a soft energy path approach propose that greater benefits would be derived if a diverse mix of renewable energy sources were matched in scale, location and quality to specific end-use needs. The debate has shown a tendency to become polarized, as much of the conventional wisdom has been institutionalized within provincial power utilities, some of which are experiencing growing public pressure to justify their project plans in light of disputed demand forecasts. Some recent initiatives reflect a growing recognition of the potential impact of large-scale projects, whether nuclear or hydroelectric, and the implications of electrical energy planning for provincial economies and societal values. For example, a Royal Commission on Electric Power Planning was appointed by the Ontario government in 1975 to examine the broader issues associated with the long-range electric power planning of Ontario Hydro. (A subsequent amendment of the broad terms of reference called for specific reports on nuclear generation as well as regional power requirements.[39]) The Commission, under the chairmanship of Arthur Porter, held a number of public meetings and published interim reports to encourage public debate and participation, and intervenors were granted funding to prepare presentations for the formal hearings. A key feature was that the Commission was able to insist upon full disclosure of Ontario Hydro information. On February 29, 1980, after a series of often contentious hearings, the Porter Commission submitted its recommendations to the Ontario government. It concluded that there should be a reorientation to end-use demand management, a moratorium on additional nuclear power stations if there is insufficient progress in solving both the technical and social aspects of nuclear waste disposal by 1990,[40] demonstration of alternative technologies (particularly solar and biomass), more attention to land-use environmental concerns, and a greater commitment to energy conservation and effective public participation in planning.

Although it is too soon to foresee the extent to which the Porter Commission recommendations will be incorporated into energy planning in Ontario, which faces a growing energy deficit, there are some initial signs of institutional change in British Columbia, which has a considerable and diverse energy potential, including hydroelectric power, wood waste from the forest products industry, natural gas, coal, solar, and geothermal sources, but which imports an increasing share of its oil requirements. In December 1978, the Ministry of Mines and Petroleum Resources was given the broader responsibility of integrating energy policies and programs and became the Ministry of Energy, Mines and Petroleum Resources. A new Energy Policy Committee was established in order to coordinate the programs of the Ministry and two Crown Corporations, B.C. Hydro and Power Authority and B.C. Petroleum Corporation. Two years later, the government introduced a new policy framework with the stated aim of achieving energy security in accordance with other social, economic and environmental objectives.[41] Although the policy statement lacked detail, a number of specific objectives were identified. These included a reduced dependence on oil via substitution of natural gas, promotion of energy conservation, increased research and development, a new energy project review process which would now assess project justification as well as potential impacts within a broader social and environmental context, and an energy pricing system which would reflect long-term replacement costs. A new B.C. Utilities Commission took over the functions of the pre-existing B.C. Energy Commission and acquired full responsibility for electricity and gas regulation from the Crown corporation, B.C. Hydro. This changed the autonomous position of the power utility, which had been criticized by environmentalists, politicians and journalists for its energy demand forecasts, rate structure, and active consideration of large-scale hydroelectric schemes on B.C.'s undeveloped northern rivers. Although the most recent forecast of a 3 percent annual growth in electricity demand between 1978 and 1996 is well below the historic growth rate,[42] the challenge facing the new policy framework and institutional arrangements will be to integrate total energy planning and to respond to proposals as diverse as the development of northeastern coal deposits for export to Japan, a coal liquefaction project at Hat Creek, increased use of biomass energy by the forest products industry, and geothermal power.

At the national level, the choice of policies and programs is made more complex by the existence of jurisdictional conflicts and differences in provincial interests, particularly with respect to the split between energy-surplus and energy-deficit regions. For example, the federal government is caught between Alberta and eastern consuming provinces over the question of oil price increases, while both Alberta and British Columbia oppose a recent federal proposal to provide a new source of revenue by imposing an indirect tax on natural gas exports. As energy projects grow larger and more capital-intensive, impacts upon regional economies and the environment become more pervasive. Social and environmental impacts are being borne in more distant energy hinterlands as projects are developed further away from centres of demand. This is particularly the case in northern petroleum development and large-scale hydroelectric projects such as James Bay, where the long-term interests of native communities are affected. Drilling programs in the Beaufort Sea and Arctic Islands challenge not only our technological capability but also the institutional processes established to evaluate potential impacts on highly sensitive environments. The increased tempo of the exploration effort following the recent Hibernia oil discovery close to the 200-mile (322 km) limit off the coast of Newfoundland signals the importance of devising regional economic policies and planning programs in order to absorb related onshore developments. There is also the issue of reconciling perceived immediate benefits with the long-term interest. For example, the National Energy Board's approval, in July 1980, of the prebuild of the southern portion of the Alaska Highway pipeline could enable Albertan producers to increase gas exports to U.S. markets, but raises the question of meeting domestic requirements in the more distant future. The delays and uncertainty regarding the U.S. commitment to complete the Alaskan section of this pipeline underlines the important role of external relations with respect to Canadian energy policy decisions.

A predominant theme of recent statements has been a quest for energy self-reliance. The challenges in the 1980s will be to develop effective means of responding to changes in the international scene, to reconcile regional interests, to demonstrate new supply and conversion technologies, and to remove the institutional and social barriers to demand reduction and the development of more conserving lifestyles.

Energy Research in Canada

Government and industry investment in energy research and development in Canada reflects the evolution of the predominant energy supply mix and the relative costs of developing specific energy technologies. Even after the international energy crisis, in a period of rising concern about securing costly oil imports, the research effort continued to be oriented towards increasing supplies rather than reducing demand (Table 5.2). Investment in renewable energy research tripled (and doubled in the case of conservation) between 1976 and 1979, but nuclear power continues to receive a lion's share of federal energy R & D funding. Fossil fuel research dominates the energy industry sector, which has intensified its efforts to develop improved offshore drilling and northern gas pipeline technologies and, together with governments and provincial utilities, has shown an increased interest in exploring coal gasification and liquefaction technologies. Provincial government and power utility involvment tends to reflect regional energy supply priorities. For example, Alberta is investing 144 million dollars over five years in oil sands research, while utilities such as Ontario Hydro and Hydro Quebec play a leading role in research aimed at reducing capital costs of electricity generation and improving long-distance transmission. By comparison, the research effort in nonhydro renewable energy and demand management remains small.

Although there has been some shift in focus, particularly at the federal level, in response to threatened energy shortages and impressive international oil price hikes, there continues to be a gap between technological innovations, existing institutional arrangements and changing social needs. The physical and natural sciences will continue to play a crucial role in developing nonconventional fossil fuel and renewable energy supplies, and in improving our ability to predict, avoid or mitigate adverse environmental impacts. However, the nature and scale of social and economic changes implicit in developing new technologies and different patterns of energy consumption call for a much better understanding of the processes involved and therefore more, and more effective, social science research. The extent to which the existing state of the art will be able to meet this challenge continues to be a topic of debate, but a number of potential contributions have been identified. These include expanding the range of choice (particularly with respect to identifying means for overcoming institutional barriers to technological and social change), monitoring shifts

Table 5.2
Energy Research and Development
Expenditures of the Federal Government
and Energy Industries

	Energy Industries[1] 1977-78 (percent)	Federal government (percent)	
		1977-78	1978-79
Renewable energy	5.5	6.0	9.0
Conservation	4.7	9.0	12.0
Fossil fuels	65.0	10.0	11.0
Transportation & transmission	18.7	5.0	5.0
Nuclear power	6.1	69.0	62.0
Coordinating & monitoring	—	1.1	1.0
Total (million dollars)	113.0	129.9	144.5

[1]Includes oil companies and provincial utilities.
Source: Canada, Department of Energy, Mines and Resources, *Energy in Canada: An Overview* (Ottawa, 1978), p. 54.

in social values, technology assessment, environmental and social impact assessment and ex-post evaluations of policies and programs.[43]

By nature of their expertise and range of cross-disciplinary interests, geographers could make an important contribution to these endeavours. However, with a few exceptions, the discipline has generally neglected energy-related research until very recently. In a 1961 issue of *The Canadian Geographer*, Chapman identified some key characteristics of the energy field which would be attractive for geographical analysis.[44] While not entirely indicative of the academic research effort, only nine articles in *The Canadian Geographer* have addressed energy topics since that time, six of them referring to Canadian energy developments. A lack of ready-made theory and research methodology has been cited elsewhere as partial explanations of neglect,[45] but these cannot be the only factors. The central interest of human and economic geographers in the urban processes of southern Canada, the sheer scale of energy technologies, and the centralized and technological nature of energy industry decision making may also have contributed. The energy events of the mid-1970s have provoked a growing geographical research effort, particularly with respect to policy, institutional and behavioural studies. The nature and scale of energy-related technological and social change in the future provide an exciting challenge for the physical, natural and social sciences. Will geographers respond to it?

Postscript

On September 3, 1981, eighteen months after negotiations began, an energy-pricing agreement was settled between the federal government and the government of Alberta. The agreement, which extends from September 1, 1981 to December 31, 1986, ends the 120,000 barrels/day cutback in oil production introduced by the Alberta government earlier in the year. Under the terms of the agreement, the price of gasoline will increase to an estimated four dollars a gallon by 1986, not including provincial taxes. The wellhead price of conventional "old" (pre-1981) oil will increase from 18.75 dollars to 21.25 dollars a barrel on October 1, 1981 and to 25.75 dollars in 1982. From January 1, 1983 until July 1, 1986, the price of old oil will increase by eight dollars a year until it reaches 57.75 dollars a barrel. (These prices are not to exceed 75 percent of the world oil price.) The price of newly discovered oil and of oil from the Albertan tar sands will be determined by a new formula, and it can reach the world price level. The oil revenue shares of the federal and Alberta governments will increase while that of the petroleum industry will be lowered. Finally, the federal export tax on Albertan natural gas will be removed, thus paving the way for similar action in the case of British Columbia.

Notes

[1] John Davis, *Canadian Energy Prospects*. Report prepared for the Royal Commission on Canada's Economic Prospects (Ottawa: 1957), p. 116.

[2] Canada, Department of Energy, Mines and Resources, *Energy in Canada: An Overview* (Ottawa: 1978), p. 26.

[3] British Columbia, Coal Task Force, *Coal in British Columbia: A Technical Appraisal* (Victoria: 1976), p. 75.

[4] John Davis, *op. cit.*, p. 99.

[5] Canadian Arctic Resources Committee, "Canada's energy crisis: a bizarre case of bungling," *Northern Perspectives* 4 (1976), p. 10.

[6] Kenneth North, "Canada's oil and gas: surplus or shortage?" in *Energy Policy: The Global Challenge*, ed. Peter N. Nemetz (Montreal: Institute for Policy Research, 1979), p. 53.

[7] Canada, Department of Energy, Mines and Resources, *op. cit.*, p. 22.

[8] Kenneth North, *op. cit.*, p. 57.

[9] Ontario, *Report of the Royal Commission on Electric Power Planning* (Toronto: 1980), Volume 1, pp. 105, 216.

[10] John Davis, *op. cit.*, p. 375.

[11] Canada, Department of Energy, Mines and Resources, *An Energy Policy for Canada—Phase 1* (Ottawa: 1973), Volume 1, p. 34.

[12] Canada-Alberta-Saskatchewan, *The Peace-Athabaska Delta: A Canadian Resource* (Ottawa: Peace-Athabaska Delta Project Group, 1972).

[13] See John V. Krutilla, *The Columbia River Treaty: The Economics of an International River Basin Development* (Baltimore: Johns Hopkins Press, 1967); and Neil A. Swainson, *Conflict over the Columbia: The Canadian Background to an Historic Treaty* (Montreal: McGill-Queen's University Press, 1979).

[14] Canada, Department of Energy, Mines and Resources, *An Energy Strategy for Canada: Policies for Self-Reliance* (Ottawa: 1976), p. 106.

[15] Joel Darmstadter, Joy Dunkerley, and Jack Alterman, "International variations in energy use: findings from a comparative study," *Annual Review of Energy* 3 (1978), p. 203.

[16] Canada, Department of Energy, Mines and Resources, *Energy Futures for Canadians* (Ottawa: 1978), p. 85.

[17] Statistics Canada, *Quarterly Report on Energy Supply-Demand in Canada* (Ottawa, 1979), Catalogue No. 57-003, pp. 2–3.

[18] The federal government retained such proprietary rights in Manitoba, Saskatchewan and Alberta until 1930.

[19] These were Atomic Energy of Canada Ltd., Eldorado Nuclear Ltd., Eldorado Aviation Ltd. and the Dominion Coal Board. Eldorado Nuclear had been acquired during the Second World War to ensure a supply of refined uranium. Atomic Energy of Canada was established in 1952 to develop and promote commercial use of the CANDU reactor technology.

[20] Canada, Department of Energy, Mines and Resources, *Annual Report 1970-71* (Ottawa), p. 3.

[21] Edgar J. Dosman, *The National Interest: The Politics of Northern Development 1968-1975* (Toronto: McClelland and Stewart, 1975).

[22] John B. Robinson, "Policy, Pipelines, and Public Participation: the National Energy Board's Northern Pipeline Hearings," in *Resources and Environment: Policy*

Perspectives for Canada, ed. O.P. Dwivedi (Toronto: McClelland and Stewart, 1980), p. 181.

23 Canada, Department of Energy, Mines and Resources, Annual Report 1974–75 (Ottawa), p. 6.

24 Industry rivalries are discussed in Peter Foster, The Blue-Eyed Sheiks: The Canadian Oil Establishment (Toronto: McClelland and Stewart, 1979).

25 For a review of actors and their positions, see John B. Robinson, op. cit.; David W. Fischer and Robert F. Keith, "Canadian energy development: a case study of policy processes in northern petroleum development," in The Energy Syndrome, ed. Leon N. Lindberg (Lexington, Mass.: Lexington Books, 1977), pp. 63–118; and W.R. Derrick Sewell, "The Berger Inquiry," in Environmental Policy Review and Project Appraisal, eds. T. O'Riordan and W.R.D. Sewell (London: John Wiley and Sons, forthcoming).

26 The Alaska Highway Pipeline Inquiry, under the chairmanship of Dean K. Lysyk, was much foreshortened, being limited to a three-month period compared to the fifteen months of Berger Inquiry hearings.

27 W.R. Derrick Sewell and Neil A. Swainson, "West coast oil pollution policies: Canadian responses to risk assessment," in Resources and the Environment: Policy Perspectives for Canada, ed. O.P. Dwivedi (Toronto: McClelland and Stewart, 1980), pp. 216–242.

28 The Canadian public's perception of energy shortages has declined in recent years because of conflicting announcements about oil and gas reserves, oil prices maintained well below international levels, and a widespread distrust of major oil companies. See Gerald Keller and Gordon H.G. McDougall, "Energy attitudes and behaviours of Canadians (1975–1979)," in Energy Attitudes and Policies, eds. Edgar L. Jackson and Leslie T. Foster, Cornett Occasional Papers No. 2 (Victoria: University of Victoria, Department of Geography). pp. 19–32.

29 David B. Brooks, "Choosing an energy future for Canada," in Energy Policy: The Global Challenge, ed. Peter N. Nemetz, op. cit., p. 75.

30 Following a decline in offshore effort in recent years, as a result of low success rates and jurisdictional disputes, 56 million dollars were spent on exploratory drilling in 1976, all off the east coast. There was a significant discovery of natural gas on the Labrador Shelf, but jurisdictional disputes continued to cloud the situation.

31 The policy came under early review when the Conservatives, who won the federal election in May 1979, proposed to accelerate the price change to 2 dollars every six months. Following the Liberal return to power after the federal election in February 1980, Prime Minister Trudeau argued in favour of some form of price blend between domestic and imported oil. The federal government was unable to reach agreement with the leading producer province, and Premier Lougheed unilaterally raised the price by 2 dollars to 16.75 a barrel, effective August 1 (still far below the world price of approximately 36 dollars). The federal-provincial dispute over oil pricing is not resolved and further action is likely in the near future.

32 Amory B. Lovins, "Energy strategy: the road not taken?" Foreign Affairs 55 (1976), pp. 65–96.

33 For example, the provision of matching grants to encourage energy-conserving process changes, and assistance to Prince Edward Island and Nova Scotia to establish an energy-audit and public awareness program similar to Ontario's energy-bus idea.

[34] In 1968 it was concluded that a proposed Bay of Fundy tidal power project was not economically competitive with alternative energy sources. However, the impact of post-1973 oil price hikes in the Atlantic Provinces has resulted in reconsideration and a detailed federal-provincial review.

[35] In November 1977, an independent panel's report had concluded that the nuclear program need not be delayed provided that work was begun immediately on a national plan for nuclear waste disposal. See A.M. Aikin, J.M. Harrison, and F.K. Hare (Chairman), *The Management of Canada's Nuclear Wastes* (Ottawa: Department of Energy, Mines and Resources, 1977).

[36] Canada, Department of Energy, Mines and Resources, *New Energy/New Opportunities: Programs to Develop Renewable Energy and Conservation* (Ottawa: 1979) Report E179-1; and *Tree Power: An Assessment of the Energy Potential of Forest Biomass in Canada* (1978) Report ER78-1.

[37] W.R. Derrick Sewell, *Accelerating the Acceptance of Solar Heating: North American Experience and International Implications* (Ottawa: Department of Energy, Mines and Resources, 1979) Report ER79-7; and M.K. Berkowitz, "A review of Canadian and U.S. solar energy policies," *Canadian Public Policy* 5 (1979), pp. 157-162.

[38] For example, see Science Council of Canada, *Canada as a Conserver Society: Resource Uncertainties and the Need for New Technologies* (Ottawa, 1977), Report No. 27; Ontario, *The Report of the Royal Commission on Electric Power Planning*, Volume 1 (Toronto, 1980); two special issues of the journal *Alternatives* on Soft Energy Paths in 1979 (Vol. 8, No. 3/4) and 1980 (Vol. 9, No. 1); and the International Symposium on Energy Conservation through Land Use Planning, Montreal, March 1980.

[39] Ontario, Royal Commission on Electric Power Planning, *A Race Against Time, Interim Report on Nuclear Power in Ontario* (Toronto, 1978).

[40] Note the contrast with the findings of Aikin, Harrison and Hare, *op. cit.* The Commission also recommended a down-scaling of funding for nuclear power research and development, unlike the Science Council of Canada which recently called for 3.8 billion dollars to be spent on demonstration projects over the next 30 years: 59 percent on nuclear and only 3.6 percent on renewable technologies. (It assumed that nonhydro renewable sources could contribute up to 7.7 percent of the total energy mix by the year 2000.) See Science Council of Canada, *Roads to Self-Reliance: The Necessary National Demonstrations* (Ottawa, 1979), Report No. 30, pp. 12 and 29.

[41] British Columbia, *An Energy Secure British Columbia: The Challenge and the Opportunity* (Victoria, 1980).

[42] British Columbia, Ministry of Energy, Mines and Petroleum Resources. *British Columbia Energy Supply and Requirements Forecast, 1979-1996* (Victoria, 1980), Summary Report, p. 7.

[43] W.R. Derrick Sewell, "Societal problems and scientific research: the case for a re-ordering of priorities," paper presented at the Science Forum of the Conference on Security and Co-operation in Europe, Hamburg, 18-24 February 1980.

[44] John D. Chapman, "A geography of energy: an emerging field of study," *Canadian Geographer* 5 (1961), pp. 10-15.

[45] Anthony Hoare, "Alternative energies: alternative geographies?" *Progress in Human Geography* 3 (1979), p. 506.

3/Northern Resources Development
William C. Wonders

In many ways the story of Canada is the story of resource development, and from the earliest years this has had a strong northern orientation. Though it was fish that first drew significant numbers of Europeans to Canada's eastern margins, it was fur which led them westwards and northwards across the continent. In the process, not only was the major geographic framework of the nation delineated, but the enormity of distance and area was established. Resource development, like political development, depended upon the evolution of a transportation net that could cope with these latter geographic characteristics. Though such a net was established, it still is far from perfect, as the ongoing debate on quality and frequency of service demonstrates, in all parts of the country but particularly in the North.

One of the most troublesome aspects of "northern resource development" is the imprecision associated with the term. While many other resource issues are complex, there is general appreciation of the core problems involved. "Northern resource development" like "northern development" has been an oft-used phrase over the past quarter century, yet there still is no consensus on what exactly is involved. "Northern" is geographically imprecise and suffers from a wide range of interpretations.[1] "Development" is seen by some as a positive, desirable objective, though subject to a variety of interpretations also, while others view it as nondesirable if its further manifestations repeat past patterns. It is unlikely that there ever will be universal agreement on these two critical elements—what is "northern" for one person is not for another, what is "development" for one is seen as exploitation and perhaps even regression by another.

The Problem
Like most vexatious issues, the problem of northern resource development has many facets, even if it were agreed that the term implies the orderly utilization of natural resources of our northern areas for optimum benefit (social? economic?) of all (Canadians? northern residents? company stockholders?).[2] In that utilization, several related aspects immediately are involved, each contributing to the problem.

Vast Space, Small Population

No other part of Canada still finds itself endowed to the same degree with such vast distances and area as does the North. These increasingly are viewed as positive attractions for much of the world, but when coupled with a very small resident population, they make for formidable basic difficulties in the development of northern resources (Table 1.3). Significant improvement has been effected in recent years in transportation facilities in the North, for example scheduled airline service into the Arctic Islands from both western and eastern parts of the country, northward extension of road linkages. The fact still remains that Baffin Island, for example, covers about twice as much area as all of Great Britain or four times that of southern Ontario, yet has a total population of only about one-half that of Cobourg, Ontario![3]

In recent years, reflecting the combined effect of improved health services and new resource developments, population increases in the territories have been the highest relatively in Canada, about three times the national average.[5] While this is significant, particularly in the resultant demands already felt and to be expected for northern education facilities and employment opportunities, it is not likely to change the overall man/land ratios. Recent population projections for the Northwest Territories place the 1985 figure at 57,355, or at 62,037 depending on differing starting points, with an average annual increase just over 3 percent.[6]

Table 1.3
Land Area and Population Distribution,
Canada and Provinces, 1977[4]

	Land area (km², '000s)	Population ('000s)	Population density (persons/km²)
Canada	9,205	23,291	2.5
Newfoundland	372	564	1.5
Prince Edward Island	6	120	20.2
Nova Scotia	53	835	15.8
New Brunswick	72	686	9.5
Quebec	1,358	6,283	4.6
Ontario	917	8,374	9.1
Manitoba	548	1,031	1.9
Saskatchewan	570	936	1.6
Alberta	638	1,900	3.0
British Columbia	893	2,498	2.8
Yukon Territory	532	21	0.04
Northwest Territories	3,246	43	0.01

Given the basic problem of enormous space and small population, any transportation in the North must be expensive. Two additional regional characteristics add to this: the length and severity of northern winters and the fragmented nature of much of Canada's most northerly area in the Arctic Archipelago. Even in the southern Yukon and in the Mackenzie Valley where an elementary road net has been established and where the majority of the territories' population is located, vehicle operating costs remain disproportionately high for fuel and oil, maintenance, tires and insurance for commercial motor carriers, with additional expenses for custom heater equipment, rock shielding, chains, tarpaulins and communications equipment necessary in the North. Podmore established "that line-haul costs for northern carriers (in the Mackenzie Valley area) average at least 15 to 20 percent higher than similar costs incurred on southern Canadian operations. However, the average operating ratio, and, therefore, revenue generation, is higher for northern carriers. Considering the unique difficulties of northern operation, and the vulnerability of demand for carrier services on some routes to short-term changes in the level of mineral or hydrocarbon exploration, northern motor carriers may be entitled to an equal rate-of-return on their investments,"[7] pushing charges still higher.

Northern resource development obviously requires transportation facilities, yet these always will continue to be relatively expensive, with little opportunity to offset the costs by a large resident population in a compact area of small distances. Technical limitations no longer are insurmountable. As Marsden concluded, "The real problem lies in moving materials at costs low enough to allow northern residents a competitive place in the national economy and access to external markets."[8]

Political Fragmentation of the North

The federal government still retains essential control of the territories lying north of 60°N, just under 40 percent of the total area of Canada. There is consensus that "northern Canada" extends well south of 60°N, of course, though there is considerable divergence of opinion on the precise location of its southern boundary. Hamelin's recent attempt at dealing with this perennial problem is shown in Figure 1.3.[9] Only the three Maritime Provinces are excluded from partial inclusion within the limits of northern Canada. Northern resources development concerns all Canadians directly and indirectly.

Involvement of most provincial governments as well as the federal government complicates the problem of northern resource development. While cooperation can and does occur between governments, difficulties and potential difficulties exist. Resource ownership by the provinces makes cooperation all the more desirable, yet frequently all the more difficult as negotiations between Alberta and Ottawa reveal in the matter of oil and

Figure 1.3

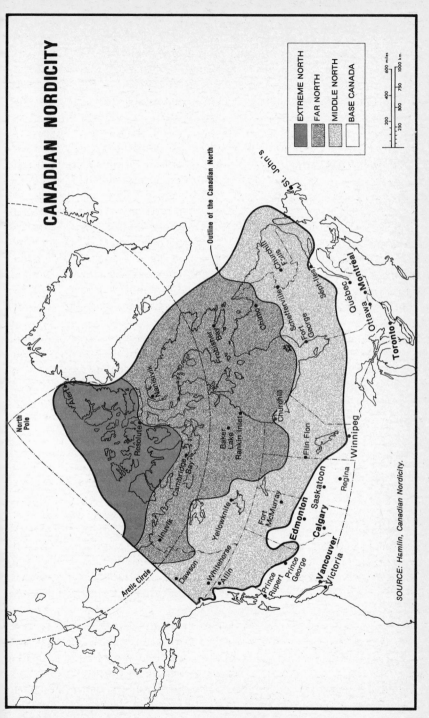

CANADIAN NORDICITY

Outline of the Canadian North

EXTREME NORTH
FAR NORTH
MIDDLE NORTH
BASE CANADA

North Pole

Arctic Circle

Alert
Resolute
Inuvik
Cambridge Bay
Nanisivik
Frobisher Bay
Baker Lake
Rankin Inlet
Chimo
Churchill
Schefferville
Fort George
Sept-Îles
St. John's
Québec
Montréal
Ottawa
Toronto
Winnipeg
Flin Flon
Dawson
Whitehorse
Atlin
Yellowknife
Fort McMurray
Prince Rupert
Prince George
Victoria
Vancouver
Calgary
Edmonton
Saskatoon
Regina

SOURCE: Hamlin, Canadian Nordicity.

gas. The debate between Quebec and Newfoundland on Labrador hydroelectric resources illustrates that political difficulties may involve province
versus province, as well as Ottawa versus province. The federal government is under strong local pressure from the territories to transfer control
of their natural resources to them as they press towards provincial status,
adding a federal versus territorial dimension. Finally, there is the potential
at least for future national versus foreign political confrontation in
northern resource development. Foreign utilization of northern marine
resources during the whaling era of the past occurred before governmental
presence, though in its final phase it resulted in the despatch of the RCMP
to Herschel Island in 1903 (as they earlier had established Canadian legal
presence in the Yukon during the Klondike Gold Rush). The Arctic marine
resource exploration for oil and gas will make for increased official contact
between Canada and its northern neighbours, the United States in Alaska,
and Greenland, in related exploration, production and transportation.

Demand for Northern Resources

It has been said, "Resources *are* not, they *become!*"[10] This is particularly true
of those of the North. Because of their remoteness from the main centres
of demand, only those resources of high value/low weight or bulk could
warrant the high costs of development. Traditionally, furs in our history
were such a useable northern natural resource. In the latter part of the
nineteenth century gold brought in the first of the miners. A broadening
base of northern resource development occurred in the present century,
chiefly in additional mines and forest products along the more accessible
southern margins of the region.[11] Since World War II the enormous
growth in demand for industrial raw materials and power by the industrial
nations, particularly by the United States and Japan, has led to world-wide
search and development programs, with northern Canada included, both
south and north of 60°N. Even the most remote Queen Elizabeth Islands of
the "Extreme North" are involved in the current search for fuel resources.

Among the most important of postwar northern resource developments have been the iron ore mines of Labrador, the expansion of older
mines and opening of new ones in northern Quebec and Ontario, the nickel
mines of northern Manitoba, the uranium mines of Saskatchewan, the
varied new mines of northern B.C., the lead-zinc mines at Faro in the
Yukon and at Pine Point in the Northwest Territories, with expanded gold-
silver production in the Yellowknife-Great Bear Lake area and tungsten
near the Yukon border. Even the Arctic has been included: the Rankin Inlet
nickel mine (now closed); lead-zinc is in production from the Nanisivik
mine on northern Baffin Island and is scheduled for production from the
Arvik mine on Little Cornwallis Island. Forest resource industries have
been expanded and new ones begun across the southern sectors of the area.
Massive hydroelectric projects have been brought into production in

Labrador, northwestern Quebec, northern Manitoba and northern British Columbia. Demand for hydrocarbon fuels has involved northern Alberta (from both conventional and oil sands sources), northeastern British Columbia and the Mackenzie Valley, and also the Canadian Arctic in the Beaufort Sea, Sverdrup Islands, and Baffin Bay sectors.

We no longer are speaking of "potential" resources of the North—it already has been incorporated into the national and the world industrial systems in recent years. From all evidence, that process will be intensified in the future. The oil and gas industry is the focus of much attention in its exploration activity in the North. That activity and subsequent production are essential in its opinion, for our well-being even in the 1980s. In late 1976 Govier warned, "It is evident that even if oil sands production occurs at the maximum rate now expected, and the threshold reserves to permit production from both the East Coast and North of 60° are developed, production from these sources will barely maintain Canada's crude oil productive capacity after 1985 at about two-thirds of its total requirements."[12]

A note of caution should be added for those who envisage the North as a cornucopia to provide for all our future resource needs. One often hears the Canadian Shield especially referred to as a "storehouse of mineral wealth." It does indeed provide an abundance of minerals, but it must be noted that the areas of potential mineral importance are not universal and occur only in limited extent. Those which realistically may support productive mines are even more limited. Similarly, other northern resources are not distributed with convenient uniformity, whether they be fur, forests or anything else. Hare suggests that "Instead of praising in fulsome language the prodigality of nature, Canadians should perhaps wonder how nature managed to put so little of use into an area so large."[13] Finally, because of the high costs involved in northern resource development, a deterioration in market demand or introduction of a cheaper product or new technology often results in early withdrawal of the resource activity from the northern scene unless additional government assistance is forthcoming.

Northern Resource Development and the Environment

The same modern technology which increasingly needs the resources of the North and which has provided the means to develop them brings with it the threat of radical transformation of the environment and of the traditional way of life of northern residents. No aspect of the problem is more difficult than this, nor arouses more heated debate. It is likely to continue indefinitely.

In an effort to offset the high costs involved in northern resource development, the scale of operations has become enormous for most projects. Yesteryear's commercial utilization of the fur resource did not radically alter the environment, though it may have affected the relative numbers of species locally and also started the process of concentration of native population into permanent communities which has accelerated in recent decades. Even the first mining operations resulted in but a temporary alteration of the environment. Not so the increasingly massive developments of today and tomorrow. Two projects illustrating something of this magnitude are the James Bay Power Project of northwestern Quebec and the Syncrude oil sands plant of northeastern Alberta.

The area involved in the James Bay Project is some 410,000 km^2, about one-quarter of the total area of Canada's largest province and over five times as large as New Brunswick! The ultimate power to be generated by the La Grande River complex will be over ten million megawatts. The largest single unit (and world's biggest underground hydroelectric plant), LG 2, officially opened in October 1979, required construction of a three-kilometre-long dam forming a reservoir half the size of Prince Edward Island. Flooding, river diversion, road and plant construction have had major environmental and social impact on the area and its native inhabitants, but are simply the latest in a series of very large hydroelectric projects across northern Canada (Churchill Falls, Nelson River, Peace River). The disastrous impact of the Bennett Dam on the Peace-Athabaska Delta region was particularly noticeable.[14] The Yukon River figures in proposed projects from time to time, while a seven million dollar feasibility study was underway on the Slave River in 1980. Whether the financial benefits outweigh the ecological disruption is highly controversial.[15]

About 60,000 km^2 of oil sands occur in northern Alberta. The potential oil reserves in this form are estimated to be twice as large as known recoverable reserves in the Middle East, though technological and cost factors have delayed development. Increasing demand and prices have made it possible to start on commercial extraction from the Athabasca oil sands, the largest of the four major deposits. Presently two plants are in production, with a third (of perhaps ultimately ten?) scheduled for completion in 1985 if oil pricing disagreements can be resolved. What is noticeable is the increasing scale of operation considered commercially essential for what was even initially a very large development. The initial plant to go into production (in 1967) can recover 10,300 m^3/day of "synthetic crude." The second plant began in 1978 with a recovery rate of 20,000 m^3/day; the third is planning on a daily recovery rate equal to the combined output of the first two. Apart from the area actually taken up by the plants which is localized, the situation of the sands astride the Athabasca River gives cause for concern about the far down-stream environmental repercussions. Present recovery methods have drawbacks in that they require huge tailings ponds to hold liquid wastes, and they also discharge large volumes of sulphur dioxide, causing fears of long-range water and air pollution, despite control measures and on-going research.

Figure 2.3

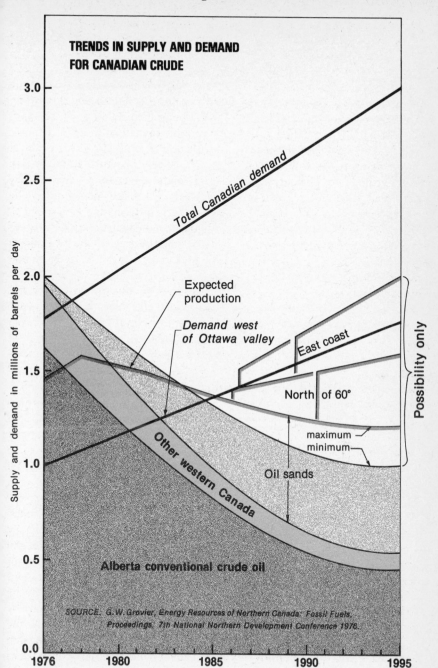

TRENDS IN SUPPLY AND DEMAND FOR CANADIAN CRUDE

Total Canadian demand

Expected production

Demand west of Ottawa valley

East coast

North of 60°

Possibility only

maximum
minimum

Other western Canada

Oil sands

Alberta conventional crude oil

Supply and demand in millions of barrels per day

3.0
2.5
2.0
1.5
1.0
0.5
0.0

1976   1980   1985   1990   1995

SOURCE: G.W. Grovier, Energy Resources of Northern Canada: Fossil Fuels, Proceedings, 7th National Northern Development Conference 1976.

Others fear for the stability of the particularly sensitive environment in the unique sand dunes south of Lake Athabasca, with the inevitable population surge linked with additional oil sands plants in the vicinity.

It is in the Arctic that confrontation between "resource developer" and "environmental conservationist" stands in sharpest relief. While costs are high throughout the North, they are particularly so in the Arctic. Yet resources are even more limited than in the subarctic. If they were originally sufficient to support the Inuit through an especially delicate man/land relationship, the old way of life is irrevocably gone and the indigenous people presently are struggling through the difficult transitional cultural stage. Furs remain a significant resource only locally, most notably on Banks Island. Minerals, metallics and fuels are the only other major resource possibility for the Arctic to provide economic return from the area. Every government encouragement has been extended to such exploration and development with, it should be acknowledged, promotion of associated native employment so far as possible.

Many consider the Arctic to be our last opportunity to "develop" in a responsible manner a hitherto little affected large region of Canada, with attempts to preserve at least some natural sectors. Concern has been expressed about the particular fragility of the Arctic ecology—the reduced number of species of plants and animals within the ecological systems and the potentially disastrous impact of the elimination of any one species with no substitute regionally available, the slow rate of growth which greatly extends the replacement time (if ever), and the potential ground damage in permafrost with a high ice content.[16] In 1970 the Canadian Wildlife Federation called unsuccessfully for a partial moratorium on northern mineral exploration in what it considered "truly a time of crisis in northern Canada."[17]

Widespread concern about the future of the North and particularly about northern resources policies led to formation of a citizens' organization in 1971, the Canadian Arctic Resources Committee, which continues to monitor, report on, and make representations on such policies. In October 1978, it made a submission to the National Energy Board hearings expressing concern about the impact of natural resource development on the High Arctic environment. Among the most significant categories of impacts identified were: "disturbance of land or marine mammals and birds; pollution of air and/or water through emissions of chemicals or other substances which are toxic in themselves, or when concentrated through a food chain, or when combined synergistically with other naturally occurring or emitted substances; damage to the habitat of significant members of a food chain, with resulting ramifications; and accidental disaster, for instance an oil blowout or accidental spill of fuel oil, particularly if offshore and/or under ice cover."[18]

There is in addition to these considerations a growing appreciation of the aesthetic and spiritual importance of wilderness environment in a world increasingly caught up in uniformity and "the system." Large areas of comparatively little disturbed landscape are only to be found in Canada in our northern and in our mountain regions. Increasing numbers of people seek in the North an opportunity to enjoy its beauty and distinctive qualities, because it is "undeveloped" and natural. This quality thus has become and will be increasingly valuable as a northern resource in itself.

The Beneficiaries of Northern Resource Development

No view is more widespread among northerners than that the resources of their region have been developed or exploited for the benefit of southerners and for stockholders often not even resident in Canada. Such a view is well founded. The Ontario Royal Commission on the Northern Environment agreed that "In the minds of most people in southern Ontario, the northern half of this province is a vast hinterland region of unlimited treasure, an area openly inviting entrepreneurs to explore, develop and exploit natural resources for shareholder profit, with neither a thought for the future of the area nor for the long-term needs of the people who live there."[19] It is sometimes facetiously suggested that resentment of Toronto is one of the chief cementing agencies in holding Canada together. While most northerners view that city as the chief symbol of past exploitation, a similar north versus south antagonism exists on similar grounds on the part of the residents of Labrador towards St. John's, of Ungava towards Montreal, of northern Manitoba towards Winnipeg, of northern Saskatchewan towards Regina, of northern Alberta and the Mackenzie Valley area towards Edmonton and Calgary, and of northern British Columbia and the Yukon towards Vancouver and Edmonton. Northern alienation from southern Canadians also is aggravated by the boom and bust phenomenon of past resource developments in northern areas,[20] though the magnitude of capital investments for many recent and future projects may reduce the frequency of future close-downs.

A new type of northerner has emerged recently. Better educated and more articulate than their predecessors, northern residents no longer are prepared to accept past practices for the future. In its 1977 and 1978 hearings in northern Ontario "the message of most speakers addressing the Royal Commission (on the Northern Environment) was clear. Northerners are no longer willing to take a back seat in decision making affecting their lives. Northerners wish to be consulted in future regarding development proposals for their areas and wish to know in advance in which direction their northern economy is being pointed."[21]

Yet a further complication has been introduced into northern resources development recently. Increasing confrontation is observable between the indigenous peoples of the North and the non-native incomers whether the latter be resident in the North or not. Until recently development occurred or did not depending primarily on the values attached to it by non-natives. (It should be acknowledged that past governments have launched some programs in the North with the stated objective of improving conditions for the native people, e.g., the Mackenzie Delta reindeer project.) More often than not private resource developments have occurred with little if any thought given to the impact they would have on the natives.

That "new type of northerner" to whom reference already has been made also includes native peoples, who have benefitted from the much-improved postwar educational facilities throughout the North and who now can and do articulate points of view (which their people long have held, but have been too reserved or unable to express) about the North very different from those of the non-natives. They demand that their rights be respected in their traditional homeland.

The 1971 Alaska Native Claims Settlement Act has had a major impact on the native peoples of northern Canada, in demonstrating what can be achieved in the face of northern resources development pressure. At a minimum, comparable benefits are being demanded in northern Canada as the indigenous peoples seek a much more influential role in the area. This goal is supported both by law and by widespread public sympathy throughout Canada. The Yukon Indians and the Nass River Indians of northern British Columbia, never having signed a treaty with the government, are in a particularly strong position. The Indians of the Northwest Territories maintain that no waiver of land rights was ever involved in their treaties, and elsewhere in the North the other Indian peoples are pressuring for a reopening of discussion. The Inuit and Métis peoples who are not bound by treaties are demanding proper guarantees for their future in the area. Clearly, native participation in future northern resources development must be a major consideration, the full significance of which is still uncertain. As with northern residents generally, it will require careful handling to minimize confrontation in favour of co-operation.

Institutional Framework of Northern Resource Development

As noted previously, the political fragmentation of the Canadian North creates complications in northern resource development in that under the BNA Act the resources within provincial territory are the responsibility of those governments. South of 60°N, policies and programs of northern resource development are considered primarily for the provincial benefits which may accrue, rather than for those of wider regional or perhaps even national advantage.

Historically, it should be borne in mind that the federal government of Canada was responsible for resource development over most of northern Canada and only since 1931 has it been restricted to the area north of 60°N.

Figure 3.3

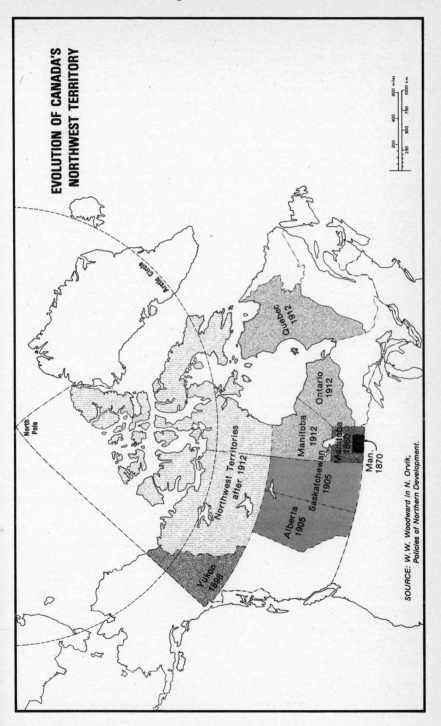

EVOLUTION OF CANADA'S
NORTHWEST TERRITORY

North
Pole

Arctic Circle

Northwest Territories
after 1912

Yukon
1898

Quebec
1912

Ontario
1912

Manitoba
1912

Manitoba
1880

Man.
1870

Saskatchewan
1905

Alberta
1905

200   400   600 miles

250   500   750   1000 km.

SOURCE: W. W. Woodward in N. Orvik,
Policies of Northern Development.

Over the previous thirty years the "Northwest Territories" gradually retreated to the northwest as new provinces were created and old ones were enlarged from federal territory. Only British Columbia remained unaffected among the provinces now included within the geographic area of northern Canada. In the case of the Prairie Provinces, the federal government retained control of their natural resources until 1930, long after their political creation, in part as a carry-over of its original "purposes of the Dominion" to forestall the potential American thrust northward in the plains.[22]

The general development of northern resources up to World War II has been set out in the classic studies of Lower[23] and of Innis,[24] while Rea has presented a more recent overview of northern development themes and trends to the present.[25] Canada has seen such development as a combined private enterprise-government policy operation. If private enterprise "has emphasized the monopolistic, large-scale and externally directed character of the businesses which have shaped the economic history of this area," Rea points out that "goverment in northern Canada has shared these characteristics to a remarkable extent" and that the "structural similarity between the business enterprises and the public decision-making bodies is reinforced by the similarity of the interests of the two groups."[26] In the area of public policy, however, there has been a significant change since World War II.[27]

Prewar Government Northern Development Policies

Until World War I, federal government development policies in the North were largely incidental to its focus on prairie settlement, and its main role within the region was regulatory, its emphasis on preserving stability. Though the Klondike Gold Rush resulted in the carving out of a separate territory and creation of a local council, the federal government retained control of the natural resources. The mining developments of the 1930s in the Mackenzie Valley were to force new policies to meet demands for more modern services, but though some changes occurred in Yellowknife, the wartime emergency delayed things. Modern industrial development was not sought and such developments as did occur were closely controlled through regulations.

Rea contrasts the federal government's emphasis on east-west development with the south to north development focus of provincial governments. In part this was linked with their territorial extensions, noted previously. Newfoundland, beset with its own economic and political crises, took little official interest in Labrador, leaving it in large measure to go its own way. Quebec and Ontario sought similar objectives in their northern development, providing support to private enterprise undertakings in mining and forestry and also pushing agriculture into the North. In the latter policy, Quebec sought to extend French culture primarily, in contrast to Ontario's hopes for expansion of a commercial agriculture. Whereas Québec sought to encourage private funding for such support facilities as hydroelectric power and railways, Ontario was prepared to use public enterprise.

In the Prairie Provinces the belated transfer of natural resource rights to the provinces meant that provincial policies came late, and even then the focus remained on the southern grain-producing sectors, particularly in Manitoba and Saskatchewan, though the former did support railway extension to the Flin Flon mining district. In Alberta, already envisaging a grand northern extension of its tributary area, and endowed with better agricultural lands in the North, the provincial government vigorously supported northward extension of railways, only to see most of its hopes crushed by drought and Depression years.

Holding its northern territory from its original entry into Confederation, yet with its population concentrated in the extreme southwest and coping with an incredibly complex and fragmented area, B.C.'s policies from the start sought to contend with the "omnipresence of the United States"[28] on both its southern and northwestern doorsteps. A series of mining developments widely scattered over the length of the province drew large numbers of American miners on whom Victoria's political and legal supremacy was impressed. Zaslow notes the success of provincially appointed gold commissioners in this regard.[29] In the far northwest, the Atlin gold area developed rather as an offshoot of the Klondike rush, and in many ways federal decisions and actions were more significant there than provincial. In the southeastern part of the province a CPR railway branch checked American presence in the Kootenay mining area, as the main line earlier had tied the Pacific outpost with eastern Canada. Railways were seen as the key to effective settlement of British Columbia as in the Prairie Provinces, though there is disagreement as to the effectiveness of provincial resource policies.[30] With the core area on the Pacific shore and abundant coastal resources, the distant northern sectors isolated by mountains often felt they received minimal attention. Government grants were made for some colonization roads and trails in the northern interior, but the limited northward construction of the Pacific Great Eastern Railway reflected the government's interest elsewhere as much as the terrain difficulties of the route.

World War II and Postwar Government
Northern Development Policies

The impact of World War II on the Canadian North was far-reaching. Directly, it introduced massive modernization of transportation facilities over much of the area from Labrador to the Yukon through such military projects as the Northeast Staging Route, Northwest Staging Route, Alaska Highway, Canol Project and the supporting Mackenzie Valley Waterway system, and improvement of the White Pass and Yukon Railway. While the direct economic effects of the Northeast Staging Route and the Canol Project were short term, I can not agree with Rea that the same has been true of the others. They have provided a base for major postwar resource developments in the Canadian Northwest. At the same time "to an unprecedented degree, World War II offered the northerner (or the temporary immigrant) the opportunity of wage employement.... Even unskilled labour could obtain appreciable cash income, and for the first time a significant number of the native Indian inhabitants could see an alternative to hunting and trapping."[31]

The far-reaching cultural changes induced by World War II involved southern Canada as well as northern, and "took the form of a new public awareness of the strategic and possibly economic value of the region; a perception on the part of some specialists of how effective existing technology could be in overcoming physical obstacles to resource development so long as the necessary scale of operation could be realized; and a recognition on the part of governments that the standard of living of many northern residents was unbelievably low."[32]

Rea has pointed out that these events have transformed Canadian northern development policy. "Instead of following and supporting private investments in directly productive activities, public investment policy became more aggressive, occasionally even attempting to lead such private investment," and increasingly "the dividing line between the 'public' and 'private' sectors of the northern export-base economy became more and more difficult to define."[33] Transportation and electric power facilities have been major elements in this process.

The Federal Government and Northern Resources Development*

The federal government from the beginning has been concerned with delineation of natural resources, and commentary on these as perceived by explorers forms a fascinating element of government reports, for the North as well as the West. Administratively, the North bulked large in the responsibility of the Geological Survey of Canada (established in 1842), the Department of the Interior (established in 1873), the Department of Mines and Resources (established in 1873) and its successor, the Department of Resources and Development (established in 1950). Federal recognition of the importance of the North and its resources was demonstrated by the creation in 1953 from Resources and Development of the Department of

* The author appreciates the information made available to him by both the federal and provincial government officials and regrets that fuller coverage can not be provided here because of space limitations. Interpretation of the information is his own, and not necessarily shared by the officials concerned.

Northern Affairs and National Resources, renamed in 1966 the Department of Indian Affairs and Northern Development. The present name for the department also is a reminder that federal presence in the North extends south of 60°N because of its responsibility for treaty Indians in Canada.

The "northern vision" of Canada which captured public imagination and support in the 1950s and which was reflected in reshaping government structure was linked closely with northern resource development. The department noted that "This new preoccupation with the North, as it happened, coincided with the discovery that, on a long-term basis, new sources of raw materials were a prime necessity to the whole civilized world. This was particularly true of minerals," and that "In the long-term view ... it is in its economic importance that the Northland acts as a permanent magnet; in its role as a supplier of mineral wealth. It is the development of this wealth that constitutes the real challenge of the North to Canada."[34] Every encouragement was extended to facilitate development of the North's resources, particularly mineral—an attitude which continues to the present, with some later qualifications added. The Commissioner of the Northwest Territories reported to the Royal Commission on Canada's Economic Prospects that this was considered "Entirely in line with sound economic progress, a great deal can be done by national policy to hasten and extend our northward development."[35] That development was seen as important in offsetting some of the increasing government expenditures in the North,[36] and also in providing employment opportunities for northerners.

The enormous federal government outlays in the North in the past two decades reflected both the need to build an infrastructure to facilitate northern resource development and the necessity of improving the social service facilities for northern residents. Administrative changes of very great importance have occurred at territorial, regional and local levels, particularly in the Northwest Territories, the Yukon having gained some of these earlier. Many of these resulted from the 1966 *Report of the Advisory Commission on the Development of Government in the Northwest Territories.*[37] In 1945 the "government" of the Northwest Territories was based in Ottawa with a Council consisting of an interdepartmental committee of appointed civil servants. "The progressive establishment of the Council as an elected body, the move to the new capital, Yellowknife (in 1967), the rapid growth in programs, budgets and the territorial civil service and the beginnings of ministerial government are seen as milestones in the Territories' growth to what has been termed a 'quasi-provincial' status"[38] for both the N.W.T. and the Yukon. Despite strong territorial pressures, however, the federal government retains control of northern natural resources.

In 1972 a major policy statement was made by the Government of Canada regarding northern development in the 1970s.[39] Seven major objectives were identified for the North, which were seen to "reflect economic conditions and policies in the South." Briefly, and in order of priority, these were:

1. To achieve a higher standard of living, quality of life and equality of opportunity for northern residents.
2. To maintain and improve the northern environment with due allowance for economic and social development.
3. To encourage systematically and within selected regions of the North viable economic development.
4. To enable northern Canada to contribute to the social and cultural development of the country as a whole.
5. To aid in the evolution of local self-government in the North.
6. To maintain the sovereignty and security of Canada in the North.
7. To develop the leisure and recreational opportunities in the North for the benefit of all.

Provincial Governments and Northern Resource Development

It has been noted that much of Canada's North falls within provincial boundaries. With the bulk of the population strung along the southern international boundary, it also has been noted that the focus of provincial governments has been there also, with the northern segments receiving irregular and scanty attention as distant semi-colonial appendages (at least in the opinion of their northern residents). Greatly increased demands for northern resources, primarily minerals and hydroelectric power, and some measure of the national "northern vision" have resulted in greater recognition of their northern areas by almost all provincial governments in the postwar years.

The Newfoundland government became directly involved in trading and then in much wider operations (including housing) on the northern Labrador coast as early as 1942, of necessity, when the Hudson's Bay Company closed down its operations as uneconomic. The Northern Labrador Trading Operations (later Services) Division of the Department of Natural Resources bore some similarities to the Royal Greenland Trade Department of Denmark. Significantly, by agreement, the federal government has covered all medical and hospital costs for Inuit and Indian peoples, and also provided large grants for native community projects. In 1976, the Labrador Services Division became part of the Department of Rural Development. In 1979, that department was restructured to include a Northern Development Branch and became the Department of Rural, Agricultural and Northern Development.[40] In addition to several other provincial government departments involved in northern parts of provincial territory (as in other provinces), one may note the Crown corporation,

Newfoundland and Labrador Hydro Corporation, which acquired the hydroelectric resources of Labrador from Brinco, the developer of Churchill Falls hydro. Symbolically reflecting the postwar recognition of its northern resource base and its determination to stand firm in the face of Quebec's official refusal to recognize the judicial decision on the Labrador boundary, was the province's action in officially enlarging its name to the "Government of Newfoundland and Labrador."

The gigantic James Bay power project in Quebec has resulted in the greatest changes administratively (as well as in many other ways) for a provincial government with respect to its northern territories in the postwar years. The full significance still remains to be seen. In initiating the project the Quebec government chose to establish yet another Crown corporation, the James Bay Development Corporation, rather than work through the existing Quebec Hydro-Electric Commission (Hydro-Québec). The new corporation, established in 1971, holds overall responsibility for total development of its enormous area—energy, mining, forestry, tourism, etc.—through its own subsidiaries, e.g., the James Bay Energy Corporation in which Hydro-Québec holds 51 percent control. Before the project could be completed, agreements had to be reached with the native peoples on their land claims. Resolution of Alaskan native land claims shortly before strongly influenced the Quebec indigenous peoples before signing the James Bay and Northern Quebec Agreement in 1975,[41] providing them with a cash grant, exclusive land rights over a fraction of the area and some measure of control over administration of the wider area. (In 1978, a Northeastern Quebec Agreement was signed to complete the northern areas of the province.) It has put into place two regional "governments" or authorities, Cree and Inuit, which administer their own compensation funds ($250 million) as well as social, health and education programs.[42] To coordinate the activities of government departments and agencies when they have work to do among the native peoples of Quebec, to draw up desirable polices, etc., the government created the "Secrétariat des activités gouvernementales en milieu amérindian et inuit" (SAGMAI) in 1978.

In Ontario, the most obvious provincial administrative actions in recent years specifically identified with the North were the appointment of a Royal Commission on the Northern Environment, and the creation of a Ministry of Northern Affairs, though as in other provinces there are many other related elements, for example the joint northern programs with the federal Department of Regional Economic Expansion. The Royal Commission and the Ministry were established in 1977, the former stemming in large part from the outcry arising from industrial pollution of the English-Wabigoon River system and Indian objections to proposed timber grants. The Commission's recommendations in its interim report were endorsed by the government in 1978.[43] "The Ministry has two basic functions: to ensure that residents of northern Ontario have the same access to the programs and services of government as those elsewhere in the province and to ensure that the special needs and conditions in the North are considered and accommodated in all policies and programs developed by government."[44] Northern development is seen to be "virtually the entire mandate" of his ministry by the minister involved,[45] as demonstrated in the discussion paper, *Northwestern Ontario, A Policy for Development.*[46]

In the Prairie Provinces, all three governments have made use of royal commissions and/or public inquiries in postwar years to consider various facets of northern resource developments,[47] but only Manitoba and Saskatchewan have established separate provincial departments designated for their northern districts. The departments concerned are very different in role. The Department of Northern Affairs was established in Manitoba in 1974. "The major thrust and direction taken by the Manitoba government in delivering services to the North is to reduce costs and avoid duplication. . . . The Department of Northern Affairs, as the coordinating agent for some 50 Northern Remote Communities, is in liaison with numerous other Departments both Provincial and Federal on an ongoing basis and as the needs arise."[48] In Saskatchewan the government also was concerned about the widening disparities between the residents in the opposite halves of the province, but decided that coordination of many departments was not adequate to eliminate the fragmented and often inappropriate programs there, establishing instead a single agency. The Department of Northern Saskatchewan, formed in 1972, is "responsible for accelerating political, economic and social development in order to bring services and opportunities to a level comparable with those of the South."[49] Alberta does not have a separate department dealing with the northern part of the province. In 1963, a Northern Alberta Development Council was created as a five-member advisory body to the provincial government. In 1973, the Council was enlarged to ten members appointed on a yearly basis from across the North under the chairmanship of a full-time northern MLA. It has direct access to the provincial cabinet through the "Minister responsible for Northern Development"—presently the Minister for Tourism and Small Business. A primary objective of the Council is to increase the amount of public participation in the planning and design of delivery systems for government services in northern Alberta and to this end holds public meetings in northern communities and sponsors various conferences and seminars. Because of the massive developments in the Athabasca oil sands area in 1974, the provincial government in a unique action passed the Northeast Alberta Regional Commission Act. Under this it appointed a commissioner responsible directly to the cabinet, to ensure orderly development in the area.

Among the provinces with significant northern lands, only British

Columbia has not formally designated a special administrative unit for those sectors, though the previous government did have a separate division responsible for northern development. This is seen as a reflection of the complex geographic nature of that province. In the words of the minister designated to comment on northern resource development, "British Columbia has avoided legislating the creation of a separate class of citizens by reason of location. More homogenous provinces may find it feasible to establish such a division but in British Columbia it makes little sense. The problems facing residents of relatively isolated or single-resource towns in the Kootenays, for example, are little different in most respects—including weather—from those of 'northern' communities."[50] The present government does attempt to decentralize staff, however, and as in other provinces seeks to bring equal opportunities to all residents outside the major urban centres, i.e., Vancouver and Victoria.

The Record of Northern Resources Development

Viewed overall, one would have to acknowledge that there has been no "strategy" of northern resource development. Developments were dealt with as they occurred and on an *ad hoc* basis. Since World War II some strategies have emerged, chiefly in the area administered by the federal government, with the provinces displaying much greater diversity in their approach to the problem. Yet even in the area of federal public land policy in the North, as recently as 1976 Naysmith considered it to have "been essentially a series of responses to demands for land, rather than a framework within which decisions respecting use and management are made on the basis of the land itself . . . [and proposed] a new course for the administration and management of public land in the north based first on a consideration of the nature, capability and limitations of the land."[51]

Judd's forecast of a decade ago that "It is probable . . . that in the future, the economic motive will become more important and that in government policy the development of northern resources will be given a high priority"[52] has been borne out and there seems no reason to expect a change. At the same time, as Lloyd has pointed out,[53] resource development projects which were initiated even into the 1950s without local involvement and environmental impact assessments are a thing of the past. The very different requirements demanded before approval of the Nanisivik lead-zinc mine on northern Baffin Island compared with the Rankin Inlet nickel mine on Hudson Bay reflected the much more stringent government controls which have been introduced over the two decades separating the start up of the two operations (mid-70s and mid-50s).

The single most publicized reflection of the federal government's announced policy on northern development was the 1974 appointment of the Berger Commission to inquire into the impact of the proposed

Mackenzie Valley Pipeline to transport Alaska and Western Arctic Gas southwards (and in some measure the subsequent Lysyk Commission for the Alaska Highway pipeline proposal). The extent of public hearings, the degree of participation by native and public interest groups, as well as by the oil and gas industry, the extensive research data presented, all represented a new level of participation in northern resource development debate. Acceptance by the government of the recommendation to defer construction of a pipeline for at least ten years until native land claims were settled,[54] despite great industry pressures because of the critical international situation in fuels, greatly heartened among others, those who seek a more orderly and planned development of northern resources.

In reviewing the situation over 1972-78, Lucas and Peterson recognize the continuation of *ad hoc* approaches to land-use decisions,[55] the strengthening of legislation to afford more environmental protection (e.g., the 1977 revision of the Territorial Land Use Regulations, the 1972 proclamation of the Arctic Waters Pollution Prevention Act, the 1977 strengthening of the Fisheries Act, the 1973 Territorial Environmental Protection Ordinance), and the modification of natural resource development legislation, e.g., the new leasing rules in 1977 for oil and gas which permit in theory environmental and social factors to be considered in issuing rights. Nevertheless there still are gaps in legislation and in procedures. The federal Environmental Assessment and Review Process (EARP) in place since 1973, for example, to look into environmental impact of all new federal projects is the result of policy only, not of law, so that its recommendations in the final analysis lack legal enforceability.

While northern resource development in the past has been almost entirely designed for the benefit of "outsiders," it now is viewed as desirable and even necessary for northern residents. Hunt considers "that the question is not *whether* the North should be developed, nor *how* the North should be developed. It is the time factor that is becoming more and more essential."[56] At most, if one agrees with Armstrong's "assumption . . . that whatever development is physically possible and economically justifiable at any given time will tend to occur,"[57] government policy may only delay or modify development under a free enterprise system—thereby challenging some of those values which it has accepted in its 1972 policy statement. This apparent paradox is exemplified in the Baker Lake case of 1979, wherein the Inuit took the government to court to protect their land from the mining companies and to clarify the issue of aboriginal rights,[58] with the decision really not resolving the problem. Construction of the Dempster Highway between Dawson and Inuvik (completed in 1978) is another illustration of apparently conflicting government policies and actions.[59]

Despite frequent appeals over the years for comprehensive, integrated planning for the North,[60] this has not materialized. "There is no compre-

hensive land-use planning for Canada's North at the present time."[61]
Richard Rohmer's personal Centennial project, the "Mid-Canada Development Corridor,"[62] was an imaginative attempt along these lines, daringly
sweeping across provincial and territorial boundaries, but has had little ongoing impact. Even in the area north of 60°, where the Department of
Indian and Northern Affairs plays the leading role, it is only one of several
federal departments with northern responsibilities, and despite the existence of a federal interdepartmental Advisory Committee on Northern
Development there is no guarantee of a unified approach or activity in
practice. Similar difficulties occur within many provincial governments as
well.

Research Into the Problem

It could be argued that all research into the Canadian North is ultimately of
significance directly or indirectly in northern resource development. The
price paid for the hastily implemented emergency projects of World War II
soon became evident. Much of the damage, environmental and social, was
the result of very limited knowledge about the area. Even in 1952 the
navigator on the U.S.C.G. icebreaker *Eastwind* heading up the coast of
Ellesmere Island to Alert advised us we were ten miles inland according to
the best charts available! After a thorough review of Canadian northern
research in 1961 Lloyd reported that "Northern Canada remains one of the
world's scientifically underdeveloped regions. Basic research there concerning the land, the seas and the atmosphere is urgently needed. Only
since World War II has the Canadian Government shown any serious and
sustained interest in the task."[63]

Within the next ten years this had changed. In 1972, it was noted that
"During the past decade, social programs, exploration and resource
development in northern Canada have expanded greatly. Efforts to further
scientific knowledge of the North have also increased, but not at a rate to
keep pace with demands for scientific information to support this social and
economic development."[64] During the 1970s there has been a near-
explosion of research into the Canadian North, carried on by governments,
by universities and by private companies, both for their own information
and to meet the increasingly required impact studies for northern resource
development.[65]

Research has taken place over a wide range of topics, both theoretical
and applied. Fortunately, much of the essential scientific framework on
which much northern resource development is based was launched by
federal agencies relatively early—accurate mapping of the North, accelerated geological surveys, extended and improved meteorological facilities, including the Joint Arctic Weather Stations project,[66] etc. These also
have made possible further more specialized research by such bodies as the
Polar Continental Shelf Project,[67] the Defence Research Board, the Arctic

Institute of North America. Sea ice conditions, transportation studies, regional economic resources studies, environmental management mapping in the northern land use program, northern community housing programs, and many other research projects have been launched. The northern residents themselves, particularly the native peoples, have been the focus of much research, to the point that they have become increasingly resentful of the apparently inevitable appearance of yet another social scientist among them. In this surge in northern research geographers have played and are playing a significant role—in government bodies both federal and provincial, in universities and in the several northern institutes now associated with them, and in work for private companies engaged in northern resource development. The geographic research involved has spanned the entire spectrum of the discipline.

The diversity of past research has reflected partially the large gaps in our basic knowledge. It also has reflected the lack of a well-defined plan for the North and for the development of its resources. Lloyd stated that "The most urgent requirement is a clear formulation of objectives and allocation of responsibility for carrying them out whether within the government services or in universities, private organization or industry."[68] In summing up the results of the 1972 "Science and the North" seminar, Solandt again emphasized the "need for better and closer coordination of research in the Arctic."[69] The situation remains essentially the same today, though the 1972 Policy Statement of the federal government has provided more clearly stated goals. In 1976 the federal Advisory Committee on Northern Development published a fourteen-point "Guidelines" for scientific activities in the North.[70] While guidelines are useful, they still are only guidelines.

Given the fragmented political structure of the North and the administrative divisions within governments (provincial as well as federal), each with its own priorities and jealously guarded "empires," it may be unrealistic to expect otherwise, even if there were consensus on northern development and on priorities for related research. As it is, there are many illustrations of what Solandt has termed the "rediscovery of the wheel," which he reckons occurs at half-hourly intervals at any Arctic research conference.[71] Again, it can be noted that Alberta is spending enormous amounts of money directly through departmental research and indirectly through consultants in connection with its northern resource developments. The volume of reports and data is overwhelming, yet much of this seems without integrated direction. (An early attempt to coordinate government, university, and private research into the Athabasca oil sands collapsed.) Many of the public feel that "research" serves as a convenient deflector of criticism, with no necessary resultant decisions being based upon it.

The Science Council of Canada recently noted that "The recent history of the North has been the product of two major and apparently conflicting trends. The trend that predominates in many discussions of northern development is the thrust toward large-scale exploitation of natural resources. The second is the desire to continue traditional resource harvesting activities, such as fishing, hunting and trapping. The latter trend would lead to northern development based on smaller scale projects, locally controlled."[72] While the former is currently more dominant, the Council urged a transition to a more balanced "strategy of mixed development" to accommodate both trends, with income from the first assisting the second "which, in terms of square miles of land use and the participation of northern peoples, should constitute a major element of northern development."[73] With the Alaskan and James Bay precedents, this mixed development trend appears most likely for the Canadian North generally, ensuring a need for geographic research into both facets of the problem of northern resource development. Given the basic facts in the North, any research must be expensive, but this can not excuse lack of support.

One can only hope that the need for delicate handling of this complex problem will be appreciated by all parties concerned. With the experience and knowledge now at our disposal, all Canadians have the opportunity of demonstrating a responsibility in the North that will be viewed with satisfaction and pride in the years to come.

Notes

[1] For a recent summary of the problem of defining the North, and a suggested solution, along with a stimulating discussion of many northern topics, see Louis-Edmond Hamelin, *Canadian Nordicity: It's Your North, Too* (Montreal: Harvest House, 1978).

[2] In this essay the focus is on the area north of 60°N, while acknowledging the inclusion of much provincial lands within the geographic reality of the North.

[3] Baffin Island: 507,467 km²; 1976 population 6,525—*1976 Census of Canada* (Ottawa: Statistics Canada, 1978).

[4] Statistics Canada, *Canada Handbook* (48th annual) (Ottawa: Minister of Supply and Services Canada, 1979), p. 40.

[5] Mean Annual Percentage Change of Population 1966-71 in Canada 1.6, Y.T. 5.7, N.W.T. 4.1; 1971-77 in Canada 1.3, Y.T. 2.8, N.W.T. 3.8—Statistics Canada, *loc. cit.*

[6] Louis-Edmond Hamelin, *Contribution to the Northwest Territories Population Studies 1961–1985* (Yellowknife: Science Advisory Board of the Northwest Territories, 1979), pp. 12–16.

[7] David Reed Podmore, "An Examination of Motor Carrier Operations in the Mackenzie Valley Area" (Edmonton: unpublished Master's thesis, Department of Geography, University of Alberta, 1974), p. 212.

[8] Michael Marsden, "Transportation in the Canadian North," *The North*, ed. William C. Wonders, "Canadian Studies in Geography" (Toronto: University of Toronto Press, 1972), p. 67.

9 Hamelin, *Canadian Nordicity*. . . ., p. xiv.

10 William M. Gilchrist, "About Our Untold Resources," *People of the Light and Dark*, ed. M. Van Steensel (Ottawa: The Queen's Printer, 1966), p. 37, and in *Canada's Changing North*, ed. William C. Wonders (Toronto: McClelland and Stewart, 1971), p. 201.

11 W.C. Wonders, "The Forest Frontier and Subarctic," *Canada, a Geographical Interpretation*, ed. John Warkentin (Toronto: Methuen Publications, 1968), pp. 473–507.

12 G.W. Govier, "Energy Resources of Northern Canada: Fossil Fuels," *Proceedings Seventh National Northern Development Conference 1976*, ed. W.H. Johns (Edmonton: Edmonton Chamber of Commerce and Alberta Northwest Chamber of Mines-Oils-Resources, 1977), p. 42.

13 F. Kenneth Hare, "Canada," *Canada, a Geographical Interpretation* . . ., p. 7. For an overview of Shield resources, see J. Lewis Robinson, *Resources of the Canadian Shield* (Toronto: Methuen Publications, 1969).

14 E.R. Reinelt, ed., *Proceedings of the Peace-Athabasca Delta Symposium* (Edmonton: Water Resources Centre, University of Alberta, 1971).

15 Don Gill and Alan D. Cooke, "Controversies over Hydroelectric Developments in Sub-Arctic Canada," *Polar Record*, 17 (May 1974), pp. 109–128. See also Boyce Richardson, *James Bay, the Plot to Drown the North Woods*, "A Sierra Club Battlebook" (Toronto: Clarke, Irwin & Company Ltd., 1972).

16 "L.C. Bliss, "Oil and the Ecology of the Arctic," *Transactions of the Royal Society of Canada*, Series IV, VIII (1970), pp. 361–362.

17 "Crisis in the North" (editorial), *The Arctic Circular*, XX (May 1970), p. 24.

18 "High Arctic Natural Gas Considerations," *Northern Perspectives*, 6 (1978), p. 3.

19 "North of 50—Its Industry and Commerce," *Issues*, Chapt. 2 (Toronto: Royal Commission on the Northern Environment, n.d.), p. 47.

20 In 1959, for example, there were nine uranium-producing mines in the Beaverlodge area of northern Saskatchewan and the district population was estimated at 4,600. Great constriction in the American market for uranium resulted in the closure of all but one mine, with the district population falling to an estimated 2,250 in 1971.

21 "North of 50. . . .," *op. cit.*, p. 46.

22 Chester Martin, *"Dominion Lands" Policy*, "Canadian Frontiers of Settlement Series" (Toronto: Macmillan Co. of Canada Ltd., 1938).

23 A.R.M. Lower, *Settlement and the Forest Frontier in Eastern Canada*, "Canadian Frontiers of Settlement Series" (Toronto: Macmillan Co. of Canada Ltd., 1936).

24 Harold A. Innis, *Settlement and the Mining Frontier*, "Canadian Frontiers of Settlement Series" (Toronto: Macmillan Co. of Canada Ltd., 1936).

25 K.J. Rea, *The Political Economy of Northern Development*, "Background Study No. 36" (Ottawa: Science Council of Canada, 1976).

26 *Ibid.*, pp. 76–77.

27 *Ibid.*, pp. 78–136 *passim*.

28 H.F. Angus, ed., *British Columbia and the United States*, "The Relations of Canada and the United States Series" (Toronto: The Ryerson Press, 1942), p. 184.

29 Morris Zaslow, *The Opening of the Canadian North, 1870–1914*, "The Canadian Centenary Series" (Toronto: McClelland and Stewart, 1971), pp. 50–51.

30 Compare Cail's evaluation, "A detailed examination of past government policy

in handling mineral lands, timber lands, and water rights reveals how painstaking were the efforts made to encourage enterprising individuals willing to face the hazards of a new country; to discourage those bent only on speculation and, at the same time, obtain sufficient revenue to develop a remote and sparsely populated part of the world." (Robert E. Cail, *Land, Man and the Law: The Disposal of Crown Lands in British Columbia, 1871–1913* [Vancouver: University of British Columbia Press, 1974], p. 70) with Zaslow's comment, "The speculative character of much of this settlement (along the second, northern transcontinental railway route) was recognized even at the time. The newly-appointed preemption land inspectors, who examined every holding, estimated that fewer than one-third of the occupants had serious intentions." (Zaslow, *op. cit.*, p. 206).

31 William C. Wonders, "The Canadian Northwest: Some Geographical Perspectives," *Canadian Geographical Journal*, LXXX, 5 (May 1970), p. 153.

32 Rea, *op. cit.*, p. 91

33 *Ibid.*, p. 90.

34 Anon, "The Northland—Canada's Challenge," *The Canada Year Book 1955* (Ottawa: Queen's Printer, 1955), p. 23.

35 R.G. Robertson, *The Northwest Territories, Its Economic Prospects* (Ottawa: Queens Printer, 1955), p. 5.

36 In 1972-73 for example, federal government expenditures in the two Territories amounted to almost $300 million—Hamelin, *Canadian Nordicity. . . .*, p. 99.

37 A.W.R. Carrothers (chm.), *Report of the Advisory Commission on the Development of Government in the Northwest Territories* (Ottawa: 1966).

38 F.A.E. Cserepy, "New Styles in Administration since 1945," a paper presented at The Royal Society of Canada's Symposium, *A Century of Canada's Arctic Islands, 1880–1980*, Yellowknife, N.W.T., August 11-13, 1980.

39 Hon. Jean Chrétien, Minister of Indian Affairs and Northern Development, *Canada's North 1970–1980* (Ottawa: Information Canada, 1972).

40 Letter from Conrad Hiscock, Director of Development, Newfoundland Department of Rural, Agricultural and Northern Development, Happy Valley, Labrador, June 20, 1980.

41 *The James Bay and Northern Quebec Agreement* (Quebec: Éditeur officiel du Québec, 1976).

42 Letter from Gaston Moisan, S.A.G.M.A.I., Conseil exécutif, Gouvernement du Québec, Québec, July 7, 1980.

43 Mr. Justice E.P. Hartt, *Interim Report and Recommendations* (Toronto: The Royal Commission on the Northern Environment, 1978).

44 Hon. Leo Bernier, Minister of Northern Affairs, *Remarks* for an opening statement to the Conference of Northern Ministers, Fort McMurray, Alberta, September 27, 1978.

45 Letter from Hon. Leo Bernier, Minister of Northern Affairs, Government of Ontario, Toronto, June 9, 1980.

46 Government of Ontario, *Northwestern Ontario: A Policy for Development* (Toronto: Queen's Printer, 1979).

47 For example: A.V. Mauro, *Report of the Province of Manitoba Royal Commission Inquiry into Northern Transportation* (Winnipeg: Queen's printer, 1969); "Churchill River Special Issue," *The Musk-Ox*, No. 15, 1975; "Special Issue: Uranium Inquiry," *The Musk-Ox*, No. 23, 1978, and No. 24, 1979; *Report of the*

Royal Commission on the Development of Northern Alberta (Edmonton: 1958); *The Peace-Athabasca Delta, A Canadian Resource: Summary Report, 1972* (Ottawa: Information Canada, 1972).

48 Letter from Dale Stewart, Deputy Minister, Department of Northern Affairs, Government of Manitoba, Winnipeg, July 9, 1980.

49 Timothy Myers, *Five Years After . . . A review of the Department of Northern Saskatchewan's first five years* (La Ronge: Department of Northern Saskatchewan, 1979), p. 1.

50 Letter from Hon. Don Phillips, Minister of Industry and Small Business Development, Government of British Columbia, Victoria, June 10, 1980.

51 John Kennedy Naysmith, *Land Use and Public Policy in Northern Canada* (Ottawa: Department of Indian and Northern Affairs, 1976), p. 3.

52 David Judd, "Canada's Northern Policy: Retrospect and Prospect," *Polar Record*, 14, 92 (May 1969), p. 602.

53 Trevor Lloyd, "Canadian Policies in the North," *The Arctic Circle: Aspects of the North from the Circumpolar Nations*, ed. William C. Wonders (Toronto: Longman Canada Ltd., 1976), pp. 35–48.

54 Mr. Justice Thomas R. Berger, *Northern Frontier, Northern Homeland: the Report of the Mackenzie Valley Pipeline Inquiry* (Ottawa: Minister of Supply and Services Canada, 1977).

55 A.R. Lucas and E.B. Peterson, "Northern Land Use Law and Policy Development: 1972–78 and the Future," *Northern Transitions, Vol. II: Second National Workshop on People, Resources and the Environment North of 60°*, eds. Robert F. Keith and Janet B. Wright (Ottawa: Canadian Arctic Resources Committee, 1978), pp. 63–93.

56 A. Digby Hunt, "The North in Canada's National Policy: Problems and Approaches," *Policies of Northern Development*, ed. Nils Ørvik (Kingston, Ontario: Department of Political Studies, Queen's University, 1973), p. 13.

57 Terence Armstrong, "Ethical Problems of Northern Development," *Polar Record*, 19, 118, (January 1978), p. 4.

58 "The Baker Lake Decision," *Northern Perspectives*, VIII, 3 (1980), pp. 1–12.

59 William G. MacLeod, *The Dempster Highway*, "Research Monograph Number One, Yukon Series," (Ottawa: Canadian Arctic Resources Committee, 1979).

60 A brief sampling could include William C. Wonders, "Our Northward Course," *Canadian Geographer*, VI, 3–4 (Winter 1962), pp. 96–105; Robert D. Franson *et al.*, "Legal Problems in the Canadian North," *Arctic Alternatives*, eds. Douglas H. Pimlott *et al.* (Ottawa: Canadian Arctic Resources Committee, 1973), pp. 312–340; Louis-Edmond Hamelin, "Développement Nordique et Harmonie," *Cahiers de Géographie de Québec*, 18, 44 (September 1944), pp. 337–346.

61 Julian T. Inglis, "Land Management in Northern Canada and Fenno-scandia," *Polar Record*, 19, 123 (September 1979), p. 544.

62 *Mid-Canada Development Corridor . . . A Concept* (Toronto: Acres Limited, 1967).

63 Trevor Lloyd, "Northern Research Review and Forecast," *Resources for Tomorrow Conference Background Papers*, Vol. 1 (Ottawa: Queen's Printer, 1961), p. 607.

64 *Science and the North: A Seminar on Guidelines for Scientific Activities in Northern Canada 1972* (Ottawa: Queen's Printer, 1973), p. 6.

65 In the past decade the companies involved in the Arctic Petroleum Operators' Association have funded some 170 research projects into Arctic environmental

studies. It is estimated over $800 million has been invested in preliminary work into petroleum and natural gas resources in the area.—Gordon H. Jones, "Economic Development—Oil and Gas Industries," a paper presented at The Royal Society of Canada's Symposium, *A Century of Canada's Arctic Islands, 1880-1980,* Yellowknife, N.W.T., August 11-13, 1980.

66 For an overview of the historic development of mapping in the Arctic Archipelago see William C. Wonders, "Scientific Progress—Geographical Mapping," a paper presented at The Royal Society of Canada's Symposium, *A Century of Canada's Arctic Islands, 1880-1980,* Yellowknife, N.W.T., August 11-13, 1980. "Geological Mapping" was covered by Ray Thorsteinsson and J. William Kerr, "Meteorology" by Sven Orvig, "Oceanographic Research" by Maxwell J. Dunbar, "Biological Research" by S.D. MacDonald, etc. For an assessment of the significance of the JAWS project, see W.C. Wonders, "The Joint Arctic Weather Stations (JAWS) in the Queen Elizabeth Islands" in *Essays in Meteorology and Climatology in Honour of Richmond W. Longley,* eds. K.D. Hage and E.R. Reinelt (Edmonton: Department of Geography, University of Alberta, 1978), pp. 399-418.

67 In 1980, it is expected that the P.C.S.P. base at Resolute will serve as the staging area for 164 scientific expeditions for example, involving more than 700 researchers. *News of the North* (Yellowknife), August 8, 1980.

68 Lloyd, *op. cit.*

69 O.M. Solandt, "Summary Statements" in *Science and the North. . . ., op. cit.,* p. 12.

70 Advisory Committee Northern Development, *Guidelines for Scientific Activities in Northern Canada* (Ottawa: Minister of Supply and Services Canada, 1976).

71 *Ibid.,* p. 13.

72 Science Council of Canada, *Northward Looking: A Strategy and a Science Policy for Northern Development,* Report No. 26 (Ottawa: Minister of Supply and Services Canada, 1977), p. 44.

73 *Ibid.,* p. 45.

4/Coastal Management in Canada*

Peter Harrison and Felix A. Kwamena

Introduction

Canada is a coastal nation despite its vast land mass. The saltwater shoreline of the Atlantic, Pacific and Arctic oceans is exceeded in length only by that of the USSR, and few countries can boast of such freshwater bodies as the Great Lakes and the myriad smaller lakes which dot the landscape. Access to water and to trade routes has been a key element in the economic development since Confederation. It is thus no historical accident that many of Canada's major cities and much of its economic activity are located in coastal areas.[1]

A good deal of Canada's shoreline, especially in the Arctic and northern latitudes, remains undeveloped. But in well-settled areas and around urban centres, the use and development of the shoreline presents a major problem of resource allocation between many competing and even conflicting uses. A more affluent and mobile population views the shoreline as a prime location for living and for recreation; many industrial establishments depend on a coastal location for their very livelihood; energy producing and transforming plants prefer the lakeshore or seashore as a base of operations; and traditional activities such as port factilities and fishing and shell-fishing operations can hardly locate anywhere else. It is not surprising that concern over the use and abuse of such a valuable resource as the shoreline and the coastal zone has grown apace in recent years. Nor is it unusual that this concern is shared by the general population, industry and government alike. What is surprising to many observers is the fact that unlike the United States to the south, Canada has no clear and well-identified set of coastal management programs.[2]

Being concerned about the situation is not sufficient. What is needed is a reasonable attempt at solving some of the problems which arise in coastal

* The research on which this chapter is based was funded, in part, by a Social Sciences and Humanities Research Council of Canada sabbatical research grant. The opinions expressed in this chapter are those of the authors and do not necessarily represent the official view of the Government of Canada.

areas in more than an *ad hoc* fashion, and at defining objectives for the type of coastal environment which society is willing to accept. Unfortunately, there is little agreement as to what these objectives are, how they should be enunciated, and who should promote their realization. The very field of coastal and shoreline management in Canada, as in most countries, is typified by confusion—over definitions of what constitutes the shoreline and the coastal zone, over conflicting requirements between different resource users, over government agency responsibilities, and even as to how to approach the possibility of "managing" a resource area which is difficult, if not impossible, to define. Nevertheless, some progress has been made in Canada in the past several years.

Because of an increased awareness of the value of resource systems to society, extensive discussion has taken place in Canada concerning the whole question of coastal zone/shorezone/shoreline management. Among other things several major conferences have been held at which many of the issues and possible solutions have been brought forward.[3] The largest, most recent, and certainly the most comprehensive discussion of coastal zone/shorezone management in Canada took place at the "Shorezone Management Symposium" held in Victoria in October 1978 under the auspices of the Canadian Council of Resource and Environment Ministers (CCREM).[4] Formal papers discussing the general principles of shorezone evolution and shorezone management were complemented by other presentations highlighting a series of case studies from and initiatives taken in a variety of places in Canada. Workshop discussions on major issues in shorezone management resulted in a series of general recommendations. Since those attending the conference came from a wide set of different backgrounds and professions, the *Proceedings* of the symposium can be taken as reflecting the type of concerns which currently exist in Canada concerning coastal areas. They also show the wide diversity of opinion as to how to approach the various problems and what to do about them.

In summarizing the discussions held at the symposium, the Steering Committee presented sets of principles for a "nationwide" (as opposed to "national") shorezone policy.[5] These principles range from a "recognition of the importance of shore areas" through calls for greater intergovernmental and program coordination to the questions of area preservation, public access, and cooperative information systems. Priorities attached to these principles stress the need for coordination and for the definition of lead agencies in each jurisdiction which would be charged with the task of promoting reasonable coastal development patterns. Although some change has resulted from the symposium in the form of white papers, new governmental units and specially created information centres,[6] the review to be presented to CCREM at its 1981 meeting will show the exact extent and importance of these changes.

Coastal Management: a Central Problem

The problem of managing coastal areas in Canada has been extensively researched over the past decade. Effort has been focused in a variety of areas including coastal land and water use,[7] conflict development and resolution,[8] oil spill problems and contingency planning,[9] shoreline protection,[10] recreational access,[11] as well as the difficult problem of identifying the nature, extent and importance of different coastal resources.[12] Certain themes have been more fully studied than others, including the problem of port development on urban shorelines[13] and the problem of institutional arrangements within coastal areas.[14]

Cooperative research between the federal and provincial governments (and certain research establishments such as the Westwater Research Centre) has taken as its focus the major estuaries in Canada—particularly the St. Lawrence and Fraser estuaries.[15] This is an important thrust which differs from that in other countries. The United States, for example, following the passage of the 1972 *Coastal Zone Management Act*, and the various pieces of State legislation enacted slightly before or in compliance with the federal act, has tended to concentrate on the problem of defining the coastal zone in legal terms and then creating land-use controls and permit systems aimed at directing coastal development. Some commentators feel that the United States has ignored completely the problem of *estuarine* management. In Canada it could be argued, the situation is the opposite.

Most, if not all, management studies of the Canadian situation come to a similar conclusion once they are faced with the problem of defining who is responsible for various aspects of coastal/estuarine management, due to the number, complexity, and overlapping nature of public institutions at the federal, provincial, municipal and special unit (e.g., Conservation Authority) levels making integrated coastal management difficult if not impossible.[16] Though there may be general agreement about the central problem, there is very little as to the solutions which should be attempted. It is no wonder that widespread concern and intensive research on the question of coastal zone management in Canada has not been followed up by the creation of new or revamped management agencies.

The problem can best be seen by looking at the various federal and provincial agencies which have a role in coastal management and the various functions assigned to them. The information given here relates only to major institutions such as Ministries. If the level of analysis were more detailed (e.g., by a discussion of relevant Acts and departmental programs), then the situation would be seen to be even more complicated— and this chapter would be four times longer.[17]

Table 1.4 outlines the major federal departments and their different roles in the coastal zone. Any particular development may be affected by a variety of these departments. For example a new harbour facility which

Table 1.4
Federal Departments Involved in the Coastal Zone

Departments Canada	Functions						
	Overall Federal Coordination & Planning	Environmental Protection	Land use Urbanization & Industrial Development	Mineral Development	Ports and Transportation	Recreation	Renewable Resources and Agriculture
Agriculture							X
Energy, Mines and Resources				X			
Environment		X	X		X	X	
Fisheries and Oceans							X
Indian Affairs and Northern Development			X	X			
Industry, Trade and Commerce			X				
Privy Council Office	X						
Public Works			X				
Regional Economic Expansion			X		X		
Transport		X			X		

Table 2.4
Provincial Departments Involved in the Coastal Zone

Departments	Functions						
	Coordination and Planning	Environmental Protection	Land Use and Urbanization	Mineral Development	Ports and Transportation	Recreation	Renewable Resources and Agriculture
NEWFOUNDLAND							
Culture, Recreation and Youth						X	X
Development						X	
Environment		X	X				X
Fisheries							X
Forest Resources and Lands			X				X
Mines and Energy				X			X
Municipal Affairs			X				
Public Works and Services			X				
Rural, Agricultural and M. Development							X
Transportation					X		
NOVA SCOTIA							
Agriculture & Marketing			X				X
Culture, Recreation Fitness						X	
Development					X		X

Environment
Fisheries
Lands & Forests
Mines & Energy
Municipal Affairs
Public Works
Tourism
Transportation

NEW BRUNSWICK

Agriculture &
Rural Development
Cabinet Secretariat
Environment
Fisheries
Municipal Affairs
Natural Resources
Tourism
Transportation
Youth Recreation
Cultural Resources

PRINCE EDWARD
ISLAND

Agriculture and
Forestry
Community Affairs
Fisheries

(Table 2.4 continued)

Departments	Coordination and Planning	Environmental Protection	Land Use and Urbanization	Mineral Development	Ports and Transportation	Recreation	Renewable Resources and Agriculture
Highways and Public Works			X		X		
Tourism, Industry and Energy				X		X	X
BRITISH COLUMBIA							
Agriculture							
Energy, Mines & Petroleum Resources		X	X				X
Forests			X				X
Lands, Parks and Housing			X				X
Municipal Affairs			X			X	
Tourism						X	
Transportation & Highways					X		

Functions

combines commercial, recreational, and fishery support facilities may well come under the aegis of the departments of Transport, Environment (small harbours), Fisheries and Oceans, Public Works (construction), and Regional Economic Expansion (development incentives). It could also be affected by policies developed by Crown Corporations such as the Canada Mortgage and Housing Corporation, Canadian National Railways and the National Harbours Board which, although responsible to various federal Ministers, can follow particular and unrelated policies.

At the provincial level the situation is in some ways more complex (Table 2.4) since not all provinces have a similar departmental structure or distribution of mandates. As can be seen in Table 2.4, the number and types of department vary widely. For operations within a province this may pose little problem other than that of defining who is in charge. But for operations in several provinces, this can become a real stumbling block because of the different policies followed. Furthermore, federal and provincial requirements, which exist simultaneously, are not necessarily in concordance.

Varied institutional structure is inherent in the system of Confederation, and as such reflects the multiplicity and complexity of Canadian society. Nevertheless, the complex arrangements affecting the coastal zone have led to many cries for new, amalgamated, or streamlined institutions. A lot of attention has thus been given in recent years to the manner in which coastal management should take place. Opinions on the matter differ widely. Some see a very direct interventionist role by government agencies, while others stress a more laissez-faire attitude. Over the years a variety of approaches has been suggested for dealing with the coastal zone. Perhaps the most "traditional" is that based on the principles of "environmental planning." This approach takes as its premise that coastal resources should be used in a manner compatible with the functional and natural ecosystem. To the advocates of the environmental approach, who are mainly natural scientists, land-use planners, landscape architects and systems engineers, the aim of coastal zone management should be to guide coastal use to *ecologically* suitable locations in order to avoid disruption of natural environmental processes. This, in effect, means the government must take an active role in planning, regulating and managing coastal uses in order to accomplish this goal. The government must therefore not just respond to coastal development. This contemporary version of coastal zone environmental planning and management is based on concepts derived from *ecological theory*, which views the coastal environment as a complex and interconnected system of physical and biological relationships. Any planning and management system that is devised for the coastal zone must therefore reflect ecological processes and should not be designed on the basis of "man-oriented processes."[18] According to this argument, an estuary must be viewed as a natural unit around which planning and management should evolve. This will then eliminate a piecemeal approach. The problem, however, is that decision-making units (political boundaries) do not usually coincide with ecological units.

Focusing entirely on physical criteria in the management process does not necessarily give rise to adequate institutions for management purposes. One approach to institution building which has seen a certain amount of ascendancy and which is considered by some to be more directly related to the physical, economic and institutional complexity of the coastal zone is referred to as "public choice theory."[19] This approach takes the view that government organizations are in many ways similar to those in the private sector—they have operating costs and production constraints, are subject to political pressure (political external costs) and develop particular sets of expertise (product). In applying "efficiency" and "productivity" criteria to government operations the conclusion is drawn that duplication and overlap, and the competitive and responsive situations they create, is not always inefficient. To many this comes across not as the good sense of political economy (which its proponents would claim), but rather as partisan politics which go against the somewhat generally held belief that government centralization, a reduction in the complication of governmental arrangements, and clear hierarchies are "good things." In addition, this approach has itself been guilty of several errors and omissions. The gravest is that it has rarely been extended into defining ideal and acceptable institutions and has concentrated on status quo solutions, together with criticism of "centralist" behaviour. Less grave, but of importance, is the fact that the approach has been well-developed both theoretically and empirically within the sphere of urban government arrangements.[20] Clear applications to natural resource situations are not as numerous as they should be.

Despite vast differences in the perception of solutions there does seem to be a consensus emerging. The approach to institutional arrangements in the Canadian situation should (a) focus on coordinating existing agencies and programs and (b) relate to specific "areas" and their groups of problems, rather than dealing with extensive coastal/estuarine areas. This has led to the suggestion that management councils should be formed either to manage specific coastal regions[21] or somewhat wider ocean areas.[22] These councils would, in general, be made up of interested parties and would act to coordinate existing programs and advise government on development proposals and policies. To date no such institutions have been created, other than at the planning level, and they most likely will not for a long time to come.[23]

Nevertheless, it seems clear that one of the on-going research needs in Canada is in the realm of institutional arrangements for coastal zone management. Development problems are intensifying and the number and extent of coastal uses increasing apace. The management problem will not go away, and thus consideration of new institutional mechanisms is of

crucial importance and must be added to the on-going resear
structure and functioning of coastal/estuarine ecosystems.

New Institutions

New institutional arrangements relating to coastal zone manage
virtually nonexistent. However, there have been changes in the realm of
environmental and ecological management which are directly applicable to
the coastal zone.[24] In particular, most provinces and the federal government have instituted environmental assessment procedures whereby
proposed developments are analyzed in terms of their potential impact on
the physical and socioeconomic environments.

The federal Environmental Assessment Review Process (EARP),
administered by Environment Canada, was created in 1973 following a
Cabinet decision to that effect. If a project is undertaken on any Canada
lands or under the sponsorship of a federal department and will probably
cause some environmental or social deterioration, then it is expected that
the sponsoring agency will submit the project for environmental assessment. Under the procedures the proponent of the project, in concert with
the sponsoring agency, prepares an environmental impact statement (EIS)
which is developed according to the guidelines set up by an independent
assessment panel. This panel advises the proponent of any deficiencies in
the EIS, requests changes and eventually publishes its findings following
public hearings and briefings on the issue.

A variety of Panel reports has already been prepared under the EARP
process, and several are under way especially for the Hibernia hydrocarbon
development off the east coast of Newfoundland and for the proposed
Beaufort Sea oil-producing areas. One panel report is of particular interest
to the question of coastal zone management—the one relating to the
National Harbours Board (NHB) proposal to expand the Roberts Bank
(B.C.) bulk-loading facility.

The existing coal-handling facility at Roberts Bank (Westshore Terminals: see Figure 1.4) began operation in 1970. The Port of Vancouver
(NHB) had extended its boundaries to allow the development to take place
outside the traditional port area. In 1967 British Columbia had also set up
its own Crown Corporation, the British Columbia Harbours Board to
reclaim land and promote the new "superport." The first phase consists of a
5 km causeway to the mainland which services the 20 ha landfill facility by
a new rail link. Kaiser Resources Ltd., of which Westshore is a subsidiary, is
the sole user and operator of the facility from which it plans to have
shipped 15 million long tons of coal to Japan by 1985.

In 1973 the NHB initiated its second phase of development (Figure 2.4)
which would have included four more 20 ha terminals, administrative
facilities, and a turning basin capable of accommodating 150,000 dead-
weight-ton tankers. Road and rail links to the mainland would be upgraded

Figure 1.4

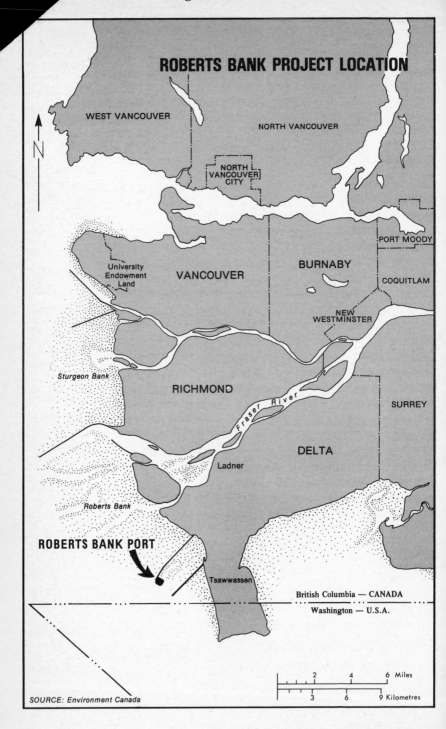

Figure 2.4

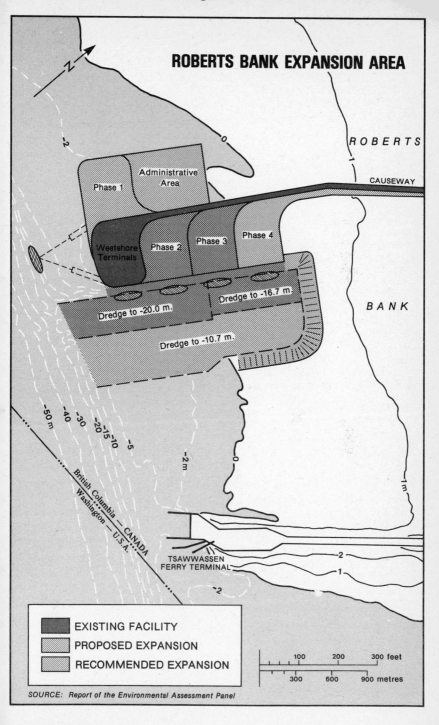

ROBERTS BANK EXPANSION AREA

ROBERTS

CAUSEWAY

Phase 1

Administrative
Area

Westshore
Terminals

Phase 2

Phase 3

Phase 4

BANK

Dredge to -20.0 m.

Dredge to -16.7 m.

Dredge to -10.7 m.

-50 m

-40

-30

-20

-15

-10

-5

-2 m

0

1 m

British Columbia — CANADA
Washington — U.S.A.

TSAWWASSEN
FERRY TERMINAL

2

1

2

1

-2

EXISTING FACILITY

PROPOSED EXPANSION

RECOMMENDED EXPANSION

| 100 | 200 | 300 feet |
| 300 | 600 | 900 metres |

SOURCE: Report of the Environmental Assessment Panel

728 ha of industrial land would be prepared on the adjacent coast-
he attempt was to create a multifunction superport complete with
n-, coal-, and bulk liquid-handling equipment.

In 1975 the NHB submitted its proposals to the EARP process and
hired Beak-Hinton to prepare the necessary EIS. Following the submission
of a variety of briefs, the EARP panel published a set of deficiencies
(February 1978), which were replied to four months later. Six days of
public hearings were held in the fall of 1978, other briefs were submitted,
and in March 1979 the Panel report was published.[25] Because of potential
deleterious environmental and social impacts the Panel recommended a
significantly reduced expansion scheme (Figure 2.4) which would reduce
annoyance to local communities, minimize environmental impact and yet
allow the development of those facilities which seemed to be justified.

The story of the Roberts Bank scheme is both long and complicated.
Nevertheless, on August 29, 1980 the Federal Minister of Transport and
the B.C. Ministers of Industry and Small Business Development, and
Lands, Parks and Housing announced that the project would go ahead "in
line with the principles established by EARP in its 1979 report." To some
extent a form of coastal management had been achieved.

EARP, however, does not constitute coastal zone management. It is a
project-specific process whose guidelines and requirements can be highly
variable depending upon the Assessment Panel chosen. Furthermore the
very uncertainty of the EIS process, combined with lack of data in many
instances, make certain Panel conclusions rather tenuous. Some also see
the lack of statutory/judicial authority of EARP as a difficulty in getting the
recommendations of the Panels accepted.

Clearly, environmental and social impact assessment is the rule of the
day, and yet a vast amount of research is needed on the problems of
assessment methodology, public participation, and decision making under
uncertainty. Furthermore, approaches to environmental management,
and coastal zone management in particular, need to be defined such that
wider questions of environmental and socioeconomic interdependency are
addressed. EARP is just one small move in this direction, and until more
experience is gained the criticism that the process is *ad hoc* will remain.

Energy Facility Siting: An Emerging Issue

In recent years urbanization, industrialization pressures and the question
of access to the shoreline have been in the forefront of coastal management
concerns, as has the process of conflict development between multiple and
occasionally mutually intolerant types of resource use.[26] These problems
have not gone away and, if anything, are intensifying. But they have not
been sufficient to give rise to coastal zone management programs other
than those developed from existing land use and resource management
regulations—and of course the old favourite, zoning. Certain sensitive

areas have indeed come in for specific consideration—such as the Gulf Islands of British Columbia—and others, including a variety of urban waterfronts, have been the scene of intensified regulatory, control and promotion activities. True, the urban areas around such metropolitan centres as Halifax, Montreal, Toronto and Vancouver are still managed in the same fashion as they were, despite some adaptations to the needs of urban waterfront redevelopment interests.[27] But in all of this, the focus has been quite definitely upon *land*-based impacts on the coastal and marine environment, whether in the form of use-patterns, pollution, congestion and the like. Certain marine activities, especially transportation, shell-fishing and the fishery, have been viewed in a different light. But since they are "traditional" or "historic" activities, they have been considered to the extent that they are dependent on the human ecumene on land and on land-based interests in certain estuarine environments.

One issue which is growing in importance more than others is the siting of energy-related facilities in the coastal zone. Energy transhipment proposals such as the extension of coal-loading facilities at Roberts Bank (B.C.) discussed above or the recently announced plan to ship liquid natural gas (LNG) to Japan from a still to be decided B.C. terminal give rise to major concern over the physical and social impacts on the coastal zone. Even wider impacts are to be expected in various parts of Canada because of the promise of offshore oil and gas production. In the future this may well be *the* issue in coastal zone management in Canada, as it is elsewhere in the world. After years of drilling (Figure 3.4), significant commercial finds of oil off Newfoundland are imminent, as suggested by tests of the Hibernia P-15 well. Similarly, Nova Scotia is poised for "big events" based on the promise of natural gas at the Venture D-23 well off Sable Island. The Arctic (Beaufort Sea and High Arctic Islands) will eventually contribute to the same saga depending not only on the commercial feasibility of finds but also upon the transportation systems built to deliver the hydrocarbons to market. With renewed exploration activity on leased tracts in the British Columbia offshore, the west coast may also be added to this list before long.

Although the precise size and productivity of currently known offshore deposits of hydrocarbons is open to speculation, one thing is certain. Should commercial amounts be declared and should the oil/gas interests proceed to the production phase, the pressure on Canada's coastline and coastal communities and environments will increase dramatically.[28] Existing supply bases will need to be complemented by a whole set of other land using operations with significant potential positive and negative effects. Fabrication yards of various kinds, pipe-coating facilities, storage and pumping installations and eventual production units and pipeline landfalls are all within the realms of possibility.[29] Hence the foreseeable shift in the source of pressure for coastal zone development: current land and water-based pressure will be augmented considerably by

Figure 3.4

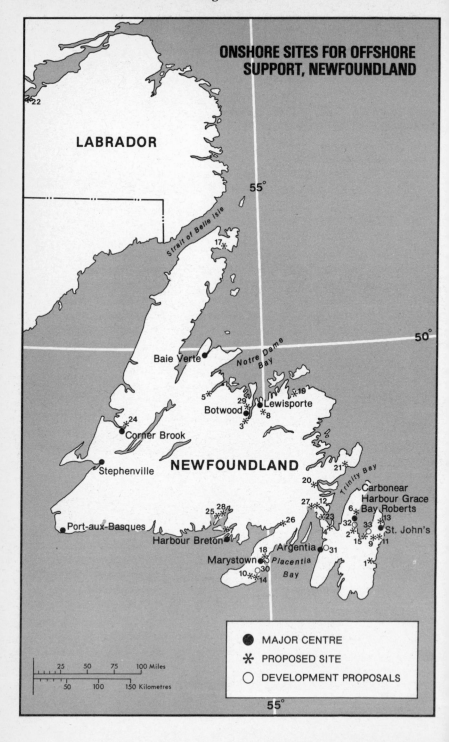

ONSHORE SITES FOR OFFSHORE SUPPORT, NEWFOUNDLAND

Figure 4.4

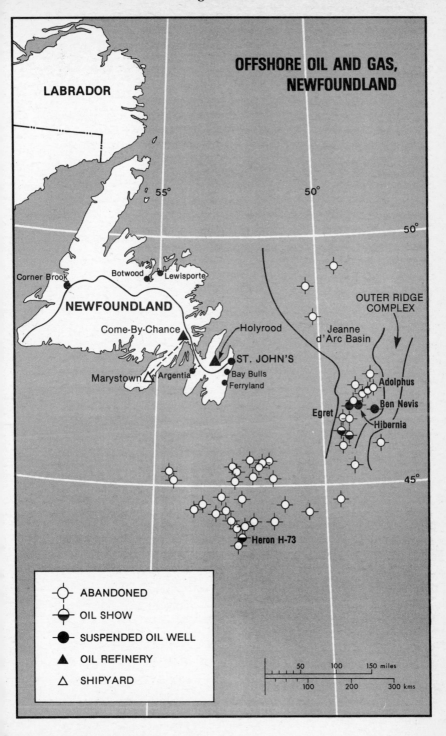

outer continental shelf (OCS) operations in a form not previously experienced in Canada. The argument can thus be made that in default of any other substantial reason, *offshore energy development is the most potent rationale for managing the Canadian shoreline.*[30]

Nevertheless, two aspects of these impacts can be identified as being somewhat more critical than the others. First, the land use and environmental impacts of onshore facilities for OCS activities need to be pre-identified and a suitable series of locations for these facilities defined *in advance* of the potential developments. In this way reasonable solutions to future difficulties may be found. It is suggested that this is the essence of OCS impact planning—the definition of procedures and the identification of institutional arrangements to deal with the elemental problem of location.[31] Secondly, the landing of offshore hydrocarbons will have significant impacts on coastal economies and communities. In one sense these could be the "shot in the arm" needed for certain economically deprived regions, within Newfoundland and Nova Scotia in particular.[32] They may even result in development processes which, if carefully managed using a "staged development process," can accomplish more "naturally" than all the federal and provincial regional development programs put together. Unfortunately, they could also give rise to a massive "balance of imports" problem (both nationally and provincially) because of the equipment and expertise needed to sustain OCS activities, and could further accentuate the "boom-bust" cycle of certain provincial economies which are based on natural resource extraction and export. Added to this could be the tremendous drain on local and provincial purses required by the extension and even creation of infrastructural services. These services range from such mundane things as land preparation to water supply, roads, schools for the increased population, and added housing facilities.

Clearly, onshore impacts of offshore oil and gas can be a mixed blessing, as is borne out by certain experiences elsewhere (e.g., the Cooke Inlet, Alaska; and certain parts of Scotland).[33] Local populations, because of the skills required, may be left out entirely of the new market for labour—and also suffer from such effects as increased prices (locally) for land and houses. It has been reported that such effects are already being felt in Newfoundland, and even traditional sectors such as the fishery are suffering because they cannot offer competitive rates—and this in a situation of sporadic sectoral growth resulting from the 200-mile (322 km) fishing zone declared in 1977. In an attempt to maximize local benefits, the government of Newfoundland has instituted strict "content requirements" especially for labour—but in the current situation this could be counter-productive for the fishery given its relative lack of attraction to the sea-going and professional population. Retraining and various types of educational programs would seem to be required as quickly as possible should the desire to reduce unemployment be a real one.

Conscious of the real problems which can arise because of unplanned development of offshore supply facilities in the coastal zone—especially speculation and land price inflation—the Newfoundland government has taken steps to control the situation. On October 17, 1980, an executive order (Newfoundland Regulation 279/80—304/80)[34] was published announcing the "freezing" of land sales/development in thirteen different locations. As can be seen in Figure 3.4 and Table 3.4 not all of these areas are on the coastline, and each is viewed as having a different role to play in offshore support. Upon the publication of these "government sites," private parties and municipalities were given until December 5, 1980 to present the Minister of Development with different or alternative proposals. On this date another seventeen sites were nominated (Table 3.4) making a total of 30 sites selected.

Site nomination does not necessarily mean that development will take place, but it seems to have fired the imagination of many sectors of Newfoundland society. The reasons for site selection, however, are by no

Table 3.4
Proposed Sites for Supporting Hydrocarbon
Development Off the Coast of Newfoundland

A. *Sites designated by the Newfoundland Provincial Government*

1. Bay Bulls	8. Lewisporte
2. Bay Roberts-Spaniards Bay	9. Long Pond
3. Botwood	10. Mortier Bay
4. Gasters Bay	11. Octagon Pond
5. Halls Bay	12. Sunnyside
6. Harbour Grace	13. Torbay airport
7. Hermitage Bay	

Source: *Newfoundland Gazette.*

B. *Sites nominated by other groups (independently)*

14. Mortier Bay	22. Goose Bay
15. Seal Cove	23. Bull Arm
16. Hopedale	24. Corner Brook
17. St. Anthony	25. St. Albans
18. Main Brook	26. Terrenceville
19. Carmanville	27. Come-by-Chance
20. Clarenville	28. St. Albans
21. Shambler's Cove	29. Botwood

Source: Ministry of Development.

C. *Development proposals*

30. Mortier Bay (DAC Ltd.)	32. Bay Roberts (Port Atlantis Ltd.)
31. Argentia (Atlantic Seacave)	33. Seal Cove
	(McNamara—Winnipeg)

Source: Ministry of Development.

means clear. Some criticism has already emerged. For example, the Bay Bulls development area is considered by most people to be an ideal site for the landing of a production pipeline from the Hibernia area. But it is doubtful that transportation of crude will take this form for a long time to come simply because of the technological problems associated with burying the line in bedrock. The current thinking is to employ a single-buoy mooring system (SBM) at the production well and to ship the oil by tanker (to a location yet to be determined). Bay Bulls may never be needed as a development area. A similar negative appraisal has been made of other sites for other functions. It has been argued that *existing* sites available in St. John's harbour and the surrounding urban area may well be sufficient for a long time to come.[35] Added to this are the obvious benefits to be gained by having facilities in a major urban area where the provision of housing and infrastructure facilities—a major problem—poses less difficulty.

Contingency planning at all levels is required if the Canadian offshore is not to be a fiasco of resource exploitation. Surely this is the challenge which will breathe life into otherwise faltering, if not moribund, attempts at management. Despite the definition of probable sites, the issues which need to be faced and the research questions which need to be dealt with in the Newfoundland situation include:

—definitions of potential resource finds and identification of requirements for labour/equipment related to each scenario;
—identification of the types of onshore facilities which will be required, their location requirements, and the sites possible for their accommodation;
—definition of potential landfalls, including the use of feeder-tankers in the short run and pipelines in the long;
—the identification of infrastructural requirements and the relationships between these requirements and existing infrastructure supply;
—the positive and negative impacts to be expected both in environmental and economic terms;
—definition of controls, if any, which need to be defined for onshore facilities;
—measures which need to be instituted in order to mitigate possible negative effects, and the clear identification of institutional responsibilities in the matter.

The task ahead is obviously massive and involves a whole host of existing public bodies and agencies, various industrial interests, the general public, and the scientific community. Coordination of these concerns is not evident at the present time.

The above list implies that some well-performed but traditional planning analyses of labour supply, infrastructure, industrial structure and the sensitivity of the environment be undertaken. But it also implies something more, and that is the development of some form of coastal management strategy and the definition of key institutions to go with it. In the case of Newfoundland a variety of "planning committees" has been set up as has a "Petroleum Directorate," all with the aim of promoting a "staged development" process rather than one which is totally uncontrolled.

Offshore hydrocarbon development off Canada's east coast provides an interesting example of the challenge of coastal management. The "region" to be managed is a potentially vast one, since the location of offshore reserves and the location of landing sites are intimately tied to the eventual impact areas. But not all areas require the same type or the same amount of management. Furthermore, the elements which make up the coastal zone themselves have very different needs in a purely sectoral sense. For example, the regions needed and used for inshore and offshore fisheries management are very different from the leasing areas for offshore exploration, and the land-based economic linkages relating to community economic and social development are different again. It would be difficult, therefore, to conceive of a coastal zone management area which is all-inclusive; a spatially polycentric or "nesting" of specific problem areas would seem to be more relevant. Concerning the offshore, the jurisdictional dispute between Newfoundland and the federal government obviously ranks high in people's minds at the present time, but roles other than the jurisdictional one have and will continue to have high importance. For example, the economic and social impact on a developed area such as St. John's implies the use of the powers of various governments and their agencies to control and promote development. But in outlying areas where few infrastructure services are available, the public sector will necessarily be involved in single or joint ventures to produce and provide needed goods and services. In such areas the management problem is completely different and requires suitably different strategies. Since it is generally considered that most impacts, whether economic or environmental, associated with offshore hydrocarbon development are felt along coastal areas and in coastal communities of all kinds, the public sector needs to give great attention to defining such strategies.

Conflicts, and the need for their resolution, will become ever more numerous and complex. In many ways offshore oil and gas development is a mixed blessing, because the potential negative environmental and economic impacts on other sectors may outweigh some of the benefits. Add to this the fact that many benefits (including from taxation) can occur outside the impacted communities and areas and the potential for conflict is seen to rise. One of the key impacts is on the inshore and offshore fishing sector because of the disruption of fishing grounds, potential damage to equipment, and the economic difficulties arising from local inflation of labour and land costs. It has taken some countries with experience in offshore hydrocarbon production a long time to create management mechanisms and funding schemes which help in solving conflicts. Given the importance of the fishing sector (see Chapter 5), attention to the creation of such mechanisms in eastern Canada should be the highest item on the public agenda, along with mechanisms to control, direct, and even be involved in onshore development schemes.

Conclusion

Old problems of coastal zone development, including urbanization, industrialization and recreation uses, are increasing in importance. But they are being added to by the location in the zone of energy-related facilities—specifically those related to offshore oil and gas exploration and development. This new pressure is seen as giving renewed life to the argument that coastal zone management of one form or another is required, and it also suggests a series of specific research endeavours which are badly needed.

Unless preplanning takes place, the onshore impacts which Canada will experience because of the offshore will not all be positive. There is thus a key role for governments to be involved in problem-oriented planning at the earliest stages possible. In the Canadian case this is complicated by complex and overlapping jurisdictions. New solutions are needed, and the EARP process is a move in this direction. However, new problems, such as offshore hydrocarbon development, can have massive impacts not previously experienced, and further research into a variety of coastal zone management issues is urgently required if coastal resource use is to be the key to a better life and not the source of inequity.

Notes

1 For a more complete discussion see: J.C. Day and J.G.M. Parkes, "Canadian freshwater lake and marine-shore areas use and management," Proceedings, *Shore Management Symposium* (Toronto: Canadian Council of Resource and Environment Ministers, 1979), pp. 56–120.

2 This comment is not meant as a criticism of the Canadian situation. Nevertheless, there has been a tendency for commentators to compare Canada with the United States despite the vast differences in problems, opportunities, existing planning frameworks and legislative procedures. For a discussion of the situation in the United States see: U.S General Accounting Office, *The Coastal Zone Management Program: an Uncertain Future*, Report to the Congress by the Comptroller General of the United States, GGD-76-107, 1976, and U.S. Senate, Committee on Commerce, National Ocean Policy Study, *Legislative History of the*

Coastal Zone Management Act of 1972 as Amended in 1974 and 1976 with a Section by Section Index (Washington D.C.: U.S. Government Printing Office, 1976).

3 Environment Canada, Atlantic Unit, Water Management Service, *Coastal Zone*, Proceedings of a seminar held at the Bedford Institute of Oceanography, Dartmouth, N.S. (Ottawa: Environment Canada, 1972), and Institute of Public Affairs, Dalhousie University, *Shoreland: Its Use, Ownership, Access and Management*, Proceedings of a seminar held at Amherst, N.S. (Halifax: Institute of Public Affairs, 1972).

4 Canadian Council of Resource and Environment Ministers, *op. cit.*

5 The difference between "national" and "nationwide" is not trivial. Despite suggestions that a national and therefore a coordinated policy be defined across the country, it was argued that a set of policies adapted to different provincial requirements is preferable—but that all provinces be encouraged to derive such policies.

6 British Columbia, for example, published: *Shore Policy for British Columbia: A White Paper Prepared for the Minister of the Environment* (Victoria, B.C.: Ministry of the Environment, 1979).

7 M. Barker, *Water Resources and Related Land Uses: Strait of Georgia-Puget Sound Basin* (Ottawa: Environment Canada, Lands Directorate, Geographical paper no. 56, 1974).

8 The problem of defining, assessing and measuring conflicts is discussed in P. Harrison, "Les conflits d'utilisation des ressources engendrés par le développement d'une région côtière: le cas du Puget Sound," *Cahiers de géographie de Québec* 19 (1975), pp. 475-488.

9 W.R.D. Sewell and N.A. Swainson, "West Coast oil pollution policies: Canadian responses to risk assessment," in *Resources and the Environment: Policy Perspectives for Canada*, ed. O.P. Dwivedi (Toronto: McClelland and Stewart, 1980),pp. 216-242.

10 The whole question of hazard zone protection, especially in coastal areas, ranks high as a public priority. This "traditional" form of coastal zone management is discussed by Parkes, *op. cit.* (1978), p. 15, who notes the importance of dyking in marine and freshwater environments. Under the Canada Water Act the federal government is shown as having spent over $67 million on this form of control.

11 D.W. Dusik, *Shoreline for the Public* (Cambridge, Mass: The MIT Press, 1974).

12 A.H.J. Dorcey, ed., *Coastal Resources in the Future of B.C.* (Vancouver: Westwater Research Centre, and University of British Columbia Press, 1979).

13 The whole question of port management in Canada is inextricably related to the question of coastal zone management not only because of the economic importance of ports but also because they are major coastal land owners. Port management procedures, including the role of the National Harbours Board, have been under review for some time and new proposals are expected imminently. References on the matter can be found in P. Cunningham, *Canada's Changing Port Scene: an Annotated Classified Bibliography* (Toronto: University of Toronto/York University Joint Programme in Transportation, research report no. 54, December 1978).

14 The most widely recognized study on institutional relationships is: D.M. Johnston, A. Paul Pross, and I. McDougall, *Coastal Zone: Framework for*

Management in Atlantic Canada (Halifax: Institute of Public Affairs, Dalhousie University, 1975).

15 Environment Canada, *Final Report, St. Lawrence River Study Committee,* (Ottawa: Environment Canada, 1979) and A.H.J. Dorcey, ed., *The Uncertain Future of the Fraser* (Vancouver: Westwater Research Center and University of British Columbia Press, 1976).

16 This question is underlined most eloquently in M. Sproule-Jones, "A fresh look at an old problem: Coordinating Canada's Shore Management Agencies," *The Western Political Quarterly,* 32 (1979), pp. 278-285.

17 The complexity of agency responsibilities is outlined in D.M. Johnston *et al., op. cit.,* Appendices I and II. The specifically federal role is presented in J.G.M. Parkes, "The federal role in shorezone management," in *Marine Studies and Coastal Zone Management in Canada,* ed. R.J. McCalla (Halifax: Department of Geography, St. Mary's University, Occasional Paper no. 2, 1978), pp. 1-18.

18 A.W. Cooper, "Ecological considerations," in *Coastal Zone Resources Management,* eds. J.C. Hite and J.M. Steep (New York: Praeger, 1971).

19 This approach is developed in the context of coastal zone management in: R.L. Bish, R. Warren, L.F. Weschler, J. Crutchfield and P. Harrison, *Coastal Resource Use: Decisions on Puget Sound* (Seattle: University of Washington Press, 1975), especially Chapter 5.

20 R.L. Bish, *Understanding Urban Government* (Washington D.C.: American Enterprise Institute, 1973). A review of public choice theory can be found in: D.C. Mueller, "Public choice: a survey," *Journal of Economic Literature* 14 (1976), pp. 395-433.

21 D.M. Johnston *et al., op. cit.* and D.M. Johnston, "Coastal zone management in Canada: purposes and prospects," *Canadian Public Administration* 20 (1977), pp. 140-151.

22 The whole issue of ocean management is discussed more fully in B. Johnson, "Governing Canada's economic zone," *Canadian Public Administration* 20 (1977), pp. 152-173. A more general discussion of legislation affecting ocean management can be found in P. Harrison, "Managing our vast new 3-ocean domain," *Canadian Geographic* 99 (January 1980), pp. 10-17. Specific research questions are raised in P. Harrison, "Geographers and the Management of Canada's Ocean Resources," *The Canadian Geographer* 36 (1980), pp. 111-113.

23 The interesting case of regional planning strategies being employed in the Lancaster Sound area is presented in: Indian and Northern Affairs Canada, *All About the Green Paper, Lancaster Sound Regional Study* (Ottawa: Department of Indian and Northern Affairs, 1980).

24 This section is based on research performed for the York University Canada Ports Project (director: H. Roy Merrens) and can be found in more detailed discussion in: P. Harrison and K. Beattie, *The Exurbanization of Port Facilities: Location Conditions and Relocation Problems.* Internal report (mimeo), Canada Ports Project, Department of Geography, York University, October 1980. Proposals (October 1980) to ship liquid natural gas to Japan raise the whole issue once again of where the terminals should be located along the British Columbia coast. This subject has already been studied in depth during the West Coast Oil Port Inquiry. For a discussion see: A.R. Thompson, *West Coast Oil Ports Inquiry:*

Statement of Proceedings (Vancouver: West Coast Oil Ports Inquiry, February 1978).

[25] Federal Environmental Assessment Review Process, *Report of the Environmental Assessment Panel, Roberts Bank Port Expansion* (Ottawa: Environment Canada, March 1979).

[26] This problem has been stressed time and again, and especially in CCREM *op. cit.* However, new energy demands and a new geography of energy production and use are going to add to these pressures.

[27] Urban waterfront renewal is an area of intense interest in North America. For a complete literature review see: R. Merrens, *Urban Waterfront Redevelopment in North America: An Annotated Bibliography* (Toronto: University of Toronto/York University Joint Programme in Transportation, Research report no. 66, April 1980). Waterfront redevelopment in a variety of Canadian cities was the subject of a seminar organized by the Demonstration Group of the Canada Mortgage and Housing Corporation in March 1980. A report of the discussions can be found in: D. DeGenova, *Housing and Waterfront Redevelopment*, currently an in-house document and forthcoming as a published report.

[28] This phenomenon has been experienced elsewhere, and such experiences are frequently treated as "lessons" for those areas which are about to be impacted. A lot of attention has been given to the Scottish case. See: P.L. Baldwin and M.F. Baldwin, *Onshore Planning for Offshore Oil:* Lessons from Scotland (Washington D.C.: Conservation Foundation, 1975) and U.S. Senate Committee on Commerce and Ocean Policy Study, *North Sea Oil and Gas: Impact of Development on the Coastal Zone* (Washington D.C.: U.S. Government Printing Office, 1974).

[29] The type, size, number, and location of such support facilities is a function of many factors including the size and location of the offshore fields and the availability of land-based infrastructure. For a discussion of various methodologies relating to the identification of facility requirements see: U.S. Department of the Interior, *Onshore Impacts of Offshore Oil: A User's Guide to Assessment Methods* (Washington D.C.: U.S. Government Printing Office, May 1979).

[30] The details of OCS oil and gas impacts on the coastal zone cannot be fully developed here. Such impacts have been recognized in the United States in an institutional fashion. Amendments to the Coastal Zone Management Act of 1972 which were approved in 1976 created a Coastal Energy Impact Program (CEIP), whereby the federal government gives grants and low-interest loans to states and local communities which experience negative economic impacts because of coastal energy facility development (amendments, sec. 308). $1.2 billion were appropriated for the ten years 1977–87 and of this $125 million were authorized for 1977-78. For a recent discussion of coastal management and the CEIP arrangements see: I.R. Manners, W. Dietrich and T. Keen, "Energy development and coastal zone management in Texas," *Texas Business Review* (Jan.-Feb. 1980), pp. 45–52.

[31] The question of preplanning is discussed more fully in: J.T.E. Gilbert and P. Harrison, "Environmental planning and management of offshore hydrocarbon operations: the development of environmental guidelines," paper presented to the workshop on the geology and hydrocarbon potential of the South China Sea and possibilities of joint research and development (Honolulu: Environment and

Policy Institute, East-West Center, mimeo, Aug. 1980).

32 Government of Newfoundland and Labrador, *Economic Analysis of the Hibernia Discovery and Related Provincial and Federal Positions* (St. John's: Petroleum Directorate, Sept. 1980). Government of Nova Scotia, *Offshore Oil and Gas: a Chance for Nova Scotians* (Halifax: Department of Mines and Energy, 1980).

33 Council on Environment Quality, *Oil and Gas in Coastal Waters* (Washington D.C.: U.S. Government Printing Office, April 1977).

34 *The Newfoundland Gazette*, Friday, October 17, 1980, pp. 1–42.

35 K. Storey, "Offshore Oil: Regional Impacts for the Avalon Peninsula," Paper presented to the "Offshore Environment in the 80s" conference, St. John's, Newfoundland, Dec. 2–4, 1980.

5/Oceans Exploitation: Efficiency and Equity Questions in Fisheries Management

Dianne Draper

As we study how men have used the resources available to them we do distinguish between good and bad husbandry, between economical or conservative and wasteful or destructive use ... We are aware that what we do will determine for good or evil the lives of those who will come after us. And therefore we geographers, least of all, can fail to think on the place of man in nature, of the whole ecology.

> Carl O. Sauer, 1956, "The
> Education of a Geographer,"
> *Annals AAG*, 46, 299.

Man's role in changing the seas has only recently begun. If man's impact on the face of the earth is any guide, the potential for intentional and unintentional change in the oceans is monumental. With continued world population growth, pressure on the oceans to provide additional food, energy, mineral and space resources will be increased. Floating cities in the sea and ocean food and energy farm units are among the concepts proposed to meet such expanded world requirements.[1] Already, artificial offshore islands have been constructed in the Beaufort Sea for oil drilling and production operations, and low levels of active commercial marine mining are underway.[2]

Worldwide, oceans exploitation appears to be inexorable. In Canada, oceans are a highly complex, incompletely understood, but rapidly developing part of of the environment. Since 1970 when the Science Council of Canada described the national interests in undertaking oceans development,[3] and the Ministry of State for Science and Technology announced a national Oceans Policy on July 12, 1973,[4] there has been a dramatic increase in our technological capacity to use ocean resources. But perhaps the most significant challenge remains—stewardship. Canada faces an increased international responsibility to manage ocean resources more effectively, not only for the benefit of Canadians, but also in the interests of all mankind who share a common heritage in the oceans.

Excellence in stewardship demands a great deal of knowledge and competence on the part of resource managers. Frequently, they are faced with the dilemma of needing to make policy decisions in a pressure situation while lacking an adequate data and knowledge base to justify their actions. Roots identified this difficulty in relation to the development of high Arctic marine transportation:

Such apparently simple questions as whether a dock can be built at Nanisivik without affecting the hunting of seals, or whether a single hole can be drilled safely in the middle of Lancaster Sound lead . . . to the admission that we do not know enough about the seals or the ice or the birds to answer what started out to be a question of engineering design, safety and cost. Furthermore, we find both the experts and the public agreeing that we do not know whether it will take one year and $100,000 or ten years and $10 million to be able to address such questions any better.[5]

In the face of multiple, often conflicting, usually interdependent uses of common property ocean resources (Table 1.5), wise policy and management decisions are difficult to reach. More than biophysical and technological dimensions enter the process. Ideally, economic, social, political, legal and institutional perspectives, as well as temporal and spatial dimensions, are accounted for in decision making. In practice, these factors and their interrelationships are not easily accommodated. In part, the difficulties in reaching responsible and responsive policy decisions come from the need to coordinate a broad range of separate environmental factors and activities, each with different potential side effects and externalities, to calculate costs and benefits over the long term, and to ensure input from individuals affected by resource decisions. Optimum net benefits from oceans exploitation (on both national and international scales) will be achieved only through implementation of effective management policy and careful stewardship.

To date, Canada's ocean policy has supported primarily technological research. Granted, such knowledge is necessary to decision making. But that is an insufficient base from which to achieve stewardship. It is essential that decision makers bring an understanding of "nontechnical" components to their deliberations. Again in an Arctic context, Roots noted the difficulty and importance of incorporating such factors:

We shy away from serious investigations of the relationship between sea birds and a social value system, or research about the right of some to a clean environment compared to the right of others to make a profit, because these investigations probe into jurisdictions, legalities, rights, and the subjective areas of politics and ethics. We are afraid to make openly planned experiments on people or their institutions, yet we take tremendous risks with social values and entire cultures through our present trial-and-error method.[6]

Even though there are serious deficiencies in our scientific knowledge, it appears that biophysical and technological dimensions are more easily handled than any other aspects of oceans management. Some of the most difficult questions lie in the socioeconomic and political-institutional dimensions. To demonstrate the problems and prospects associated with these vital concerns, the remainder of the chapter focuses primarily on the commercial fishery resources of the Atlantic and Pacific coasts, and on the need for increased geographic attention to these matters.

Isolating fisheries development and management issues from other uses and users of ocean resources is both impossible and unwise. Within a Canadian oceans context, however, the fisheries sector is important. Despite continued management problems, fisheries constitute the Canadian ocean resource with the longest history of extractive use and contribution to the country's economic development. Fisheries not only reflect the uncertainties and conflicts characterizing many ocean resource exploitation and management issues, fisheries management also presents an almost totally neglected research challenge to the discipline.

As recently as 1967, Sewell and Burton indicated that no studies dealing with purely Canadian fisheries problems existed in North American geographical literature.[7] While that is no longer the case, both the opportunity and the need[8] for theoretical and applied geographic contributions[9] to oceans planning and management decisions exist *now*. If it is to be meaningful, disciplinary response must be swift.

To appreciate the challenge the fisheries sector alone provides to the stewardship of Canadian ocean resources, the nature of fisheries management objectives and strategies are identified. A brief section on the application of certain geographic skills to fisheries questions precedes consideration of selected recent management efforts. This provides the context for the final section of the chapter which identifies past performance and potential contributions of geographers to Canadian fisheries management.

Dimensions of Canadian Fisheries Management Issues

The historical development of Canadian fisheries management strategies and policies may be divided into three major periods. The first, Confederation to 1965, was characterized by a biological emphasis. Responses to fisheries problems and pressures were primarily reactive and *ad hoc*. The second phase, 1965 to 1976, saw the addition of economic and social considerations to the biological basis of management. The recent period, 1977 onward, is associated with implementation of the "200 mile limit."[10] An overview of some important aspects of Canada's attempt at fisheries (and to some extent, oceans) stewardship is provided for reference (Table 2.5).

The 1976 policy for Canada's commercial fisheries developed in response to concerns about serious troubles in the Atlantic fishery, as well as the common property nature of the resource. Problems in the Atlantic fisheries related partly to the escalation of effort by foreign fishing fleets off our shores since the 1950s. That overexploitation led to a dramatic decline in total catch volume and to greatly increased costs per unit of output.

Table 1.5
Ocean Uses and Potential Conflict[1,2]

A. Ocean Uses and Stresses

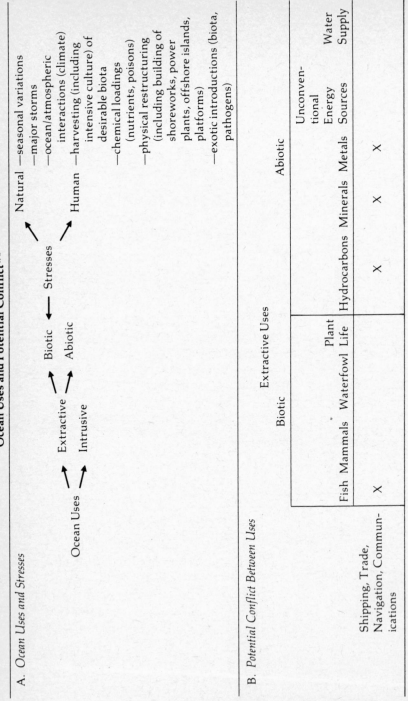

Ocean Uses → Extractive / Intrusive → Biotic / Abiotic → Stresses → Natural / Human

Natural
— seasonal variations
— major storms
— ocean/atmospheric interactions (climate)

Human
— harvesting (including intensive culture) of desirable biota
— chemical loadings (nutrients, poisons)
— physical restructuring (including building of shoreworks, power plants, offshore islands, platforms)
— exotic introductions (biota, pathogens)

B. Potential Conflict Between Uses

| | Extractive Uses | | | | | | | | |
| | Biotic | | | | Abiotic | | | | |
	Fish	Mammals	Waterfowl	Plant Life	Hydrocarbons	Minerals	Metals	Unconventional Energy Sources	Water Supply
Shipping, Trade, Navigation, Communications	X				X	X	X		

X = area of potential conflict or interference between uses	Waste Disposal	Public Recreation, Marine Parks	Scientific Research	Military Uses	Governance — coastal zone management	— protection of marine environment	— Law of the Sea	— international cooperation and coordination
Intrusive Uses								
Public Recreation, Marine Parks	X							
Scientific Research	X	X						
Military Uses	X	X	X					
Governance including — coastal zone management	X	X	X	X				
— protection of marine environment	X	X	X	X	X			
— Law of the Sea	X	X	X	X	X	X		
— international cooperation and coordination	X	X	X	X	X	X	X	
— socioeconomic development of coastal communities	X	X	X	X	X	X	X	X

Notes

[1] Interdependencies are not identified here, nor are all possible conflicts between uses.

[2] D.J. Rapport and H.A. Regier, "An ecological approach to environmental information," *Ambio* 9 (1), (1980), pp. 22–27 provided some material for compilation of this table.

Table 2.5
Historical Development of Canadian Fisheries Management: Some Major Events

Time Period	Action/Issue	Comments

STAGE 1: CONFEDERATION TO 1965

1867	BNA Act, Section 91 "sea coast and inland fisheries" placed under federal jurisdiction	
1868	Fisheries Act provided for active federal regulation of the catching of all living aquatic resources, protection of their environment from pollution, conservation of exploited fish stocks.	i. emphasis on biological conservation; legislation established minimum net mesh sizes, prohibited destructive gear types, set closed fishing seasons. ii. fishing *time* limited, but no attemp made to limit entry; reflected opinion that anyone could participate in fisheries as a matter of right and also revealed lack of recognition of common property characteristics of fisheries.
1920s through 1940s	increased fishing pressure on (eg.) Atlantic cod stocks	i. measures to restrict fishing *effort* initiated, such as prohibiting use of highly productive gear-like traps, weirs, monofilament line. ii. Such measures dissipated resource rents and encouraged some fishermen to leave the industry, discouraged others from entering. iii. No formal attempts to limit *entry* or *amount* of fishing until late 1960s.
Post World War II through the early 1960s	1. rapid expansion of fishing due to advances in technology for catching, processing, storing and transporting catches.	i. much of the increased world fishing effort took place on Newfoundland Grand Banks.
	2. Newfoundland joined Confederation 1949;	i. great increase in foreign fishing power and catch,

Grand Banks became of direct national importance as an oceans frontier.

widespread overfishing, impacts of these events on local fishing communities and reactions of provincial administrations to these effects combined to force greater federal attention to fisheries issues, particularly in the Northwest Atlantic.

3. in 1950s and 1960s, concentrated foreign fishing of codstocks *offshore* Newfoundland reduced catches by about 80 percent (with approximately same effort) for *inshore* fishermen. Newfoundland government demanded federal assistance (fisheries an important sector of provincial economy, providing source of employment in area of few alternative income opportunities).

i. biological issues of more effective regulation of fishing to maintain or restore yields remained prime federal concern, but Newfoundland fisheries received assistance in the form of direct or disguised income support measures such as boatbuilding subsidies and seasonal "unemployment" benefits.

ii. Such developmental assistance created a major management problem. Federal goverment lacked insight into common property problem of fishery, therefore unable to clearly define development policy and forced to respond in *ad hoc* fashion to provincial demands for fisheries assistance. Assistance schemes were largely ineffective and created some negative side effects. For example, economic externalities frequently ignored; subsidies granted to all to improve boats and gear but total catch could not increase (inshore stocks fully exploited) so fishermen collectively took same total catch but with more expensive gear and at higher public and private cost.

Time Period	Action/Issue	Comments

4. fishing explosion re-sulted in development of greater *international* cooperation in fisheries management: Interna-tional Commission for the Northwest Atlantic Fisheries (ICNAF) es-tablished 1949.

i. establishment of ICNAF first step toward regulation of *amount* of fishing (through catch quotas) and paved way for inclusion of economic factors in estab-lishing policy.

ii. total fishing effort in the Northwest Atlantic esca-lated rapidly after mid-1950s, catches peaked in 1968. Early in 1960s ICNAF member countries recognized need for catch quotas, but mandate from members to establish total allowable catches (TACs) for herring and other groundfish stocks did not come until 1971. Separate national allocations were established on a scientific (rather than political) basis, beginning 1973. To secure agreement, and pending unilateral extension of fishing limits, Canada agreed to curtail domestic offshore fishery effort.

5. nationally, the 1950s and 1960s saw expan-sion of provincial inter-est in fisheries develop-ment.

i. generally, the federal gov-ernment has provided most of the financing for east coast fisheries develop-ments. In British Colum-bia, governments have tended to let the federal government administer marine fisheries.

6. in the mid 1950s, the common property na-ture of fisheries began to be explored.

i. lag-time of about a decade before policy prescriptions (based on better under-standing of common property characteristics) developed in federal plans.

7. 1958, 1960 First and Second Law of the Sea (LOS) Conferences

i. Canada contributed to 'functionalist' concept (distinction between territorial sea with sovereign jurisdiction and contiguous zone with limited state jurisdiction) and to development of fishing zone concept. In 1964 Canada proclaimed a 12-mile fisheries zone, and straight baselines and in 1970 declared a full 12-mile territorial zone with fisheries closing lines to enclose (e.g.) Gulf of St. Lawrence, Bay of Fundy on east coast and Dixon Entrance, Hecate Strait on Pacific coast for exclusive Canadian use.

8. 1963 the Newfoundland government appealed for federal government to design and activate a national fisheries development policy.

9. January 1964, Ministerial Conference convened: Federal-Provincial Conference on Fisheries Development.

STAGE 2: 1965 to 1976

1. increased knowledge of common property characteristics of fishery lead federal authorities to strive to reduce numbers of inshore fishermen on east coast and increase offshore fleet (See Note 4 under Post World War II heading, above).

i. Federal government's 1964 commitment to active (not reactive) fisheries development employed new insights of fisheries economics in efforts toward rationalization of fishing industry. Efforts included 1965 Newfoundland Fisheries Household Resettlement Program, 1969 re-

Time Period	Action/Issue	Comments

		development plan for Prince Edward Island fishing industry (which included restricted entry to over-exploited fisheries such as lobster, salmon). Some subsidy schemes dropped as counter-productive.
	2. economic analyses concluded excessive numbers employed in inshore fisheries of Atlantic Provinces, but social and political constraints made rationalization very difficult.	i. on Atlantic coasts, two major reasons for ineffectiveness of rationalization schemes: (a) uncontrolled foreign fishing effort, (b) high unemployment rates in Atlantic Provinces.
	3. on Pacific coast, 1968 Salmon Vessel Licence Control program established (limited entry) and later a buy-back program to remove excess fleet capacity: an *unprecedented* step.	i. program established licence fees for vessels; anticipated reduction in number of vessels designed to increase returns of remaining fishermen. Unexpected complications (such as "expectations trap," "transitional gains trap," saleability of licences, increased fishing capacity due to "capital stuffing") reduced success of program. Solutions being sought to these and other "second generation" management problems.
	4. 1973 Canada at LOS III	i. international political climate toward expanded economic zones was such that Canada moved toward unilateral declaration of a 200-mile fishing limit; Canada had agreed to negotiate allocation of surplus fish to countries

agreeing in advance to respect Canada's anticipated extension of jurisdiction.

5. 1975, 1976 ICNAF set TACs below maximum sustained yield.

i. designed to reduce overfishing, permit stock recovery.

6. May 1976 "Policy for Canada's Commercial Fisheries" published.

i. this represented the first comprehensive analysis of fisheries and policy ever issued federally. It acknowledged the need for economic rationalization, totality of limited entry, reduction of excessive manpower in inshore fishery, rationalization of processing sector.

ii. Policy strategies noted were:

a. The guiding principle in fishery management no longer would be maximization of the crop sustainable over time but the best use of society's resources. "Best use" is defined by the sum of net social benefits (personal income, occupational opportunity, consumer satisfaction and so on) derived from the fisheries and the industries linked to them.

b. while private enterprise, individual, cooperative and corporate, would continue to predominate in the commercial fisheries, fundamental decisions about resource management and about industry and trade development would be

Time Period	Action/Issue	Comments

reached jointly by industry and government.

Clearly, social concerns (for costs/benefits) were incorporated.

iii. The 1976 policy, plus the use of the 200-mile restrictions to reduce both foreign and domestic fishing (to permit stock recovery) was seen as improving long-term performance of fishing industry, particularly on east coast if inshore crowding could be reduced by move to offshore fishery and processing sector.

iv. a continuing, significant obstacle to achievement of rationalization is unemployment levels in Atlantic region; large numbers unemployed and surplus inshore labour cannot all find employment in expanded offshore sector. There is a political and social bias, especially in Newfoundland, toward maintenance of traditional inshore fishery on largest possible scale. Contradictions exist between permitting inshore fishery to absorb labour, achieving "best use" of fishery, and avoiding subsidization of fishery to dispense social welfare.

STAGE 3: *1977 to present*

January 1, 1977 — Canada extended its jurisdiction over fisheries to 200 miles.

i. Canadian share of yield from fisheries within 200 miles assured; in some stocks fully used by Canada, foreign fishing eliminated. In recognition of obligations under the LOS III Informal Composite Negotiating Text rules, Canada continues to provide foreign fleets access to stocks surplus to immediate requirements. Industry benefits through (e.g.) processing foreign catches, access for Canadian fish products to foreign markets. Some call to ban completely foreign vessels from within 200-mile zone.

ii. some stocks outside Canadian limits subject to increasing fishing pressure (e.g.) salmon. Transboundary stocks between Canada and U.S.A. subject to dispute (e.g.) halibut.

January 1, 1979	Northwest Atlantic Fisheries Organization (NAFA) organized to replace ICNAF.

Notes

[1] This table highlights only some of the major policy developments in Canadian fisheries management.

[2] More complete information may be found in the sources of information for this table; P. Copes, *The Evolution of Marine Fisheries Policy in Canada* (Burnaby, B.C.: Simon Fraser University, Department of Economics and Commerce: Discussion Paper Series 79-3-1, 1979); G.R. Munro, "Canada and fisheries management with extended jurisdiction; a preliminary view," in *Economic Impacts of Extended Fisheries Jurisdiction*, ed. L.G. Anderson (Ann Arbor, Michigan: Ann Arbor Science Publishers Inc., 1977), pp. 29–50; and A.W.H. Needler, "Evolution of Canadian fisheries management towards economic rationalization," *Journal of the Fisheries Research Board of Canada*, 36 (July 1979), pp. 716–724.

Fisheries also faced special problems due to their dependence on a common property resource. The tendency for excessive manpower and capital to enter the industry and result in congestion and low returns to labour and capital was evident. However, most of the fishing industry on the Atlantic coast was and is located in areas that have few alternative employment opportunities.[11] Fishermen, generally reluctant to leave their occupation or their communities, remain in the industry despite its low returns, because fishing communities perceive employment as a benefit. Profit levels are secondary.[12] Given modern welfare standards, though, the income earned from fishing in the Atlantic region was too low. The estimated 1976 net annual earnings averaged less than $3,500 per individual fisherman.[13] To raise income, various forms of governmental assistance were made available. This had the effect of slowing the reduction in excessive manpower from the industry.

Solutions widely advocated to reduce excessive manpower and capital inputs, and to increase productivity, involve entry control and access allocation in the harvesting sector. As well, centralization of processing facilities to remove overcapacity and inefficiency is considered important. Effective limited entry schemes depend on competent legislation and enforcement for regulations. They also require coordination and cooperation between federal and provincial governments, fishermen's unions and associations, fishing companies, community organizations and so on. These conditions are difficult to achieve on the domestic level. On an international scale, the difficulties are even greater

Until 1977, most Canadian fishermen harvested stocks that were at least partly international. Both Pacific salmon and Atlantic groundfish stocks were vulnerable to uncontrolled foreign fishing. For this reason the International North Pacific Fisheries Commission and the International Convention for the Northwest Atlantic Fisheries undertook international agreements to safeguard stocks. Unfortunately, inadequate enforcement of international regulations enabled national rivals to exceed allocated quotas.[14]

These and other events led to the unilateral declaration of full Canadian fisheries jurisdiction in a 200-mile (322 km) coastal zone by January 1, 1977.[15] Some people expected the extension of jurisdiction to be the panacea for all Canada's fishing industry problems. Virtually exclusive Canadian access to fishing grounds previously fished heavily by foreign fleets, plus the effects of stock recovery which began about 1975, combined to make the fishing industry a promising sphere of economic development.

Along with that promise came the need to make some critically important decisions about the "best use" of the "new" resource. Which segments of society would control the fishery resources and benefit from their future growth? Would the new wealth generated through the fishing industry be spread among all groups involved or concentrated in the hands of a select group? To a greater extent than ever before, major questions facing policy makers embodied social equity implications in addition to economic efficiency considerations. The choices made could drastically alter the traditional way of life in many fishing communities and have lasting effect on settlement patterns, particularly in the Atlantic region.

While all dimensions of fisheries have seen varying degrees of policy and administrative reorientation and restructuring, the most significant problems and prospects for management and stewardship over the next ten to twenty years concern efforts associated with *economic rationalization* and *extension of jurisdiction*. Of the many fisheries problems which exist (examples are noted in Table 3.5), satisfactory evolution and/or resolution of these two issues is fundamental to achieving management goals, including the apparently divergent goals of *efficiency* and *equity*.

Economists have wrestled for years with problems of economic efficiency in a common property resource like the fishery. Only recently has the preoccupation with efficiency broadened to include awareness and analysis of what is socially preferred in fisheries management policies.[16] In recognition that economic efficiency is not the only criterion on which fishery resources are allocated, concern has been expressed about the *goals* which are (or ought to be) pursued in management and the *methods* of achieving them

This concern has stimulated difficult questions such as the following. By what criteria are domestic and international fisheries and oceans resources to be allocated optimally? What are the economic, social and political implications of different patterns of use of fisheries and oceans resources? How is the well-being of fishermen ensured? For whom is efficiency to be defined? What are the relationships between fisheries and other sectors of the economy, such as offshore hydrocarbon development? In what ways can management of marine areas and resources be integrated and coordinated effectively? What conflicts are likely to occur as concepts such as coastal zone management are brought to bear in the policy process?

These few questions illustrate the enormous complexity of fisheries management issues.[17] That complexity may slow analysis and decision making, but it does not permit inaction. Geographers have neglected fisheries issues; that can and must change.

Geographers and Fisheries Management Research

As resource analysts,[18] geographers are well aware of the complex network of interrelated variables which must enter decisions on oceans and fishery resource management and development. We know that developing an in-depth knowledge of the dimensions of a resource management issue—of even a single one of the spatial scales, time periods,

Table 3.5
Examples of Canadian Fisheries Problems and Issues

Perspective[2]

Dimension[1] Biophysical	Social and Economic	Legal/Political/Institutional	Technological
—living marine resources; status of stocks and catches	—fishing effort; investment, historical patterns of fishing, foreign fleet fishing	—regulations; jurisdiction established by international agreements and enforcement	—countries fishing east and west coasts; types of vessels and gear
—areas fished/rate of fishing (productivity)/incidental catches	—marketing, product distribution	—200-mile economic zone; catches beyond 200 miles	—innovation; development of domestic capabilities (e.g., freezer trawlers)
—resource conservation; establishment of TACs, quotas	—impacts of international fishing on Canadian industry, particularly import/export sectors	—continental shelf; implications of management	—gear and vessel, areal type conflicts
—ocean dynamics and climatic effects	—common property resources; public trust and public property ownership questions and decisions	—allocation and distribution of stocks, rights to fish	—clean up facilities for pollution (from processing, petroleum exploration)
—pollution; fish processing ships, petroleum offshore, land-based.		—fish vs. power and other conflicts in choice of use	—port facilities and access
—petroleum exploration/sea ice/shipment: catch relationships		—LOS III; major international conflicts	
		—unresolved policy problems; areas, disputes, and proposed solutions	
		—influence of international politics on problem resolution (e.g., ICNAF/NAFO)	

International

National

—fisheries resources identified as to types, distribution, economic importance
—stock productivity; enhancement
—overfishing (economic and biological); stock failures
—environmental degradation, particularly water quality
—multiple-use conditions
—off-and onshore impacts of oil exploration and development
—CZM: on communities, shores, marine services
—climate effects; length of season, gear
—multiple species interactions

—recreational vs. commercial fishing; part-time vs. full-time fishermen; definition of fisherman
—employment in fishing activities and investment trends
—imports/exports and Canadian consumption; demand
—regional character of fishing industry; similarities and differences must be reflected in national policy
—historical fishing patterns; disruption from oil development
—processing and marketing; regional income, locational decisions, individual fishermen's incomes
—regional development strategies; conflicts in use
—market competition
—rationalization
—fishing effort/quota relationships

—philosophy of resource use; economic rationalization, regional and social development, trend toward extended jurisdiction and full utilization of Canadian stocks by Canadians
—jurisdiction over shared stocks; enforcement
—delimiting boundaries to territorial waters, economic zones
—multiple use conflicts
—limited entry; licencing
—marketing (role of industry: government)
—public participation in policy making
—policy initiatives
—definition of fisherman
—performance of subsidy strategies

—gear disposal on grounds; damages
—conflicts in gear use and area
—processing technology
—role of fisheries loan boards in economic waste, inefficient production
—multiple-gear vessels; built-in monitoring equipment for biophysical data collection
—gear restrictions; development of improved efficient technology

Perspective[2]

Dimension[1]	Biophysical	Social and Economic	Legal/Political/Institutional	Technological
Regional	—stock movements; inshore/offshore —fishing grounds; quality, quantity, location	—employment; historical pattern, changes, settlement and regional development implications —processing locations: rationalization and regionalism —capital and manpower requirements	—concurrency (management rights) negotiations —native food fishery; socio-economic development —limited entry; equity considerations —goals for regional fisheries development in a national context	—overcapacity (harvesting and processing) —gear limitations and area restrictions

Notes

1. Spatial dimension: ramifications of problems and issues are visible throughout the system (on all scales and across all perspectives).
2. Perspective: management issues incorporate the resource base (exploitation), harvesting, processing, and marketing components.

or specific perspectives (Table 3.5) and their interactions—is a difficult, time-consuming task.[19] Yet, this is precisely the challenge we face if the opportunity to improve our performance in and contributions to fisheries and oceans analysis, planning, policy and management is to be met. The need for a comprehensive, flexible policy framework, one which accounts for the constant changes in every dimension of fisheries management, is recognized. But how is that awareness to be operationalized, to make meaningful contributions to policy? What lines of geographic research have been and might be pursued profitably in the quest for responsive and responsible fishery and ocean resources decisions?

Integrative, prescriptive models of resource policy and decision-making processes formulated by geographers indicate that the ideal management process begins with a statement of desirable goals and problem identification. Further stages include consideration of constraints, drafting of potential solutions, formulation of alternative strategies, assessment of alternatives, selection of a solution and review after implementation.[20] When combined with Mitchell's analysis of geographers' orientations to resources research,[21] such policy models provide an indication of the scope for application of geographic skills to the problems and prospects for fisheries policy (Table 4.5).

In terms of Canadian fisheries management goals, the 1976 policy statement incorporated economic efficiency and social equity objectives in resource use and allocation, economic development and social/cultural development spheres. Both objectives were and are perceived as desirable, but conflicting. There remains considerable concern and uncertainty among economists and policy makers over the best way(s) to proceed to achieve these objectives.[22] Thus, the strategies associated with economic rationalization and extended jurisdiction continue to be scrutinized and evaluated.

Influencing the actions taken in concern for the industry's economic organization and performance, and the impacts of extended jurisdiction, is the fundamental problem of the traditional common property nature of the resource. Over the past ten to twelve years free access to all important Canadian fisheries has been reduced or removed through restrictive licencing and rationalization programs (see Table 2.5). Complicating the process are the differing physical and socioeconomic characteristics of the B.C. and Atlantic coast fisheries. For example, on an industry-wide basis, questions of economic rationalization are of greater economic and social significance in the Atlantic than the Pacific region. This is due to conditions such as higher unemployment, lower real income levels, and greater labour force immobility in the Atlantic inshore fisheries. The Pacific fisheries, based on salmon, are relatively more prosperous and employment alternatives are more numerous. On an individual basis, of course, economic rationalization can be as significant for certain British Columbia fishermen as for those in the Atlantic fisheries.

Table 4.5
Scope for Application of Geographic Skills to Fisheries Policy

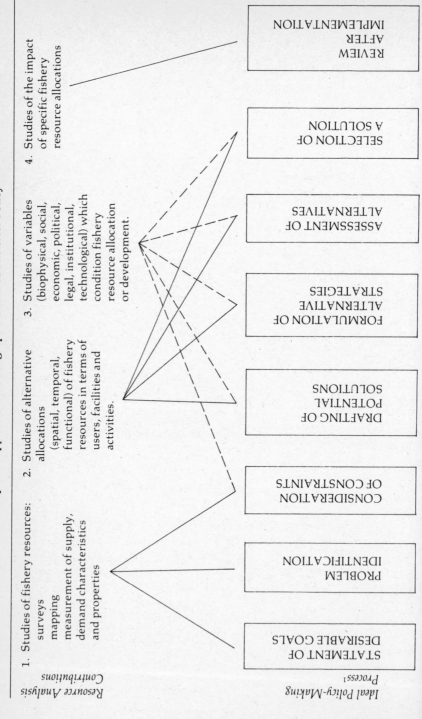

Resource Analysis Contributions

1. Studies of fishery resources: surveys mapping measurement of supply, demand characteristics and properties

2. Studies of alternative allocations (spatial, temporal, functional) of fishery resources in terms of users, facilities and activities.

3. Studies of variables (biophysical, social, economic, political, legal, institutional, technological) which condition fishery resource allocation or development.

4. Studies of the impact of specific fishery resource allocations

Ideal Policy-Making Process[1]

STATEMENT OF DESIRABLE GOALS

PROBLEM IDENTIFICATION

CONSIDERATION OF CONSTRAINTS

DRAFTING OF POTENTIAL SOLUTIONS

FORMULATION OF ALTERNATIVE STRATEGIES

ASSESSMENT OF ALTERNATIVES

SELECTION OF A SOLUTION

REVIEW AFTER IMPLEMENTATION

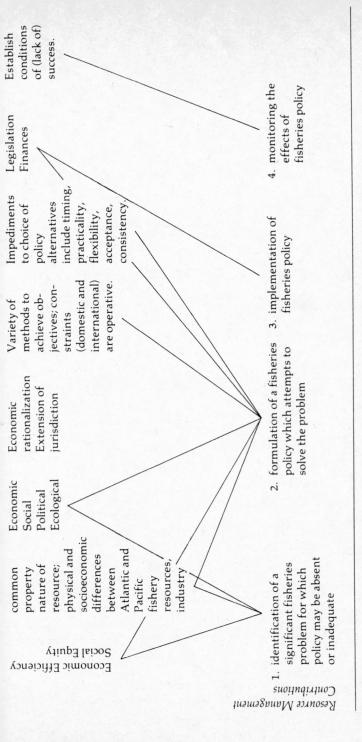

Notes

1. Policy-making processes are continuous and iterative; no flows or feedbacks are shown here.
2. This table illustrates some possible applications of geographic skills to fisheries research. It is not meant to be limiting or inclusive.

Source: Bruce Mitchell, *Geography and Resource Analysis* (London: Longman, 1979), pp. 3, 7 and Bruce Mitchell, "Models of resource management," *Progress in Human Geography* 4 (1980), p. 45.

Similarly, the variance in continental shelf structure on Pacific and Atlantic coasts gives rise to different impacts of extended jurisdiction. The Atlantic continental shelf slopes off much more gradually than the Pacific shelf, which is only 40 to 50 miles (65 to 80 kilometres) wide. Consequently, important Atlantic groundfish stocks extend beyond the 200-mile (322 km) limit, particularly on the "tails" of the Grand Bank and the Flemish Cap areas (Figure 1.5). Regulations and quota restrictions resulting from extension of jurisdiction have a more direct and critical effect upon Atlantic coast fisheries than upon those of the Pacific coast.[23]

Formulation and assessment of alternative strategies to achieve efficiency and equity objectives require understanding of constraints. For example, the social desirability of limiting negative impacts of economic rationalization on British Columbia Indian fishermen, and the necessity to avoid massive dislocation of fishermen in the Atlantic region, must be addressed. On a domestic level it will be important to ensure existence of alternative arrangements for planning and coordination of offshore developments as they relate to fisheries. Likewise, the presence of international conflicts over allocation of stocks (Canadian-American tuna "wars"), or for control over ocean space (George's Bank area), is important in formulating alternative management strategies.

To varying degrees, matters of timing, administrative practicality and flexibility, and public as well as private sector priorities expressed through participation in and acceptance of alternative strategies, will act as impetuses or impediments to effective policy making. Such variables may play a considerable role in influencing the success or failure of any particular policy and/or strategy selected.

Selected Fisheries Management Problems, Strategies and Outcomes

Economic rationalization and extended jurisdiction, while not perfect strategies, do represent the presently implemented "best" thinking about methods to achieve desired goals. These two strategies have demanded and continue to require significant choices and decisions, and have resulted in some important changes in the fishing industry. Two examples are illustrative. One concerns the socioeconomic implications and ramifications of a limited entry program for B.C. Indian fishermen. The other relates to the continuing difficulties experienced in Newfoundland in making economic rationalization decisions in the light of extended jurisdiction opportunities. Both examples are discussed with a view toward illustrating the nature of the conflicts and problems encountered, and noting the kinds of research that have contributed or may point toward problem resolution.

Figure 1.5

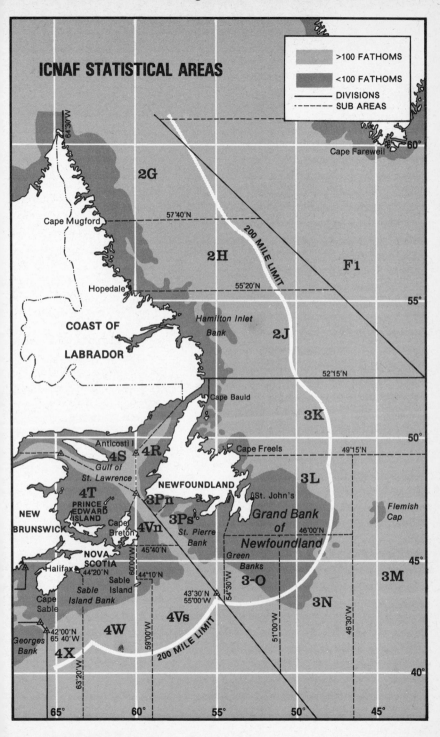

Economic Rationalization in the B.C. Fishing Industry; the Native Indian Fishery

Since the early days of the commercial fishing industry, the history of Indian participation has been one of almost continuous decline. By 1967, the situation for Indians in the fishing industry was one of continuing displacement because of increasing mechanization, larger-scale operations, industry consolidation and competition from other ethnic groups. The Indians' relative lack of geographic mobility and general lack of alternative employment opportunities also contributed to increasing rates of unemployment. This was particularly detrimental to the economic well-being of village residents dependent upon fishing as a livelihood.[24]

By 1968 the B.C. commercial fishery was experiencing the cumulative effects of a number of problems. Primarily, overcrowding and overcapitalization were dissipating the economic rent accruing from the fishery. All fishermen, including Indians, suffered poor returns relative to their labour and capital inputs. In September 1968, the federal government announced its Salmon Vessel Licence Control Program, a plan to limit entry to the fishery. Under the program the number of salmon vessels was frozen and a system of "A" and "B" licences instituted. Boats that had landed 10,000 pounds (4536 kg) or more of salmon in 1967 or 1968 and were still operating in 1969 were given "A" licences. These were renewable annually. Other vessels not meeting these qualifications were given "B" licences. Later regulations limited "B" licenced vessels to a maximum ten year industry participation period. Other modifications followed.[25]

Federal officials realized implementation of the licence control program would have direct negative impacts on the lives and economic futures of Indian fishermen. For example, the difficulties they were having in acquiring equipment and techniques for effective competition was reflected in the poor quality of their boats and production records.[26] This fact, coupled with their declining participation (Table 5.5) and the ten-year limitation on "B" licenced vessels meant that many Indians would lose their livelihood when required to retire their boats from the industry. The federal Fisheries Service attempted to offset the negative effects of phasing out Indian vessels with special regulations, reduced licence fees, and an Indian Fishermen's Assistance Program. None of these strategies were entirely successful.[27]

Many Indians perceived that their displacement from the fishery was a result of the licence control program. Economic rationalization measures, in fact, were the prime cause. In 1969, for example, four large fish processing plants on the north and central coasts had closed through company consolidation efforts (Figure 2.5). Over 76 percent of displaced workers were Indians.[28]

A group of north coast Indians reacted against such external forces contributing to their decline in the fishery. For over three years the Indians

Table 5.5
Indian Participation in the B.C. Salmon Fishery

Year	Estimated number of Indian fishermen	Total Indian boats in fishing fleet	Total B.C. fleet	Percentage Indian fleet of total fleet
1963	2300	1213	7766	15.61
1964		1284	7341	17.49
1966	2100	1075	6784	15.84
1969	1800	917	6317	14.51
1970	1700	980	6350	15.43
1971	1650	855	5958	14.35
Percent Decline 1963–71	28.26	29.51	23.28	
Percent Decline 1969–71	8.33	6.76	5.68	

Source: Canada, Department of Indian Affairs and Northern Development, *Review of the B.C. Indian Fishermen's Assistance Program*, (Ottawa: Queen's Printer, 1972), Appendix 'D', p. 1.

negotiated a proposal for funding their own fish cannery operations, first with federal and later with provincial government agencies. A study of the events leading to establishment of an "Indian owned and operated" cannery at Port Simpson, British Columbia, revealed the importance of "nontechnical" variables such as political, personality and cultural differences which conditioned fishery resource development decisions.[29]

Despite its responsibility for Indian affairs, the federal government refused to fund the cannery, indicating the operation would be counterproductive to biological effectiveness and economic efficiency considerations in the B.C. fishery. Particularly with regard to Indians in the fishing industry, economic and social objectives have conflicted in the policymaking process. Decisions have tended to be made in favour of economic criteria. In this case, federal and provincial management objectives polarized almost completely.

In agreeing to provide funds for construction of a cannery and for purchase of vessels with salmon licences to develop a core fishing fleet for the project, the provincial government explicitly ranked socioeconomic factors above economic feasibility and efficiency. A ten to twelve million dollar (1973–1976) social development effort in the fishery, the project was to provide employment for unskilled workers, keep families off welfare, and maintain a traditional way of life for the Indian population.

Figure 2.5

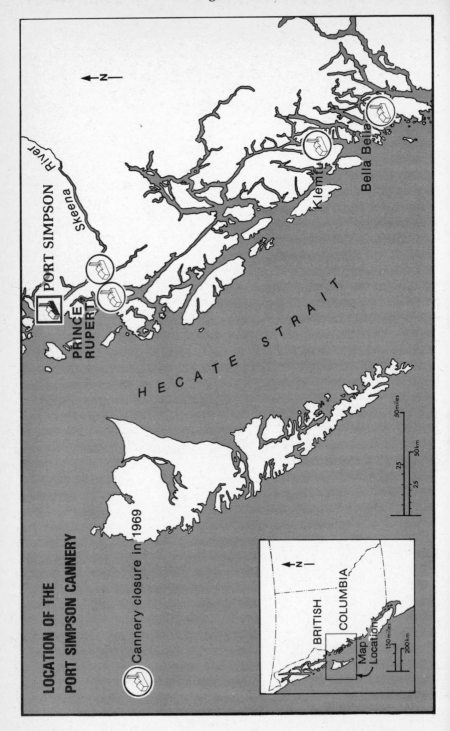

As such, the cannery development proved to be a challenge to the manner in which B.C. fishery resources had been used. The province's action upset the traditional pattern of federal dominance in fisheries management. Not only did the unprecedented action force the issue of social responsibility in fishery resource use to the fore, it also highlighted the need for a participatory, coordinated and comprehensive management approach to the resource.

The federal government's 1976 policy document stated that fundamental restructuring of the fishing industry through rationalization was inevitable. At the same time, perhaps reflecting management needs encountered in cases like Port Simpson, the document noted that "best use" objectives applied. These objectives aimed, among other things, to provide relief for income-deficient fishermen, to facilitate individual and community adjustment to economic and social change, and to integrate programs for fishery development with those designed for regional economic development. Coastal areas were to be revitalized and regional cultures and lifestyles advanced. These objectives were to be reached with the fullest possible involvement of all people concerned with fisheries.

For both B.C. and Newfoundland/Atlantic regional fisheries, these objectives raise many questions vital to achieving improved management. How are the conflicting values of industry interests to be reconciled in management? How can (or should) a definitive policy regarding security for fishery-dependent peoples be developed? How may regional and community development be attained through a coastal strategy for the industry? Another important question is how the federal and provincial fishery agencies may cooperate and coordinate their social and economic development programs. These kinds of questions offer many research opportunities.

Before discussing the ways in which geographic research has and may contribute to more effective fisheries management, it is useful to consider the efficiency-equity dilemma in the Newfoundland context.

Economic Rationalization and Extended
Jurisdiction In Newfoundland Inshore Fisheries

Traditionally, fisheries in the Atlantic region and Newfoundland have been divided into offshore and inshore sectors. The offshore fishery is capital intensive, consisting mainly of company-owned trawler fleets which are vertically integrated with the processing plants in about 30 large ports. Trawlers (vessels over 150 gross registered tons) can yield substantial catches per fisherman and generally have produced much larger incomes per man employed than the inshore sector.

In the inshore fishery, small fisherman-owned boats (generally under 25 tons) requiring only modest levels of capital investment are scattered through hundreds of small, often relatively isolated, communities. Inshore fisheries are seasonal; incomes are low. There is a third, more recent, category known as the nearshore fishery. This type developed from the inshore fishery as independent fishermen acquired larger, more sophisticated vessels that enabled them to travel further and exploit a greater variety of fish species.[30]

Questions of efficiency and equity arise in the inshore fisheries where alternative work opportunities are limited. In this respect, the Newfoundland situation is quite like that experienced by the B.C. Indian fisheries. Beyond this similarity, Newfoundland's inshore fishing industry is much more complex. A greater number of species is pursued (up to ten or twelve per individual) by more fishing units (Table 6.5) and there are distinct patterns of specialization or diversification according to species, vessel class and areal differences. This complexity gives rise to numerous interest groups, each of which has reacted in different ways to federal and provincial government policies and toward extended jurisdiction.[31]

Table 6.5
Characteristics of the Newfoundland
Fishery in 1973

Vessels		Fishermen	
motorboats	9,325	full time	903
10-25 T	382	part time	3,996
over 25 T	318	casual	10,414
	10,025		15,313

Source: Canada, Department of Fisheries and Oceans, Economic Policy Branch, "Annual Statistical Review of Canadian Fisheries" Vol. 7, 1974.

The above figures include all vessels and fishermen, i.e., for both inshore and offshore fisheries. For inshore fishery, trawler vessels and fishermen should be excluded:

Newfoundland Inshore Fishery in 1973

Vessels		Fishermen	
motorboats	9,325	full time	824
10-25 T	382	part time	3,572
over 25 T	250	casual	9,341
	9,957		13,737

Source: Unpublished DFO statistics

Note: In comparison in 1973 British Columbia had 11,717 men and 5,560 vessels engaged in the fisheries. (Source: H.S.Y. Hsu, *An Analysis of Gross Returns From Commercial Fishing Vessels in B.C.* (Vancouver: Environment Canada, 1976), p. 22, and Fisheries and Environment Canada, *Statistical Review of Canadian Fisheries* (Ottawa, Environment Canada, 1977), p. 123.

Extended jurisdiction has brought inflated notions of increased resource availability, although the outlook for cod stocks in the Hamilton Bank and adjacent areas appears promising. If there is an expanding fishery, several management problems need to be solved in order to realize "best use" and maximum social benefit. Who will have access to any increased stock? How can equitable decisions be made between inshore and offshore sectors or between gear types? How can the need to rationalize harvesting and processing capacities to presently available resources be reconciled with the employment levels and livelihoods of those dependent on fishing?

Present federal and provincial policy makers do not know how to manage fishery resources for maximum social or economic benefit, although they are aware of the importance of policy decisions on the lifestyle and socioeconomic structure of rural Newfoundland. Newfoundland's provincial fisheries development documents place considerable emphasis on the maintenance of existing lifestyles and settlement patterns.[32] If inhabitants of coastal fishing communities intensely value their way of life, then federal thrusts toward "human" aspects of fisheries management seem compatible with these provincial goals. (This may be one area of common ground in the federal-provincial power struggle over future development of the East coast fisheries.) If outport community lifestyles based on inshore fishing were no longer highly valued, or became impossible to maintain due to inadequate fishing returns, how could economic and social policy objectives be reconciled?

Provincial objectives for fishery development already conflict. On the one hand the province has emphasized retention of the decentralized nature of the fishing industry. On the other, the province (with DREE assistance) has instituted a series of regional developments known as Fisheries Marine Service Centres. This Program has contributed to regional shifts in fisheries development in the province.

The Fisheries Marine Service Centre Program commenced October 15, 1974, with the signing of a subsidiary agreement to the Canada-Newfoundland General Development Agreement of February 1, 1974. The Program was designed to improve the impact of the fishing industry on the provincial economy by promoting the more efficient and effective use of the longliners employed in the inshore and nearshore fishery. Longliners, which range from 35 to 65 feet (10 m to 20 m) are larger and more sophisticated than the smaller traditional boats, and cannot be hauled up on the beach for shelter or repair. Until 1974, there was little in the way of an infrastructure to support the expanded longliner fleet.

An initial twelve million dollars was provided to establish marine service centres throughout the island and Labrador (Figure 3.5). Located in areas where major concentrations of longliners existed, these marine service centres have improved the operational efficiency of the fleet, reduced depreciation on the vessels, and increased the length of the fishing season in some areas. They appear to be acting as a geographic centralizing force. For example, longliner operators from the Flowers Cove to Port Saunders area wintered over in Isle aux Morts in 1978, conducting repairs at the marine service centre and contributing to the major winter fishery there. This was a new venture for the Northern Peninsula fishermen that led not only to an increased productivity for the fishermen, but also to an increased fish supply and to greater employment for fish plant workers in the southwest coast area.

To what extent, and in what locations, are such social and economic effects of the Fisheries Marine Service Centre Program manifest? Of what magnitude are these regional changes? In Newfoundland, fisheries operations have been decentralized for centuries. What long-term changes might centralization bring through marine service centre facilities? And what will be the impact on the inshore fishery of further expansion in both the longliner fleet and marine service centres? These concerns constitute areas for research consideration.

The strategies by which any fisheries management goal will be achieved must recognize and deal with the inevitable interest group conflicts. In Newfoundland there is "class" conflict of interest between those who own and manage processing facilities and trawler fleets, and those engaged in wage labour in these operations. Simultaneously, there is competition between inshore, nearshore and offshore modes of production. Naturally, each group attempts to influence the policy-making process in its own interest. This has served to pit one group of fishermen against another,[33] and to encourage distrust between fishermen, industry and government interests. Time has entrenched these group positions. Do geographers dare to investigate people and their institutions?

An awareness of policy makers' attitudes toward various fishing interests is instructive in analyses of policy decisions and regulations. Le Blanc, for example, has publicly acknowledged a bias in favour of inshore fishermen.[34] As federal Fisheries Minister, his support of inshore fleet development over the offshore fishery (and of fishermen over processors) has lent weight to the social dimensions of commercial fisheries policy.

On the other hand, Copes, an economist, felt that rationalization of the industry could be achieved only by shifting emphasis from inshore to offshore fisheries. In pointing out that rationalization limited the number of fishermen employed in the industry, Copes identified the stumbling block of unemployment pressures in Newfoundland:

... a deliberate rationalization of the fishery that bars a proportion of the fishing population from the only employment available to them is socially and politically unacceptable. For this reason it appears almost impossible to achieve substantial rationalization of the fishing industry before the general employment situation ... has been improved.

Figure 3.5

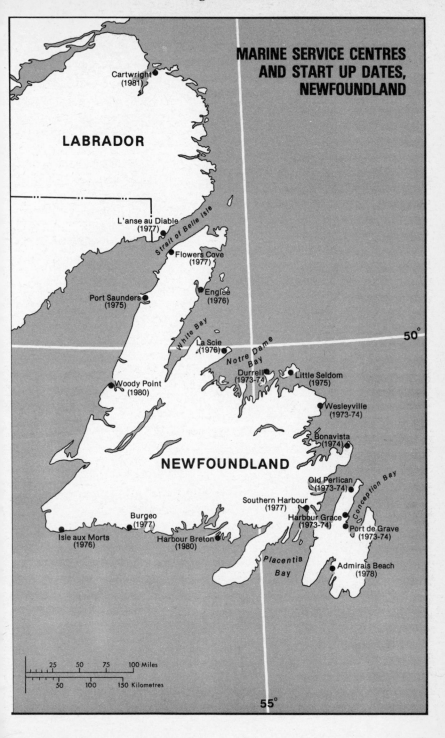

MARINE SERVICE CENTRES
AND START UP DATES,
NEWFOUNDLAND

LABRADOR

Cartwright
(1981)

L'anse au Diable
(1977)

Strait of Belle Isle

Flowers Cove
(1977)

Englee
(1976)

Port Saunders
(1975)

White Bay

La Scie
(1976)

Notre Dame
Bay

50°

Durrell
(1973-74)

Little Seldom
(1975)

Wesleyville
(1973-74)

Woody Point
(1980)

Bonavista
(1974)

NEWFOUNDLAND

Old Perlican
(1973-74)

Conception Bay

Southern Harbour
(1977)

Harbour Grace
(1973-74)

Port de Grave
(1973-74)

Burgeo
(1977)

Isle aux Morts
(1976)

Harbour Breton
(1980)

Placentia
Bay

Admirals Beach
(1978)

25   50   75   100 Miles

50   100   150 Kilometres

55°

. . . unemployment pressures in Newfoundland are likely to remain substantial in view of high rates of natural increase in population, repeated failure to sustain viable secondary manufacturing industries and a strong official and popular bias against out-migration of surplus labour. Therefore the pressure on the inshore fishery to accommodate an excessive complement of manpower is likely to remain great.[35]

Recent developments in offshore petroleum exploration, while improving the provincial employment situation for skilled labour, might have a fundamental effect on the fishery and upon community life based on the fishery. There could be a loss from fishing labour into oil of wage earners such as trawlermen and fish plant workers. If the oil industry were to offer better wages and working conditions for skills these individuals possessed, these workers might leave the fishing industry.

Employment in the oil industry might be appealing to fishermen also. Given the seasonal nature of the fishery in Newfoundland, particularly in regions subject to ice packs, the security of full-time jobs in the oil industry could be attractive. While the majority of inshore fishermen appear to be committed to and proud of their fishing heritage, many of them have combined fishing with other wage work. This occupational pluralism may pave the way for fishermen to join the oil industry.

Past difficulties in the industry, including resource base problems from overfishing, may have weakened fishermen's desire to pursue the fishery and might make oil employment tempting.[36] Likewise, present difficulties in obtaining licences to enter restricted fisheries may "force" fishermen out of the industry. Ultimately, labour shifts could impact on fishery management policies.

How, for example, are Newfoundland's fisheries to be protected during any oil development area? The fisheries deserve preservation in terms of their protein contribution to world food supplies alone. Is this viewpoint incorporated in current policy? Other nuisance factors such as loss of access to fishing grounds, reduction in fish stocks due to petroleum-induced pollution, and gear loss caused by debris from rigs or supply vessels can affect the fishery. These problems illustrate the need for clear policy directives, strict regulations on ocean exploitation activity, and careful planning to avoid or mitigate negative impacts, particularly in the coastal zone.

Whether fishing communities are restructured as a result of rationalization in the fishing industry or in response to oil development, decision making is more than a cost-benefit exercise and matter of economic efficiency. Nonmaterialistic values must be accounted for, and the people most directly affected by change must be involved in planning their community lifestyle as it depends on fish. Given the choice, coastal communities might specify decentralization as an appropriate management goal for a region. It could be argued that, in addition to contributing to equity concerns, decentralization increases efficiency in resource use through better utilization and more rapid processing of local stocks. Simultaneously, use of numerous smaller processing facilities would have implications for transportation systems which would alter the efficiency situation.

Clearly, some challenging problems derive from the establishment of efficiency and equity goals in fisheries management. Trade-offs are real and difficult. The following section considers the contributions geographers have made to fisheries management through research, and offers some suggestions for research and research support.

The Past and Potential of Geographic Research on Fisheries Management

As noted earlier, relatively little research has been conducted by Canadian geographers on commercial fisheries and oceans management issues. Those efforts which employ socioeconomic and political-institutional perspectives differ widely in their research approach, as well as time and space dimensions.

Much of the research has employed the case study approach. Some examples include Mitchell and Huntley's analysis of the strengths and weaknesses of three international fishery organizations related to the west coast fishery; O'Riordan's consideration of the Anglo-Icelandic cod war for the future of Pacific salmon management; and Mitchell's study of the implications of the British-Icelandic cod war for the resource management process.[37] Other general studies, such as those by Harrison and Kwamena, have begun to identify management frameworks for offshore resources and ocean space, and to suggest approaches for integrated planning of ocean resources.[38]

In resource management research in geography, much time has been spent in identifying the nature and key variables of a problem.[39] The first three studies noted above exhibit this pattern. The other two studies, building upon such a research base, sought new frameworks to understand and explain relationships among variables that would assist in management.

In 1978, the first special session on "Marine Studies and Coastal Zone Management in Canada" was held at a Canadian Association of Geographers' Annual meeting. Of the eight papers published from the session, four dealt with socioeconomic and political-institutional perspectives. These papers evidence a similar emphasis upon identification of variables and their relationships. Parkes, for example, discussed the federal role in shore zone management and highlighted the problem of cooperative management in a system of divided jurisdiction. Harrison and Sewell considered the relationships between coastal zone management institutions and the definition of appropriate areal units for management.

Draper's analysis of the relationships between the actors, their personalities and behaviours in the Port Simpson cannery case highlighted the socioeconomic aspects in resource management. Ross noted the domestic and international conflicts resulting from the interception and allocation of west coast salmon.[40]

These papers, and others like them presented at various conferences and developed through institutions such as the Dalhousie Ocean Studies Program, are continuing to stimulate an increased understanding of significant factors and alternative strategies in management of fisheries and ocean resources. Such studies must continue, if the generally neglected state of marine geographic research in Canada is to improve. In addition, as Sewell noted in both 1973 and 1976, much more research needs to be done toward improved evaluation of alternatives, including assessment of the social impacts of resource decisions.[41]

In contemplating research, geographers should heed the words of other researchers in fisheries management. The significance of "nontechnical" components is emphasized frequently. For example, McCracken and Macdonald identified research into ". . . questions about equity and democratic participation and responsibility that are too often ignored in our pursuit of efficiency and full utilization"[42] as an important need. In terms of human elements in Atlantic fisheries, they also noted:

The key question is, "Can the regional economies of the Atlantic coast, in particular those of the inshore fisheries communities, follow the conventional route of economic development and industrialization and avoid the negative consequences of industrialization—in particular the low productivity, low relative incomes, and high unemployment to be found in depressed regions?
. . . It is the question of how fish and other resources are managed, who makes the decisions about the community viability, and what the process of selection is, which we feel is important and not yet adequately answered.[43]

Other authors have noted similar gaps in fisheries management abilities and knowledge. Fletcher suggested fisheries management had yet to deal "satisfactorily on a continuing basis" with questions of overall direction. To answer the value questions of *where* we should be going in fisheries management, and *why*, he felt input was required from human, social and natural sciences.[44] How best to integrate socioeconomic and ecological factors into fisheries decision making was uncertain. However, the decisions that were taken could prove instructive to managers. Fletcher suggested that such decisions could serve not only as a guide to future management, they could also help identify "knowledge and intelligence needs and priorities."[45]

As Canadian control of fisheries increased, Regier and McCracken indicated changes could be expected in both management style and types of information input:

Management will have to become more extensive, flexible and responsive. Scientific analyses will have to include inputs from sociologists, political scientists, economists as well as resource-oriented science. In fact there will probably be a greater need for insight and input from different information sources. These will include better researched marketing, socioeconomic possibilities, political impacts, as well as resource assessments and ecological responses.[46]

On a regional level, Loftus, Johnson and Regier confirmed such changes. They indicated that attempts to define and understand Ontario fisheries problems and issues required considerations of a larger system. "This system includes, among other components, fish communities, conflicting users of land, water, and air, and fisheries agencies themselves."[47] Some of these broader information needs could be fulfilled through geographic research. Certain specific research projects such as the priorities Regier placed on mapping, monitoring and modeling of resource stocks and socioeconomic characteristics, also could help meet the challenges facing fishery managers.[48]

Geographers frequently pride themselves on their methodological ability to be comprehensive, to synthesize and to generalize. Surely enough possibilities have been raised thus far to suggest that these and other geographic skills outlined (Table 4.5) are relevant in fisheries management research. With such a wide array of research topics available, and because of the complexity of fisheries issues, careful selection of projects is a necessity. As an aid to identification of research priorities, geographers might consider undertaking a classification of fisheries management problems similar to what Anderson has done.[49]

This kind of exercise would facilitate recognition of research issues which ought to receive simultaneous study. For example, existing inter-relationships between maintenance of stock productivity and prevention of excess capacity in harvesting would indicate these topics should be tackled together. Likewise, joint study of local conditions and their effects on decision making could help clarify how management decisions are made. Other relevant research efforts should emerge from such a classification exercise. One area of study which could improve geographic contributions to fisheries management would be an increased understanding of fishermen's behaviour.[50]

In this context, a paper by Bromley and Bishop noted clearly the need to consider the nature and extent of immobility among low-income Indian and other fishermen. Such knowledge could assist in determining the effects of limited-entry schemes on fishermen excluded from access. Concerned that limited entry may cause greater social and financial inequalities, these two economists noted that the present literature does not answer questions like whose real income would be affected and to what extent, or how fishermen feel about the regulations which affect their potential welfare.[51] Geographers can and should explore such areas, including the issues of inshore-offshore trade-offs, unemployment problems, and the difficulties of transnational stocks. In particular, the extreme political sensitivity of inshore-offshore trade-offs in the Newfoundland and Labrador areas, combined with the domestic-foreign allocation problem on the east coast, will need to be analyzed in a broad way in recognition of regional economic differences.[52]

A clear research priority for geographers, if we are to understand and contribute to fisheries management, is to conduct hindsight evaluations of specific resource allocations, and to relate these to the needs of future organization for fisheries management. Pontecorvo, Johnston and Wilkinson suggested that more thinking needs to be done about recommendations for future organization dealing with fisheries. They based their conclusion on the fact that questions like the following cannot be answered now:

Who, for example, will reconcile conflicting interests of fishing, oil and gas exploration and shipping control, and how? Will fishery management continue to be thought of as a separate unifunctional activity, now to be conducted far out at sea under national concepts and procedures of public administration and under the direction of a single federal agency? Or will it be conceived also as an integral part of coastal zone management and planning, and to that extent integrated with the management functions of nonfishery agencies. If the latter course is to be adopted, will it not involve the provincial authorities, and possibly also the municipalities, in at least certain aspects of fishery management, or in other activities that have a bearing on the options available in fishery management?[53]

Geographers should give some serious thought to investigating such questions.

Given the discipline's lack of apparent interest and research in fisheries in the past, it will be necessary to convince fishery managers that, as resource analysts, geographers have a valuable contribution to make to stewardship. In order to demonstrate our competence—we have the skills, even if we must adapt them to a marine orientation—small-scale research projects should be attempted initially. Studies of the socioeconomic impact of access restrictions to high-value Atlantic fisheries such as lobster, herring and crab could prove useful input to ongoing decisions regarding equity and effectiveness of licencing systems. Lessons from analysis of the British Columbia Salmon Enhancement Program for other stock rehabilitation programs; insights into the inability of the Salmon Vessel Licence Control Program to reduce excessive capitalization in that B.C. fishery; and studies of the potential impact of oil development on Atlantic and Newfoundland fisheries would all be relevant to establishing the validity of geographic contributions. (This assumes adequate attention to research design and detail.)

Once these types of studies have proved effective, rather more substantial funding may be sought from organizations such as the Social

Sciences and Humanities Research Council or the Natural Sciences and Engineering Research Council. If geographers are to determine "for good" the lives of those now dependent upon fisheries, as well as those who will inherit the oceans commons, we will be required to contribute to solutions to the difficult socioeconomic and political-institutional problems facing fisheries and oceans exploitation.

Notes

1 Adrian F. Richards, "Energy from the ocean: requirements and capabilities," in *Ocean Resources Utilization,* ed. Neil T. Monney (New York: American Society of Mechanical Engineers, 1976), pp. 91–129; John B. McAleer, "Ocean engineering capabilities and requirements for artificial islands and platforms," in *Ocean Resource Utilization,* ed. Neil T. Monney (New York: American Society of Mechanical Engineers, 1976), pp. 63–89.

2 Raymond Kaufman, "Ocean engineering capabilities and requirements for the offshore mining industry," in *Ocean Resource Utilization,* ed. Neil T. Monney (New York: American Society of Mechanical Engineers, 1976), pp. 49–62; John B. McAleer, "Ocean engineering capabilities and requirements for artificial islands and platforms," in *Ocean Resources Utilization,* ed. Neil T. Monney (New York: American Society of Mechanical Engineers, 1976), p. 67.

3 Science Council of Canada, *Canada, Science and the Oceans* (Ottawa: Information Canada, 1970).

4 Ministry of State for Science and Technology, *New Oceans Policy,* news release (Ottawa: July 12, 1973).

5 E.F. Roots, "Environmental aspects of Arctic marine transportation and development," in *Marine Transportation and High Arctic Development: Policy Framework and Priorities; Symposium Proceedings* (Ottawa: Canadian Arctic Resources Committee, 1979), p. 82.

6 E.F. Roots, "Environmental aspects of Arctic marine transportation and development," in *Marine Transportation and High Arctic Development: Policy Framework and Priorities; Symposium Proceedings* (Ottawa: Canadian Arctic Resources Committee, 1979), p. 87.

7 W.R. Derrick Sewell and Ian Burton, "Recent innovations in resource development policy," *Canadian Geographer* 11 (Winter 1967), p. 339, footnote 27.

8 One recent call for geographic involvement in oceans resource management issues is: Peter Harrison, "Geographers and the management of Canada's ocean resources," *Canadian Geographer* 24 (Summer 1980), pp. 111–113.

9 Taafe, for example, called upon the discipline to demonstrate "pragmatic pluaralism," to devote attention to both theory and relevance in research. Fisheries and oceans exploitation questions are highly promising research areas to permit both to advance. See, E.J. Taafe, "The spatial view in context," *Annals of the Association of American Geographers* 64 (1974), pp. 1–16.

10 Parzival Copes, *The Evolution of Marine Fisheries Policy in Canada* (Burnaby, B.C.: Simon Fraser University, Department of Economics and Commerce: Discussion Paper Series 79–3–1), p. 39.

11 W.C. MacKenzie, "Rational fishery management in a depressed region: the Atlantic ground fishery," *Journal of the Fisheries Research Board of Canada* 36 (July

1979), pp. 811–813, correctly identifies an exaggerated claim to dependence on fishing for a livelihood in Atlantic Canada. In 1972, just under 10 percent of all participants in the fishery earned more than half their total income directly from fishing. Considerable diversification exists. Fishing has been combined with a variety of sources of livelihood, such as logging and trapping in the off-season, since early days of the industry. Unemployment insurance benefits have become a respectable source of annual income supplements for many fishermen, particularly in the Gulf of St. Lawrence and northeast coast of Newfoundland areas.

12 A.W.H. Needler, "Evolution of Canadian fisheries management towards economic rationalization," *Journal of the Fisheries Research Board of Canada* 36 (July 1979), p. 723; and Ralph Matthews, *There's No Better Place Than Here: Social Change in Three Newfoundland Communities* (Toronto: Peter Martin Associates Limited, 1976), p. 138.

13 W.C. MacKenzie, "Rational fishery management in a depressed region: the Atlantic ground fishery," *Journal of the Fisheries Research Board of Canada* 36 (July 1979), p. 811 and Appendix table p. 819.

14 B. Mitchell and H. Maureen Huntley, "An analysis of criticisms of international fishery organizations with reference to three agencies associated with the Canadian west coast fishery," *Journal of Environmental Management* 5 (1977), pp. 47–73; and David H. Wallace, "Management of marine fisheries resources," in *To Stem the Tide: Effective State Marine Fisheries Management*, eds. R.J. Marcelli and R.D. Matthews (Lexington, Kentucky: The Council of State Governments, 1975), p. 82.

15 The preceding discussion was based, in part, upon Parzival Copes, "Canada's Atlantic coast fisheries: policy development and the impact of extended jurisdiction," *Canadian Public Policy* 4 (Spring 1978), pp. 155–171; and C.L. Mitchell, "The 200-mile limit: new issues, old problems for Canada's east coast fisheries," *Canadian Public Policy* 4 (Spring 1978), pp. 172–183.

16 Daniel W. Bromley and Richard C. Bishop, "From economic theory to fisheries policy: conceptual problems and management prescriptions," in *Economic Impacts of Extended Fisheries Jurisdiction*, ed. Lee G. Anderson (Ann Arbor, Michigan: Ann Arbor Science Publishing Inc., 1977), pp. 281–301; J.A. Crutchfield, "Economic and social implications of the main policy alternatives for controlling fishing effort," *Journal of the Fisheries Research Board of Canada* 36 (July 1979), pp. 742–752; Anthony Scott, "Development of economic theory on fisheries regulation," *Journal of the Fisheries Research Board of Canada* 36 (July 1979), pp. 725–741.

17 In concentrating on problems encountered in socioeconomic and political-institutional dimensions, the importance of other factors is not being underestimated. There could be no fishery without fish. Clearly, there is insufficient biological knowledge of stocks on which to construct accurate models of fish population dynamics. Predictive capacity is thus reduced. Oceanographic changes and environmental factors which influence fish and fisheries are incompletely understood. Even with better basic data, management improvement will be gradual. Some geographers might contribute toward these basic data needs. For example, in March 1980, an "Ocean and Fisheries Climate Workshop" was hosted by the Director-General, Ocean and Aquatic Sciences, Atlantic division of Fisheries and Oceans. At that workshop, data needs were

discussed as well as the effects improved climate data would have on fisheries management. Geographers in attendance at the workshop assisted in identification of ocean/atmospheric research needs in the context of fisheries management. For example, climatologists could assist fishermen through provision of better meteorological information. Data on location of frontal zones plus eddy information in conjunction with biological knowledge of tuna could assist west coast fishermen in determining areas in which to set their long lines. Climatic data may be used to correct catch-per-unit data; a large increase in catch may be due to frontal systems temperatures rather than to an increased biomass. These basic data needs, of both the manager and fishermen, may be met (partially) by geographic research.

[18] Mitchell has noted that geographers may be active in resource management as analysts, managers or developers. As analysts, geographers aim to understand the essential characteristics of natural resources and to determine the processes through which resources are allocated and utilized. Generally, this is the role for which initial geographic education (in resources) provides sufficient background. To qualify as managers, geographers would have to be directly involved in the actual decisions regarding policies, conditions or practices for the allocation and development of resources. Usually such decisions are made by elected or appointed officials. Resource analysts may provide input to such a decision process. Resource developers actually use a resource to produce a commodity or build a facility to service human wants and needs. Each role implies a distinctive application of geographic skills to the process of managing resources; resource analysis is emphasized here. See Bruce Mitchell, *Geography and Resource Analysis* (London: Longman, 1979), pp. 2–8.

[19] Ralph R. Krueger and Bruce Mitchell, *Managing Canada's Renewable Resources* (Toronto: Methuen, 1977), p. 6.

[20] Bruce Mitchell, "Models of resource management," *Progress in Human Geography* 4 (1980), p. 45.

[21] Bruce Mitchell, *Geography and Resource Analysis* (London: Longman, 1979), pp. 3, 7.

[22] See, for example, papers in the "Symposium on policies for economic rationalization of commercial fisheries," *Journal of the Fisheries Research Board of Canada* 36 (July 1979), pp. 711–866; and, Notes for a speech by Mr. Gary C. Vernon, Assistant Deputy Minister, Fisheries Economic Development and Marketing, to the Annual Conference of the Association for Canadian Studies on Canada and the Sea, Simon Fraser University, Burnaby, B.C., July 12, 1979.

[23] Gordon R. Munro, "Canada and fisheries management with extended jurisdiction: a preliminary view," in *Economic Impacts of Extended Fisheries Jurisdiction*, ed. Lee G. Anderson (Ann Arbor, Michigan: Ann Arbor Science Publishers, Inc., 1977), p. 32.

[24] H.B. Hawthorn, ed., *A Survey of the Contemporary Indians of Canada: A Report on Economic, Political, Educational Needs and Policies* (Ottawa: Indian Affairs Branch, Vol. 1, 1966), pp. 106, 119, 146; and W.F. Sinclair, *The Importance of the Commercial Fishing Industry to Selected Remote Coastal Communities of B.C.* (Vancouver: Department of the Environment, 1971), p. 96.

[25] For further details, see: B. Mitchell and W. Ross, "Problems of evaluation in resource management as illustrated by the British Columbia Salmon Licence

Program," *Geographical Interuniversity Resource Management Seminars* (GIRMS) 4 (1973-74), pp. 83, 84 and references cited in bibliography pp. 94, 95; B. Mitchell, "Hindsight reviews: the B.C. licence program," in *Pacific Salmon Management for People*, ed. D.V. Ellis (Victoria: University of Victoria, Western Geographical Series, Volume 13, 1977), pp. 148-186.

26 Although the majority of Indian fishermen had poorer quality boats and production records, some Indians were (and are) among the top fishermen on the coast, owning equipment worth hundreds of thousands of dollars and earning among the highest incomes. See also, D. Draper, "Resources Management, Socio-Economic Development, and the Pacific North Coast Native Cooperative: a Case Study" (University of Waterloo, 1977, unpublished Ph.D. dissertation).

27 See, for example, D. Draper, "The British Columbia Indian Fishermen's Assistance Program," *GIRMS* 4 (1973-74), pp. 96-108.

28 N. Hall, Chairman, Joint Consultative Committee on Manpower—West Coast Fishing Industry, *Report* (Vancouver, B.C., 1970), p. 4.

29 D. Draper, "Resources Management, Socio-Economic Development, and the Pacific North Coast Native Cooperative: *A Case Study*" (University of Waterloo, 1977, unpublished Ph.D. dissertation).

30 P. Copes, "Canada's Atlantic coast fisheries: policy development and the impact of extended jurisdiction," *Canadian Public Policy* 4 (Spring 1978), pp. 155-171; R.D.S. Macdonald, "Inshore fishing interests on the Atlantic coast: their response to extended jurisdiction by Canada," *Marine Policy* 3 (July 1979), pp. 171-189; W.C. MacKenzie, "Rational fishery management in a depressed region: the Atlantic ground fishery," *Journal of the Fisheries Research Board of Canada* 36 (July 1979), pp. 811-826; C.L. Mitchell, "The 200-mile limit: new issues, old problems for Canada's east coast fisheries," *Canadian Public Policy* 4 (Spring 1978), pp. 172-183; and W.F. Sinclair, "Management alternatives and strategic planning for Canada's fisheries," *Journal of the Fisheries Research Board of Canada* 35 (July 1978), pp. 1017-1030.

31 In particular, R.D.S. Macdonald, "Inshore fishing interests on the Atlantic coast: their responses to extended jurisdiction by Canada," *Marine Policy* 3 (July 1979), pp. 180-189, has identified responses of inshore fishing interests.

32 Government of Newfoundland and Labrador, *White Paper on Strategies and Programs for Fisheries Development to 1985* (St. John's, Newfoundland, 1978), p. 4. See also, R. Andersen, "The need for human sciences research in Atlantic coast fisheries," *Journal of the Fisheries Research Board of Canada* 35 (July 1978), pp. 1031-1049.

33 One of the clearest expressions of the importance of interest group conflict and policy makers' views and actions in the east coast fishery is found in R. Matthews, "Class interests and the role of the state in the development of Canada's east coast fishery," *Canadian Issues: Journal of the Association for Canadian Studies* 3 (1980), pp. 115-124.

34 LeBlanc's public statement of support for inshore fishermen is cited in R. Matthews, "Class interests and the role of the state in the development of Canada's east coast fishery," *Canadian Issues: Journal of the Association for Canadian Studies* 3 (1980), pp. 117-119. See also, R.D.S. Macdonald, "Inshore fishing interests on the Atlantic coast: their responses to extended jurisdiction by Canada," *Marine Policy* 3 (July 1979), p. 179.

35 P. Copes, "Canada's Atlantic coast fisheries: policy development and the impact of extended jurisdiction," *Canadian Public Policy* 4 (Spring 1978), pp. 162, 168.

36 These effects have been suggested by D. House, Sociology Department, Memorial University, based on a comparison of oil and fishery interrelations in southern Norway, northeast Scotland and Shetland.

37 B. Mitchell and H.M. Huntley, "An analysis of criticisms of international fishery organizations with reference to three agencies associated with the Canadian west coast fishery," *Journal of Environmental Management* 5 (1977), pp. 47–73; T. O'Riordran, "Resource management in a global commons," in *Pacific Salmon Management for People*, ed. D.V. Ellis (Victoria, B.C.: Western Geographical Series, Vol. 13, 1977), pp. 229–259; B. Mitchell, "Politics, fish, and international resource management: the British-Icelandic cod war," *The Geographical Review* 66 (April 1976), pp. 127–138.

38 F.A. Kwamena and P. Harrison, *Canada's Offshore Resources: Frameworks for Management* (Ottawa: University of Ottawa, Research Note 25, 1979); P. Harrison, *Managing Canada's Ocean Area: Institutions, Client Groups, and Coordination* (Ottawa: University of Ottawa, Research Note 26, 1979); F.A. Kwamena, *Canada's Offshore Resources: the Problem of Integrated Planning in Canada's 200-Mile Economic Zone* (Ottawa: University of Ottawa, Research Note 27, 1979).

39 T.S. Kuhn, *The Structure of Scientific Revolutions* (Chicago: University of Chicago Press, 1970), pp. 23–34.

40 The following papers, presented at a special session of the Canadian Association of Geographers Annual Conference at London, Ontario, May 1978, were published in R.J. McCalla, ed., *Marine Studies and Coastal Zone Management in Canada* (Halifax: St. Mary's University Occasional Papers in Geography Number 2, 1978): J.G.M. Parkes, "The federal role in shore-zone management," pp. 1–18; P. Harrison and W.R.D. Sewell, "Appropriate areal units for resource management: the case of the coastal zone," pp. 19–25; D. Draper, "Decision making in resources management: the patron-broker-client framework applied to a fish cannery establishment and operation," pp. 26–40; and W.M. Ross, "International interception and allocation of west coast salmon," pp. 41–54.

41 W.R.D. Sewell, "Broadening the approach to evaluation in resources management decision-making," *Journal of Environmental Management* 1 (1973), pp. 33–60; and W.R.D. Sewell, "The changing context of water resources planning: the next 25 years," *Natural Resources Journal* 16 (October 1976), pp. 791–805.

42 F.D. McCracken and R.D.S. Macdonald, "Science for Canada's Atlantic inshore seas fisheries," *Journal of the Fisheries Research Board of Canada* 33 (September 1976), p. 2121.

43 *Op. cit.*

44 H.F. Fletcher, "Toward a relevant science: fisheries and aquatic scientific resource needs in Canada," *Journal of the Fisheries Research Board of Canada* 34 (July 1977), p. 1064.

45 *Ibid.*, p. 1056.

46 H.A. Regier and F.D. McCracken, *Science for Canada's Shelf-Seas Fisheries* (Ottawa: Environment Canada, Fisheries and Marine Service, Fisheries Research Board of Canada Report Series Number 3, 1975), p. 28.

[47] K.H. Loftus, M.G. Johnson and H.A. Regier, "Federal-provincial strategic planning for Ontario fisheries: management strategy for the 1980s," *Journal of the Fisheries Research Board of Canada* 35 (June 1978), p. 921.

[48] H.A. Regier, *A Balanced Science of Renewable Resources: With Particular Reference to Fisheries* (Seattle: University of Washington Press, 1978), pp. 85-87.

[49] L.G. Anderson, "A classification of fishery management problems to aid in the analysis and proper formulation of management problems," *Ocean Development and International Law Journal* 4 (1977), pp. 113-120.

[50] See, for example, J.A. Gulland, "Fishery management: new strategies for new conditions," *Transactions of the American Fisheries Society* 107 (January 1978), pp. 1-11; and D.G. Moloney and P.H. Pearse, "Quantitative rights as an instrument for regulating commercial fisheries," *Journal of the Fisheries Research Board of Canada* 36 (July 1979), pp. 859-865.

[51] D.W. Bromley and R.C. Bishop, "From economic theory to fisheries policy: conceptual problems and management prescriptions," in *Economic Impacts of Extended Fisheries Jurisdiction*, ed. L.G. Anderson (Ann Arbor: Ann Arbor Science Publishers, Inc., 1977), pp. 281-301.

[52] G.R. Munro, "Canada and fisheries management with extended jurisdiction: a preliminary view," in *Economic Impacts of Extended Fisheries Jurisdiction*, ed. L.G. Anderson (Ann Arbor: Ann Arbor Science Publishers, Inc., 1977), pp. 29-50.

[53] G. Pontecorvo, D.M. Johnston, and M. Wilkinson, "Conditions for effective fisheries management in the Northwest Atlantic," in *Economic Impacts of Extended Fisheries Jurisdiction*, ed. L.G. Anderson (Ann Arbor: Ann Arbor Science Publishers, Inc., 1977), p. 91.

6/River Basin Development in Canada
Donald Tate

Water resources form an important and probably underplayed component of the natural resource base of Canada. With 1 percent of the world's population and 9 percent of the world's annual runoff, the country's water endowment is clearly a generous one. These assets have a substantial value in economic terms. For example, the value of exported hydroelectric power in 1979 totalled just under three-quarters of a billion dollars.[1] Further, a federal study estimating the value of water in all of its various uses placed this value at between $10 billion and $20 billion for 1980.[2] Also, there has always been a strong relationship between the distribution of major lakes and rivers and the location of municipal, industrial and other activities,[3] although other influences are also important, such as markets, transport costs and capital availability.

In view of the importance of water, the nature of the water management process in Canada has considerable interest and implications for resource management in general. This chapter reviews river basin development in Canada, focussing on the post-1945 period. It begins with a brief outline of the jurisdictional background of Canadian water management and then presents an overview of major developments during this period. The discussion of these two matters is brief, principally because both topics have been covered adequately elsewhere.[4] The chapter then continues with an outline of a framework within which to view river basin development in general and a number of case studies in particular. The case studies have been chosen from a wide variety of settings which reflect the diversity of Canadian experience in water management. The chapter closes with observations on the process of river basin development, and about its implications for both resource management and geographical research.

Jurisdictional and Historical Background
The British North America Act, plus many years of judicial amplification, serves as Canada's constitution. Rather than describe the various legal arrangements with respect to water,[5] it is sufficient to note one or two of the most important points. Ownership of the resource is vested in the provinces, giving them a large share of the legislative authority over water

Table 1.6
Status of Federal and Federal-Provincial Cost-Shared Programs Under the Canada Water Act

CONTINUOUS MONITORING AND SURVEY PROGRAMS

Under Negotiation	New during 1979–1980	Ongoing during 1979–1980	Completed
		Prairie Provinces Master Apportionment Agreement Water Quantity Survey Agreements	

PREPLANNED STUDIES

Under Negotiation	New during 1979–1980	Ongoing during 1979–1980	Completed
	Thompson River basin	Winter River basin	Lower Saskatchewan Basin Task Force (1979) Yukon River basin (1979)

PLANNING STUDIES

Under Negotiation	New during 1979–1980	Ongoing during 1979–1980	Completed
Yukon River basin	Lake Winnipeg Water Quality** Fraser River Estuary Waterford River basin (Nfld)	Planning Committee on Ottawa River Regulation Shubenacadie-Stewiacke basin Mackenzie River basin English-Wabigoon Mercury Contamination	Peace-Athabasca delta (1972) Qu'Appelle basin (1972) Saskatchewan-Nelson basin (1973) Okanagan basin (1974) Saint John basin (1975) Lake Winnipeg, Churchill, and Nelson Rivers (1975) Fraser River Upstream Storage (1976) Flow Regulation—Montreal Region (1976) Churchill River (Sask.-Man.)

IMPLEMENTATION AGREEMENTS

Under Negotiation	New during 1979–1980	Ongoing during 1979–1980	Completed
Souris basin (Manitoba)	Floodproofing—Red River Valley	Lower Fraser Valley Flood Control Program	Peace-Athabasca delta (1976)
Lake Winnipeg, Churchill and Nelson Rivers	Souris basin*** (Saskatchewan)	Okanagan basin	Metropolitan Toronto (CWCAA)*(1978)
		Qu'Appelle basin	Upper Thames (CWCAA)* (1979)
		Canada-Ontario Agreement on Great Lakes Water Quality	Southwestern Ontario Dyking (1979)
		Saint John (being implemented under regular programs)	Northern Ontario Water Resources (1978)
			St. Lawrence River Water Quality (1973)
			Souris basin (1978)

FLOOD DAMAGE REDUCTION PROGRAMS

Under Negotiation	New during 1979–1980	Ongoing during 1979–1980	Completed
Programs with Alberta, British Columbia, Newfoundland and Yukon Territory	Program with Northwest territories	Programs with New Brunswick, Nova Scotia, Quebec, Manitoba, Saskatchewan and Ontario	Southeastern New Brunswick Dyking (1978)
		Memorandum of Understanding, NWT (Hay River)	
		Flood Management—Marsh Creek, N.B.	
		Dykes and Flow Regulation Works, Montreal Region	
		New Brunswick Flood Forecasting	

OTHER COOPERATIVE ARRANGEMENTS

Under Negotiation	New during 1979–1980	Ongoing during 1979–1980	Completed
		Follow-up Programs, Canada-Ontario Great Lakes Shore Damage survey	Canada-Ontario Great Lakes Shore Damage Survey (1975)
		Water Quality Monitoring	
		Garrison Diversion	
		North Shore (St. Lawrence) Ecological Inventories	
		Technical Working Group on Water Quality in the Ottawa River	

* negotiated under the Canada Water Conservation Assistance Act
** deferred for the present
*** conducted under a DREE Subsidiary Agreement

Source: The Canada Water Act Annual Report—1979-1980

within provincial boundaries. In addition, however, the federal government has certain legislative rights, such as over fisheries and navigation and shares in the legislative authority with respect to other uses, for example, agriculture. This distinction between ownership and legislative rights is unimportant only in the northern territories, which are under federal control. Thus, in many large Canadian river basin developments, cooperation between the two levels of government has been one of the keys to success. That this arrangement has been successful is shown by the number of river basin studies which are currently underway or have been completed in the past (Table 1.6).

Table 1.6 also bears testimony to the diversity of river basin developments which are taking place in Canada. Actually, an examination of the history of this development reveals three distinct phases since 1945, a brief description of which follows.[6]

In the first stage, which lasted to the mid-sixties, water developments were oriented largely to supply management. Many of the large mega-projects developed in Canada (e.g., the St. Lawrence Seaway, Churchill Falls, Columbia River) were either authorized or committed during this period. Water was viewed philosophically as a resource to be manipulated for man's advantage. Broadly, it was seen as a resource without social cost, with little attention being given to the analysis of management alternatives beyond fairly limited benefit-cost analyses of different structural configurations. Little attention was paid to the demand side of management, to water quality issues, or to wider environmental relationships.

Discontent in some quarters with this basically mechanistic approach and advances in management techniques (principally in the United States) gave rise in the mid-sixties to a short period of ferment and radically changed approaches. The words "multiple purpose" and "comprehensive" had been applied to river basin planning and development for some considerable time before this period, but largely as theoretical constructs or as models for smaller developments. Large projects, as we have seen, still had a single-purpose nature. However, during this mid- to late-sixties period, this terminology and the approaches they stood for received the important impetus of being the basis for the Canada Water Act, an important piece of legislation by the federal government. The Act, which embraced totally the comprehensive approach to river basin development, came to be an important instrument for increased federal-provincial cooperation in water management. The nation and the water managers awoke also to the fact that water quality deterioration was a pressing national concern. In some respects, and on a small scale, Ontario had anticipated the national thrusts of this time by several years, mainly due to the Conservation Authorities program and the Ontario Water Resources Commission. During this period, or as a result of it, both the federal and most of the provincial governments institutionalized water management within environment departments. A number of comprehensive river basin planning studies was also developed during this evolution.[7]

No sooner had these new approaches been established, and new paths charted, than currents began to flow toward consolidation and retrenchment. The large cost of the comprehensive approach, government budget limitations, the diversion of water management resources into seemingly more important areas, and the failure or inability of the comprehensive approach to deal expeditiously with some pressing water problems (e.g., Great Lakes water quality), all contributed to a move back to the more single-purpose planning and development study. The Canada Water Act came to be more applied to single-purpose issues, such as water quality deterioration,[8] environmental impact[9] and flood mitigation.[10] One legacy of the second period remains, however, namely the tendancy to view water resource developments in their wider context as they affect many water use sectors and the environment in general.

While the Canada Water Act had important impacts upon approaches to river basin development, it was by no means the "only game in town." Indeed, as outlined earlier, the Ontario Conservation Authorities had anticipated comprehensive basin planning by several years, and continues to carry out these types of programs, while the federal interest has shifted. Such studies are ongoing, for example, in the Grand, Thames and South Nation basins. Alberta has also instituted a very active river basin planning program in all of the province's large basins.[11] In British Columbia, basin planning as such has been downplayed recently to some extent in favour of an approach to regional development, which sees water as only one, albeit important, regional resource requiring planning and development.[12]

Framework for Analysis

The foregoing brief historical sketch suggests that river basin management in Canada has fluctuated between single and multiple purposes; further, approaches have become more comprehensive in scope. Even where studies have addressed a single purpose, solutions have increasingly been analyzed in terms of their broad impacts on the economy, society and environment. Analyzing this process in more detail requires a framework which (a) describes the planning and implementation process itself, and (b) provides a classification within which the large number of past studies can be placed.

The water planning and implementation process generally followed in Canada can be summarized in the following manner.[13] Studies generally begin with one or a number of *purposes* aimed at solutions to existing water problems. Purposes may be defined at the political level, as is usually the case, or at the professional level of government agencies. Next, *objectives* are set, which form the basis for evaluation at later stages in the process. At the federal level, economic efficiency, regional development, environmental protection and enhancement, and, less frequently in the water resource field, equity in income distribution are common objectives. At the provincial and local levels, these objectives can also be adopted, but often more limited ones are also important. Examples of the latter are support of community growth, attraction of industry, creation of recreational areas, and so forth. Following the setting of objectives, *techniques* are selected to analyze the resource characteristics of the area and to evaluate any plans forthcoming from the study. In any planning exercise, a *range of alternative solutions* may be considered. The study results in the *plan* itself. Is it structurally oriented, or are there also nonstructural components? Which objectives are satisfied? Is the plan justified by the techniques used? Finally, the plan undergoes an *implementation* phase. Each of these steps is addressed below.

In categorizing the types of river basin development in Canada, White's six strategies of water management have been used.[14] In this context, strategy means a characteristic combination of goals (single or multiple), means (construction, regulation, research or some combination), and decision-making milieu (private or public). Although White's framework was developed in the United States in the mid-sixties, it nevertheless appears to be an adequate mechanism for categorizing Canadian experiences also. Under this framework, six management strategies dominate present-day water management:

—single-purpose construction by private agencies
—single-purpose construction by public agencies
—multiple-purpose construction by public agencies
—single-purpose projects by public agencies employing multiple means
—single-purpose, public projects employing multiple means where research is a principal component of the analysis
—multiple-purpose, public projects using multiple means.

Clearly, it is not possible to deal with every river basin development in Canada. Instead, a case example approach has been adopted. For each type of strategy one example will be assessed in some detail with respect to how the various elements were approached. Other examples are mentioned where appropriate. This method will lead to conclusions about the planning process itself, the implications of each type of study for resource management, and the implications for geographical research.

Case Examples of River Basin Development in Canada

For each of the six management strategies outlined in the last section, a representative case study has been compiled (Figure 1.6). The single-purpose private type of development is represented by management of the Saguenay River for power generation. Single-purpose public developments are exemplified by the planning and development of the Red River Floodway at Winnipeg and associated upstream works. The South Saskat-

Figure 1.6

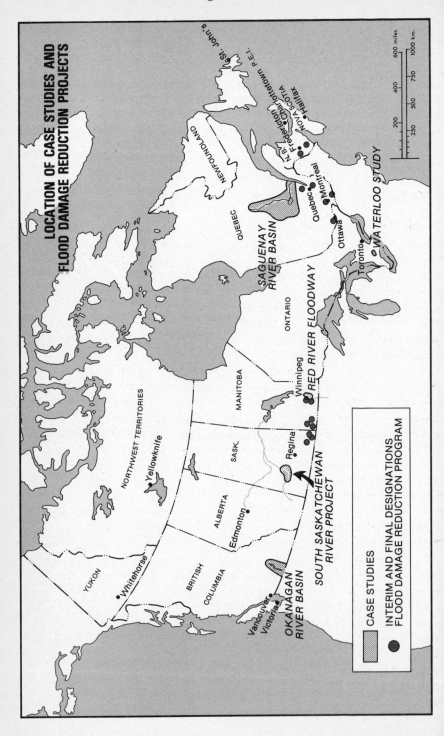

chewan River project constitutes an example of the multiple-purpose construction strategy common among public agencies. Single-purpose projects employing multiple means are represented by the recent federal-provincial programs to mitigate flood damage throughout Canada. The efforts to deal with emerging water supply problems in the Regional Municipality of Waterloo, Ontario, illustrate the fifth management strategy, a single-purpose public strategy, using multiple means where research is included as an important component. The sixth, and to date most complex strategy, multiple-purpose public projects with multiple means of achieving goals, is represented by the comprehensive river basin planning and implementation program in the Okanagan River Basin of British Columbia.

Single-Purpose, Private Construction

In common with experiences elsewhere this strategy was the earliest to develop in Canada. In the first three hundred years of settlement, individual action by private interests shaped many of the patterns of water uses. Water resources were seen to be virtually limitless, with no thought given to the effects of private actions on other users. A prime example of this type of action was in the location of industrial operations along watercourses, where natural processes were relied upon to carry away waste materials. The "commons" character of industrial water resource use generated few serious problems while establishments were widely dispersed,[15] and the assimilative capacity of the environment was not exceeded. However, as Hardin has pointed out, overuse of common property resources eventually leads to serious problems. In the case of industry, for example, it has lead to water pollution problems of significant proportions. In fact, the problems ensuing from industrial use of water for waste disposal was one factor generating the adoption of more complex water management strategies.

The case selected here for more detailed discussion focusses not upon the industrial pollution problem, but on the use of water by the Aluminum Company of Canada (Alcan) to generate the large amounts of power required by its refining operations in the Saguenay Valley of Quebec.[16] Alcan's requirement for firm power in this region averages about 2,000 megawatts annually. To generate this amount of power, the company manages the Saguenay River system, whose basin covers a 51,800 km^2 area of central Quebec. The power system in place is composed of six generating stations and three reservoirs to stabilize the river flow throughout the year. All electric power needs of the Saguenay and Chibougamau regions are served by Alcan including the demands of several municipalities, plus, in addition to the aluminum refineries, other heavy industrial operations of the copper mining and pulp and paper sectors. The company's system also feeds power into the Hydro Quebec system via 345 KV and 240 KV tie lines.

In terms of the framework adopted here, the purpose of Alcan's management is rather limited, namely to assure a firm power supply. Although other users are served, their requirements are secondary to averting the economic repercussions of shortages in firm power. In terms of broader objectives, economic efficiency in terms of supplying power at least cost to the company best describes the overall aim of system operation. The means for achieving this end is principally structural in nature, with power stations constructed to take advantage of the large head and flow of the Saguenay River.

Given the size and complexity of the Alcan system, the company developed a dynamic programming computer model to assist in its water management decisions.[17] This programming approach develops the optimal rule curve for reservoir releases, the aim being to optimize the amount of firm power available to meet demands, while minimizing reservoir outflow. The latter is particularly important during the December to mid-April period of low flows and consequent reservoir drawdown. Despite being representative of the most simple of water management strategies, the Alcan system employs advanced computerized techniques in achieving its principal end, the assurance of adequate firm power in a multi-reservoir power system. Alternatives are considered insofar as system operation is concerned; but no evidence is available that alternatives to river development were considered beyond the use of the river for power generation.

Single-Purpose Public Construction
One of the most common types of water management strategies has been the single-purpose public construction project. Often, these projects are associated with an engineering bias and a narrow focus in terms of alternatives considered prior to development. In the late sixties and early seventies, it was fashionable to term such projects "ad hoc." And yet, many of these single purpose projects have paid back large dividends in terms of net benefits, as has the one selected for the case example, the Red River or Winnipeg Floodway and associated works in southern Manitoba.

Historically, the Red River, which flows northward through a very flat lacustrine plain, has experienced periodic flooding.[18] The 1950 flood, the one perhaps best remembered for its disastrous effects, produced a flood crest of 104,000 cfs, but had been preceded by even higher flows at least three times, in 1826, 1852 and 1861. The 1950 flood, which, as later calculated, caused damages of $114 million (1957 prices), is noteworthy because it led to actions culminating in the construction of the Floodway, plus complementary works known as the Portage Diversion and the Shellmouth Reservoir.[19] Together these projects provide protection against flows of up to 169,000 cfs, the 1:165 year flood in stochastic terms. In terms of broad objectives, the aim of protection against one type of extreme environmental event, flooding, consistent with the attainment of economic efficiency, was most important.

The only alternatives considered to the Floodway were structural in nature. Upstream storage structures were investigated, but discarded because of the potential loss of valuable agricultural land. Channel modifications were also considered, but found to be ineffective in solving the problem. The possibility of flood insurance was suggested, but not pursued because of both difficulites in gaining public acceptance and also technical problems. Thus, this project can be characterized as being narrow in terms of the range of alternatives developed in that nonstructural alternatives were not considered in detail. In this case, however, even after twenty years of hindsight, it is difficult to envisage an effective set of nonstructural measures to protect such a heavily urbanized area. A major innovation was achieved during this development by the provincial Royal Commission on Flood Cost-Benefit.[20] Not only did it attempt to apply the economic principles of cost-benefit analysis in a rigorous manner, but it also set a new pattern for federal-provincial negotiations for financial assistance in water projects.

The Floodway was constructed between 1962 and 1968, at a cost of just over $63 million (1957 prices) shared by the federal and provincial governments (58.5 percent and 41.5 percent respectively). A post-audit completed during 1980 verified the economic justification of the project. Even with a rise in the discount rate from the 4 percent level used by the Royal Commission to 10 percent, the rate commonly used now,[21] the benefit-cost ratio for the Floodway itself is still greater than one. The Portage Diversion and the Shellmouth Reservoir both retain their ratios significantly greater than one, even with 10 percent and 13 percent discount rates. The effectiveness of this flood control system was amply demonstrated through the prevention of flooding in the 1974 and 1979 runoff seasons, when flows attained the hydrologic severity experienced in 1950.[22] Without the system, it is estimated that these damages would have totalled over $1 billion (1979 prices). As Mudry, Rosenberg and Reynolds conclude, "Great credit should be given to the Royal Commission for its achievement in identifying and justifying the feasible components. This conclusion is based upon economic considerations which give little credit to the human suffering which would have resulted without the works."[23]

Multiple-Purpose Construction by Public Agencies

Multiple-purpose construction by public agencies is, by now, a well-established water management strategy. In North America, one of the first large multiple purpose programs was the Tennessee Valley Authority's system of dams and reservoirs built to harness the power potential of the Tennessee River, to control floods, to provide navigation and to supply water to municipalities and industries.[24] Another such early project was the Hoover Dam construction on the Colorado River. In Canada, also, many of the projects developed during the supply orientation period were multi-purpose construction projects. For instance, the St. Lawrence

Seaway had two principal purposes, improvement of navigation and power generation. Similarly, the Columbia River development was primarily justified on the basis of power production, but also involved substantial downstream flood control benefits. The case selected for discussion here involves the South Saskatchewan River Project, a scheme which was intended to assist in diversifying the agricultural economy of the region in which it is located.

After being discussed for a considerable period of time, work was begun on the Gardiner Dam, a large earthfill dam on the South Saskatchewan River near Outlook, Saskatchewan.[25] Project authorization was given in 1958, the result of a political promise by the incoming Diefenbaker government. The purposes of the project were five in number: to create a large area of irrigated agriculture; to provide a significant hydroelectric power generating capacity; to augment low flows during the winter months for downstream abatement of pollution and for power generation purposes at the downstream Squaw River plant; to increase municipal and industrial water supplies in the Qu'Appelle Valley, especially in Regina and Moose Jaw; and to provide recreational benefits.[26]

The primary focus, or objective, of the project was regional development. As in most multi-purpose construction, an attempt was made to pick the most efficient construction alternative, given the overall decision in favour of the construction alternative. However, in the broader sense, economic efficiency was a secondary goal. For example, the expansion of irrigated land was a primary rationale for the project. No consideration was made of the cheapest means of obtaining the primary end, namely increasing food supplies, or whether, indeed, such an increase was a desirable end.

The project has met with mixed success. In terms of irrigation, expectations have yet to materialize. The original plans called for about 202.3 thousand hectares of irrigated land to be developed, with the initial block of 20.2 thousand hectares to be commenced with upon project completion. To date only about 6.5 thousand hectares have been developed, far short of the initial plans. Richards suggests a number of reasons for this failure,[27] among them being the high costs (e.g., $270,000 per 162 hectare farm) of developing irrigation structures, the reluctance of the farmers to bear those costs, the lack of markets for specialty crops originally used to justify the project, and the difficulties which arose in persuading dry land farmers to switch into irrigation. The anticipated population stabilization has also not materialized. The area is still experiencing a decline in farm population,[28] despite earlier claims of regional growth were the project to be built. Recreation has also been a disappointment thus far. Difficulties have arisen due to erosional processes which occurred as Lake Diefenbaker formed, to lake level fluctuations which occur as the lake is used to generate power, and to difficulties in creating an attractive recreational area. The parks around Lake Diefenbaker still rank low among Saskatchewan provincial parks in terms of attendance.[29]

The project has been a success in terms of power generation, especially with the dramatic rise in generation costs since 1973. In a province where much of the power is derived from thermal plants, the Gardiner Dam power is considerably cheaper.[30] The project supplies, however, only about 7 percent of Saskatchewan's power requirements. In addition to power generation at site, power production at the downstream Squaw Rapids plant has been enhanced through flow regulation, especially the provision of increased flows during the winter season.

In summary, the South Saskatchewan River project is typical of many multiple-purpose river development projects. In developing plans for multiple-purpose projects, the developing agency has often been overly optimistic in term of benefit assessment. Day,[31] for example, found that many of the anticipated benefits from development of the Deer Creek reservoir in the Lake Erie area of southern Ontario failed to materialize, seriously questioning the benefit-cost analyses carried out beforehand. This same finding applies to the South Saskatchewan River project. However, because the project was quasi-political in nature, analytical rigour was probably downplayed.

Single-Purpose Public Projects Using Multiple Means

One of the legacies of Canada's experience with the comprehensive approach to river basin development has been the realization that broadened perspectives are valuable even in solving single-purpose problems. Structural measures can be effectively augmented with a variety of nonstructural approaches, which, in addition to improving effectiveness, may also reduce costs substantially. In the public arena, the latter is an increasingly important goal as the competition for limited funds intensifies.

Efforts by all levels of government to lower flood damages illustrates well the use of multiple means in approaching a serious national problem.[32] Flood control in many regions of the country has historically involved structural approaches (e.g., dams, dykes), emergency measures and the payment of ever-increasing amounts of post-disaster assistance. For instance, it has been estimated that the property damage in Canada due to flooding totalled in excess of $100 million, ignoring inflation, for the period 1948–1973. Some $60 million worth of damages occurred in 1974 alone; by contrast, the 1975 bill for damages totalled $10 million.[33] Thus, the annual flood damage totals are highly variable, depending of course on the extent and location of flooding. Costs of mitigating flood damages are also expensive. For example, the total cost of the Lower Fraser Flood Control Program, begun in 1968 and shared by Canada and British Columbia, now stands at $61 million, up from the original estimate of $36 million at the project's inception.[34]

Yet, despite expenditures in the order of those noted for the Lower Fraser Program, damages have continued to increase. Increasing flood damages in the midst of greatly escalated mitigation expenditures is a characteristic which Canada shares with the United States, and has been the subject of much research by geographers. One of the principal theoretical contributions to have developed is that the range of choice in approaching flood damage reduction has been conceived too narrowly.[35] Recent shifts in the philosophy of public programs in the flood damage reduction area are grounded in this theory.

The federal-provincial Flood Damage Reduction Program, initiated in 1975, and currently including the provinces of Nova Scotia, New Brunswick, Quebec, Ontario, Manitoba and Saskatchewan, as well as the Northwest Territories, has as its objective the lowering of flood-related losses. One of the program's initial steps is the careful delineation on maps of flood risk areas, using hydrologic criteria.[36] Once this has been accomplished, further development of structures within this hazard zone is discouraged through the cooperation of all three levels of government through instruments such as zoning ordinances, public land acquisition, restrictions on the provision of publicly supported mortgages and exemption of new developments in the floodplain from the payment of disaster relief. Positive steps are also taken in the form of improved flood warning systems, increased education about flood hazards and the provision of expertise and financial aid to the floodproofing of existing structures. Structural measures have a place also in this program where they are warranted, but not to the exclusion of other alternatives. Thus, under this management strategy a wide range of alternatives and techniques is considered in solving the problem.

Some recent research has suggested that this approach,[37] with its emphasis on adjusting to instead of conquering the problem, may be experiencing some difficulties. Although increasing use is being made of institutional arrangements such as zoning, building regulations and flood warning systems, there still seems to be an overriding commitment to structural measures. This is reinforced by cost-sharing arrangements, which see the senior levels of government bearing most of the structural but not the "regulation" costs, thus not affecting directly the local citizenry. Many of the nonstructural measures, like zoning, on the other hand have a direct local impact. This reinforces local preferences for the structural approach. Inconsistent enforcement of the new approach also seems to be a problem, with exceptions, omissions and violations being commonplace. Finally, some difficulty is arising from unclear jurisdictions of the various agencies involved in the program. The resulting lack of communication may create confusion for those involved, as residents become uncertain as to which agency has authority.

Single-Purpose Public Projects with Multiple Means Including Research
The case study selected to illustrate this strategy concerns the efforts being made in the Regional Municipality of Waterloo, Ontario to institute

reductions in water use through adoption of a wide variety of conservation measures. This case study, although not focussing on an entire river basin, is nevertheless an instructive one because it demonstrates the wide range of alternatives for reducing water demand in a municipality and, by extension, at the basin level. To achieve such an end is to reduce or postpone capital expenditures on new water supplies, thereby promoting increased efficiency in public expenditures.

The Regional Municipality of Waterloo, located in southern Ontario about 129 km west of Toronto, is the largest Canadian municipality still using groundwater as its sole water supply source. This water is relatively pure, requiring no chlorination prior to use. With recent growth, however, demands have been threatening to exceed available supplies, a situation exacerbated by the objections of rural residents in the adjoining townships to the digging of more wells to serve the municipality.[38] Structural alternatives for developing new supplies do exist, the main ones being a dam on the Grand River which traverses the municipality and a pipeline from Lake Erie. Both alternatives are expensive, however, at $17 million and $230 million respectively (1976 costs).[39] In an effort to forestall, reduce or even cancel the need for these expenditures, municipal officials and the staff and students at the University of Waterloo have instituted a program of research aimed at developing an effective water conservation program.[40] In terms of societal objectives, the program aims at economic efficiency and equity in meeting the threatened water shortages of the area, and also as support for further regional development.

The primary technique used to date has been a comprehensive research program to define and develop the options for water conservation.[41] The first component of this program has been an information/education effort to raise public awareness of the problem and of prospective solutions. A series of recommendations has been produced as a result, ranging from the need to target specific sectors of the population (i.e., high income groups) for special appeals, to the need for the program itself to be internally consistent with conservation principles (e.g., use of recycled paper). A second element of this research approach involved a residential retrofit of toilet and shower devices.[42] In a pilot study, it was found that some 50 percent of the homes involved accepted both types of water-saving devices and that residential water use was cut an average of 20 percent by those homes. A study in Pennsylvania exhibited similar results.[43] In that study, water saving devices for toilets were accepted by 74 percent of homes involved, with a 20 percent flush-water saving.

In addition to decreasing average demands, the Waterloo study also concerned itself with reducing the peaking factor of residential weather demand and with reducing large volume use. Peaking is the factor primarily responsible for design size of water systems,[44] and thus if it can be reduced so also may capital cost. Numerous studies have demonstrated that peaking is responsive to the structure of water charges.[45] The most common types of charging structure in use in Canada are the flat rate and the declining block rate structures, both of which encourage excessive water usage. A number of alternative rate structures was investigated by the Waterloo study team and two were recommended for testing,[46] a system using excessive use charges and a system of increasing block rates. These investigations are still underway. Two other facets of the water conservation problem examined legislative powers and better water management planning. These areas also are still under investigation.

In summary, the Waterloo study is a good example of a single-purpose study which was tackled using multiple means, including a significant research component. It has been successful in identifying a number of alternatives on the nonstructural side of the field which promise potentially significant water saving and probable cost savings in postponing the need for large capital works. This study is also an excellent example of the benefits which can be derived when municipal officials and local university teams cooperate to solve practical problems.

Multiple-Purpose Public Projects Using Multiple Means

The last, and most complex water management strategy, recognizes that water is a multiple-purpose resource and that a number of means exist for the solution of water management problems. Canada has been one of the pioneering countries with respect to this strategy, with the example of the Ontario Conservation Authorities being widely recognized.[47] The province of Alberta also has an extensive program of comprehensive river basin planning, covering all of the major river basins in the province. In view of the rapid economic development of the province, and the emerging demands on a water resource in short supply, this type of planning is especially important in Alberta.[48] The comprehensive river basin planning studies carried out under the Canada Water Act are also examples of this type of strategy in operation nationally, and one of these, the Okanagan River Basin study, is used as the case example in this chapter.[49]

The study was launched jointly by the federal and B.C. governments in response to several water problems in the Okanagan Valley in the southern interior of British Columbia. These problems included impending water shortages in this semi-arid area, an incipient and costly plan to divert water from neighbouring Shuswap Lake, a growing water quality problem exemplified by eutrophication and accompanying taste and odour problems, the adverse effects of deteriorating water quality on recreation, an important Valley industry, and periodic flooding problems in the lower part of the basin. The international character of the basin imposed an additional factor to be taken into account in managing the area's water resources.

Multiple-objective planning was a noteworthy characteristic of this study. The realization was implicit in the exercise that the shape of the final plan would be dependent upon which objectives were given as the overall priority. Three such objectives were adopted: a status quo scenario, which would allow the basin to continue on its historic development path; a maximum economic growth scenario, which would reflect the economic efficiency objective; and a scenario oriented to a lower rate of growth but the enhancement of environmental quality.

The planning task was organized around the need to consider a wide variety of alternatives in developing the best plan for the basin. Four distinct components for study were used: water quantity, water quality, fisheries, and water-based recreation. For each component, goals and methodologies were adopted that would help to formulate and evaluate alternative development plans, or "futures." Implicit in each of these four components was the incorporation of socioeconomic methods such as benefit-cost analysis, forecasting, evaluation of intangibles and public participation. Considerable basic research of both a physical and socio-economic nature was built into the plan of study. Public participation played a significant role in the selection of the scenario, emphasizing environmental quality as the recommended development plan for the basin.

The plan which materialized covered a large number of areas deemed essential for management of the basin. Among these were recommendations for a basin-wide administrative organization (ultimately rejected by both the regional districts and the province); management of available supplies, which were deemed sufficient without importation to meet all future demands; allocation of tributaries among fisheries uses on the one hand and domestic and agricultural uses on the other; flood damage abatement through zoning rather than structural measures; rehabilitation of the existing flood control system; and installation of phosphate removal facilities in the major municipalities of the basin. Other recommendations may be found in the report of the Basin Board.[50]

The Okanagan exercise incorporated an active public involvement program, which met with considerable success, and can be considered as one of the exercise's most important achievements. Early in the planning process, local citizen involvement groups were established to serve in an advisory capacity to the Board and the professional planning staff. Frequent public meetings and seminars assured a flow of information between the two groups (i.e., citizen and Board-planners). In the end, the citizen advisory groups played a strong role in the selection of the preferred development alternative, which placed its emphasis on protecting and enhancing environmental quality, as opposed to achieving maximum economic growth.[51]

The Okanagan is a good example of comprehensive planning on a multiple-objective basis. The advances made in several areas, such as evaluation using different frameworks, or accounts, the evaluation of intangibles, and public involvement are important for water resource planning and yet, it appears, have received little attention. Criticism has arisen on several fronts, however, relating to time lags between planning and implementation, the proliferation of the study into nonessential areas, the impracticality of reorganizing administrative boundaries, and the rigidity of the recommendation for phosphate removal as the curative measure for water quality deterioration. Thus, the planning exercise, actually an experiment, has met with mixed success and acceptance.

Observations on the Process of River Basin Development

Emerging from the case examples are several characteristics of river basin development in Canada. Based upon Table 2.6 and other material presented, several trends are discernible. While these trends do not include all of the developments during this period, they nevertheless appear to be among the most important. These trends have important implications for research and for resource management and will be brought out in the following section.

The process of basin development has changed radically over the period of study. At the end of World War II emphasis was upon supply management and the use of water development to stimulate economic growth. Little attention was paid to the wider environmental implications of harnessing water resources, often giving rise to problems in subsequent years. The environmental damage to the Peace-Athabasca Delta caused by the development of B.C.'s Bennett Dam for hydro power production is a dramatic example of this point.[52] From the supply orientation and single-purpose nature of developments in the earlier part of the period, emphasis switched to a wider view of the development process, culminating in the comprehensive river basin development process embodied in the Canada Water Act, and similar developments in several provinces, such as Alberta and British Columbia. Earlier experiences of the Ontario Conservation Authorities meant that this approach was not entirely new in Canada, but the new Act contributed significantly to the spread of the ideas contained in it. Since this wider perspective on water management developed, emphasis has shifted back somewhat to the earlier single-purpose concerns, or in some cases (e.g., British Columbia), to a view that water management and planning should be integral parts of regional economic and social development, thereby tending to downplay the river basin orientation. One important change, however, remained. The lessons learned about the value of a wider view of water problems have tended to endure, with the result that single-purpose problems now are likely to be seen in the context of their broader implications for water management. Also, environmental factors are now given much more explicit recognition than they were in earlier periods.

River basin planning has experienced parallel development. In the earlier years, planning was usually limited to specific project development, heavily oriented to the structural viewpoint and rather deficient with respect to the consideration of project alternatives or the wider spatial implications of project development. With the onset of the comprehensive model, planning, of necessity, became much more broadly based, and tended to follow too many avenues unrelated to the correction of specific water problems. Reaction to this feeling that river basin planning was going too far afield led to the failure to develop planning studies at the rate originally intended and the adaptation of the wider viewpoint to single-purpose problems.

In the studies examined in this chapter, and through a more extensive review of other studies, it seems that the most frequent emphasis of development projects has been related to the economic efficiency objective. The aim has usually taken the form of enhancing growth opportunities, increasing per capita income, or similar measures as a result of water development. This aim, however, is prone to being formulated incorrectly, as in the South Saskatchewan example. The next most frequent objective is the protection, restoration or enhancement of environmental quality, as in the case of the Peace-Athabasca, Churchill River, Lake Winnipeg-Churchill-Nelson and St. Lawrence Water Quality studies. The comprehensive studies often incorporated more than one objective, and in the Okanagan case outlined above, it was shown how plans were drawn up so as to maximize the efficiency and the environmental objectives in turn.

Taking the whole period into account, the techniques used to develop basin plans and to put the plans into operation have made heavy emphasis on engineering and physical sciences. The earlier supply-management orientation implied this type of emphasis, with the only technique adopted from the social sciences having been benefit-cost analysis. With the development of broader approaches, techniques have also broadened to include more socioeconomic analysis, for example public participation and social impact assessments, legal and institutional studies, the investigation of nonstructural alternatives and water demand forecasting. However, taken as a whole, the water management field in Canada is still dominated in most areas by the engineer and physical scientist.

As implied in the foregoing paragraph and as seen in the case examples developed earlier, the range of alternatives in Canadian river basin development has been quite narrow. In the main, structural alternatives have been seen as the solution to water management issues, and the profession has been slow to broaden its horizons. The area most advanced in its consideration of alternatives has been flood plain management, a field which has benefited from the work of many geographers.[53] The federal-provincial flood damage reduction program illustrates this broadened approach to flooding problems, as does experience in Ontario. The area of municipal and industrial water supply could also profit from a broadened approach to emerging supply shortage. Water conservation measures such

Table 2.6

Characteristics of Canadian River Basin Development Water Management Strategy

	Single-Purpose Private Construction	Single-Purpose Public Construction	Multiple-Purpose Public Construction	Single-Purpose Public Projects Using Multiple Means	Single-Purpose Public Projects Using Multiple Means Including Research	Multiple-Purpose Public Projects Using Multiple Means
Case Example	Alcan development of Saguenay Basin	Winnipeg Floodway upstream storage and diversion	South Saskatchewan River Project	Federal-provincial flood damage reduction program	Water conservation project, Regional Municipality of Waterloo	Canada-B.C. Okanagan River Basin study
Purpose(s)	Power production for aluminum smelting	Flood control for Winnipeg Metro area	Irrigation, power generation, water supply, recreation, flow augmentation	Mitigation of flood damage throughout Canada	Demand management as a substitute of supply expansion	Water supply, quality deterioration, flood control, recreation, enhancement
Objective(s)	Economic efficiency	Economic efficiency consistent with achieving flood control	Regional development	Lower the cost of disaster assistance	Greater efficiency in municipal water supply	Economic efficiency, environmental protection

Techniques Employed	Engineering and construction plus computerized optimization model	Engineering and construction plus some benefit-cost analysis	Engineering and construction plus some benefit-cost analysis	Nonstructural plus structural ways of adjusting to hazard if nonstructural unsuitable	Wide variety of nonstructural measures for water demand reduction	A very diverse range of physical and social science techniques and evaluative methods
Range of Alternatives considered	Narrow—structural only plus flow management as determined by model	Construction and physical alternatives only	Narrow—slight variations in project design	Wide range of alternative adjustments evaluated	Wide range, including economic, public information, in-house water saving methods	Three development scenarios—status quo, maximum growth and environmental protection
Type of Plan	System of six dams plus three reservoirs	One reservoir plus two major diversion routes	Dam plus large reservoir plus diversion works Qu'Appelle River basin	Maps, zoning, incentives for relocation, public land acquisition, and other means	Plan still in the research phase, but the wide degree of attention generated indicates a large potential for success	Development plan for basin based on environmental objective
Comments on Implementation	Power supplied also to regional municipalities and industries	Very successful project, with B/C ratio greater than 1 under all conditions of post-project analysis	Marginal success only in achieving many of the anticipated benefits	Fifteen designations in place and many more expected; still too early to assess long-term benefits		Some difficulties in implementation phase (see text)

as those in the Waterloo case study remain rare, but could go a long way to solving shortfalls in supply which appear to be emerging in some of the water-deficient basins of the Canadian West.[54]

A noteworthy aspect of water management has been the lack of interest among decision makers in using economic instruments as incentives to promote environmentally sound behaviour or to encourage water conservation. One of the few exceptions to this situation is the Waterloo case study, where the application of economically based rate structures was recommended as one way of achieving water demand reductions. Some other proven examples exist across Canada,[55] but generally the water industry has been slow to adopt pricing as a central instrument in sound water management.

The case is even more glaring in the water pollution control area. Water pollution basically arises from the overuse of a common property resource, resulting from the lack of any mechanism to allocate the use of water for the abatement of waste. In market economies, prices normally serve this function but, in the area of pollution control, no such prices exist. This suggests that the basic cause of water pollution is economic in nature, and further that actions to correct the problem should incorporate, at least in part, market pricing principles.[56] Yet, in Canada such a solution has been neglected on a comprehensive basis. This neglect has occurred despite evidence as to the effectiveness of market-based principles in pollution control, gathered from wide areas of the world,[57] including Canada itself. For example, Penman found, in connection with the system of effluent discharge fees for industrial polluters in Winnipeg, Manitoba, that fees of this nature not only reduced waste discharge to the sewer system, but also reduced industrial water demands. In fact, he stated that the fee system was effective where years of attempted regulation, litigation and fines had proven ineffective.[58]

Throughout the evolution of river basin development, in Canada and in other areas of the world, the regionalization emphasis has been on hydrologic units. This use of physical criteria to establish primary spatial units is based upon the integrating nature of surface streamflow, and fails to recognize that most socioeconomic flows and characteristics are not organized in this manner. Problems arise in planning studies related to obtaining reliable socioeconomic data on a river basin basis. Although computerized data systems are making this task easier,[59] such data systems have been developed only within the past ten years, a very short period when an analyst is relying upon long-term time trends. The time involved in adjusting older data to a river basin basis can be very long and quite costly.[60] The hydrologic regionalization common in water management also is often irrelevant when dealing with urban water resource problems. It seems that a substantial amount of work could be carried out in investigating the implications of using river basins as regional units, and, if these are shown to be effective, in recommending the best ways of adjusting data from outside the water resource area to fit the river basin system.

River Basin Development, Resource Management and Research

The field of water management is a major component of a wider area of study and application, resource management. In the past, developments in the water field have contributed to the general field of resource management in a number of ways. Three such developments are benefit-cost analysis,[61] the perception that management options should be broadened,[62] and the integration of public involvement into the planning process.[63] River basin development has produced a number of general benefits for Canadian resource management, which are dealt with in this section. Again, the purpose here is to be indicative as opposed to exhaustive, as the latter is not possible in a relatively short chapter.

One of the fundamental characteristics of Canada, and one which has particular significance at this time, is the constitutional makeup of our political structure. In water, as we have pointed out, ownership of the resource is provincial (except in the Territories), but legislative authority is shared between the federal and provincial levels of government. The challenge of working within this framework has been met particularly well in river basin development, and many significant water developments are the result of federal-provincial cooperation. The mechanisms which have been established through the years, ranging from the Canadian Council of Resource and Environment Ministers, which grew from the need to develop water resources jointly, to the cooperation between federal and provincial agencies at the detailed working level, have been effective in developing Canada's water resources.

A second benefit for resource management ensuing from river basin development arises from the attempt to consider multi-objectives and a variety of alternatives in solving resource problems. Although there remains considerable need to improve further, it is probable that these issues have been handled rather better in water management than in most fields. Many of the multi-objective evaluation techniques used, for example in the Okanagan study, have wide applicability to many areas of resource management.

All resource management fields are built upon the availability of large quantities of data and research, the benefits of which are apparent only after long periods of time. In water management, and particularly river basin development, the integration of research into the whole process of development has generally been well handled. All of the comprehensive river basin programs, both under the Canada Water Act, and outside the Act, have had substantial research components, which have benefited from a long period of data availability. The recent single-purpose studies and development have also shared this characteristic. Even private single-purpose developments may incorporate significant research activity, as was found to be the case in the Alcan case study. The lesson here for resource management is that research based upon long periods of record is an important component of the management process, and should be an integral part of management decisions.

There have also been lessons for local involvement in the planning process. First of all, the public participation programs included in each of the comprehensive basin planning studies have been variably effective.[64] For instance, in the Okanagan case, public input had a role in selecting the plan finally recommended. In other studies as well, public involvement has led to increased awareness of the study, and an increased level of public commitment to the study and its results. This experience, which was pioneered in the river basin planning field, appears to have grown into other areas of resource management, as for example in the urban field. The second implication concerning local involvement relates to financial participation in planning and development exercises. In water management, financing of studies and implementation has been borne by the two senior levels of government. This financial arrangement often led to unrealistic local demands and expectations from the development process. It is now considered by some reviewers that provision for local financial involvement may temper local expectations from development plans and implementation, making for a more responsible level of development.[65]

River basin development in Canada has become an increasingly multi-disciplinary activity. Engineers, physical and social scientists have been actively involved in the planning process and at later implementation phases. The creation of multi-disciplinary teams through these tasks has resulted in effective handling of problems and in the consideration of alternatives which would have been ignored had such teams not existed. For example, the multi-objective planning methodology used in the Okanagan study could only have been developed and implemented through the multi-disciplinary team approach, using engineers, physical and social scientists, as well as management personnel. This is an important finding and flows from recommendations made frequently in the past.

In addition to implications for resource management in general, the Canadian river basin development experience also has implications for research. Of particular interest in this connection are research problems which could be dealt with by geographers.

The current focus in resource management is clearly the energy field. Major supply areas are located in river basins which have significant water problems such as too little water, fragile ecosystems and populations which depend upon *in situ* use of the water (e.g., fishing). Research issues here range from assuring sufficient water to satisfy future needs, to investigating the integration of ground and surface water, to examining systematically the environmental impacts of energy developments, and to finding methods of harmonizing future developments with ways of life oriented to maintaining intact the natural environment. In all of these areas, the geographer can apply skills acquired from both the physical and the socioeconomic sides of the discipline.

In the areas of institutional and legal arrangements, also, important issues must be addressed. For instance, the success of water management was outlined earlier in working within the administrative framework of Canada. The precise reasons for this success are uncertain. Research should be addressed to assessing these reasons and to defining those areas of the experience which are transferable to other resource management areas.

Another institutional area relates to the apportionment of streamflow and benefits when water flows across international and interprovincial boundaries. Flows of some international streams are already apportioned, either by treaty, as in the case of the St. Mary's and Milk Rivers,[66] or by administrative arrangement, for example in Souris.[67] Others, such as the Niagara, are apportioned with respect to streamflow benefits.[68] In the case of the Saskatchewan River basin, streamflow on the mainstem of the river is apportioned under the Master Apportionment Agreement administered by the Prairie Provinces Water Board.[69] In the future, pressure on water supplies might result in requirements for apportionment on other inter-jurisdictional rivers, most notably the Mackenzie system. Work needs to be carried out on the apportionment principles which both have underlain and should underlie such arrangements. Day and Friesen have made a start in this area, but more work will be required.[70]

The area of water demand also promises to be one of increasing importance and one in which geographers can contribute usefully. One task relates to research on the instruments of demand management, such as pricing, rate structuring and water conservation measures. Another relates to overcoming the professional reluctance to develop demand management as a full-fledged equal to supply manipulation in developing or expanding water services. Another concerns forecasting of future water demands and relating these to available supplies. In each of these areas, geographers have made important contributions,[71] but have really only begun to investigate the subject in detail.

Data availability is an integral and vital part of the planning process. As outlined earlier, the procurement of socioeconomic statistics on a river basin basis has proven a difficult task in the past. Geographers can usefully contribute to the technology for assuring that data can be derived in the future on a variety of spatial bases, including the river basin.[72]

In this outline, the need for further research has been assumed in the now-traditional areas of water resource management, such as broadening the range of alternatives and public participation. Thus the opportunity for both "lateral" and "vertical" thought by geographers in the field of river basin development will continue to be important in the future.[73]

Notes

1 Canada, National Energy Board, *Annual Report, 1979*, Ottawa, 1980, p. 26.
2 For example, according to Young and Gray, the average value of an acre-foot of water used for hydro power production in the United States was $1.50 in 1971. Assuming that this value applies to Canada, and making the conversion from U.S. to Canadian dollars and from 1971 to 1980 dollars, the unit value of water for hydro usage in 1980 would be $4.24 per acre-foot. An internal study by the federal Department of the Environment estimates the total water use for hydro power generation at 2,366 million acre-feet (2.92 x 10^{12} m^3). Multiplying this total usage by the unit value of water in hydro power production yields a total value of just under $10 billion dollars. See R. Young and S.L. Gray, *The Value of Water in Alternative Uses*, Washington, U.S. National Water Commission, 1971; and Canada, Environment Canada, Inland Waters Directorate, "Energy from Water-Section 2; Technology and Resource Potential", unpublished working paper, 1980; and Statistics Canada, *Electric Power Statistics*, Ottawa, Catalogue No. 57-001 Monthly, July, 1980, p. 11.
3 Canada, Environment Canada, Inland Waters Directorate, "Water and the Canadian Economy," unpublished working paper, 1979.
4 See for example: Quinn, F., "Notes for a National Water Policy," in R.R. Krueger and B. Mitchell, *Managing Canada's Renewable Resources*. (Toronto: Methuen, 1977), pp. 230–235; and Canada, Environment Canada, Inland Waters Directorate, *Canadian Water Management Policy Instruments* by D.F. Bellinger (Ottawa: Social Science Series No. 13, 1975), p. 20.
5 For more detail, see B. Laskin, "Jurisdictional Framework for Water Management," in Canada, Department of Northern Affairs and Natural Resources, Resources for Tomorrow Conference, *Background Papers, Volume 1*, Ottawa, 1961, pp. 211–225; and Canada, Department of Energy, Mines and Resources, Canadian Committee for the International Conference on Water for Peace, "Water Resource Development in Canada: A Perspective," in *Canadian Papers for the Conference*, Document 50, p. 8.
6 For more detail, see Quinn, *op. cit.*, p. 229.
7 In 1967, while initial development of the Act was underway, the federal government offered to fund the cost of one comprehensive river basin planning project in each of the regions as a prototype of the new water management approach. Three such studies were initiated, covering the Saint John's, Qu'Appelle and Okanagan River Basins, although funding was shared by the federal and provincial governments.
8 The Canada-Ontario Great Lakes Water Quality Agreement and the Canada-Quebec St. Lawrence Water Quality Agreement are examples of this type of study.
9 See for example: Canada-Alberta-Saskatchewan, Peace-Athabasca Delta Project, *The Peace-Athabasca Delta: A Canadian Resource*, Ottawa, 1972.
10 The federal-provincial efforts at flood mitigation are described on pages 163–64.
11 Alberta, Alberta Environment, *Water Resource Management Principles for Alberta*, undated, p. 10.
12 Information derived from conversation with Dr. F. Quinn, member of an Environment Canada team evaluating the River Basin Planning Program under the Canada Water Act.

[13] Environment Canada, Inland Waters Directorate, *Canada Water Yearbook, 1976*, Ottawa, 1976, pp. 9-13.

[14] White, G.F., *Strategies of American Water Management* (Ann Arbor: University of Michigan Press, 1971), p. 13.

[15] G. Hardin, "The Tragedy of the Commons," *Science*, Vol. 162, pp. 1243-1248.

[16] R.J. Silver, M.H. Okun, and S.O. Russell, "Dynamic Programming in a Hydroelectric System," in Environment Canada, Department of Environment, *International Symposium on Modelling Techniques in Water Resources*, Ottawa, 1972, pp. 423-436.

[17] *Ibid.*, see also D.K. Se, R. Thompstone, M. Kermani and B. Divi, "An Explicit Stochastic Optimization Approach to Develop Operational Policies for a Multi-Reservoir Hydroelectric System," *Proceedings*, Joint National ORSA/TIMS Meeting, Atlanta, 1977, pp. 1-17.

[18] N. Mudry, H.B. Rosenberg and P.J. Reynolds, "Post-Project Evaluation of the Red and Assiniboine River Flood Control Projects in the Province of Manitoba, Canada," pre-print of a paper to be presented at the 11th International Congress, International Commission on Irrigation and Drainage, Grenoble, France, 1981, pp. 3-7.

[19] T.E. Weber, "The Red River Floodway and Related Flood Control Works," in *Canadian Papers for the International Water for Peace Conference, op. cit.*, Paper 480, pp. 3-5.

[20] Manitoba, Royal Commission on Flood Cost-Benefit, 1956.

[21] Mudry, Rosenberg and Reynolds, *op. cit.*, pp. 23-26.

[22] W.F. Ranie, "The Red River Flood Control System and Recent Flood Events," *Water Resources Bulletin*, A.W.R.A., Vol. 16, #2, April 1980, pp. 207-214.

[23] Mudry, Rosenberg and Reynolds, *op. cit.*, p. 26.

[24] G.R. Clapp, "An Approach to the Development of a Region," in I. Burton, and R.W. Kates, *Readings in Resource Management and Conservation*, (Chicago: University of Chicago Press, 1965), pp. 298-307.

[25] South Saskatchewan River Development Commission, *South Saskatchewan River Development Project*, Regina, 1964.

[26] Canada, Department of Agriculture, Prairie Farm Rehabilitation Administration, The South Saskatchewan River Dam, Queen's Printer, Ottawa, 1959.

[27] J.H. Richards, "Is Lake Diefenbaker Justifying Its Planners?" *Canadian Geographical Journal*, Vol. 91, #6, Dec. 1973, pp. 22-31.

[28] *Ibid.* p. 28. This trend has continued in the 1971-1976 period. For example in 1971, the number of census farms in the census subdivisions bordering Lake Diefenbaker totalled 1,732; this total fell to 1,548 by 1976. See Statistics Canada, *Census of Agriculture, 1971*, Catalogue #96-709, Vol. 4, #3, 1973; and *idem, Census of Agriculture 1976*, Catalogue #96-808, Vol. 13, 1978.

[29] Richards, *op. cit.*, p. 29. These findings were still valid as of 1979.

[30] Calculated from: Statistics Canada, *Electric Power Statistics, 1977*, Catalogue #57-206 Annual, Vol. 3, Ottawa, 1979, p. 58.

[31] J.C. Day, "Benefit-Cost Analysis and Multiple-Purpose Reservoirs: A Reassessment of the Conservation Authorities' Branch Deer Creek Project, Ontario," in F.M. Leversedge, ed., *Priorities in Water Management*, Western Geographical Series, Vol. 8, University of Victoria, 1974, pp. 23-36.

[32] R.B. Maclock, and G.A. Page, "Cutting Our Flood Losses," in W.R.D. Sewell, and M.L. Barker, eds., *Water Problems and Policies*, Cornett Occasional Papers, #1, University of Victoria, 1980, pp. 7-12.

33 R.A. Spargo, and W.E. Watt, "The Canadian Flood Damage Reduction Program," in Environment Canada, Inland Waters Directorate, *Canadian Background Papers for the World Water Conference*, Ottawa, 1976, p. 74.

34 Canada, Environment Canada, *Canada Water Act Annual Report, 1979–80*, Ottawa, 1980.

35 A great deal of literature is available on this subject. See for example: G.F. White, *Human Adjustments to Floods: A Geographical Approach to the Flood Problem in the United States*, Research Paper #29, Department of Geography, University of Chicago, 1942; B. Mitchell, *Geography and Resource Analysis*, (London: Longman, 1979), pp. 206–209.

36 Spargo and Watt, *op. cit.*

37 B. Mitchell, J. Gardner, R. Cook and B. Veale, *Physical Adjustments and Institutional Arrangements for the Urban Flood Hazard*, Department of Geography, University of Waterloo, Publication Series #13, 1978.

38 J.E. Robinson, "Demand Modification as a Supply Alternative: A Case Study of the Regional Municipality of Waterloo, Ontario, Canada," unpublished manuscript, Department of Man-Environment Studies, University of Waterloo, 1979, pp. 1–2.

39 *Ibid.*, p. 2.

40 *Ibid.*, pp. 3–12.

41 W. Ashton, S. Howard-Ferreira, and L. Bond, *An Incomplete Guide to Water Conservation, Residential Water Conservation*, Department of Man-Environment Studies, University of Waterloo, undated.

42 *Ibid.*, pp. 27–50.

43 W. Sharpe, "Selection of Water Conservation Devices for Installation in New or Existing Dwellings," as quoted in Ashton, Howard-Ferreira, and Bond, *op. cit.*, p. 36.

44 A.P. Grima, *Residential Water Demand: Alternative Choices for Water Management* (Toronto: University of Toronto Press, 1972), Chapter 1.

45 See for example: W.R.D. Sewell, and L. Roueche, "The Potential Impact of Peak Load Pricing on Urban Water Demands," in F.M. Leversedge, *op. cit.*, pp. 141–161; also A.P. Grima, *op. cit.*

46 J. Gold, "The Effect of Water Rate Structures on Water Conservation," Department of Man-Environment Studies, University of Waterloo, 1979.

47 J.S. Anderson, "Conservation Authorities and Water Management," Soil Conservation Society of America, *Proceedings of the 34th Annual Meeting*, Ottawa, 1979, p. 15.

48 Alberta, *Water Resource Management Principles for Alberta*, *op. cit.*

49 Canada-Ontario Okanagan River Basin Board, *Final Report*, Penticton, B.C., 1974.

50 *Ibid.* See summary chapter.

51 *Ibid.*

52 *The Peace-Athabasca Delta: A Canadian Resource, op. cit.*, pp. 65–90.

53 B. Mitchell, *Geography and Resource Analysis, op. cit.*

54 In an internal Environment Canada study, it was found that the Okanagan, North Saskatchewan, South Saskatchewan, Milk and Red-Assiniboine basins could experience chronic water shortages by the year 2000. See: Environment

Canada, Inland Waters Directorate, "Water and the Canadian Economy," unpublished working paper, 1980.

[55] Grima, *op. cit.*, and Sewell and Roueche, *op. cit.*

[56] For example: J.H. Dales, *Pollution, Property and Prices* (Toronto: University of Toronto Press, 1971), pp. 77–100.

[57] A.V. Kneese, and B.T. Bower, *Managing Water Quality: Economics, Technology and Institutions* (Baltimore: Johns Hopkins Press, 1968).

[58] A. Penman, "The Experience with the Effluent Discharge Fee Scheme of the City of Winnipeg," a paper prepared for and presented to the Inland Waters Directorate, Environment Canada, February, 1974.

[59] Statistics Canada, Office of the Senior Advisor on Integration, *Selected Thematic Maps of Man's Activities in Canadian Watersheds*, by B. Mitchell, Ottawa, 1980.

[60] For example, the cost of obtaining population age-sex, income, agricultural, mining and manufacturing data for the ongoing Prairie Provinces Water Demand Study was well over $50,000. This study covered the period 1951–1976.

[61] W.R.D. Sewell, J. Davis, A.D. Scott and D.W. Ross, *A Guide to Benefit-Cost Analysis*, Resources for Tomorrow Conference, *op. cit.*, 1961.

[62] Mitchell, *Geography and Resource Analysis, op. cit.*, p. 222.

[63] See discussion in B. Mitchell, *Geography and Resource Analysis, op. cit.*

[64] Information derived from internal files, Inland Waters Directorate, Environment Canada, and particularly "An Evaluation of the Qu'Appelle Public Involvement Program," by D. Vindasius, 1976.

[65] Information derived from interviews by a team evaluating the comprehensive river basin program under the Canada Water Act. The evaluation is being conducted under the auspices of Environment Canada, by a team of independent reviewers.

[66] L.M. Bloomfield, and G.F. Fitzgerald, *Boundary Waters Problems of Canada and the United States, (The I.J.C 1912–1958)* (Toronto: Carswell Co., 1958), pp. 210–211.

[67] *Ibid.*, p. 154.

[68] J.C. Day, and B.F. Friesen, "Aesthetics, Hydroelectricity and International Equity in the Niagara Basin," an unpublished paper prepared under contract with Environment Canada, 1976, pp. 7–9.

[69] Canada-Alberta-Saskatchewan-Manitoba, Prairie Provinces Water Board, *Annual Report, 1977–78*, Regina, 1978, pp. 42–53.

[70] Day and Friesen, *op. cit.*

[71] See for example: Canada, Department of Energy, Mines and Resources, Policy and Planning Branch, *Forecasting the Demands for Water* by W.R.D. Sewell and B.T. Bower, eds., Ottawa, 1968; Canada, Department of the Environment, Inland Waters Directorate, *Industrial Water Demand Forecasting*, by D.M. Tate and R. Robichaud, Social Science Series #10, Ottawa, 1973; and A.P. Grima, *op. cit.*

[72] Statistics Canada, *Selected Thematic Maps of Man's Activities in Canadian Watersheds, op. cit.*

[73] According to de Bono, vertical thinking occurs when researchers analyze existing concepts and problems to greater depth or breadth; lateral thinking is the process of developing new problems areas or concepts during the research process. See B. Mitchell, *Geography and Resource Management, op. cit.*, p. 55.

7/Rehabilitation—Towards a Wiser Usage of Our Land Resources

Alexander G. McLellan

Definitions, Concepts and Scope

Introduction

The word "rehabilitation" is more familiar in the medical and psychological connotation, where it roughly describes the process of returning a person to good health physically or mentally. The usage with which we are concerned in this chapter concerns rather our landsurfaces—the impacts we have had and continue to have on them. The parallels, however, with the word of medical and psychological origins are both more fundamental and diverse.

Rehabilitation in the medical sciences in brought into play after the sickness has ensued. Until recently, landscape rehabilitation has also been a process implemented after the fact. Today's generation is perhaps more cognizant of preventative approaches, and rehabilitation in the future will be more apparent in preparatory planning than in recuperative curing of past despoilation.

Land As a Basic Resource

In dealing with our land resource, it is clear that we have not always acted wisely in the past, despite basic veneration of land in many indigenous cultures.

Biblical admonitions towards wise stewardship of the land reflect the significance attached to the latter in the Covenant between man and God. In more contemporary times, Aldo Leopold has perhaps best stated this symbiosis in his land ethic. "All ethics so far evolved rest upon a single premise: that the individual is a member of a community of interdependent parts. His instincts prompt him to compete for his place in that community, but his ethics prompt him also to cooperate (perhaps in order that there may be a place to compete for). The land ethic simply enlarges the boundary of the community to include soils, water, plants and animals, or collectively: the land,"[1] Thus land becomes the stage for our ecological interelationships with the other animate and inanimate objects of our environment. Today, in the era of a vanished frontier with virtually no new virgin lands to add to our ecumene, with a society now questioning its former consumptive viewpoints and being forced by attitudes related to a new conservation ethic and perhaps even more currently simple economic hardships related to energy costs, cavalier attitudes to land use are no longer tolerable.

In Canada planning regulations are designed to avoid the many forms of land abuse. Indeed, the last twenty years have seen the removal of private ownership rights to do with "our land" as *we* see fit. Attention seems to have been successfully diverted more to the *responsibilities* as well as the *privileges* of private land ownership.[2] In the future, increasing public and governmental concerns should be directed to higher use, misuse and underuse, as well as abuse of our land resource and the responsibility of handing on to future generations a land surface which can sustain food production, natural and human life forms and other activities necessary for national well-being.

Land Disturbing Activities—Terminology and Goals

The traditional land areas requiring rehabilitation are those that have been "drastically disturbed" (North American usage[3]) or made into a condition of "derelict land" (U.K. usage[4]). Regardless of the preferred terminology, there is agreement that the extreme end product of such abuse is "land so damaged or otherwise affected by industrial or other development that it is incapable of alternative use without further treatment."[5] A more ecological restatement of this might be "if the native vegetation and animal communities have been removed and most of the topsoil is lost, altered or buried, these drastically disturbed sites will not completely heal themselves within the lifetime of man through normal secondary successional processes."[6]

Some forms of agriculture can quickly lead to a degradation of our landscape and its productive ability, particularly in the face of adverse climatic or topographic circumstances. Examples are the Dust Bowls of the thirties and the overgrazing of foothill ranges. However, the "traditional" degrading practice of the notorious coal mining practices in Appalachia resulted in landscape degradation to an extent where remedial rehabilitation was almost impossible (Figure 1.7).[7] The lesson is that we should consider rehabilitation procedures *before* commencing land disturbance activities.

In a 1974 publication, the National Academy of Sciences proposed the following definitions:

Restoration means that the exact conditions of the site before disturbance will be replicated after the disturbance. Thus, complete restoration is seldom, if ever, possible. . . .

Reclamation implies that the site will be habitable to organisms originally present in approximately the same composition and density after the reclamation process has been completed. . . .

Rehabilitation means that the disturbed site will be returned to a form and productivity in conformity with a prior use plan. It implies that a stable condition

Figure 1.7

MINING PRACTICES

a] LANDSCAPE BEFORE

COAL SEAM

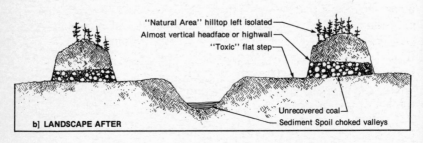

"Natural Area" hilltop left isolated

Almost vertical headface or highwall

"Toxic" flat step

Unrecovered coal

Sediment Spoil choked valleys

b] LANDSCAPE AFTER

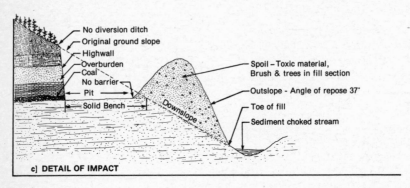

No diversion ditch

Original ground slope

Highwall

Overburden

Coal

No barrier

Pit

Solid Bench

Downslope

Spoil – Toxic material, Brush & trees in fill section

Outslope – Angle of repose 37°

Toe of fill

Sediment choked stream

c] DETAIL OF IMPACT

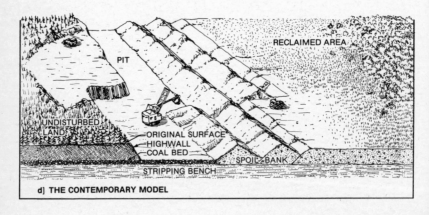

RECLAIMED AREA

PIT

UNDISTURBED LAND

ORIGINAL SURFACE

HIGHWALL

COAL BED

SPOIL BANK

STRIPPING BENCH

d] THE CONTEMPORARY MODEL

will be established that will not deteriorate substantially with the projected land use ... consistent with surrounding aesthetic values. It also suggests that the selected land use should be both ecologically stable and of high value to society.[8]

An important principle here is that while the current use of land may be appropriate for this point in time, it is wise to maintain as wide a range of alternatives as possible for the future. A rehabilitation technique that precludes certain alternatives removes future possibilities. The acceptance of rehabilitation ethics and techniques implies the acceptance of land stewardship for the present and the future.

The lessons of the past should not be forgotten. The admirable management (=rehabilitation?) of grouse moors and tree planting practices in Scotland and the reclamation of Fen-marshlands in England indicate that wise estate management practices, if ongoing, can produce admirable financial returns even from land which is severely disadvantaged. Rehabilitation should not be considered as a "once only" experience, but one in which we discover the benefits of long-term ecological and economic thinking!

Land Use Activities Demanding Rehabilitation Considerations
A Comprehensive List?

The degree of disturbance, degradation or dereliction depends largely on the land use activity, its practices and procedures, how long it has been operative, and the recuperative ability (with or without human stimulation) of the local environment to reinstate natural conditions. Let us look first then at the activities which have caused most harm to our landscape.

Chemically Contaminated Landscapes

Today we use more toxic materials, have created more synthetic noxious products and as a result produce more contaminated waste products than any other civilization in history. Some 35,000 of those used in the United States are classified by the Federal Environmental Protection Agency as being either definitely or potentially hazardous to human health.[9] The inauguration of "the good life" has inadvertently produced the disposal problem of chemical compounds, liquid and solid, which are not very easily reducible to a neutral state by normal environmental conditions.

In the past, discharge of small amounts of these materials into lakes, rivers and seas, and percolation below the ground surface in deep wells, shallow reservoirs and directly onto the soil surface was accepted and "seemed" to do little harm. Increasing concentration and the slow decay period of such toxic wastes have changed all that. The list of harmful effects of such discharges on soil, crop growth, ground and surface water qualities is horrifying enough, but the recently documented impact on human beings, including birth defects in the unborn generation, have indicated that sincere attention to disposal of chemical wastes is long overdue. The indictment of publicized sites such as Elizabeth, New Jersey and Love Canal, Buffalo, New York, can be multiplied a thousandfold in the North American continent.

Canada, too, has its "time bombs." Inadequate surface and shallow subsurface disposal of atomic wastes in at least two sites in Ontario has forced the government into compensatory payments, purchase of affected lands and homes and wholesale shipping of the contaminated soils for "safe" burial elsewhere. Even the time-honoured sanitary landfill disposal techniques are no longer unquestioned. Enforced school and home evacuation due to methane gas buildups and migration through the subsurface in Kitchener, Ontario, is only one example of constrained land use due to ineffective disposal techniques. In the summer of 1980, the Ontario Environment Ministry initiated a crash program to reexamine 190 known sanitary landfill sites. Contamination of formerly clean subsurface wellwater by leachate is becoming an increasing problem in urban fringe locations. Rehabilitation of such problems may never achieve complete success and is incredibly costly. Perhaps the greatest impasse in land rehabilitation today concerns this area of chemically contaminated land. Throwing money at the problem and using outdated and ineffective technologies is no longer acceptable to the public. A massive research effort is required immediately in this area.

A further distinction between chemical dump areas and sanitary landfill sites is that the latter will probably involve some landform change. The possibility of creative landscape architecture for producing a new landscape which is both aesthetically pleasing and functionally useful (e.g., parkland, ski hills) is an attractive but still elusive goal.

We in Canada have been lucky to have avoided the nuclear holocausts of Bikini and other Pacific Atolls which have so completely refuted the recent U.S. land rehabilitation and resettlement attempts or the several centuries of industrial revolution and decay which contaminated and indeed sterilized so much of the landscape of the Black Country of the U.K. But with the recent revelations in North America, we have no cause for complacency!

Surface Mining Industry

Until the advent of the previously described activities, surface mining was the traditional *bête noir* of land degrading activities.

Surface Mining of Coal

Perhaps the focus of much of the early public wrath was the wanton destruction of Appalachian landscapes due to contour strip mining of coal. The practice shown in Figure 1.7 (while often leaving the vast bulk of the coal untapped because current technology/machinery was unable to remove the increasing thickness of overburden covering the commercial coal seam), caused (a) sterilization of the use of the hilltops by their being rendered inaccessible, (b) the production of relatively restricted flat areas of coal debris and subsurface rock now highly acid and without weathered material or topsoil to enhance rehabilitation possibilities, (c) steep valley sides covered by dumped debris, and (d) valley bottoms and streams choked by overloaded silt and sediments. New attitudes towards stewardship, conservation ethics and environmental consciousness have combined with greater public involvement to ensure that this situation will no longer be tolerated. One of the most influential of all public statements was the 1967 U.S. Department of the Interior Report which pointed out that the United States had by 1965 1.3 million ha of land disturbed by surface mining.[10] In addition, the concern over the West as the last bastion of relatively untouched wilderness and its huge reserves of easily accessible coal has seen a flood of environmental control and regulatory rehabilitation impositions undreamed of in the early sixties. In the West where acidity and occasionally toxic sodic subsoil conditions create additional difficulties, rehabilitation methodology and success have made admirable progress in the last ten years. Personal observations at Colstrip, Montana, revealed progressive rehabilitation programs based on thorough preplanning inventories which allow very close approximation to the original landscape conditions. The most telltale feature of rehabilitated land surfaces is often the greener, more lush conditions of vegetation enriched by nonindigenous species.

The ultimate in huge-scale rehabilitation is in the West German lignite fields of the Cologne-Aachen-Dusseldorf triangle. From five huge opencast mines, 130 million tons of coal are produced. Rheinbraun, the coal company, works hand in hand with government and local authorities, and has worked over 18,833 ha of land, of this 12,675 have been reclaimed, 5,591 to forests for recreation, 5,445 to agricultural activities, 700 to artificial lakes and ponds, seven of which are now available for fishing and water sports. In all of this an integrative approach which ensures appropriate compensation and settlement for the 25,000 persons already affected is used in long-term planning.[11] Perhaps such integrated efforts where government, industry, and local authorities work together for the public interest is an appropriate lesson for the North American future.

Ore Mining

Problems of dereliction and rehabilitation with mining tend to be highly localized. In Canada, the geological formation of the Laurentian or Canadian Shield has led to the vast majority of our mines, although not all are of the surface variety. Where open ore mines exist (Falconbridge, Sudbury), they are often deep and restricted in extent with 6- to 10- metre galleries or steps of decreasing radius down to depths of several hundred metres. This poses special problems and restrictions on rehabilitation possibilities. The inadequacy of preexisting topsoil and the increased surface area created through mining, and the likelihood of penetrating regional groundwater tables, severely constrain future "land use" possibilities.

In areas degraded by ore mining activity much of the research attention has focussed on the tailings or waste debris left after removal of the commercial metals and minerals. This is frequently an infertile, if not highly acidic and even toxic material. On the optimistic side, it can easily form landscapes of suitable scale and slope for many subsequent uses. Its revegetation has been problematic, but has benefited from extensive research by many individuals and agencies. One of the most successful and enterprising efforts has been that of T. Peters and the International Nickel Company (INCO) at Coppercliff/Sudbury, Ontario.[12] Here decades of open ore roasting and chemically contaminated rains have resulted in a "moonscape of barren rock." The ore refining process resulted in a slurry of mine tailings which then had to be disposed of. The drying out of this material created a barren wasteland subject to blowing conditions resembling desert dust storms. After numerous unsuccessful efforts, INCO, by keeping the water table high and the tailings moist, by using copious applications of fertilizer, and by establishing rye/grass vegetation, has successfully stabilized the surface. Commercial cropping, natural woodland successions and the reentry of wildlife species have all occurred. Soil horizons with humus layering prove that even inert materials can be rehabilitated. Apart from the successful technology involved, one of the most exciting prospects of the project (now with more than a thousand hectares rehabilitated) is the potential land-use contribution the aesthetically pleasing prairie-like landscape can make to the city of Sudbury, where steep rocky hills make most urban land uses prohibitively expensive.[13]

The Aggregates Industry

Like other surface mining industries, the sand and gravel and quarry stone (aggregate) extractive industries normally effect a considerable change in landscape configuration. It is in consequence not possible to consider the NAS restoration definition, but rather to consider some form of rehabilitation. Again the activity is concentrated where the deposits exist in nature and local impacts can have extensive far-reaching results. In Figure 2.7, the progress and scale of extraction for aggregate materials can be seen over a twenty-year period in Uxbridge township, Ontario. Here one complex glacial landform, the Oakridges Interlobate moraine, provides the resource base. While not necessarily the best of aggregate deposits,[14] its location closer to the huge Metro Toronto market (consuming 35–40 million tons of construction aggregates per annum) than any alternative sources gives it a market advantage.

Naturally occurring sand and gravel and crushed stone aggregates,

Figure 2.7

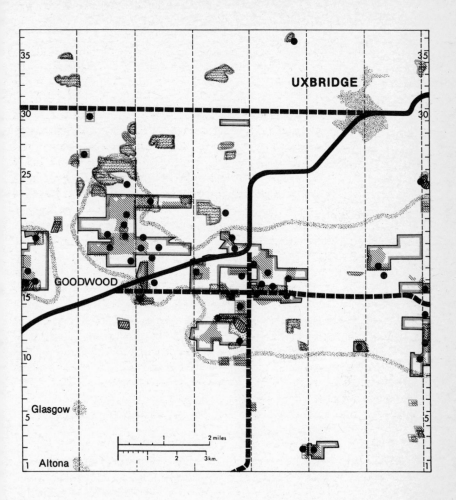

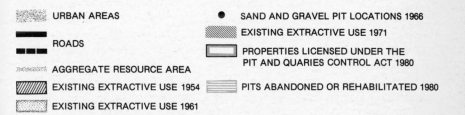

URBAN AREAS

● SAND AND GRAVEL PIT LOCATIONS 1966

EXISTING EXTRACTIVE USE 1971

ROADS

PROPERTIES LICENSED UNDER THE
PIT AND QUARIES CONTROL ACT 1980

AGGREGATE RESOURCE AREA

PITS ABANDONED OR REHABILITATED 1980

EXISTING EXTRACTIVE USE 1954

EXISTING EXTRACTIVE USE 1961

while properly considered as surface-mined resources, have distinctive characteristics which demand different resource use policies and rehabilitation objectives. McLellan outlines the differences in this way:

The excavations produced are frequently shallow—rarely more than 50–60 ft. in depth—and therefore the industry is an extensive land user with a major surface impact—the commodities produced, sand, gravel and crushed rock are bulky, low cost and not easy to transport, most of the production tends to be oriented very closely around its urban markets. ... This unlike the hard rock mining operations of northern Ontario means expansion in S. Ontario—the most populated and extensively used part of this province. The aggregate industry therefore operates in a very competitive and high priced land use market. ... This is the crux of the aggregate industry crisis in Ontario; increased public awareness and concern for the quality of the environment, particularly that on the doorsteps of urban municipalities has resulted in a decreasing availability of reserves for an industry engaged ... in expansion to meet public demands—an interesting conflict of interests.[15]

The urban fringe localities of most pits and quarries demand an immediacy of solution not just because of high visibility and public activity, but also because of rapidity of extraction processes, shorter life, urban expansion market potential, and competitive land use alternatives. Normally toxicity and ground water contamination problems will not be involved, and conditions are perfect for creative landscape shaping to dovetail with future intended uses. It is probably true that in many parts of actively expanding urban Canada the rehabilitated land has produced a net market value exceeding the profits from the longer term sales of the aggregate resources from the site. Rehabilitation in this case is not just a result of government and public pressure. Marketability and economic benefits are becoming uppermost in developers' minds.

In a recent study of the after-use fate of former aggregate extraction sites in the rapidly expanding Metro Toronto, the authors found for a change some reassuring and positive evidence. Of 67 sites investigated 34 percent are now used for recreation, 27 percent for residential purposes, 13 percent are educational or institutional uses, 10 percent are used by industry, 8 percent for commercial purposes, 5 percent are sanitary landfill sites and the remaining 3 percent is land now seeded, cropped and left in open space.[16]

The three types of surface mining discussed above and the chemical contamination of landscapes are our major sources of degraded land requiring rehabilitation. However, many other activities have landscape impacts demanding attention and specific rehabilitation responses.

Pipelines and Exploration
In Canada, pipeline construction, largely for oil and gas transport but also for water, utilities and sewage, unfortunately has created a not entirely

invisible network across the land. So much more important then that we consider our errors before implementing the huge networks contemplated in bringing our oil and gas resources from untapped Arctic and East Coast areas to the markets. Any one who has investigated air photos of our land surface can readily pick out such pipeline routes—permanent linear swathes cut through wooded areas, left hopefully to be encroached on by natural reforestation. All too often the precious topsoil is not separated from the infertile overburden and in the infilling process is subsequently buried. (Farmers too might have less complaints about fertility loss.) Simple techniques such as this and greater preplanning, coupled with backhoe ripping of soils, soil preparation and speedy ground cover reestablishment and avoiding compaction by heavy equipment present a commonsense solution which has too infrequently been used in the past.

Another activity which we should concern ourselves with is oil and mineral exploration. Few of us (while walking in the supposed isolated wilderness of the Canadian Shield, the Rocky Mountains or the High Arctic) have not come across evidence of survey lines, past exploration camps, dumps and other visually repellent scenes of past and often brief periods of human exploration activity. In such environments with slow regenerative rates or precarious and fragile fertility, recovery is a slow process which a little thought could expedite. Without regulatory explicitness it appears such thoughtlessness will persist, a small reminder of the importance of legislation, despite its bureaucratic burdens, to protect us from ourselves, and why more sensitized legislation which stimulates acceptable and creative rehabilitative practice will be one of the most productive and necessary areas of research in the near future.

"Acceptable" Degrading Practices?

Some activities which we condone as eminently important in our everyday lives can clearly have derogatory landscape impacts without good management practice and rehabilitative technique. We have already mentioned degraded farm and rangeland. Our stewards and husbanders of the majority of our land surface sometimes have more in common with their "coal mining" cousins than they care to admit.

Our recreation activities which we find so energizing, refreshing or relaxing can frequently have disastrous consequences on our land surfaces. Four-wheel drive, all-terrain vehicles, and "dune and marsh buggies" permit access to ecosystems which are in no respect tolerant of these activities. In the United States, particularly severe disturbances have been found due to off-road vehicle use around such modern mining boomtowns as Rock Springs, Wyoming, and Vernal, Utah. Related vegetation disturbance and increased sediment load in nearby rivers is perhaps greater than that caused by the mining operations themselves.[17]

The concern of those interested in park management over acceptable carrying capacities, vandalism, habitat destruction, and loss of specific interpretive trail opportunities due to excessive pedestrian traffic is symptomatic of the loss of human opportunities and decrease in personal satisfaction when specific scenic, ecological or recreational resources become degraded. With so much focus of public activity in such designated parks there is no doubt that rehabilitation will become a recurrent and ongoing preoccupation of park managers.

Urban Expansion and Alteration

While planners have for many years decried the exploitative, wasteful aspects of urban growth and designed green belts and zoning policies to curb it, it is rare that landscapes, their redesign and the land-uses they are to provide are thought of in a comprehensive way.[18]

Even steep slopes that provide alpine skiing opportunities require grooming and reshaping. Similarly, when a subdivision is planned the natural topographic expression often requires considerable transformation. This form of regrading is significant in that it is instrumental in providing an appropriate landscape for the intended use. It may be fruitful therefore to examine a fairly typical subdivision development from this perspective. (Figure 3.7)

In this kame-moraine the sands and gravels were easy to remove. No glacial till areas (difficult to remove and expensive to reshape, therefore often left intact by the prudent developer with adequate preplanning information) exist. Similarly, the ground water table lies well beneath the development zone and no swampy pockets exist (usually difficult to drain, expensive to infill, easily impacted by surrounding development and therefore often, not necessarily on good planning principles, left intact to meet municipal open space requirements, despite the fact they hardly satisfy the recreational open space objectives the bylaw anticipated).

The reasons for the preferred slopes (Figure 3.7B) become immediately apparent. Two to six degree slopes provide (a) adequate drainage; (b) suitable terrain for minimum cost constuction; (c) slope angles appropriate for safe driving road gradients in central in Canada's icy winters; and (d) avoidance of the other problems presented by the nonpreferred slopes (0-5° provide inadequate drainage slopes, in excess of 10° produce problems for safe handling of mechanized equipment and are excessively expensive in terms of cut and fill requirements. At the extreme, such steep slopes (Figure 3.7B) may be left intact, often with their original vegetation intact for public enjoyment.

Geomorphologists might well turn their knowledge of foundation materials and slope stabilities to questions posed by the developer and planner. Their absence from this creative area of landscape rehabilitation design will see the loss of this exciting potential in their discipline to help resolve the problems of others. Engineers, landscape architects and planners are beginning to become aware of the challenges.

Figure 3.7

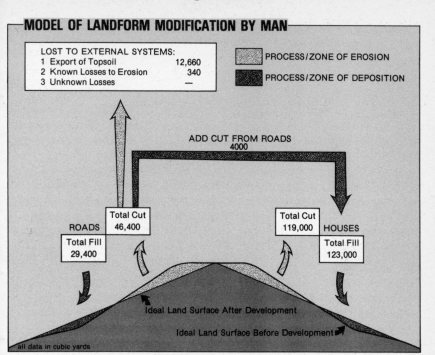

MODEL OF LANDFORM MODIFICATION BY MAN

LOST TO EXTERNAL SYSTEMS:
1 Export of Topsoil   12,660
2 Known Losses to Erosion   340
3 Unknown Losses   —

PROCESS/ZONE OF EROSION

PROCESS/ZONE OF DEPOSITION

ADD CUT FROM ROADS
4000

ROADS

Total Cut
46,400

Total Fill
29,400

Total Cut
119,000

HOUSES

Total Fill
123,000

Ideal Land Surface After Development

Ideal Land Surface Before Development

all data in cubic yards

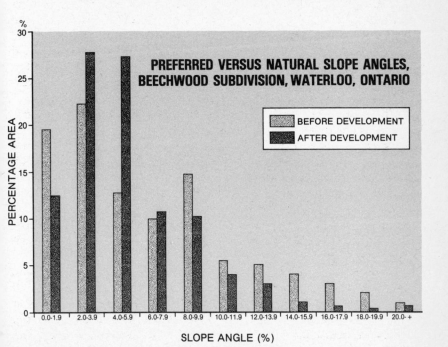

PREFERRED VERSUS NATURAL SLOPE ANGLES, BEECHWOOD SUBDIVISION, WATERLOO, ONTARIO

BEFORE DEVELOPMENT

AFTER DEVELOPMENT

PERCENTAGE AREA

SLOPE ANGLE (%)

It may not be too farfetched to suggest that the extensive hectares of land banked, often for many years, for speculative purposes amounts to a dereliction condition. Farming, if it continues at all, is sporadic or rapacious. The knowledge that the land will soon be developed does not engender quality farming practices. The land often lies idle and slowly returns to a scrubby unkept appearance while vandalism and decay and often outright destruction see the loss of farm buildings. Could temporary rehabilitation for recreation open space be a more acceptable alternative? Can planners find some way of overcoming questions of liability, and public interference that in the minds of developers preclude this form of temporary rehabilitation?

While new urban expansion creates exciting challenges, the inner areas of cities are also the subject of rehabilitation questions. Restoration of historically significant structures, period houses and grand estates has long been an estabished practice. The Grange in Toronto, Louisville in Nova Scotia, Hudson's Bay and RCMP posts in the West, are only some examples. However, with aging inner cities, consequent decay, loss of function and obsolescence, the absence of true social and entertainment stimulus, on the one hand and the spending power of the wealthy young single on the other, the value of central downtown urban locations has seen an awakened interest in the rehabilitation of old buildings and "downtown" spaces.

Whole blocks of urban properties, particularly former factories whose functions had run their course, have suddenly been rehabilitated for restaurants, disco dance spots and bars. Nearby properties have been converted into parking facilities to handle the new-found popularity. Montreal's "Vielle Ville," Toronto's O'Keefe Centre area, and Vancouver's Gas Town are all good examples. Other properties, many originally residential, have been "brownstoned" (a term used to describe the rehabilitation process of brownstone tenements in New York, Brooklyn, Boston and elsewhere). People tired of the wearisome daily commuter flights to the suburbs have become aware of a return to pleasant living and the renewed excitement of the city core.

Decay, obsolescence and dereliction of old industrial sites, mill buildings, railway yards, dock frontages, and their resulting decrease in real estate value combined with an often convenient and highly accessible location have made many prime targets for revitalization through the rehabilitation process. Toronto's Harbourfront with light opera lunches, pleasant walks, parks and restaurants, craft centres and new hotels, condominiums and shopping areas is being transformed. The process of urban rehabilitation is still in its infancy.

Road, railway and canal systems, pipeline and power utility corridors have performed tasks in the past, but perhaps we can add new life to them. They provide linear corridors often traversing the superimposed myriad of street blocks and private properties that destroy free nonvehicle movements throught cities. Would recreation and exercise activities, jogging, bicycling and walking prevent their functions to continue? Would rehabilitation through multiple use and some redesign provide a range of activities easily available to the public without great additional costs in land purchases? In days of economic constraint, and government difficulty in providing further park/open space opportunities, creative rehabilitative exercises on such properties provide a worthwhile challenge. Considerations such as these suggest that multiple-purpose activity and the achievement of higher productivity and usage are basic concepts in the question of rehabilitation.

Highway Construction

A vast land-use which causes extensive disturbance but does not evoke the frightening prospects of surface mining is road construction. Clearly any new highway development withdraws land from other uses. The resulting scars have to be regraded and revegetated. This is not always successfully done. Despite the well-established geomorphology of highway slope design, the number of slope failures, choked drainage areas, degraded and dead woodland associated with highways is surprising. The different degree of rehabilitative success can be readily observed when moving from job to job or jurisdiction to jurisdiction. The amount of land which is "sterilized" from other uses by our highway networks is staggering. Perhaps it is not too much to hope that more creative thinking might go into rehabilitation considerations at the preplanning stage, rather than to wait until the errors become obvious and in ecological respects irreversible.

The Scale of Land Degrading Activities

Given the diversity of land degrading activities and the disparate jurisdictions under which they are "controlled," it is perhaps understandable that no federal or provincial body has ever attempted a comprehensive survey of derelict land and the progress or otherwise of its rehabilitation.

This section cannot remedy this omission—hopefully the various Canadian provincial governments will see the value of such documentation in the near future. However, some data will be presented in order to give the reader a more refined picture of the scale of the various activities.

Some U.S. Information

In March 1978, the Presidents of the American Society of Agronomy, the Crop Science Society of America and the Soil Science Society of America were able to report that in "the United States alone, over 1.76 million hectares of land have been disturbed by surface mining, about half of this by coal mines. Every year about 40,470 hectares of land are disturbed by coal mining. It is estimated that over 10.8 million additional hectares of land can be stripmined for coal . . . over 10.5 million additional hectares of land have been used for rural transportation right-of-ways. Approximately 27,000 hectares of land are required each year to handle the dredged material for waterways."[19] If scale is a determining factor in developing priorities for research and problem resolution, we need look no further!

In a U.S. Bureau of Mines 1931–1971 survey the domestic minerals industry in that period utilized 1.48 million ha, while 591,000 ha (40 percent) was reclaimed. In 1971 alone 83,000 ha were utilized and 66,000 ha were reclaimed. Thus the ratio between land used and reclaimed doubled in 1971 compared to the ratio for the 41-year period.[20]

These figures avoid definitional problems of degree of rehabilitation and its success. The U.S. Bureau of Mines clearly has no interest or authority over the other forms of degrading activity mentioned in the previous sections, but we may yet be appreciative of the increased regulatory powers of the seventies in avoiding unacceptible practices in the increased consumption of coal-bearing lands in the eighties.

Of particular significance to Canadians in the next decade might be a survey conducted by Brown, Johnston and Van Cleve. They were interested in Arctic and Alpine rehabilitation problems and in trying to define the nature and extent of the problem. A U.S.-wide survey was undertaken of all land management agencies known to administer tundra lands. Responses revealed that the following are the major causes of land disturbance: (i) grazing; (ii) recreation, including trail campsite and trampling disturbances; (iii) mining past and present, and mineral exploration sites, construction sites; (iv) roads, and off-road vehicle disturbances; (v) pipelines; (vi) powerlines; (vii) reservoirs; (viii) other causes such as fire and landslides. Note the perhaps unexpected diversity of disturbing activities and the precedence of grazing and recreation! Of the approximately 2.9 × 10^6 of alpine tundra in the western United States, almost 12 percent has been disturbed and requires rehabilitation.[21]

The most alarming disclosure of the Alpine survey is the apparent lack of regard by land managers for disturbed alpine land. In a few cases, land managers are totally unaware that tundra ecosystems even exist within their areas of responsibility. The major concern, perhaps understandably, seems to be for resources of high economic return, such as timber and rangelands. It seems absolutely essential that the watershed, wildlife habitat, aesthetic, and other values of tundra environments in both Alpine and Arctic regions be managed with the same degree of concern given other resources.[22]

Derelict Land in Canada

The disarray of information is quickly recognized when assessing the Canadian picture. In 1973, McLellan reported that all of the debates concerning surface mining impacts have characteristically suffered from the lack of any precise data on the impact of mining on the landscape.[23] To the writer's knowledge, no data have ever been produced nor any Canadian report ever published indicating the relative or absolute acreage of land injured by these so-called degrading activities. It is for these reasons that a pilot survey was undertaken in Waterloo County. Further objectives were to evaluate and implement a simple methodology which could be used to produce an inventory of derelict land in Ontario, and to assess the relative importance of the various derelict land-producing processes and the potential efficiency of the new government ordinance aimed at terminating this abuse of land.

The survey revealed that 360 ha of this prosperous fertile agricultural part of southern Ontario were abandoned and in a derelict condition. A further 800 ha are being used in ways which could add to this acreage. Surface mining (for aggregate materials) has been the major cause of land dereliction in Waterloo County (93 percent of occurrences and 78 percent of acreage). Without entering into the general merits or drawbacks of the Ontario Pits and Quarries Control Act, several notable omissions emerged from the evidence of this study. The multiplicity of extraction sites clearly presents a problem to the land-use planner. The abandoned pit sites average a little over 2 ha, clearly limiting rehabilitation alternatives. Not only this, but they are completely outside the authority of the legislation which applies only to pits licensed at present.

Another significant point is that 71 percent of all abandoned pits in the county are visible from the road. In a county where tourism and pleasure driving are significant income sources, should this be tolerated? The indefinite legal responsibility and costs involved in rehabilitating 127 abandoned pits suggest that only direct action and subsidy by provincial authorities will lead to significant improvement.

Newer operations are larger and less numerous. Trends in this direction with concomitant greater planning control of progressive, more financially sound units will hopefully ease past problems. In 1979 the Ontario government released plans designed to "clean up" the legacy of past abandonment.[24]

Other such localized studies exist but the data base is still woefully inadequate. Thirgood recognized this and along with other correspondents attempted to achieve some comprehensive vision of the "Extent of Disturbed Land and Major Reclamation Problems in Canada."[25] They found that in eastern Canada the main problem is the extent and difficulties in rehabilitating coal mine wastes. Generally, low pH values make revegetation difficult. At Minto and Sydney, coal mine wastes with a pH below 4 are not self-revegetated and attempts at planting have not succeeded. In some cases, heavy sulphide concentrations have resulted in pH values of 2-0, which are toxic to any vegetative growth. At Knob Lake, Quebec, there are thirteen major iron ore open pits, some down to 200 metres below surface, and there are over 50 rock dumps frequently over 50 metres high. Elsewhere, disruption of the land surface is less spectacular. Land affected by iron mining in hectares is as follows: open pits, 1,260; tailings, 790; and rock wastes, 930. In Labrador at Carol Lake and Wabush, tailings disposal is into lakes, but elsewhere it is on land. Tailings dams occupy appreciable areas. At Gaspé the three tailings dams cover 780 ha, while the remaining mines have sulphide tailings over a total of about 320 ha. As the acid mine drainage from certain base metal mines, particularly in New Brunswick, would contaminate the drainage system unless controlled, collection systems treat all water before it leaves the property.

The waste from gypsum operations is the unconsolidated overburden of glacial origin. It is the only type of mining where broken or finely crushed rock is not part of the mining waste. Gypsum quarries and waste dumps occupy about 1,000 ha in eastern Canada.

While the reclamation results are considered encouraging, they appear to be simply geared at revegetation, with pine plantations dominating (Jack, Red and Scots pine) and some ground cover successes with white dutch, sweet clover and bird's-foot trefoil. The long-term success and commercial competitiveness of such rehabilitation sites has not yet been assessed. The opportunities for other land uses (recreation, urban expansion and agriculture) do not seem to have been considered as real possibilities. Perhaps it should be in the light of a broader assessment that the success or otherwise of rehabilitation efforts in Canada should be viewed.

In Ontario, the problems seem to be divided between the effects of hardrock mining in the north (Canadian Shield) and aggregate extractive industries in the south (southern Ontario lowlands). In the latter it would be safe to say that Ontario has taken a leadership role in North America in promoting progressive rehabilitation methods in aggregate operations.

In southern Saskatchewan in 1975 Anderson et al. reported 4,300 ha of severe disturbance due to strip mining with an annual rate of increase of 150–280 ha/year. Prior to 1973, areas stripped had a "surface configuration of chaotic to parallel ridges or interconnected cones with steep slopes and open pits. Natural revegetation, although its quality is not stated, has occurred on only 16 percent of the area but selectively on the best low sodium and salinity loamy areas."[26]

In Alberta altitudinal, topographical, climatic and other aspects of environmental diversity result in at least ten ecological zones. Our current knowledge of rehabilitation technique is probably too crude to adequately respond with a set of guidelines or practices to deal with them all in a sophisticated manner. We are still in the stage of trial and error. Indeed some researchers complain that "unfortunately, applied research is rapidly outdistancing its needed support from basic research."[27]

One of the peculiarly Albertan problems is the spectre of a hugely expanded oil sands problem. "It has been estimated that with a production target of one million barrels of crude oil per day, approximately 1,000 ha of land will have to be cleared every year, most of the disturbed areas eventually must be vegetated again; these include the overburden piles and the tailings sand. In vegetating such areas several problems such as salinity, low fertility, erosion and unfavourable soil reactions have to be contended with. There has been some success in the general vegetation program on the Great Canadian Oil Sands Ltd. lease, but the problems listed above still have to be studied and solutions for them found."[28] The emphasis in the recommendations of this report on ground cover, native indigenous species and fertilizer application emphasize the decreased opportunities for rehabilitation compared with the sand and gravel sites of southern Ontario.

In British Columbia attention is again drawn to the differing requirements of the diverse biogeoclimatic zones.[29] While an attempt has been made to establish general reclamation criteria and standards, personal observations of indifferent success compared with Ontario have been recently echoed by Thirgood who cited a "failure to establish satisfactory standards, adequate enforcement or staffing and technical expertise."[30]

The main activities have concentrated in the "Coal block" areas of southeastern British Columbia. Particular significance is attached to rehabilitation efforts because the grass shrub communities there support large wildlife populations (deer, bighorn sheep and elk). It has already been found that well rehabilitated and successfully revegetated spoil heaps with their flat surfaces being relatively uncommon in that topographical region become local feeding focii. In addition, watershed values are vital to the continuance and well-being of the important sport fishery industry on such rivers as the Columbia.

In northern Canada permafrost conditions have demanded special adaptations even to machinery. "Mushroom shoes" allow bulldozer blades to scrape up trash and debris without destroying fragile underlying vegetation mats. In heavily trafficked areas, thick layers of gravel or wood chips are used to protect ground surfaces and provide for thermal stability.

Responses to Rehabilitation
Researchers and Their Roles

As with many contemporary environmental problems, it is clear that the issues involved in rehabilitation research do not dwell within any one discipline. Colloquia, where scientists (physical and social) and experts from diverse fields can come together and talk about mutual interests, are frequent. A few examples are The Derelict Land Symposium, University of Leeds, U.K. 1969; Mid Atlantic Regional Conference on Surface Mined Lands for Outdoor Recreation—sponsored by the Bureau of Outdoor Recreation, NE Office Bureau of Mines and Pennsylvania State University,

1973; International Symposium on the Recovery and Restoration of Damaged Ecosystems, 1975 and 1977, Virginia Polytechnic and State University; Municipal Waste Water and Sludge Recycling on Forestry and Disturbed Land Symposium, Pennsylvania State University, 1977; Reclamation of Western Surface Mined Lands, 1976, Colorado State University; and the Annual Conference of the New Canadian Land Reclamation Association. The U.S. Congress has had an annual conference on Surface Mining Control and the Reclamation Act since 1977. Major geographical associations now include frequent special sessions in their regional and national meetings. New journals, "Canadian Land Reclamation" 1975— and "Minerals and the Environment" 1979—provide publication outlets for specialists in rehabilitation research.

The 1976 symposium on the "Reclamation of Drastically Disturbed Lands," so widely used in this chapter, was sponsored by no less than ten different agencies (American Society of Agronomy, Crop Science, Soil Science and Soil Conservation Societies of America, the American Society of Agricultural Engineers, the Societies of American Foresters and for Range Management, the U.S. Environmental Protection Agency and the Ohio Agricultural Reserach and Development Center. The experts who attended could be classified as follows—soil scientists of all sorts, agronomists, foresters and plant physiologists, hydrologists and sanitation scientists and engineers (civil, chemical, water resources, soil, agricultural and mining), geologists, industrial and agricultural economists, remote sensing experts, resource managers, irrigation, park and range specialists, conservationists, planners and civil servants, landscape architects, surface mining specialists and scientific officers for private coal companies. The preponderance of technological scientists was obvious, but it is often universities and academics who provide the venue for the discussions— perhaps the basic academic research will yet get done!

Regardless of how the work is done it is clear that it should: (a) have comprehensive goals, (b) be integrative and transcend narrow disciplinary boundaries, (c) be cognizant of governmental and public concerns in its implementational strategies, (d) not ignore true analysis of the important questions of short- and longterm cost/benefit analysis, (e) bring the results and problems of research into the hands of appropriate persons in industry, government and public areas, as well as "academic" journals.

Government Involvement and Legislation

Government has a role to educate as well as to govern. Stimulation of research through the provision of funds and facilities, design of provincial and national policies, and the determination of minimum acceptance standards of rehabilitation performance are all important. It is clear that there is a large and growing diverse body of scientists willing to undertake appropriate studies! The design and passing of suitable regulatory controls and enforcement procedures is another area of concern. Do security rehabilitation deposits work better than the posting of performance bonds? Are the imposition of fines or penalty closures justified and effective? What other measures can be considered? Comparative assessments of different control mechanisms could be an effective government research exercise.[31]

A major question for private companies revolves around the approvals process. Legitimate environmental constraints and public involvement have enormously protracted this process. Rapidly rising sophistication of research and related costs increase private enterprise anxieties. With some legitimacy they feel that the deck may be stacked against them. Will they be provided with a fair hearing? Does investment of time, money and effort assure a normal progression towards approval? In Canada the onus of proving minimal impact rests with the applicant. However, with local authority and zoning decisions being separated from licensing/approval procedures the risks are perceived as high. Corporate complaints suggest a bewildering multiplicity of overlapping government controls.

In Alberta the Land Surface Conservation Regulation Act 1972, in the Northwest Territories the Territorial Lands Act 1971, in Ontario the Mining Act 1970 and the Pits and Quarries Control Act in 1971, are the most pertinent legislation. However, in all provinces other acts and specific planning regulations can have great import. For example, in Ontario the Niagara Escarpment Commission has control over an extensive area of mineral resources. The Environmental Protection Act provides some guidelines. Local areas have some jurisdiction for protecting environmentally sensitive and heritage areas, as do federal statutes. Perhaps new regulatory control should have as an objective streamlining the approvals examination process without removing its sensitivity.

Special Roles for the Public, Politicians and the Planner

The Public

In North America resource decisions are now of great interest to the public. Any government or private development proposal which does not permit public participation usually is doomed to a stormy passage. Unlike forestry and agriculture which may in fact perpetuate very harmful processes and effects but are considered directly beneficial to our human and economic condition, surface mining is not perceived as vital to any individual, and the total disruption of such mining, especially in the past where rehabilitation efforts have been mere tokenism, has caused greatest outcry. The result is that the public no longer feels protected by the scrutiny of appropriate governmental agencies. Individual members of the public who have concern about direct or indirect effects of mining on their lifestyle demand their "day in court" as objectors or participants. Groups occasionally hire experts and lawyers to present their "concerned citizens" viewpoint. At another level public organized bodies speak to major policy decisions and guidelines for operational control. Many reviews of statements by public bodies can be found, only one is quoted here.

In regard to a "Federal Regulatory Program," the Sierra Club (1973) states:
Given industry and government's shallow commitment to total reclamation, the absence of federal or state land use planning, the absence of federal law and state enforcement of existing laws, and the primitive state of existing technology, it is not unreasonable to conclude that strip mining should be prohibited. Perhaps not for all time and in all places, but prohibited until there exist even the most rudimentary means of making strip miners accountable to a broader public standard of care and caution.

Short of total prohibition the federal government should:
—Phase out contour strip mining on steep slopes.
—Apply a moratorium to new strip mines pending a determination of where reclamation is possible or feasible and capable of being enforced.
—Establish comprehensive land use and energy policies.
—Provide for citizen participation in the environmental regulations of coal strip mining.
—Establish a nationwide program for orphan (abandoned or completed operations) mine reclamation.
—Develop incentives for research and development of environmentally sound underground mining methods.
—Reassess coal export policies.
—Prohibit government purchases of strip-mined coal.[32]

So far these groups have probably made less concrete and innovative suggestions concerning rehabilitation than the experts mentioned previously. With more experience, more organization and the increasing acceptance of public participation this could change. The difficult question of the conflict between private or greater public interests remains.

The Politician

With such an angry outburst of public emotion, the "uncharacteristic" enthusiasm with which politicians have been prepared to act should not surprise us. Legislative control spread as fast as any bushfire and will continue to be amended. Perhaps it is now time for sanity. Should companies which have demonstrated a track record of commendable rehabilitation be dealt with in the same way as those who have consistently left a trail of dereliction and refused to live up to previous agreements? Should stepped progressive rehabilitation programs be mandatory for continued extraction permits in the long term? When are so-called "public interests" just as private and self-serving as those of the developers? What research should government sponsor and how should private corporations contribute? Some of these questions may not have the emotional or vote-gathering attraction of the "environmental bandwagon" of the past few years, but they are probably more important in creating an innovative and pragmatic future! In the West German example, the government has recognized that the national significance of the resource and the disruptions caused to the environment and lifestyles of the people demand *cooperative* rather than adversary roles between bureaucracy and business!

The Planner

Planners have not been highly responsive to the innovative challenges of surface mining and rehabilitation. In a general way, two features could account for this surprising lack of necessary leadership from the profession. Firstly, many professional planners act in an advisory and permission-granting role similar to government. Given the unpopularity of landscape reshaping uses—sanitary landfill, pits and quarries, coal mines—it has not been an attractive prospect for planners to deal with. The profession with its incredible overload of ongoing zoning and permissions work has not undertaken any considerable amount of research. Indeed, the detailed knowledge of underground reserves and physical environmental conditions is normally outside the expertise of planners and is often the priviliged information of the developer. With this background in mind and the anti-environmental and nonrehabilitative past track records of surface mining, it is hardly surprising that planners rarely show enthusiasm for incorporating adequate provisions for future mineral supplies in official plans.

From a professional viewpoint, two other difficulties make such applications difficult to handle. Firstly, the life period of mining sites often exceeds the 25-year life of most official plans. Also the economic vagaries of our contemporary world make future projections difficult. Secondly, zoning—the "universal instrument" of planning technique—refers to the use of the land surface. Surface mining involves consideration of the use of the subsurface. Legal and practical difficulties exist for interim uses which may cause only temporary disruption of the pre-existing land uses. Questions of multiple resource use, interim zoning, and implementation of progressive rehabilitation planning may suggest that here lies a series of questions worthy of the research role of the profession. Any clear innovative role by the profession would be a refreshing change according to Canadian developers long used to negativism and obstacles rather than creativity.

Rehabilitation: Types, Techniques and Creative Possibilities
A Concerted Effort? Errors and Progress

In a remarkable series of instructional booklets designed to improve "Mining and Reclamation in the West," and published by the Surface,

Figure 4.7

LANDFORM MODIFICATION

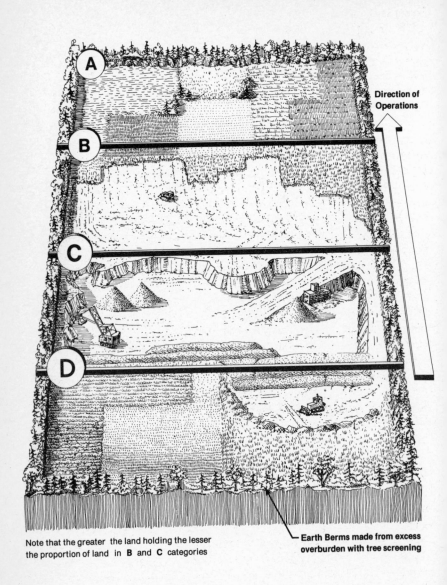

Direction of Operations

Note that the greater the land holding the lesser the proportion of land in **B** and **C** categories

Earth Berms made from excess overburden with tree screening

(A) Land in agricultural use as yet untouched

(B) Land being stripped of overburden/topsoil transferred to area **D** for renewed agricultural use

(C) Land containing actual active face, plant/equipment for removal of aggregate materials

(D) Land which has been extracted, now being regraded with topsoil transferred from area **B** for renewed agricultural use

Environment and Mining (SEAM) Program of the U.S.D.A. Forest Service—User Guides to "Engineering," "Vegetation," "Reclaiming Small Tailings Ponds & Dumps" and to "Soils," the following quotation is found. "The long-standing premise that mineral activity is always the most valuable use of a tract of land is increasingly being challenged. Many mineral deposits being discovered today are of lower grade and located at greater depths, and are therefore more expensive to mine. Another significant factor is that nonmineral surface resources are now also considered to be scarce and their value has increased accordingly."[33]

Given the earlier statements on changing stewardship philosophies to land, increased legislative constraints, vigilant public scrutiny and heightened corporate awareness, wise and effective reinstatement of the land surface is more assured today than ever before.

Some basic errors perpetrated in the past are now widely recognized and universally avoided (Figure 1.7). In contour mining in Appalachia and even in strip mining in the West until twenty years ago, it was standard practice to ignore the all-important stratigraphical structure of the landscape. Thousands of years of soil-forming processes have created a situation where the most fertile materials are normally on the surface. The stripping, protection and reinstatement of this material (instead of burying it as in the past) is a major goal of most current legislation and practice (Figure 4.7). Topsoil should be regarded as a valuable biocommodity—long periods of stockpiling, heavy equipment compaction, unvegetated exposure to atmospheric elements and careless reinstatement should be avoided.

Chemical testing and fertilizer programs can expedite the return to previous agricultural levels within a few growing seasons. Continuous monitoring of excavations can identify toxicity problems and materials which should be buried in locations where their ability to affect surface vegetation or water quality will be minimized.

Rehabilitation—A Geomorphological Challenge?

Geomorphology is the study of landforms—their creation and evolution over time. If geomorphologists know so much about the shape of land surfaces, their stability and instability, it seems apparent they should be intimately involved in rehabilitation—the creation of new land surfaces. That this has not happened is a sad reflection on disciplinary conservatism. Engineers and planners have often been left to make landscape reshaping decisions. Failed highway embankments, eroded slopes, sedimentation accumulations and unsuccessful vegetation attempts point to this not always being successful.

In preparing our plans for rehabilitation, we should be cognizant of the tremendous opportunity to create landscapes which are a "better fit" for the proposed use—there is nothing in the natural landscape which necessarily suggests *it* is the best fit (Figure 3.7). Two small examples illustrate the point.

Planners are well aware that housing densities and subdivision designs should be integrated with landscape characteristics. In the subdivision regulations of the city of Los Angeles regulations are outlined to maximize slope stability and to retain topographic features of scenic and geologic interest.[34] In addition:

Where the average percent of natural slope of the land is:	The maximum density of housing units per gross acre shall be:
10 to 14.9%	1.5
15 to 19.9%	1.0
20 to 24.9%	0.8
25 to 29.9%	0.6
30 to 34.4%	0.4
35% and over	0.1

The influence of geomorphological parameters is paramount, but are these the correct parameters? In the Ontario rehabilitation legislation loose materials can be left at slope angles of 1:1 or 45°, a condition guaranteed to accelerate erosion, retard vegetation growth and promote slope failure.

In another recent example, a geomorphological site survey for a proposed new township park near Guelph, Ontario, revealed approximately half the area was composed of glacial till-drumlinoid materials and the other half of fluvioglacial sand and gravel outwash materials. This prior knowledge was instrumental in (a) satisfying the immediate demand for camp sites at a location which did not sterilize the extraction of the valuable aggregate materials, (b) the creation of level surfaces for playing fields in the easily (and profitably) removed sand and gravel area, (c) the excavation and design of below water table extraction at the location where the greatest depth of sand and gravel was found so as to produce a lake of considerable dimensions with appropriate water quality for fishing and swimming. The author's design for rehabilitation was implemented and the land reshaping costs were paid for by a nearby sand and gravel producer desperately in need of new resources. The excess sand and gravel produced (700,000 tonnes) was paid for on a royalty basis (more than 50 cts/tonne) which provided the local township with a handsome windfall (in excess of the costs of acquiring the whole property). Here is an excellent example of the benefits of integrative planning (a) preplanning survey, (b) multiple resource usage, and (c) effective rehabilitation design. The time for completion of this project was only three years from start to finish. It seems sometimes possible "to have your cake and eat it too."

Towards Some Ideal Rehabilitation Modelling

Preplanning

Preplanning should be a mandatory practice—detailed site and off-site information is necessary if the site is to be "Restored" or effectively "Rehabilitated." The associated research may in fact determine areas worthy of being preserved and being retained in their present condition. Table 1.7 is a result of the author's involvement in the preparation of over 30 site plans for new pit and quarry operations in Ontario.

The objectives of the site-planning exercise are many, but can be simply stated as (a) to render the operational programs as inoffensive to the

Table 1.7
Potential Inputs in Environmental Impact Statement of an Aggregate Surface Mining Operation

Physical Studies	*Operation Studies*
Air Photo Investigation	Market Analysis and Economic Justification
Ground Water	Transport and Haulage Routes
Surface Water	(on and off site)
Soils Analysis	Community Relationships
Ecology (Fauna and Flora) Water and Land areas	Planning Study
Geological Investigation	Attitudinal Studies of nearby residents towards mining operation
Archaeological and Historical Visual Aesthetics	Noise producton and amelioration
Preservation and buffer considerations	Site Plan design (slopes, entrances, plant machinery, etc.)
	Coordination with all planning and institutional authorities
Mining Interference and Reclamation	
Optimal phasing plan for operation Progressive rehabilitation model Agricultural interference and restoration	
Reforestation program	
Wildlife corridor maintenance and improvement	
Final land-use design	

social and physical environment of the area as possible, (b) to ensure that at any one point in time the acreage of land disturbed is minimized (i.e., that effective and progressive rehabilitation techniques are vigorously implemented (Figure 4.7)), and (c) to leave a landscape which is in all respects suitable for the intended future use(s). In all of this it is important that the research conducted and the recommendations produced be closely integrated with the implementation program and not considered as a necessary bureaucratic hardship or whitewash product.

Timing
Rehabilitation should now be considered preventative rather than corrective surgery. A longer-term view is appropriate for rehabilitation activities. The acceptance of multiple resource use, sequential phased operations and progressive rehabilitation will render such activities more acceptable to public, planner, and government alike.

Diversity of Application
It has been made clear that rehabilitation is a concept that has very wide application. Ineffective or underuse of many facilities or landscapes is a costly oversight which contemporary and future societies may not tolerate as in the consumptive/wasteful past. Urban obsolescence and landscape reshaping should be viewed as the creative opportunities they are.

The Future
In common with much practical or problem-oriented research, rehabilitation demands the integration of knowledge from many sciences and many arts. In this chapter we have only touched on some of the areas which should be covered. The author, although now working in landscape rehabilitation for over ten years, hastens to indicate the imperfection of his understanding of many essential areas, such as visual aesthetics, drainage problems, and crop fertilization considerations. Here is a challenge to integrate that knowledge and those persons which our disciplinary-oriented educational structures normally keep apart.

If there is a single primary message in this chapter, it is that we have identified a challenging problem of frightening dimensions and diversity. Such challenges are an exciting encouragement for those who wish to see improvement in the way we handle our landscape and resources—surely we can do better in the future!

Notes
[1] T.W. Box, "The Significance and Responsibilitiy of Rehabilitating Drastically Disturbed Land" in "Reclamation of Drastically Disturbed Lands" (Amer. Society of Agronomy Inc., Crop Science Society of America Inc., Soil Science

Society of America Inc., F.W. Schaller and P. Sutton, eds., Madison, Wisconsin, 1978), p. 1.

2 A.G. McLellan, "Derelict Land in Ontario—Environmental Crime or Economic Shortsightedness?" *Bull. of the Conservation Council of Ontario*, Vol. 20, no. 4, (1973), p. 14.

3 F.W. Schaller and P. Sutton, eds., "Reclamation of Drastically Disturbed Lands" (Madison, Wisconsin: American Society of Agronomy and the Crop Science and Soil Science Societies of America, 1978).

4 W.G. Collins, ed. "Proceedings of the Derelict Land Symposium" (University of Leeds, U.K., 1969).

5 A.G. McLellan, *op. cit.*, p. 9.

6 T.W. Box, *op. cit.*, p. 2.

7 The National Academy of Sciences, "The Rehabilitation of Western Coal Lands" (Cambridge, Mass., 1974).

8 T.W. Box, *op. cit.*, pp. 3–4.

9 *Time* Magazine, "The Poisoning of America" (1980), pp. 58–65.

10 U.S. Dept. of the Interior, "Surface Mining and Our Environment" (U.S. Gov't and Printing Office, Washington, 1967), p. 52.

11 Quoted from company publicity brochure, 1980.

12 An excellent documentation of the years of rehabilitation research effort conducted by INCO can be seen in their film *Rye on the Rocks* available on request.

13 Other research on rehabilitating mine tailings can be seen in P.F. Ziemkiewicz, "Reclamation research methods on coal mine wastes with particular reference to species evaluation and selection." Proceedings of the Canadian Land Reclamation Assoc., University of Guelph, 1975 and J.V. Thirgood, "Extent of Disturbed Land and Major Reclamation Problems in Canada," in F.W. Schaller and P. Sutton, *op. cit.*, pp. 45–68.

14 A.G. McLellan and C.R. Bryant, "The Methodology of Inventory: A Practical Technique for Assessing Provincial Aggregate Resources," *The Canadian Mining and Metallurgy Bulletin*, Vol. 7 (1975), pp. 113–119.

15 A.G. McLellan, "The Aggregate Dilemma: Surface Mining in Canada—The Conflicts of Public Sentiment and Industrial Conscience," *Bull. of the Conservation Council of Ontario* (1975), p. 31.

16 S. Yundt and D. Augaitis, "From Pits to Playground—Aggregate Extraction and Pit Rehabilitation in Toronto—A Historical Review," Ontario Ministry of Natural Resources, Toronto, April 1979, 51 pp.

17 T.W. Box. *op cit.*, p. 7.

18 C.R. Bryant, L.H. Russwurm and A.G. McLellan, "The City's Countryside," in Press.

19 F.W Schaller and P. Sutton, *op. cit.*, p. xx.

20 J. Paone, J. Struthers and W. Johnson, "Extent of Disturbed Lands and Major Reclamation Problems in the United States," in F.W. Schaller and P. Sutton, *op. cit.*, pp. 11–22.

21 R.H. Whittaker, *Communities and Ecosystems* (New York: MacMillan, 1970), p. 58.

22 R.W. Brown, R.S. Johnston and K. van Cleve, "Rehabilitation Problems in Alpine and Arctic Regions," in F.W. Schaller and P. Sutton, *op. cit.*, pp. 23–42.

23 A.G. McLellan, *op. cit.*, 1973, p. 9.

24 A.G. McLellan, S.E. Yundt and M. Dorfmann, *Abandoned Pits and Quarries in*

Ontario—A Program for their Rehabilitation. Ontario Geol. Survey Miscellaneous Paper 79, 36 pp. (1979), Ontario Gov't., Toronto.

[25] J.V. Thirgood, "Extent of Disturbed Land and Major Reclamation Problems in Canada," in F.W. Schaller, P. Sutton, *op. cit.*, pp. 45–68.

[26] D.W. Anderson, R.E. Redmann and M.E. Jonescu, *A Soil, Vegetation and microclimatic inventory of coal strip mine wastes of the Estevan Area, Saskatchewan* (Energy, Mines and Resources, Ottawa, Canada, 1975), pp. 140.

[27] R.W. Brown, *et al.*, in F.W. Schaller, P. Sutton, *op cit.*, p 41.

[28] S.K. Takyi, M.H. Rowell, W.B. McGill and M. Nyborg, "Reclamation and Vegetation of Surface Mine Areas, Athabasca Tar Sands," Environmental Research Monograph, 1977, p. 1, Syncrude, Alberta.

[29] J. Dick, "Criteria for Land Reclamation Standards," 1974. University of British Columbia, Vancouver, B.C.

[30] J.V. Thirgood, in F.W. Schaller and P. Sutton, *op. cit.*, p. 89.

[31] S.E. Yundt and B.E. Messerschmidt, "Legislation and Policy Mineral Resource Management in Ontario, Canada," *Minerals and the Environment,* Vol. 1, 1980, pp. 101–111.

[32] G.V. Holmberg, W.J. Horvath, J.R. LaFevers, "Citizens Role in Land Disturbance and Reclamation," in F.W. Schaller and P. Sutton, *op. cit.*, pp. 69–94.

[33] General Technical Report INT 70, "Mining and Reclamation in the West," Surface Environment and Mining Program (SEAM), U.S.D.A Forest Service, 1979, p. 1.

[34] Subdivision Regulations City of Los Angeles, Section 1-801.60.01.

8/Reducing Disaster Losses: The Management of Environmental Hazards

Harold D. Foster

Canada is an intricate risk mosaic, every region being threatened by a variety of both natural and man-made hazards.[1] While it is impossible to remove all such risk, disaster losses can be diminished by planning for security through the adoption of numerous safety strategies. This process of deliberate risk management generally involves the operation of complex decision-making networks, termed "safety delivery systems" by the author. Figure 1.8 is a heuristic model of the operation of such a system. As can be seen from this diagram, the reduction of risk from major environmental hazards involves the cooperation of a number of groups of actors. These frequently include the three levels of government, the scientific community, developers, architects, consultants, financial institutions, realtors, the media, various special interest groups, the owners and renters of private homes and commercial buildings, and the public at large.

Each safety delivery system has defined, either explicitly or implicitly, what for it is an acceptable level of risk. It then seeks to achieve this target by the implementation of strategies designed to ensure that losses from the hazards that it is attempting to manage do not rise above this threshold. In fact, Canadian society has evolved in a manner that allows it to operate within specific levels of tolerance for all natural and man-made events. Typically, boundaries to what is acceptable risk are defined either by law or by common practice. Regulations such as public health and building codes often identify the maximum event that should be guarded against and hence what losses must be accepted. The resulting level of safety reflects such factors as past experience, needs, wants and wealth.

Such safety delivery systems are not static. Social goals may alter or disasters occur which illustrate that current standards are too low. In consequence, the law or associated codes and regulations may be altered and the safety delivery system involved must then be modified to meet those new objectives. Similarly, change and resulting improvements in security can be achieved by the provision of government incentives designed to promote the adoption of innovation that would otherwise not take place, or would naturally occur more slowly. Such incentives include grants and subsidies, income tax credits and deductions, loans, accelerated depreciation, government insurance and procurement, tax exemptions and

Figure 1.8

HEURISTIC MODEL OF THE FLOOD SAFETY DELIVERY SYSTEM

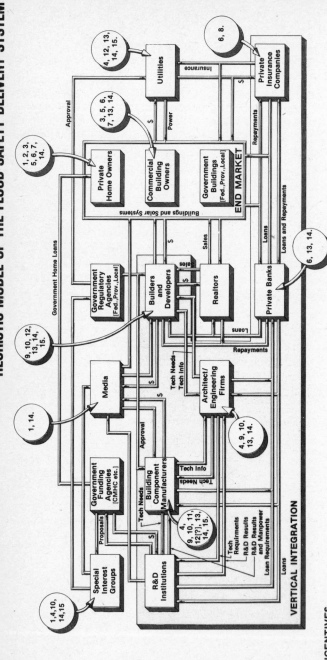

INCENTIVES

1. Grants and subsidies
2. Income tax credits
3. Income tax deductions
4. Research and development
5. Low cost loans
6. Guaranteed loans
7. Accelerated depreciation/ rapid amortization
8. Government insurance and reinsurance
9. Government procurement
10. Demonstration programs
11. Government equity investment
12. Tax exempt bonds
13. Information collection
14. Information dissemination
15. Education and training programs

research, development and demonstration programs. Education and training can also be provided to reduce risk. The points on the safety delivery system where such incentives can be used to promote safety are illustrated in Figure 1.8.

Regardless of the hazard involved, in theory, at least, every safety delivery system can choose whether or not to implement four basic groups of mitigation strategies.[2] Typically, these involve measures to modify or remove either the hazard or the infrastructure at risk, or they seek to accommodate accepted losses with minimum social disruption (Table 1.8). In practice, however, the choice of strategies may be limited by such factors as a lack of scientific knowledge about the hazard and its probable impact, an absence of appropriate technology, and high cost or legal and social objections to implementation. The selection of mitigation strategies is also influenced by the training of those involved in managing the safety delivery system and the perceptions and attitudes of various special interest groups and the general public who are served by it. In addition, some hazards strike so rarely, as for example meteorites, or cause so little damage that no safety delivery system exists for them. In such cases the typical response by those adversely affected is loss bearing.[3]

Safety Delivery Systems: Case Studies

A multiplicity of delivery systems is used in attempts to increase the safety of the Canadian public and to protect individual or corporate property. Such networks include those seeking to reduce the damage caused by tsunamis, floods and forest fires, as well as to mitigate the coastal and lacustrine erosion threat. Examples of such systems are described in detail in an attempt to illustrate the basic principles involved in their operation.

Tsunami Safety Network

Tsunamis are trains of seismically triggered sea waves, most frequently generated by submarine dip-slip faulting, which are capable of causing extensive damage in low-lying coastal areas. Although occurring in other oceans, tsunamis have been recorded most frequently within the Pacific basin where, between 1900–70, 138 were reported, 34 of which were locally destructive while 9 also caused damage at great distances from their sources. The effects of such waves in coastal areas can be very destructive. In 1964, for example, 122 people died and 200 were injured by seismic sea waves generated as the result of earth movements centred in Prince William Sound, Alaska.[4] This tsunami was the greatest of the ten seismic sea wave trains recorded on the west coast of British Columbia during the some 65 years of operation of the Tofino tide gauge. It is, therefore, not surprising that it caused widespread damage to many Vancouver Island coastal settlements. The greatest impact occurred at Alberni and Port Alberni where the first wave arrived without any official warning.

Table 1.8
Examples of Potential Adjustments to Hazards

Eliminate the Hazard	Modify the Magnitude and Intensity of Impact	Modify Damage Susceptibility	Modify Loss Burden	Bear the Loss
Melt glaciers, snow and icebergs	*Structural Protection*	*Management of High-Risk Sites*	*Emergency Measures*	Bear the loss
Pull weeds	Avalanche defences	Land-use regulation	Warning systems	
Destroy pests	Dykes, piers	Statutes	Evacuation	
Drain lakes and swamps	Floodwalls, seawalls	Zoning ordinances	Fighting the hazard	
Remove perched blocks	Channel improvements	Building codes		
Cut down trees	Floodways	Urban renewal	*Redistribute Losses*	
	River diversions	Subdivision regulations	Disaster relief	
	Reservoirs	Government purchase of land or property	Financial aid	
	Landslide barriers	Subsidized relocation	Tax write-offs	
	Fire breaks		Insurance	
	Coastal defences	*Structural Change*		
		Use of different materials		
	Land Management	Designing for safety		
	Terracing	Building underground		
	Gully control	Land elevation		
	Bank stabilization	Elevation of buildings		
	Forest Fire control	Planting resistant crops		
	Revegetation			
	Contour plowing	*Changes in Internal Fittings or Operating Procedures*		
	Crop rotation	Alter planting or cropping techniques		
	Spraying	Alter recreational or industrial procedures		
	Biological control of pests			
	Forestation			
	Weather Modification			
	Seeding of storms			
	Fog dispersal			

Including the damage to the MacMillan Bloedel and Powell River Company plants in Port Alberni, estimates of the total losses have reached as high as $10 million.[5] Houses were displaced up to 300 m and logs moving at speeds in excess of 32 km per hour were driven into buildings. As a result, 58 properties were completely destroyed, and 320 dwellings suffered damage.

The risk of tsunami destruction along the western Canadian coast has led to the development of a complex safety delivery system which includes organizations and individuals drawn from almost the entire Pacific Rim. They are involved because the tsunami warning network currently operating in British Columbia is an integral part of a larger international system covering the Pacific Ocean.[6] The headquarters of the Seismic Sea Wave Warning System is in Honolulu and is supplied with data by at least 30 seismological and some 50 tide stations. These include the Dominion Astrophysical Observatory near Victoria, and Tofino and Langara Island tide stations on Canada's Pacific coast. When an earthquake, registering 6.5 or greater on the Richter scale, is observed at any participating seismological station, this information is immediately relayed to Honolulu. Here the location of the epicentre is determined by analyzing data from several stations. If it is suspected that a tsunami may have been generated, tide stations in the area are requested to monitor their gauges for evidence of anomalous readings. If the existence of a tsunami is verified, warnings are issued to all participating countries, including Canada. Once the generation of a tsunami has been confirmed, the arrival time at various Pacific coastal points is estimated from travel time charts prepared for each tide station in the system. These travel times are considered accurate within approximately 2.3 percent. Except when close to the epicentre, threatened areas can then be evacuated and mobile infrastructure and fittings removed.

Several types of bulletins may be issued by the International Tsunami Information Center. Watch bulletins report the occurrence of tsunami-generating size earthquakes. Warning bulletins are issued when the existence of a tsunami has been confirmed, and this bulletin includes the estimated time of arrival at the tide stations. Tsunami warning supplements, giving information on reported wave heights, are issued at least hourly thereafter. A tsunami watch is cancelled when it is determined that no tsunami has been generated, but the "all clear" decision is left to the discretion of local dissemination agencies. The British Columbia Provincial Emergency Programme (PEP) receives these bulletins at it headquarters in Victoria.

If, as a result of the information received from Honolulu, the decision is made by the PEP Coordinator and the Provincial Secretary to alert coastal communities, further dissemination of the information occurs. RCMP detachment commanders are, for example, responsible for alerting the local PEP Coordinator in each community and designated municipal officials. Bulletins are also passed to the Broadcast News Service which has a teletype service to coastal radio stations. The Raven Network, an independent Indian-owned and operated radio-telephone system centred at Bowser, south of Courtenay on Vancouver Island's east coast, is also requested to pass information to its subscribers.

As with any other system, this safety delivery network is only as strong as its weakest link. The B.C. tsunami warning system is unlikely to function effectively because local government and the public-at-risk is unprepared to respond to the information the network generates.[7] There are very few tsunami risk maps available which delineate those areas in specific communities which are likely to be flooded. Only one Vancouver Island municipality, Port Alberni, has a detailed local tsunami warning plan. Its most comprehensive fanout system is used when the tsunami warning has not been preceded by a watch bulletin. Few, if any, other coastal communities in British Columbia have developed an official tsunami response plan, despite the fact that several other settlements have previously been inundated.

Flood Safety Network

Floods are a critical problem in Canada. This is because access to drinking water was a major factor in the initial location of most Canadian settlements. Silt deposited on flood plains also provided good agricultural land, while river transport made the clearing of the forest an easier proposition. As a result, most Canadian cities were sited on river banks or lakesides. Later growth, therefore, frequently took place on flood plains, and is inevitably leading to escalating losses from this hazard. Today, over two hundred Canadian towns and cities, from British Columbia to Newfoundland, face potential flooding.[8]

Five distinct types of flooding are experienced. In the west, major losses are usually associated with snowmelt and/or winter or spring rainfall onto snow or frozen soils. Such occurrences may result in flooding of long duration. In 1950, for example, the Red River reached flood stage on April 21st, peaked on May 19th, and did not fall below flood stage again until June 10th, an interval of 51 days during which time Winnipeg was severely damaged, and losses exceeded $100 million. In contrast, in the east of Canada, cyclonic storms or hurricanes spawned in the Caribbean occasionally move inland into Quebec, Ontario and the Maritime Provinces. Hurricane Hazel which struck Toronto in 1954 killed 81 people and caused in excess of $3.5 million of damage in the Don Valley alone. Much of the country also suffers from cyclonic storms of varying magnitude and duration; rainfall is less intense but large drainage basins can be affected. The flooding experienced by Timmons, Ontario in 1961 illustrated this problem. More dramatic and posing greater danger to life are the conventional storm floods caused by violent local storms. These normally result in rapid inundation in small drainage basins. Such events, although intense, are short-lived. Ice jam and ice break-up floods also occur in the spring, particularly in eastern Canada. As the ice begins to fracture, it frequently congregates against obstructions such as bridges or in bends or gorges to form natural dams. The obstructed water which is ponded behind it results in flooding upstream. Such dramatic events are usually of short duration but can cause extensive damage, as was the case at Belleville at the mouth of the Moira River in March 1936. Such flooding also occurs almost annually on the Chaudière River in Quebec, where St. Georges, Beauceville, St. Joseph, Vallee Junction, Ste. Marie, and Scott Junction suffer repeated damage.

Until the mid-1970s the Canadian safety delivery system for floods operated in a very conservative manner. The federal and provincial governments used traditional incentives such as grants and subsidies to promote the construction of engineering works and to reimburse flood loss victims. They also conducted information collection and dissemination programs on the hazard. This approach resulted in the construction of dykes, dams, floodways and other engineering structures to reduce or contain exceptionally high discharges. In addition, damages suffered when such engineering solutions failed were generally reimbursed under joint federal-provincial disaster assistance programs. Until it was repealed in 1970, the Canada Water Conservation Assistance Act provided for financial contributions by the federal government to the construction of major flood control works. Usually 37.5 percent of the cost was borne by the federal government, 37.5 percent by the province involved and the remainder by local governments in the area affected. Such flood protection schemes were implemented in Metro Toronto, in the Upper Thames and Halton in Ontario, and in Alberni, Hastings Creek and North and West Vancouver in British Columbia. More recently, a series of *ad hoc* agreements in which the federal government paid at least 50 percent of the costs of the flood control structures have been implemented. By far the largest of these have been the construction of the Greater Winnipeg Floodway and the dyking, bank protection and pumping and ditching still being carried out on the Fraser River.

Despite investments in excess of $200 million on such structures by the governments involved, flood losses themselves have continued to rise. In 1974 alone, estimated flood damage in Canada exceeded $71 million, of which some $60 million was reimbursed under government compensation schemes. By this date it was becoming increasingly clear that innovation was required if losses were not to become impossible to contain. A variety of other incentives were required. With this in mind, a national Flood Damage Reduction Program was announced in 1975 by Environment Canada. Its major objective was to discourage development on flood plains, so preventing increases in the infrastructure at risk from flooding. The principal objectives of this program are the mapping of flood risk areas; the communication of this hazard information to government agencies, industry and the public; and the discontinuance of investment of public funds in structures that are likely to suffer flood damage.[9] The program also aims at stopping flood disaster assistance for future development if it has taken place after a risk area has been determined and publicized. Efforts are also being made to encourage municipalities and provinces to place land-use restrictions on high-risk locations and to carry out environmental impact assessment and benefit cost analyses before the construction of flood control schemes. In summary, at least four new types of incentives are being adopted to influence the flood management system in Canada.

The national Flood Damage Reduction Program is being implemented by the signing of federal-provincial agreements which specify general objectives and identify which flood-prone areas are to be mapped. So far such agreements have been reached between the federal government and New Brunswick, Nova Scotia, Quebec, Ontario, Manitoba, Saskatchewan and the Northwest Territories. As of 1979, negotiations were continuing with British Columbia, Alberta, and Yukon and Newfoundland. It is estimated that the mapping program alone will take a further five years and cost some $25 million to implement. Initial federal-provincial pilot projects have already been undertaken in Fredericton, Montreal, Oshawa, Carman and Moose Jaw. These have applied a series of mapping scales and approaches.

Once the areas likely to be flooded under differing discharge conditions have been identified, the new national program permits the Minister of Environment Canada and his provincial counterparts to designate mapped flood risk areas, so effecting policies for discouraging further damage-prone development in them. Once this has been done, no structures are to be permitted in the floodway, and only flood-proofed buildings not adversely affecting flow are allowed in the outer lower risk zone. So far, however, only two such designations have been made, one in the Montreal region and the other in the Chaudière basin.

While it is still possible to criticize this approach to the reduction of flood damage by the federal and provincial governments, it does illustrate a new willingness to widen the type of incentives by those involved in the flood safety delivery system. Indeed the recent acceptance by federal and provincial governments that the best way to prevent flood damage is often to stop development in high-risk areas, represents a major change in their philosophy.

Coastal Erosion: Safety Network

Canada has a highly indented coastline and myriads of both large and small lakes. In consequence, much of its land surface is subjected to marine or lacustrine erosion. Since waterfront property is desirable for aesthetic and recreational reasons, the land lost through attrition is, therefore, often of high value. Although such erosion is a problem in all provinces and territories, it is most significant around the Great Lakes. It is there that the most complex safety network is being developed to assist in the reduction of economic loss and risk to life.

The Great Lakes, with a surface area of 246,000 sq. km are able to absorb relatively large variations in water supplies, yet still maintain fairly constant outflows. However when, as in the 1972–73 period, persistently high precipitation continues over the 764,000 sq. km Great Lakes drainage basin, lake levels rise considerably. If this increase in water height is combined with severe storms, extensive erosion damage can occur, especially along the lower Great Lakes shoreline. Such an unfortunate combination took place in 1972 and 1973.

Following the accompanying public outcry, the Ontario Ministry of Natural Resources and Fisheries and Environment Canada entered into an agreement to survey the erosion-related damage and to make recommendations on the future planning and management of such shoreline areas.[10]

The initial mapping program collected information on both erosional losses and those due to inundation from high lake levels. Early surveys permitted the exclusion of predominantly bedrock areas, such as the shores of Lake Superior and the northern margins of Lake Huron. Attention was, therefore, focussed on high-risk Canadian shores, specifically those extending from Port Severn on Georgian Bay to Gananoque on Lake Ontario. For these areas, erosion and inundation were examined together with the economic, environmental and social implications of the associated losses. This Canada-Ontario Great Lakes Shore Damage Survey included the comparison of old and new aerial photography, an inventory of shoreline property and field damage surveys. Estimates were also made of the long- and short-term erosion rates. In all, some 50,000 properties were found to be at risk along 3,570 km of shoreline. Computer data storage and retrieval was used at the Canada Centre for Inland Waters to handle the 27 variables collected for each of the properties, including information on location, ownership, land use and value. It was determined that in 1972 and 1973, 8,439 properties had been damaged at a cost of $19 million. Losses of land valued at $9 million had also taken place.

The survey results were published in a 637-page Coastal Zone Atlas, together with a technical report.[11] The latter described the amount of damage, effectiveness of past attempts to prevent it, and the nature and value of infrastructure at risk. The report was distributed to municipal and planning board offices, public libraries and to federal and provincial government departments in an effort to stimulate awareness of the nature of the hazard. It pointed out that there was the immediate potential for a further $19 million of damage to occur, either from erosion or inundation. However, it was estimated that structural protection from walls, costing about $1 billion, was uneconomic and indeed aesthetically undesirable. However, other strategies were promoted. These included detailed erosion and flood mapping, land-use adjustments through zoning, set-back requirements, some structural protection and the public acquisition of certain high-risk sites.

In 1976, the federal and Ontario governments established a task force to implement most of the technical report recommendations. Many maps of flood- and erosion-prone areas, at a scale of 1:10,000, have since been prepared based on photomosaics. These delineate the predicted 100-year erosion limit and identify highly dynamic beach areas. They are published together with a guide which is then distributed to municipalities and Conservation Authorities which are expected to use them in their planning and management programs. Special emphasis has been given to a 29 km stretch of Lake Erie's shoreline at Kingsville. For this area the program attempted to develop methodologies for the evaluation of shore management strategies in high-risk locations. It also sought to develop effective erosion reduction measures. In addition, a four-year public information program was also put into operation. A summary of the Shore Damage Survey was sent, for example, to 35,000 shoreline residents, and workshops on the erosion issue were held with representatives of local municipalities and professional associations. Various other publicly available documents, such as *Shore Property Hazards, What you Always Wanted to Know about Great Lake Levels* and *A Guide for the Use of Canada/Ontario Great Lakes Flood and Erosion Prone Area Mapping*, have also been published.[12] A federal-provincial shoreline erosion monitoring program began in the lower Great Lakes in 1976. This involves surveys of some 160 sites, together with studies of sequential oblique photographs of the shoreline. This data collection program is providing information on the rates of cliff recession and other land losses.[13]

Forest Fires: Safety Network

Organized federal forest fire control began in Canada in the late 1800s. In British Columbia, Alberta, Saskatchewan and Manitoba, a fire-ranging service started in 1901. The initial emphasis of the federal Forestry Branch of the Department of the Interior was on fire suppression. By 1914, fire protection was provided to 93,000 sq. km of Forest Reserves and 531,000 sq. km of unreserved lands or fire-ranging districts. By 1920, aircraft were in use for detection, reconnaissance and the transport of equipment and suppression crews in both British Columbia and Alberta. Fire lookouts were also widely established.

A major change occurred in 1930 with the transfer of forest resources to the provinces. Today only the forest resources of the Yukon and the Northwest Territories, together with the national parks and certain Indian lands, receive direct federal fire protection. The national role has switched to the provision of forest research in an attempt to improve the operation of the fire safey network. Most provinces, such as Alberta and Manitoba, have directly assumed the forest protection role. A few have delegated this responsibility to user agencies or municipal governments.[14]

As a result of this federal-provincial division of responsibility, forest protection in Canada is now practised with varying degrees of rigour. These usually reflect differences in wood species, economic values, existing commitments to industries and proximity to markets. During the ten-year period from 1968 to 1977, an average each year of 8,664 fires burned over 11,860 sq. km of Canadian forest and tundra. These figures have risen from 5,000 fires and 8,000 sq. km which were typical of losses in the 1930s. Comparisons were difficult to make, however, because of improvements in historical fire record keeping. Nevertheless, increases in population, tourism and mobility have continued to expand the fire hazard. Present management costs are between $50 to $100 million annually. It is of interest to note that the maximum size of individual major fires has been cut from some 10,360 sq. km in the 1920s to about 1,036 sq. km today, a reduction by a factor of ten.

Much of this change has come from the application of forest fire oriented research results. Such studies began at the Petawawa Forest Experiment Station in 1929. After greater responsibility for forests was given to the provinces, federal emphasis changed from protection in the field to research. Early work focussed on danger rating (involving small test fires), fire retardant chemicals, slash burning and the development of fire control planning procedures. In an attempt to increase federal-provincial contact and speed the application of such results, six regional forest research establishments were set up in the 1960s. These were located in Victoria, Edmonton, Sault Ste. Marie, Quebec City, Fredericton and St. John's. In addition, the Forest Fire Research Institute was located in Ottawa to conduct a nationwide research program. Numerous innovations have been developed by these centres, including benefit-cost studies of fire control and the application of new technologies—satellite imagery, computers and aerial ignition techniques. This research has led to a wider acceptance of the concept of fire management, involving giving due consideration to resource values, the environmental role of fire, the appropriate level of control, prescribed utilization to reduce fuel availability and fire impacts. This federal research by the Canadian Forestry Service is supplemented by provincial investigations and by work at Canadian universities.

Forest fire experience and research results are exchanged between provinces on an annual basis through the activities of the Canadian Committee on Forest Fire Control, an Associate Committee of the National Research Council. At a January meeting the heads of all provincial and federal forest fire control agencies and representatives of other interested organizations discuss and take action on forest fire control issues of national concern. Each presents a report on the past year's forest fire experience.[15] It is clear from the minutes of these meetings and proceedings of international workshops that fire is increasingly viewed as a hazard only under certain circumstances. In others, it is seen as a resource.[16]

Forest fire management has become very sophisticated. In British Columbia and the Yukon, for example, the Canadian Forest Fire Danger Rating System has been operationally applied by the provincial and territorial governments since 1970. This permits forestry operations, such as logging, to be regulated by the level of fire danger. To allow this to take place, an extensive computerized weather and fire danger information and mapping system is administered by the province of British Columbia. Computer-produced maps of spatial variation in fire danger are given to interested parties at the Provincial Fire Protection Branch headquarters in Victoria and at each of six regional Forest Protection Offices. These maps assist in the making of fire-related decisions, such as whether or not to move the provincial air tanker fleet to areas of anticipated fire activity. The logging industry is also regulated and its activities curtailed according to the fire danger classes computed for their areas of operation. Public warnings of fire hazard are posted and routinely handled by the media. A recent innovation is a system of quantifying and mapping lightning fire risk. This is based on a lightning detection and computer-based analysis and plotting system for cloud-to-ground lightning strikes. This system allows high-risk sites to be identified and enables air fire patrols to be routed to detect the largest number of new fires as quickly as possible.

The hazard risk is also reduced by the prescribed use of fire. Post-logging debris is burned when environmental conditions will not allow it to cause uncontrolled fires. The Prescribed Fire Predictor, a slide-rule device, enables forest managers to use the fuel moisture codes of the Canadian Forest Fire Weather Index on logged sites to predict fire behaviour.

Infrared fire detection and mapping systems, developed by the Canadian Forestry Service, are now also in use to improve the speed of discovery of new fires, the quality of the initial attack and the efficiency of the final mop-up of forest fires. In addition, the Pacific Forest Research Centre and the provincial Parks and Outdoor Recreation Division are attempting to assess, map and reduce fire hazard levels in parks and campgrounds.[17]

Safety Delivery Systems: An Overview

While there are obvious differences between the safety delivery systems for individual natural hazards, there are also major similarities. Such networks, for example, generally operate in relative isolation. They are designed to reduce the risks from a single disaster agent such as flooding, or from a group of related hazards, for example mass movement phenomena. As a result, there is often little coordination of effort between managers of such systems. Safety delivery networks also often involve various levels of government. If losses are to be reduced then cooperation is usually required between federal, provincial and municipal governments. In some cases, international coordination is also essential. Frequently, however, land-use decisions are made by municipal planners and elected officials who fail to identify the spatial distribution of hazard risk. In consequence, they often permit extensive development on high-risk sites and large losses inevitably follow. Provincial and, in certain cases, federal aid is then normally given to victims. This situation is leading to greater federal and provincial involvement in the local identification of risks and related land-use decisions. A spectrum of participation can now be identified which stretches from simple hazard data collection to federal and provincial government purchase of high-risk sites to permit them total control over their use.

A third trend is the growth of predictive capabilities based on the greater use of remote sensing and computer modelling. Decision makers can now predict when and where many disaster agents will strike. These innovations also permit forecasts of associated life and property losses. Paralleling this trend has been a growing awareness that engineering and technological strategies, such as the construction of floodways and avalanche defences can rarely provide adequate safety on their own. Infrastructure must be located in areas of acceptable risk and agricultural, industrial and commercial activities must be modified to accommodate threat. It is becoming increasingly clear that if losses from environmental hazards are to be controlled, disaster planning must involve far more than merely responding after a disaster agent has struck. Canadian society must decide that safety from hazards is a significant goal and accept alterations in land use and economic processes in order to achieve it. Ideally, community safety programs organized at the municipal level are required if losses are to be curtailed.

Community Safety Programs: The Way Ahead?

Few, if any, Canadian communities are willing to leave their futures to chance. Increasingly, comprehensive planning is being used to ensure that development is compatible with specific goals. If disaster losses are to be reduced significantly, the mitigation of risk must become a major objective at the local level and a variety of safety delivery systems must be integrated into comprehensive planning. This requires the development of a community safety plan, the various stages of which are illustrated in Figure 2.8. Such a plan might best be designed by an advisory committee reporting to elected officials whose role it is to ensure that implementation of the comprehensive plan decreases risk.

The initial step in the production of a community safety plan involves the identification of the hazards that threaten the region.[18] To this end a

Figure 2.8

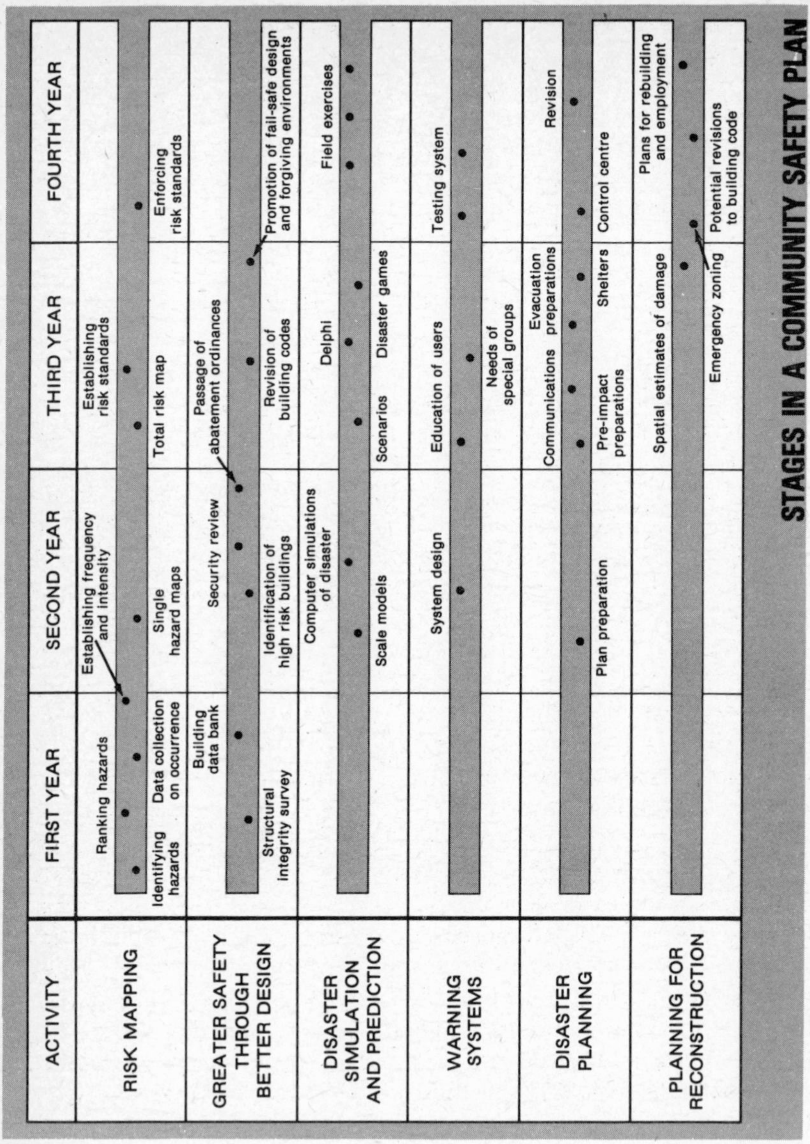

STAGES IN A COMMUNITY SAFETY PLAN

ACTIVITY	FIRST YEAR	SECOND YEAR	THIRD YEAR	FOURTH YEAR
RISK MAPPING	Identifying hazards • Ranking hazards • Data collection on occurrence	Establishing frequency and intensity • Single hazard maps	Establishing risk standards • Total risk map	Enforcing risk standards
GREATER SAFETY THROUGH BETTER DESIGN	Structural integrity survey • Building data bank	Security review • Identification of high risk buildings	Passage of abatement ordinances • Revision of building codes	Promotion of fail-safe design and forgiving environments
DISASTER SIMULATION AND PREDICTION		Computer simulations of disaster • Scale models	Delphi • Scenarios • Disaster games	Field exercises
WARNING SYSTEMS		System design	Education of users	Testing system
DISASTER PLANNING		Plan preparation	Needs of special groups • Evacuation preparations • Communications • Pre-impact preparations • Shelters	Revision • Control centre
PLANNING FOR RECONSTRUCTION			Spatial estimates of damage • Emergency zoning	Plans for rebuilding and employment • Potential revisions to building code

wide range of literature must be reviewed, data collected and interviews carried out. There are a number of sources that can be tapped for this information; these include such agencies as Emergency Planning Canada, the relevant provincial emergency program, the Canadian Geological Survey, Environment Canada and climatology, geography, geology and urban planning departments of universities and colleges.

Once the hazards that can cause disasters in a community have been identified, the losses for which they have been responsible in the past must be estimated. Until this step has been carried out, it is not possible to establish meaningful safety goals. The cause of death is recorded in Canada and medical statistics often exist for long time periods. In addition to deaths and injuries, environmental hazards are also often responsible for enormous financial losses. The safety goals of comprehensive planning should also seek to reduce this toll. Unfortunately, there is rarely, if ever, any single body that has kept a record of all hazard losses. However, insurance companies, fire and police agencies, and government disaster mitigation, economic analysis, agriculture and urban affairs and transport departments can often supply relevant data. This can be used to develop an overview of past economic losses due to environmental hazards.

Once the loss rates from hazards that a community has traditionally suffered have been established, future acceptable safety levels must be decided upon. This requires an answer to the question: How safe is safe enough? Trade-offs between goals such as those of safety and freedom or safety and economic development are inevitable. Four approaches are available for use in reaching this decision. *Risk aversion* involves a decision to achieve the maximum possible reduction of risk regardless of cost. *Risk balancing* tries to determine acceptable loss levels by comparison with reference cases, including risks from other activities. *Acceptable risk* can also be determined by using cost-effectiveness techniques. These seek to give the greatest safety for the minimum expenditure. *Cost-benefit balancing*, the fourth approach, seeks to allow the greatest risks for those activities with the highest associated locational benefits.[19]

Once current community health and economic loss levels have been established and future goals set for their reduction, a variety of potential approaches can be applied. The range of such strategies is illustrated in Table 1.8. In some cases, an attempt may be made to eliminate the hazard. Blasting can remove perched blocks and eliminate the rockfall hazard in certain areas. More frequently, however, the hazard is too permanent to eliminate and changes must be made to either the physical environment or infrastructure to reduce the magnitude and intensity of its impact. Explosives are used in Rogers Pass, British Columbia to induce a number of relatively small avalanches, rather than an occasional major snowslide.[20] One of the most expensive attempts to reduce the magnitude of impact of any Canadian hazard has been the Red and Assiniboine River flood control projects, the most significant element of which is the Red River floodway. The latter is the key to Winnipeg's flood protection.[21] There are numerous examples of land management in Canada designed to increase safety. These include the use of a variety of chemical sprays and Thuricide 16B® (a microbiological controlling bacterium *Bacillus thuringiensis kurstaki*) in Nova Scotia to combat the devastation caused by the spruce budworm.[22] Experiments have also been carried out with weather modification in western Canada to reduce the forest fire hazard. It has also been suggested that cloud seeding might increase Prairie precipitation and diminish drought losses. Strategies designed to reduce the damage susceptibility are becoming increasingly popular in Canada. To a large degree these have involved changes in land-use regulations to prevent or reduce development on high-risk sites, and the adoption of more stringent building codes, such as those which incorporate the expected forces due to earthquakes. The loss burden can also be modified by warning systems, fighting the hazard, evacuation and by redistributing losses by relief, financial aid and insurance. In addition, municipalities in every province are encouraged by both federal and provincial disaster agencies to prepare disaster plans. Such documents, for example the *Emergency Operational Plan* of the Metropolitan Corporation of Greater Winnipeg, include details of how to respond to a variety of disaster agents.[23]

In certain circumstances financial assistance is also available to victims under the federal Disaster Assistance Program. Payments to date give some idea of the scale of impact of Canadian hazards. This program is post-event and does not take into consideration the large federal expenditures that occur at the time of the crisis, for example, National Defence support. Federal funding is available to assist in peacetime disasters, which are defined as "any real or anticipated occurrence which endangers the lives, safety, welfare and well-being of some or all of the people and which cannot be brought under control by the use of all the regular, municipal government services and resources."[24] This definition tends to exclude many natural disasters such as droughts and forest fires. Nevertheless, during the past decade, 20 such disasters have been declared. These have included fishing gear damage by severe ice off Newfoundland, a Prince Edward Island windstorm and two hurricanes in Nova Scotia. In 1971, 36 homes and 32 people were buried by the St. Jean Vianney landslide. It is clear from the record, however, that flooding remains the major threat to Canadian lives and property, with extensive losses being recorded in New Brunswick, Quebec, Manitoba, Saskatchewan, Alberta and British Columbia. In total the federal government has paid in excess of $58 million to disaster victims in the past decade. In many instances this has been matched or surpassed by the provinces. In 1974, for example, Alberta farmers suffered major crop losses from flooding. They were not eligible for federal compensation but were assisted by the province's own Adverse Damage Compensation for Crops Program, which paid them some $30 million in assistance.[25]

The identification of the most desirable alternative strategies for reducing risk is largely a process of learning from the experience of others. A municipal safety committee can gain valuable insights from hazard-related literature, interviews with individuals who have survived disasters and contacts with other municipalities faced with similar hazards. The management of hazards does not take place in a vacuum and strategies should be evaluated against a series of criteria before implementation. Mitigation strategies can be selected on the basis of their impact on equity, whether or not results are achieved quickly, their leverage, cost, continuity of effect, compatibility, and expected public reaction to implementation. In most Canadian communities hazard mitigating strategies are applied on an *ad hoc* basis in an uncoordinated manner. They are far more likely to be effective, however, if they are implemented in groups to form six interrelated disaster programs. These involve the determination of the spatial distribution of risk, increasing safety through better design, disaster prediction, establishing warning systems and the preparation of disaster and reconstruction plans.

Before risk levels can be effectively utilized to control development, differing hazard zones must be delineated, the loss potential of alternative combinations of structural designs and land-use activity within these zones established, and standards set for unacceptable risk to life and property. The first step in this process, the production of maps defining spatial variations in risk, requires data from a wide variety of sources. These include direct observations of past disasters, films, photographs, newspaper files, private and public records and the logs of police and fire departments and hospitals. Archaeological data and legends, together with predictive models, may also be of value. Geological, biological and hydrological data are also of use in producing hazard maps.

Considerable reconnaissance work is in progress at the Canadian Centre for Remote Sensing, where attempts are being made to identify high-risk forest fire, flood and landslide sites from satellite imagery.[26] Various federal and provincial agencies are currently producing single-hazard maps. These include, for example, the flood hazard map of the Fredericton area, published by Environment Canada and the New Brunswick Department of Fisheries and Environment.[27] The previously described *Coastal Zone Atlas* which illustrates the risk of erosion around the Great Lakes shoreline is a further example. Wuorinen's map of the earthquake hazard in Victoria is an illustration of university sponsored research.[28] Some hazard maps attempt to illustrate more than one source of risk. Examples of this approach are the geological hazards and soil sensitivity to earthquake movement maps produced by the Resource Analysis Branch and Ministry of Transport, Communications and Highways, for the Lower Mainland of British Columbia.[29]

Certainly the most useful microzonations from a planning point of view are the multiple hazard-multiple purpose maps. These seek to show the total risk picture as a basis for rational locational decisions. To produce such maps, a common unit of comparison must be established, such as the life loss or injury potential, probable stress caused or the dollar losses to be expected from all hazards. Since such mapping is likely to be computerized, the production of a series of maps using all three of these units of measurement is almost as simple a procedure as that involved in the use of a single basis of hazard comparison. Where a selection must be made, monetary units have certain advantages over other alternatives since they allow benefit-cost relationships to be established and permit risk factors to be compared with other costs that vary with location, such as those due to transportation.

To produce multiple hazard-multiple purpose microzonations, individual disaster agents must be evaluated independently to produce a series of one hazard-one purpose microzonations. For each hazard mapped in this way the anticipated annual or other time period dollar losses per unit area are calculated. The final total risk map is then the summation of all such values. To the author's knowledge, Wuorinen's total risk map for the Saanich Peninsula is the only Canadian example of such an approach.[30] This provides a single anticipated annual loss value in dollars for soil and coastal erosion, flooding and earthquakes in the peninsula and illustrates variations in expected figures on a computer map of the area. The methodology and program developed in this study could be used by any Canadian municipality.

The major instrument for increasing safety through design is the National Building Code. This is updated every two years and is drafted in the form of a by-law to encourage adoption by local governments.[31] To allow for acceptance with a minimum of change, design requirements such as snow, wind and earthquake loads, which vary with climate, and terrain, are referenced to basic data for each locality, the latter being provided in a supplement to the Code. In this way, each municipality adopting the Code requires differing degrees of structural integrity depending on its geographical location and the magnitude and intensity of the hazards to which it is likely to be subjected. In the case of earthquakes, for example, the requirements in Canada for a specific site are based on design earthquake ground motions calculated to have an even chance of being exceeded at least once in a hundred years (Figure 3.8). This results in a risk which is analogous to that assumed in designing the building for wind resistance.

In 1980, over 70 percent of the Canadian population lived in organized areas where the National Building Code has been voluntarily accepted as the local building by-law or forms the primary basis for it.[32] Obviously a first step in ensuring greater municipal safety is adoption of the Code. A second is the establishment of sufficient building inspectors and trained technical staff to ensure that its provisions are in fact followed by developers.

Disaster prediction is an essential step in preventing major losses. A wide range of techniques is now available to permit forecasting disaster and preparing to meet it in advance. These include the use of scale and

Figure 3.8

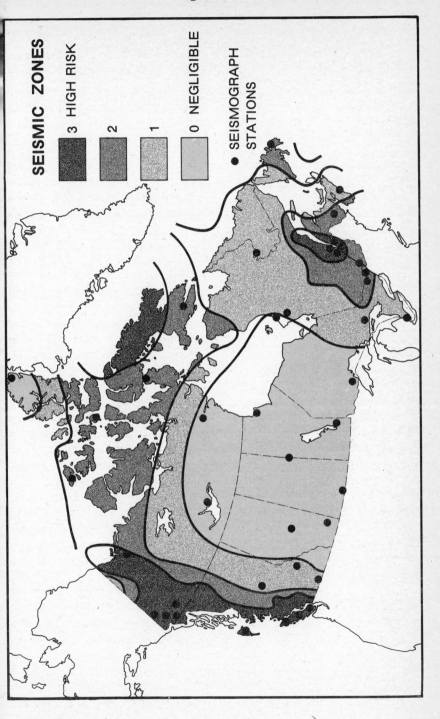

SEISMIC ZONES

3 HIGH RISK

2

1

0 NEGLIGIBLE

● SEISMOGRAPH
STATIONS

analogue models and computer simulations. Scale models, for example, have been used in an attempt to protect Port Alice, Vancouver Island from mudflows.[33] This settlement is a company town which has been built on a debris fan. Damage totalling some $800,000 was caused on December 15, 1973 by a mudflow originating at the 750-metre level on steep slopes above the town. As a result of this mass movement, one $39,000 home was demolished, nine others were uninhabitable, twenty vehicles were damaged and the town's storm drains and gas lines were rendered inoperable. A further damaging slide occurred in 1975.[34] Theoretical studies have been conducted since and a scale model of the town and adjacent slopes constructed. Mudflows were reproduced using bentonite mud with a similar viscosity to the coarse, bouldery gravel actually involved. On the basis of the information obtained, a dyking system was constructed at a cost of $250,000, designed to protect the town from slides up to 2.5 times the volume of those recently occurring. Future mudflows will be diverted into unsettled areas.[35]

Computer simulations which permit relatively accurate predictions of potential disaster losses are invaluable management tools. Regardless of the hazard involved, the construction of such models requires four common steps. The first of these is an initial analysis of the physical characteristics of the hazard which permits the subsequent development of a mathematical model capable of forecasting the severity and frequency of its impact. The approach taken is to develop a model which produces a spatial pattern of intensities with properly spaced contours which are consistent with the size, shape and configuration of observed patterns.

To predict the damage and casualties such an uneven distribution of intensities will cause, it is necessary to know the geographical distribution and characteristics of the population and infrastructure that is at risk. This can be determined by surveys of building types, occupancy rates and internal fittings. The distribution of communications, transportation and utility networks and of crops and other land uses must also be established. Such information is used to produce a geographical representation of the society threatened by the hazard. Once these two steps have been taken, the models of the disaster agent and of the infrastructure and its inhabitants must be linked by a matrix which represents the loss relationship between property type and the intensity of impact. To illustrate, it is known from widespread experience how much damage various types of buildings sustain from flood waters of differing depths and velocities or explosions of particular force. It is therefore possible to predict the degree of destruction related to particular intensities of impact on specific buildings. This technique has been used to predict the scale of damage and injuries that would occur in the city of Victoria from the 100-year earthquake and other seismic events of lesser and greater magnitude.[36] It could be applied to any hazard in any Canadian municipality.

Other techniques for predicting the potential magnitude of future disasters include scenario building, the use of the Delphi technique and game simulations. The latter provides local officials and staff the opportunity to respond to simulated disaster situations without the stress of actual responsibility for the safety of lives and property. Field exercises permit the testing of equipment and personnel under conditions which approximate those of actual disaster. In October 1974, a research team from Ottawa's Carleton University visited Sydney, Nova Scotia following a destructive wind storm.[37] They found that the community's response to this disaster had been excellent and concluded this was the result of an earlier field exercise which had simulated the collapse of a wing of the local high school.

Emergency Planning Canada is charged with coordinating planning of the federal government's response to the more than 60 natural or man-made hazards that may occur in Canada. To this end, this organization sponsors or gives more than 50 courses, conferences and seminars annually. Some 2,500 individuals, including elected officials, municipal government employees and representatives of volunteer agencies participate. The Federal Study Centre at Arnprior, 70 km west of Ottawa, is the scene of numerous disaster simulations. Organizers also provide assistance in the compilation of related disaster plans. Disaster simulations permit communities to give attention to those hazards which clearly provide the greatest threat.

Warning systems are also key elements of all safety programs. These should be established to allow the monitoring of potential disaster agents and to permit evacuation or other preventative measures to be taken when danger reaches critical levels. Response to such warnings is inevitably most successful if community awareness has been heightened and a disaster plan drawn up to ensure that all necessary tasks are accomplished with a minimum of delay or confusion. Where destruction occurs, recovery is heightened by the availability of plans designed to speed rational reconstruction and minimize delay. The consequences of implementing such programs should be assessed against the safety goals that have been set by the community. Naturally they should be designed so that they permit these to be met.

The changing nature of risk and the multiplicity of potential strategies for reducing it mandate that hindsight reviews be conducted as an integral part of every community safety plan. Progress towards the achievement of safety goals must be evaluated to enable modifications of direction to be made whenever necessary. This process requires a constant monitoring of mortality, morbidity and hazard-related economic loss in the area. While these data in themselves may be sufficient to assure safety planners and elected officials that risk is being reduced, it is useful to demonstrate this to the general public in a more easily understood manner.

One possibility is to publish a safety equivalent of the consumer price index. Such an approach would involve assigning a monetary value to life loss and injury and adding the resulting total to hazard-related property damage. The total figure could be published monthly on a per capita basis to accommodate changes in population. Stress might also be used as a unit of measurement.[38] Obviously if the hindsight review does not demonstrate that the safety goals, incorporated into the comprehensive plan, are being met then changes must be made to the strategies which have been adopted. Increasingly as the means of achieving comparative safety increase, yet the will to apply them is absent, Canadians suffer the disasters they deserve. In the final analysis, Canadian safety delivery systems will only operate effectively if local governments and the individuals they serve are willing to accept full responsibility for their own protection.

Notes

[1] Harold D. Foster, "Disaster Mitigation: A Geomorphological Contribution," *Emergency Planning Digest* 2, 5 (1975), pp. 2–9; Kenneth Hewitt and Ian Burton, *The Hazardousness of a Place: A Regional Ecology of Damaging Events* (Toronto: University of Toronto Press, 1971).

[2] W.R.D. Sewell and Harold D. Foster, "Environmental Risk: Optimizing Management Strategies in the Developing World," *Environmental Management* 1, 1 (1976), pp. 49–59.

[3] John Whittow, *Disasters: The Anatomy of Environmental Hazards* (Athens: The University of Georgia Press, 1979).

[4] W.R. Hansen and E.B. Eckel, "The Alaska Earthquake, March 27, 1964: Field Investigations and Reconstruction Effort," in *Focus on Environmental Geology*, ed. R.W. Tank (London: Oxford University Press, 1966), pp. 46–65.

[5] W.R.H. White, "The Alaska Earthquake: Its Effects in Canada," *Canadian Geographical Journal* LXXII (1966), pp. 210–219.

[6] L.M. Murphy and R.A. Eppley, "Development Plans and the Pacific Tsunami Warning System," in *Tsunamis in the Pacific Ocean*, ed. W.M. Adams (Honolulu: International Union of Geodesy and Geophysics and East-West Center, 1970), pp. 261–269.

[7] Harold D. Foster and Vilho Wuorinen, "British Columbia's Tsunami Warning System: An Evaluation," *Syesis* 9 (1976), pp. 113–122.

[8] Environment Canada, *Canada Water Year Book 1975* (Ottawa: Information Canada, 1975), pp. 202–203.

[9] R.B. MacLock and G.A. Page, "Cutting Our Flood Losses," in *Water Problems and Policies*, eds. W.R.D. Sewell and Mary L. Barker, Cornett Occasional Papers 1, 1980, pp. 7–12.

[10] Reid D. Kreutzwiser, "Might 'Management' Save Great Lakes' Shores?" *Canadian Geographic* 97, 2 (1978), pp. 60–65; Fisheries and Environment Canada, *Canada Water Year Book 1977–1978* (Ottawa: Minister of Supply and Services, 1978), pp. 102–103.

[11] Environment Canada and Ministry of Natural Resources Ontario, *Canada-Ontario Great Lakes Shore Damage Survey: Technical Report*, October 1975.

12 Fisheries and Environment Canada and Ministry of Natural Resources Ontario, *Shore Property Hazards*, n.d., 14 pp.; Government of Canada, *What You Always Wanted to Know About Great Lake Levels*, n.d., 29 pp.; Fisheries and Environment Canada and Ministry of Natural Resources Ontario, *A Guide for the Use of Canada/Ontario Great Lakes Flood and Erosion Prone Area Mapping*, March 1978, 19 pp.; Walter M. Tovell, "Not Ours to Control: Living with Changing Lake Levels," ROTUNDA 10, 3 (1977).

13 Fisheries and Environment Canada, *Canada Water Year Book 1977-1978* (Ottawa: Minister of Supply and Services, 1978), p. 103.

14 A.D. Kiil, "Fire Research Programs and Issues in Mid-Canada," in *Proceedings of the International Fire Management Workshop*, ed. D. Quintilio, May 1979, pp. 5-14.

15 National Research Council Canada, *Canadian Committee on Forest Fire Control*, Reports Tabled at 1980 Annual Meeting, Victoria, British Columbia, January 22-24, 1980.

16 Ian R. Methuen, "Fire Research at the Petawawa Forest Experiment Station: The Integration of Fire Behaviour and Forest Ecology for Management Purposes," in *Fire Ecology in Resource Management Workshop Proceedings*, ed. D.E. Bubé, December 6-7, 1977, pp. 23-27.

17 Bruce D. Lawson, Project Leader, Fire Research, Canadian Forestry Service, Pacific Forest Research Centre, Victoria, personal communication, September 3, 1980.

18 Harold D. Foster, *Disaster Planning: The Preservation of Life and Property* (New York: Springer-Verlag, 1980).

19 B. Fischhoff, C. Hohenemser, R.E. Kasperson, and R.W. Kates, "Handling Hazards," *Environment* 20, 7 (1978), pp. 16-37.

20 R. Perla, "Artificial Release of Avalanches in North America," *Arctic and Alpine Research* 10, 2 (1978), pp. 235-240.

21 N. Mudry, P.J. Reynolds, and H.B. Rosenberg, "Post-Project Evaluation of the Red and Assiniboine River Flood Control Projects in the Province of Manitoba, Canada." Paper prepared for 11th Congress, International Commission on Irrigation and Drainage, Grenoble, France, 1981.

22 Nova Scotia, Department of Lands and Forests, *Report on the 1979 Experiment with Thuricide 16B for Foliage Protection and Reduction of Population Densities of Spruce Budworm Larvae [Choristonevra fumiferana (Clemens, 1865)] Lepidoptera: Tortricadae.*

23 Winnipeg, *Emergency Operational Plan*, Metropolitan Corporation of Greater Winnipeg, 1963.

24 L.A. Swick, Chief, Environmental and Natural Plans, Emergency Planning Canada, personal communication, September 8, 1980.

25 *Ibid.*

26 A.K. McQuillan, *Benefits of Remote Sensing in Canadian Northern Resource Development* (Energy, Mines and Resources Canada, 1975); Thomas T. Alföldi, *Landslide Analysis and Susceptibility Mapping* (Energy, Mines and Resources Canada, 1974); T.T. Alföldi, "Remote Sensing of Natural Hazards for Environmental Impact Assessment," paper presented at EPS Remote Sensing Seminar, March 11, 1975, Ottawa, Ontario.

27 R.B. MacLock and G.A. Page, *op. cit.*, pp. 7-12.

28 Vilho Wuorinen, "Seismic Microzonation of Victoria: A Social Response to

Risk," in *Victoria: Physical Environment and Development*, ed. Harold D. Foster, Western Geographical Series, 12, 1976, pp. 185-219.

[29] Angela Abrams, *Present Geologic Hazards and Soil Sensitivity to Earthquake Movement for the Lower Mainland Official Regional Plan Review* (Ministry of Environment, British Columbia, 1979).

[30] Vilho Wuorinen, "A Methodology for Mapping Total Risk in Urban Areas" (Ph.D. Dissertation, Department of Geography, University of Victoria, 1980).

[31] R.S. Ferguson, "Building Codes—Yesterday and Today," *Habitat* 18, 6 (1976), pp. 2-7; H.B. Dickens and A.T. Hansen, "Canada's National Building Code: Its Development and Use," *Habitat* 18, 6 (1976), pp. 8-11.

[32] *Ibid.*

[33] H.W. Nasmith, Thurber Consultants Ltd., Victoria, B.C., personal communication, May 1979.

[34] Harold D. Foster, "Relief, Drainage and Natural Hazards," in *Vancouver Island: Land of Contrasts*, ed. Charles N. Forward, Western Geographical Series, 17, 1979, pp. 51-69.

[35] H.W. Nasmith, *op. cit.*

[36] Harold D. Foster and R.F. Carey, "The Simulation of Earthquake Damage," in *Victoria: Physical Environment and Development*, ed. Harold D. Foster, Western Geographical Series, 12, 1976, pp. 221-240.

[37] Jim Jefferson and Joseph Scanlon, *The Sydney/Big Storm Report*, Emergency Planning Canada Field Report 74/7, 1974.

[38] Harold D. Foster, "Assessing Disaster Magnitude: A Social Science Approach," *The Professional Geographer* XXVIII, 3 (1976), pp. 241-247.

9/Research in Canadian Recreational Planning and Management
Geoffrey Wall

Introduction

Discussions of recreation are plagued by imprecise terminology. Although there is a considerable body of literature which attempts to clarify the meanings of such terms as recreation and leisure, universally acceptable definitions have yet to be derived. The problem is compounded by the indiscriminate use of words such as pleasure, fun, spare time and enjoyment which are often used as synonyms for recreation and leisure and as substitutes for each other. In the interests of clear thinking it is desirable to make a distinction between the meanings of leisure and recreation. Leisure can be regarded as a measure of time: it is the time remaining after work, sleep and necessary personal and household chores have been completed. It is the time available for doing as one chooses. Leisure may thus be defined as "discretionary time." Recreation embraces the wide variety of activities which are undertaken during leisure. Outside of professional circles, there has probably never been one word or phrase in common circulation to describe that time which we think of as leisure. People talk about concrete, discrete activities, such as watching television, skiing or going to the cottage, and not about recreation or leisure. Leisure and recreation are abstractions from common experience, abstractions which only those who stand aside from that experience can perceive. The language is that of the academic and the planner rather than the participant.[1]

The simple distinction between leisure as discretionary time and recreation as activity is difficult to implement, for many activities include both obligatory and discretionary components. For instance, without food we would die and eating is a necessity; it is also a popular form of recreation from which many people derive great pleasure. Similarly, gardening and attending conventions are activities which can be both enjoyable and a chore. Such difficulties have prompted some authors to argue that leisure and recreation are states of mind and that they are best defined in psychological terms.[2] While one can be sympathetic to this viewpoint and can acknowledge that individuals recreate for a wide variety of reasons and may even derive different satisfactions from the same activity, psychological definitions have their own inherent difficulties. The designation of areas for excitement, danger or relaxation is uncommon among recreational planners and site managers who usually operate on the basis of activities, designating areas for camping, skiing or hunting. However, the psychological definitions do serve to remind us that opportunities to recreate are not provided in and for themselves; they are made available to enable participants to achieve a wide range of satisfactions.

Recreation and leisure are not the prerogative of any one discipline. Recreations in the home, such as reading and watching television, are probably best studied by sociologists and psychologists, although economists may be interested in associated spending patterns. While recognizing that other disciplines have important roles to play, it is suggested that the geographer is in a position to make a distinct and significant contribution to the understanding of outdoor recreation. Outdoor recreation is a land use. It is in competition with agriculture, forestry, mining, housing, industry and a variety of other functions for the same scarce resources of land and water. Recreation facilities such as ski areas, resorts, parks and swimming pools have service areas comparable to those of stores or ports, and recreation creates patterns of movement analagous to those associated with commuting or migration and susceptible to analysis by similar methods. From these examples alone it should be evident that the concepts and methods of the geographer are appropriate to analyses of recreation and have the potential to further the understanding of recreational phenomena.

Outdoor recreation has two basic aspects: the supply of recreational facilities and the demand for participation in outdoor recreation. Supply and demand interact to produce the pattern of outdoor recreation, which may be defined as the spatial and temporal incidence of outdoor recreation. These patterns have associated economic, environmental and social impacts and give rise to planning and management problems.

Interactions between supply and demand occur at a variety of scales reflecting the time available for outdoor recreation and the distances that can be traversed during that time. When only short periods of time are available as, for example, in the evening, recreation, of necessity, takes place in or relatively close to the home. In contrast, during vacations, when several days of leisure may be juxtaposed, it is possible to travel long distances. There is thus a continuum from recreation in the home to recreation at considerable distances from the home base, the latter often being associated with the acquisition of temporary accommodation. It follows that tourism can be regarded as an extreme form of recreation which is distinguished by relatively long lengths of stays away from home and relatively large distances travelled.[3] The literature generally focusses on either recreation or tourism but, it is argued, these are aspects of the same phenomenon which can usefully be considered together: after all, recreationists and tourists may be found together at the same sites doing similar things.

The existence of the recreational time-distance continuum draws attention to the fact that the temporal distribution of leisure may be as significant as its quantity. If, for example, the working week were reduced by several hours, it would make a great deal of difference to patterns of recreation if these hours were distributed evenly across the week, added to the weekend, or accumulated towards a longer vacation. Other things being equal, the larger the size of the unit of leisure, the smaller are the distance constraints, and the greater is the freedom of locational choice of the potential participant. However, such time-distance relationships are further modified, particularly on long journeys, by the availability of money, for wealthy travellers may increase their time at a destination by substituting fast but expensive air travel for cheaper but slower ground transportation.

Supply

The supply of recreational facilities is "the natural and man-made features which provide or could reasonably be expected to provide in the future opportunities for outdoor recreation."[4] Attention in Canada first focussed on resource allocation for recreation at the Resources for Tomorrow Conference in 1961.[5] Three related lines of investigation were recommended to effectively evaluate supply prospects:
1. basic research into the relationships of the natural environment to recreation;
2. a present recreational land-use inventory;
3. a recreational land-use capability inventory.

In spite of the large quantity of recreational research which has been undertaken, few Canadian studies have provided fundamental insights into man-environment interrelationships in recreation. However, this situation reflects the present status of recreation research internationally. On the other hand, considerable progress has been made on the classification and inventory of existing and potential recreational resources.

The climate of Canada is both a resource and a resistance. The marked spatial and seasonal variations in climate greatly influence the recreational potential of the country. Great differences between summer and winter temperatures result in seasonal variations in recreational activities and in the ability of the country to attract foreign visitors and retain vacationing nationals. Economic pressures are placed on resorts which are unable to attract visitors throughout the year because returns on capital investment must be earned over a short operating season. Unseasonal weather may spell disaster for unprepared facility operators such as the the owners of ski areas whose patronage has suffered through lack of snow in mild winters. Many recreational areas are attempting to extend their operations by developing complementary attractions in the off season. Thus, for example, Ontario summer resorts in the Bruce Peninsula and Muskoka have developed cross-country and snowmobile trails, whereas ski resorts have constructed summer attractions. The new resort at Whistler, British Columbia, will have ski slopes and a golf course so that it can cater to visitors throughout the year.

The Atmospheric Environment Service has taken the initiative in preparing a number of recreation-tourism climatic studies at a provincial scale, and reports for Ontario, the Prairie and Maritime Provinces, and the Northwest Territories have been published.[6] These reports document the season length and reliability of weather conditions for a number of popular recreational activities as they vary from place to place. Such information is of great potential utility in calculating the likely length of operating seasons before investments are undertaken.

At a different scale, microclimate information has been employed in the planning of national parks. While sufficient data are not always available to enable a numerical or quantitative approach to be adopted, it is usually possible to glean sufficient information to make recommendations concerning some aspects of site planning. For example, Findlay examined the climate of Pukaskwa National Park on the northern shore of Lake Superior and indicated how climatically desirable areas in the park change with the seasons.[7] In February the most comfortable areas are in the deep valleys perpendicular to the prevailing wind, but they are less attractive in April as the temperatures rise, snow and ice melts, and they become less easy to traverse. By May, favourable zones for recreational activities can be found on inland dry areas above the valley bottoms but away from the relatively cold Lake Superior shoreline. Such information has obvious implications for the siting of trails and other recreational facilities. Similar reports to that for Pukaskwa are available for Auyuittuq, Fundy, Kejimkujik, Kouchibouguac, Prince Albert and Riding Mountain National Parks.[8]

The Atmospheric Environment Service has extensive climatological records and has sought to encourage the application of meteorological information to recreation and tourism through the organization of conferences and the publication of their proceedings.[9] Nevertheless, there is evidence to suggest that the wealth of materials has yet to be used to their full potential.[10]

The Ontario Recreation Supply Inventory is one example of an inventory of present recreational land use.[11] It is a computer-based system which attempts to provide a record of the recreational facilities and resources within the province, as well as estimates of the recreational opportunities that they provide. In order to calculate "opportunities," it is necessary to apply various standards to the inventory data. These are the space standard, access capacity, turnover rate, season length, and an institutional factor.

The space standard is an estimate of the space required for one opportunity of recreation. It is estimated taking into account quality considerations, i.e., the amount of space required for a recreationist to comfortably enjoy the activity. Some examples of space standards are: ice skating, 50 square feet per person, canoe tripping, one-fifth of a mile per person, and hiking, one-quarter of a mile per person.

Access capacity is a standard which considers the extent to which a resource is physically accessible. For instance, in the case of boating, the access capacity is determined by the number of moorings, the number of boat ramps or hoists, and the number of parking spaces which can accommodate a car and boat trailer. The extent to which such facilities are available can limit the use of the resource which, in this case, is the water body on which boating takes place.

Turnover rate is the number of times a resource or facility can provide an opportunity for recreation of a given quality in a 24-hour period. This recognizes that a facility or resource can be, and often is, used by more than one person in a day.

Season length is the average number of days per year during which the activity can be enjoyed. In some activities, such as swimming and golf, the season length may be affected by facility management in determining the number of days of operation. In other cases season length may be restricted by the weather. For example, average annual season lengths for sailing and water-skiing in Ontario are 135 and 65 days respectively.

The institutional factor recognizes that all supply is not equally available to all people every day of the week, and takes into account such constraints as usual working hours, statutory holidays and Sunday closures.

Employing these five standards, information on supply can be generated for particular activities or for areas within the province. It was felt that such information would be valuable for comparison with demand figures and might be useful in the study of many other problems of supply. In spite of the large volume of information which has been gathered, the utility of the system has been restricted by the failure to up-date the data base.

The Canada Land Inventory preceded the Ontario Recreation Supply Inventory and was much more ambitious in scope.[12] The Canada Land Inventory is discussed in Chapter 1, so it is only necessary to mention the recreation component here. Land is designated into one of seven classes, ranging from class one with high capability to class seven, which incorporates land of very low sustained potential. In the land capability system for recreation, subclasses denote recreational features or attractions that contribute to an area's potential for supporting intensive use. Shorelands generally rank higher than uplands because of the intensive-use capability of beaches and the popularity of shore-based activities. On uplands and low-quality shorelands, the variety of activities possible and the landscape quality in terms of scenery, topography and natural history phenomena determine the rating. Water bodies are not evaluated independently; rather it was felt that the potential of water bodies would accrue to the surrounding land. In addition to published maps, the data are also available for manipulation by computer.

The Canada Land Inventory was extremely bold in its conception and it has generated a great deal of information. While some have questioned the quality of the data and the validity of the underlying assumptions, it is easy to be critical after the event.[13] It was a pioneer effort which received international acclaim. It was never intended to be used for detailed site planning, but it has utility at regional levels, as Smith has demonstrated in his study on cottaging in Prince Edward Island.[14] It should be remembered that a capability map is neither a suitability nor a feasibility study and cannot fulfill their respective roles. Any resource development plan must ultimately depend upon the sound appraisal of information gained from field work and other supplementary sources. The full potential of the computer manipulation of the data has not been realized because of the cost and because of government reorganization which eliminated the Outdoor Recreation-Open Space Division of the Lands Directorate just as it was ready to embark upon this task.

Many measures of recreational supply and potential, including those discussed above, depend upon somewhat mechanistic means of indicating the suitability of areas of recreation in numerical terms. In a somewhat similar vein, an extensive literature has developed concerning the quantitative evaluation of the quality of scenery.[15] In the past, areas have been designated as parks because of their scenic value, but in the absence of established criteria for the assessment of that scenery. Researchers on landscape evaluation are aiming to remedy this deficiency by developing techniques of evaluation which are objective and replicable. Much of the literature on landscape evaluation has emanated from Britain and the United States, although there are signs that this is changing.[16] Canadian researchers have tended to investigate specific components of the landscape such as wild rivers and scenic roads.[17] Landscape evaluation is often seen as an intractable technical problem whose solution would resolve many of the difficulties of designating areas for preservation. This is not the case, for beyond the technical problem is the issue of values. If it were possible to determine the most beautiful area in the country and all could agree on it, the problem of what to do with it would still remain. Some might wish to fence it off and prohibit visitors to avoid its desecration, while others might argue that it would be wrong to prevent people from seeing such a significant part of the national heritage.

The climate, land and water resources of Canada provide possibilities and problems for the provision of outdoor recreational opportunities, but these may be modified by human action. Artificial hills and snow can be made, artificial lakes can be created, and even wilderness areas have their complement of man-made trails. However, the emphasis on the inventory and monitoring of supply has been on the natural and nonurban. Comparatively little effort has been devoted to the inventory of recreational opportunities in urban areas, and it is proving difficult to move away from the blind application of space standards, in spite of exhortations to this effect.[18] Similarly, there has been a tendency to emphasize the public provision of recreation opportunities; much less is known about the recreation resources in private hands.[19] The lack of balance in emphasis reflects the availability of resources for research and the backgrounds of many recreation researchers, planners and managers which give them a predilection for relatively natural areas.

Demand

Demand is a term which is often associated with the discipline of economics. In that context it refers to the quantity of a product which is consumed at a given price: as the price increases, demand decreases, and as the price falls so demand tends to rise. The economic definition of demand cannot readily be employed in the study of outdoor recreation, for many forms of outdoor recreation are unpriced, or priced only indirectly, and participants do not bear the full cost of the decision to participate. Furthermore, many proponents of outdoor recreation regard it as a merit want which should be available to all sectors of the population, regardless of the ability to pay, even if this requires public subsidy.

The demand for outdoor recreation may be defined as "the use of existing facilities and the desire to use recreation facilities now or in the future" or, to put this another way, the number of people requiring to take part in an activity.[20] Demand, as defined above, incorporates three components:

1. Effective demand. This consists of those people who actually take part and is usually measured in user-days or frequency of participation;
2. Deferred demand. This refers to those people who could and would like to participate but do not, either because of a lack of facilities or a lack of knowledge, or for both of these reasons;
3. Potential demand. This consists of those people who would like to participate but are unable to at present, and require an improvement in their economic and social circumstances in order for them to be able to do so.

Unfortunately, the literature on outdoor recreation is often imprecise in the use of the word demand. Deferred and potential demand, which can be grouped together as suppressed demand, are extremely difficult to measure and, in consequence, are often ignored. Authors frequently use the word demand when they are considering only effective demand, participation or consumption. Great care, therefore, should be taken in interpreting the literature on the demand for outdoor recreation.

Considerable information is available in Canada on effective demand, but much less is known about suppressed demand. Questionnaire surveys undertaken for the Canadian Outdoor Recreation Demand Study in 1967, 1969 and 1972, and provincial surveys, such as the Ontario Recreation Survey, 1973, have generated a great deal of information on what Canadians do in their leisure time.[21] The CORDS results indicate growth in participation in most forms of outdoor recreation, but there are signs, such as stagnating rates of visitation to provincial parks, that growth rates have begun to level off.[22] The surveys also demonstrate marked regional and socioeconomic variations in participation. However, sound explanations of many of these differences remain elusive.

Secondary analyses of these large data sets is taking two major forms. Firstly, there has been an interest in focussing upon the participation rates and recreational problems of particular subgroups of the population such as apartment dwellers, senior citizens and single parents.[23] Secondly, in recognition that most people participate in a number of recreational activities, there has been a move to identify groups of activities which are commonly found in association and are frequently called activity clusters, activity packages or market segments. Romsa, for example, has undertaken such a study for Quebec.[24] While there has been some debate concerning which statistical techniques are appropriate for the grouping exercise, the move to study activities in combination appears to be a progressive step.[25]

In contrast to the considerable information which is available on effective demand, few data exist on suppressed demand. However, the Ontario Recreation Survey attempted to gain an insight into this phenomenon. It addressed the problem of suppressed demand in two main ways:

1. By examining the constraints which people currently experience and which restrict their participation in recreational activities. It is assumed that if such constraints were removed then participation would increase;
2. By asking respondents in which activities they desire more participation.

The constraints most often mentioned by respondents were insufficient time, lack of money, or lack of opportunity. However, the significance of reasons varies from activity to activity. For example, among present campers, golfers and ice skaters who desire to participate more in their respective activities, ice skaters are most likely to mention lack of opportunities and poor or crowded facilities; golfers most frequently indicate lack of time; and, of the three, campers are most inhibited by cost. Not surprisingly, the nature of the constraints varies with the socioeconomic characteristics of respondents. Thus, for example, middle-aged respondents were more likely to be constrained by lack of time than older residents, who were more likely to be restricted by their physical abilities.

The responses to questions concerning activities in which more participation is desired reveal a great variety of aspirations. More participation is often desired in activities which are already popular, and active outdoor recreations such as swimming, fishing, camping, touring and snowmobiling frequently appear high on the list of desirables. It is difficult to know how far such findings represent real desires or if they are little more than ready responses to superficial survey questions. However, there could be considerable repercussions if such proclivities were to be encouraged, for many types of active outdoor recreation consume large quantities of resources and are environmentally demanding.

Household surveys, of the type which has been discussed, have generated a great deal of information on consumption of outdoor recreation and some material on suppressed demand. Unfortunately, these data have been of less value for planning than had been hoped. The time lag between data acquisition, analysis and publication has often been so great that results have been outdated before they have been published. Furthermore, the utility of the data is often restricted by the scale at which it has been collected. Such surveys provide a general picture of participation aggregated over large areas. In spite of large initial samples, subsamples may be too small to derive meaningful analyses for smaller areas or for activities which are participated in by a minority of people. However, decisions on the provision of many facilities are local rather than national or even provincial in scale.

For planning purposes it is desirable to know the likely demand for outdoor recreation at a particular time in the future. It is extremely difficult to calculate future demand with any certainty. The magnitude and type of demand will be influenced by the nature of supply, for the provision of new recreation opportunities can create new demand, convert suppressed demand to effective demand, or divert demand to new locations or activities. The extent to which one activity or location can be substituted for another activity or location without a decline in the quality of the recreational experience has yet to be determined with any precision. In such circumstances predictions of recreational demand are little more than "guestimates."

One simple but crude means of estimating future levels of participation is to project existing participation rates. If this is to be done, a time series of information must be available and it must be assumed that rates of change will not alter in the period for which the projection is made. If participation data are not available, it may be possible to use other indices such as attendance records, membership lists, number of licences or sales of recreation equipment. The suitability of each index will vary with the recreational activity in question. The method has severe limitations, particularly in the case of informal activities such as picnicking or driving for pleasure, where little numerical information may be available. Unfortunately, the assumption that existing rates of change will remain unaltered is seldom realistic and, in fact, this is often what one is trying to predict. The method is unable to foretell sharp changes in the popularity of recreations and ignores the influences of supply upon demand. The method can provide quick, rough estimates for a few years ahead but should be avoided for longer-term projections.

Most commonly used methods of predicting future recreational participation (effective demand) are based on the relationships between participation rates and the socioeconomic attributes of participants. Three steps are usually involved:

1. The socioeconomic correlates of participation in the recreational activity under consideration must be determined;
2. The number of people and their socioeconomic characteristics must be calculated for the area in question for the time period of interest;
3. The predicted numbers of people in each socioeconomic group are multiplied by the appropriate coefficients of participation and the results of these calculations are summed.[26]

The methodology involves a number of assumptions: it is assumed that relationships between participation rates and socioeconomic variables remain constant over time; that the future socioeconomic characteristics of the population can be determined accurately; and that the supply of facilities is not critical. Unfortunately, the strength of relationships between participation rates and socioeconomic variables is not great, so that the predictive power of such methods is not particularly strong.

A variety of other forecasting techniques has been reviewed by Lehtiniemi, but they have yet to receive widespread use in recreation.[27] It continues to be virtually impossible to predict rates of participation for an area with any precision; it is even harder to predict the demand for a particular site, particularly if that site has yet to be established. Nevertheless, in both the public and private sector, it is highly desirable to know the demand for a facility before capital is invested so that one can be as sure as possible that scarce resources will not be wasted.

Patterns

This section is concerned with the distribution of recreationists and recreational structures as they vary across space and through time. There is a wide variety of studies of outdoor recreation patterns and papers on urban and rural, intensive and extensive, public and private, summer and winter, and past and present recreational land uses have been published. The reader is referred to the collection of papers edited by Wall for a selection of such studies in Ontario.[28] Rather than describe such studies in detail, a task which is beyond the scope of this review, patterns of recreation will be discussed under five major headings: description, evolution, theory, prediction and manipulation.

Description

Descriptions of patterns of outdoor recreation can be subdivided into three types according to the scale of investigation. These are national and provincial studies, site studies and regional studies. Each has its own advantages and disadvantages.

The Canadian Outdoor Recreation Demand Study and the Ontario Recreation Survey are examples of national and provincial surveys. These studies have been discussed above, so only brief mention is required here. Suffice to say that they are based on large samples scattered over wide areas and are therefore expensive to undertake. Difficulty is usually experienced in relating participation to supply, although some success has been achieved in combining data from the Ontario Recreation Supply Inventory and the Ontario Recreation Survey in the Tourism and Outdoor Recreation Planning Study.

Site studies are at the opposite end of the scale from national studies. They are investigations of particular recreational facilities or resorts. They usually begin with a detailed description of the site and situation of the facility under examination. Interviews are then conducted with users of the site to gain such information as their origins, group composition and socioeconomic characteristics; their on-site activities; their satisfactions with the experiences obtained; and suggestions concerning modifications to the site or its management to enhance future visitor satisfactions. Such data are relatively easy and cheap to collect and can be of great utility to the site manager. However, unless such studies are specifically designed to test substantive issues, they seldom generate findings of applicability beyond the site itself. In particular, since interviews are conducted at the site, no information is gained on nonvisitors, or those who chose to visit a site other than the one under examination. One consequence of this is that the majority of visitors report that they have an enjoyable experience (otherwise they would not have come!), and the opinions of those who might be more critical are not canvassed.

It is suggested that there is a need for more studies undertaken at an intermediate scale, where both household and site surveys could be employed, and where supply, as well as demand, could receive due consideration. There are few Canadian studies of this type, although the Canadian Outdoor Recreation Demand Study began with a similar objective, and the Tourism and Outdoor Recreation Planning Study goes a considerable way in this direction. Studies of the Highlands and Islands of Scotland, undertaken by the Tourism and Recreation Research Unit of the University of Edinburgh, demonstrate what can be achieved when a specific problem (the implications of oil-related development for recreation provision) is tackled using a variety of data acquisition techniques, coupled with simple but appropriate methods of analysis, and the sensitive interpretation of results.[29]

Evolution

Most studies of outdoor recreation in Canada are concerned with the present. There are not many studies which examine how existing patterns of outdoor recreation evolved and the history of recreational land use continues to be a neglected area of research. Attitudes to the land have changed considerably over the years, and the major recreation resource areas of Canada have not always been viewed as attractive recreation destinations. Positive appreciation of wilderness is a relatively recent phenomenon in the history of western civilization and of Canada. At a time when so many people are convinced of the importance of wilderness, it is sobering to think that wilderness appreciation could be little more than the latest fashion in landscape taste! Unfortunately, Canadian attitudes to the landscape have yet to be documented with the thoroughness which Huth and Nash have devoted to the task for the United States.[30] However, Foster has recently made a valuable contribution in her study of the history of wildlife preservation.[31]

The evolution of public recreational provision is better documented than the history of developments in the private sector. National and provincial parks are perhaps the most visible public recreation areas. The history of national parks, particularly western parks, has been described in a number of places.[32] Provincial parks, on the other hand, are not well documented, although a thorough study of the provincial parks of British Columbia has been undertaken by Youds.[33] This thesis is particularly interesting in that it describes how the park system contracted in response to increased pressure for resource exploitation, before expanding again in recent years. McFarland has investigated the evolution of municipal recreation in Canada and studies of the evolution of the park systems of Edmonton and Vancouver have also been undertaken.[34]

Evidence of the use of recreation resources in private ownership is much more fragmentary than that on public reserves, and studies of the topic are more limited. Wolfe and Wall have both examined cottage developments in Muskoka, and Lundgren has written on the changing distribution of hotels in the Montreal Laurentians in Quebec.[35]

Public and private responsibilities intertwine in Niagara Falls and Banff, which are two of the most noted resorts in Canada, and their prominence has attracted researchers.[36] Other less prestigious resorts have received little attention. Similarly, the history of extensive recreations, such as hunting and fishing, has not been examined, although they have always been important recreational resource uses. Overton's study of the evolution of the game laws in Newfoundland is a recent contribution to this neglected area of investigation.[37]

In summary, knowledge of the evolution of recreational land-use patterns is fragmentary, that work which exists is widely scattered, and more research needs to be undertaken if we are to understand the background to many recreational resource planning and management problems. A book on the evolution of recreational land use in Canada is currently in press, and it is hoped that this will go some way to filling some of the gaps which have been identified.[38]

Explanation

Most studies of patterns of outdoor recreation have been empirical investigations undertaken in the absence of a well-established theoretical framework, although Campbell, Rajotte and Greer and Wall have recently tried to make generalizations concerning the recreational hinterlands of cities.[39] Few researchers have attempted to relate their findings to those of others, and the employment of different questionnaires, sampling frames, survey methods and coding systems has frustrated the comparison of results and the cumulative development of knowledge. A cause and consequence of this is that theory is poorly developed in studies of outdoor recreation, and researchers have looked to concepts and methods in other disciplines and have applied them to outdoor recreation, often without adequate consideration of the underlying assumptions.

Outdoor recreation differs from many other products in a variety of ways which may have implications for analysis. For example, unlike many other products, in recreation the user visits the site of production, rather than the good being transported to the user. Furthermore, in recreation the good may not be consumed in the sense that a loaf of bread or a pair of shoes is consumed. Unlike many products, recreational opportunities cannot be readily stored: while a worker may sometimes be able to accumulate days of paid vacation, a hotel or campground operator cannot postpone his services for an empty room or a site cannot be sold twice the following night! Again, distance is usually regarded as a disutility in most economic transactions, but in the case of recreation there is often an interest in going the extra mile to see something new or exotic. Clearly, not all recreationists are distance minimizers. In such circumstances notions of intervening opportunity and distance decay may need qualification.

Prediction

The ability to predict future patterns of recreation depends upon the ability to predict demand and to assess its spatial implications. Since these tasks are difficult to accomplish, it follows that it is very hard to foretell future recreational patterns. Unexpected changes in exchange rates, political tensions or transportation costs can suddenly modify peoples' choice of destinations.[40] Even almost a decade after the 1973 energy crisis, there is still uncertainty concerning its effects, so that comments regarding the future influence of a changing energy situation must be little more than speculation.

Although systems models have been employed, the most common

method currently in use for predicting recreational travel patterns is a modified gravity model.[41] The gravity model must be modified by the inclusion of some measure of site attractiveness to replace one of the population measures, for many people are moving away from, rather than to, centres of large population but indices of site attractiveness are difficult to derive.[42] Some researchers are attempting to derive models which reflect the fact that recreationists often visit more than one destination on a single trip.[43] It should be noted that such models do not really explain anything; however, they do appear to work. A useful review of the problems in this area can be found in Coppock and Duffield.[44]

Manipulation

There are ongoing attempts to modify recreational travel patterns. Advertising is employed by both the private and public sectors to persuade potential visitors to patronize one destination rather than another, and cheap fares and packaged trips may be employed to further induce the traveller to move in a particular direction. Sometimes the motives for manipulation may be profit; at other times they may be more altruistic, as in the case where tourism development is part of a regional economic development strategy. There are few published evaluations of attempts to manipulate recreational travel patterns, and this appears to offer an interesting avenue of research. One wonders, for example, to what extent the advertising strategies of the various levels of government are competitive or complementary.

Impacts

Participants in outdoor recreation cause a variety of impacts which, for convenience, can be classified under three headings: economic, environmental and social. In reality, these categories are not distinct: for example, it may be possible to spend money to ameliorate some types of environmental impact. Nevertheless, the three-fold division is a useful one, for almost all studies of the impacts of outdoor recreation can be readily assigned to one of the categories, there being few studies which examine more than one type of impact.

Economic Impacts

As indicated earlier, many recreational facilities are provided as free goods, i.e., the consumer is not asked to pay for their use directly, although they are frequently paid for indirectly through taxes. This causes difficulties for the measurement of the value of recreation in economic terms. Nevertheless, some method is required of comparing the benefits to be derived from the use of scarce resources in outdoor recreation with the benefits to be deployed from the use of those same resources for other purposes. Also, some means is required of estimating if the potential benefits to be derived from the provision of a facility are likely to exceed the costs. It is true that many recreation benefits are intangibles and incommensurables and that this creates problems for the economic evaluation of recreation benefits, but this should not be construed as an argument for abandoning the attempt. Rather, it is an indication of the magnitude of the challenge.

Recreational benefits can be considered under two major headings: primary and secondary benefits. Primary benefits are the benefits derived by the user of a recreational area and the secondary benefits are the benefits gained by the operator of a facility and those connected with him.

Primary Benefits

In the partial absence of a market mechanism, primary benefits are probably the hardest to measure. Crude measures, such as estimating the total expenditures of visitors to a site or simply asking them how much they would be willing to pay for the use of a facility, have numerous deficiencies.[45] A slightly more sophisticated method assumes that the benefits which people derive from recreating in a given area are directly related to the distances which they are prepared to travel to the area, and hence to travel costs. If the origins of visitors to a site are known, employing the above assumption, it is a relatively easy task to draw up a demand curve and calculate the consumer surplus. Such Clawson demand curves, as they have been called after one of their more prominent advocates, have been heavily criticized and minor refinements have been suggested by other users, but they remain one of the few methods of estimating the primary benefits of an existing facility.[46] However, since the origins of visitors must be known in order to construct the demand schedule, unless one is willing to employ data from a similar, existing site, they have little utility for evaluating the primary benefits from a proposed facility.

Secondary Benefits

Secondary benefits are most commonly calculated using economic multipliers. An economic multiplier measures the change in incomes (or number of jobs) resulting from an exogenous injection of expenditure into an economy, i.e., an injection of tourist expenditure into an economy will raise personal incomes within that economy by some coefficient or multiple of itself. The income multiplier considers three types of spending:

1. *Direct spending.* Initial expenditures by visitors create direct revenue to hoteliers, service stations and other components of a local economy;
2. *Indirect spending.* The payment of salaries and wages to local employees are indirect effects of initial tourist expenditures;
3. *Induced spending.* As wages and salaries within the local economy rise, consumption expenditure also rises, providing an additional impetus for local economic activity. The income multiplier is the ratio of the direct, indirect and induced spending to the direct spending.

There is now a substantial literature on economic multipliers and the reader is referred to this for for further technical details.[47] However, a number of warnings are appropriate: there are sales and employment multipliers in addition to income multipliers; different authors calculate the multiplier in slightly different ways with major implications for results; and the size of the multiplier is greatly influenced by the definition of the region adopted for the calculation. Unfortunately, too, the multiplier calculations can only be undertaken if a large volume of data on business transactions is available and this is seldom the case.

In spite of these problems, multipliers appear to have considerable potential utility in evaluating possible investments from the perspective of regional economic devlopment. If multipliers are calculated separately for sectors of the recreation and tourist economy, such as different types of tourist accommodation, then expected benefits to alternative investment strategies can be compared. Perhaps two major conclusions can be drawn from recent multiplier studies: gross expenditures on recreation and tourism are misleading as an indication of their significance to an economy unless the size of leakages is also known, and the value of recreation and tourism to a local economy is often overestimated because economic multipliers are often small.[48]

A concise review of methods of economic analysis applicable to outdoor recreation and tourism has recently been prepared by the Canadian Outdoor Recreation Research Committee, and Mathieson has prepared a thorough statement on the economic impact of tourism.[49] These two sources constitute an excellent introduction to the literature.

Environmental Impacts

Large numbers of participants in outdoor recreation are bringing about changes in the environments to which they resort. Increased mechanization of recreation, including the growth of such activities as snowmobiling, skiing, power boating and driving dune buggies, has magnified the potential for environmental impact. Participants in informal activities such as walking, swimming and picnicking, also leave their marks. Even environmentally conscious visitors have the power to destroy the areas to which they are attracted, particularly when grouped together in large numbers over long periods of time. An understanding of the impact of visitors is a prerequisite to the sound management of recreation areas. As the need for environmental impact statements becomes increasingly recognized, and even legally required, so demands for information on the environmental effects of outdoor recreation will become more pressing.

There is a large and growing literature on the impact of outdoor recreation on the natural environment. This literature, which is largely British and American, has been reviewed by Wall and Wright.[50] Most of the findings are appropriate to the Canadian situation. They indicate that environmental changes will occur even at low intensities of use. In northern latitudes where soils are thin and growing seasons are short, soil and vegetation are particularly prone to damage and recovery rates may be very slow. In addition, the presence of snow and associated activities are complicating factors. The snowmobile and all-terrain vehicle have enabled their users to stray from the beaten track and penetrate formerly inaccessible areas. Thus, technological change has increased the potential for damage and also distributed it more widely.

In spite of the large volume of writings on the topic, research on the impact of recreation is insufficient or lacking in some areas. For instance, the impact of many recreational activities has not been adequately researched (e.g., motor boating); but in other areas there is a larger volume of literature (e.g., trampling and snowmobiling). Many of the studies are concerned with only limited aspects of the environment. For example, Liddle has pointed out that ecologists have mainly investigated the effects of trampling on vegetation and soils, and only occasionally have the associated animals been considered.[51] Few studies assess the impact of an activity on all aspects of the environment that are affected by that activity. Nevertheless, much information of value to managers is already available, although, according to Clark, greater effort is needed to bridge the gap between academic research and its practical application.[52]

Research on the environmental impact of recreation has been concentrated on accidental impacts in relatively natural environments. These impacts are quite localized when compared to the effects of acid rain, which appear to be far-reaching. Comparatively little work has been undertaken on recreational impacts on built environments, although some of the studies of vandalism may have relevance here, or on the creation of man-made recreational environments.[53]

Social Impacts

The social impact of recreation can be considered under two headings: the influence of one participant or group of participants on another individual or group of participants, and the impact of recreationists on the host communities on which they impinge.

Lucas's classic study of the Boundary Waters Canoe Area demonstrated that different groups of users have different expectations and tolerances and impinge upon each other in different ways.[54] Lucas found that paddling canoeists were very demanding, with a perceived wilderness area much smaller than the officially designated area. They were likely to be bothered by meeting other groups and disliked heavily used areas. In contrast, motor boaters were more tolerant of encounters and accepted relatively high recreation levels. Priddle and his collaborators have replicated this work in Algonquin Park and Killarney and have been concerned to translate such findings into practical application.[55] The notion of crowding, as seen in the number of group interactions that can take place before the recreational experience is impaired, has been the focus of attention, and measures have been implemented which restrict the sizes of groups and limit the number of parties in the parks. However, crowding is a complicated concept which has proved difficult to pin down.[56]

User conflicts may be expected between cross-country skiers and snowmobilers; between fishermen, sailers and power boaters; between campers with different expectations and camping styles; and even between roller skaters and pedestrians in Stanley Park, Vancouver.[57] It is not difficult to recognize the problems, but it is a challenge to come up with solutions which will satisfy all groups of participants.

The impact of visitors on host communities is an emerging research area which will gain greater practical significance as more stress is placed on the welfare of residents of destination areas. Mathieson has reviewed the literature in the context of tourism, and Butler has pointed to some of the seemingly significant variables which contribute to the magnitude of impact.[58] Doxey's study of Niagara-on-the-Lake and McFarlane's examination of the Stratford Festival are two of the very few studies of this phenomenon, although Cheng has also presented some interesting personal observations on the situation in Canmore, Alberta.[59] Studies of the impact of visitors on host communities are still lacking a well-established theoretial base, although the concept of the "resort cycle" offers promising possibilities.[60] There is also a need for more empirical work to ascertain both types of social impact and their salience for different members of society.

Commentary

As has already been indicated, most studies of the impacts of outdoor recreation have been within one of the three impact groups and there has been little attempt and no widely recognized methodology to combine economic apples, environmental pears and social plums into a composite measure to summarize the total impact of a recreational development. Similarly, there have been few attempts to assess who gains and who loses from such developments. One of the most comprehensive studies which has been undertaken to date is that by Abt Associates on the impact of tourism on Prince Edward Island.[61] In a more futuristic perspective, Butler has attempted to indicate likely impacts of various types of tourism development on the northern environment and on Inuit lifestyles.[62]

One concept which goes some way to combining environmental and social impacts in recreational sites is the concept of carrying capacity. Carrying capacity can be defined as the maximum number of people who can use a recreational site without an unacceptable alteration in the physical environment and without an unacceptable decline in the quality of the recreational experience. There is now an extensive literature on carrying capacity, but this is not the place to review it as this has been done adequately elsewhere.[63] However, several points merit emphasis. The concept appears to be applicable to both natural and man-made environments, although it has been largely applied to the former. A recreational site, be it natural, man-modified or man-made, does not have one set carrying capacity. The capacity will reflect the goals established for that site, and these should specify the degree and types of environmental modification which are acceptable and the nature of the recreational experiences to be provided. It may be influenced by such factors as capital availability and managerial experience. Carrying capacity remains an elusive concept, but the time when researchers and managers sought one mythical magic number, which could be approached with safety but exceeded at peril, has passed. Discussions of the carrying-capacity concept have focussed attention on the need for clear and precise statements of goals, and assessments of the extent to which those goals are being realized.

Canadian park systems have long had vague and contradictory goals. Both national and provincial park systems have been set the task of preserving a unique heritage and providing recreational opportunities. Some, such as the Ontario Provincial Park System, also have economic objectives. Park advocates are often at odds in their reasons for desiring more parks, some seeing them as playgrounds for people, and others regarding them as nature reserves which should not actively encourage the visitor. The tension between preservation and development is unlikely to disappear, but there is evidence that the dichotomy is being faced in a practical way. Perhaps this can be most clearly seen in the Ontario Provincial Park System, where parks have been classified into six types (nature reserves, wilderness areas, natural environment parks, recreation parks, provincial waterways and historical parks).[64] Furthermore, for each class the purpose and protection afforded by the designation, the facilities and services permitted, and their areal and locational requirements are specified through a zoning system. The classification and zoning system is an attempt to suggest the function of particular parks and areas within parks and, hence, what their management should be.

Where visitor pressures are thought to exceed the carrying capacity, as in parts of Algonquin and Killarney Provincial Parks, visitor quotas have been introduced in the interests or protecting the environment and maintaining a quality recreational experience. These schemes are still in their infancy and their operation has yet to receive full evaluation. The introduction of such management strategies vividly indicates that the resolution of the technical problem of measuring carrying capacity will lead to other problems of a less technical nature. If the number of visitors is to be restricted, how will it be decided who gains admission?

Decisions

Numerous people make decisions concerning the deployment of recreational resources. These range from the individual who has to decide when and where to participate and what activities to participate in to the numerous agencies with a responsibility for monitoring, regulating or providing outdoor recreational opportunities. The recent fashion in geography for undertaking studies of perceptions and decision making has resulted in a spate of such investigations of recreational land use.[65] There are numerous investigations of attitudes towards and evaluations of a wide variety of recreational environments ranging from national parks to non-designated recreational space in urban areas.[66] In part, these studies reflect the recognition of the failure of recreational behaviour to be adequately explained by socioeconomic variables. Such perception studies have provided interesting insights into particular recreation situations and have provided managers with useful information concerning the quality of recreational experiences to be obtained at their site and possible responses to contemplated management strategies. However, to date, the perception studies have provided few fundamental insights into what people want from their recreations or why they do particular things. In the absence of such information it is difficult to truly explain recreation behaviour. Phillips has opened up an interesting avenue of investigation in her examination of relationships between personality types and their participation in recreation, and her study appears to have implications for the substitutability of recreations and for leisure counselling.[67]

Much of the more accessible land is in private ownership, so that individual decisions of landowners have a bearing on the availability of recreational space for others. For example, most of the accessible shoreland property is in private lands and therefore public access to lakes is restricted in many areas. In some places, such as the Lake Erie shoreline and Prince Edward Island, a large proportion of the property is owned by foreigners, and this has caused local residents to feel that they are losing control of their own destiny. These concerns led to the establishment of a Royal Commission on Land Ownership and Land Use in Prince Edward Island and restrictions on the purchase of land by nonresidents of the province.[68] Another issue which has become increasingly prominent in recent years is the extent to which landowners are willing to give public access to their land for outdoor recreation. In Ontario, there have been recent revisions in the laws of legal liability and trespass in an attempt to facilitate the public use of private land for recreation.[69]

Although it would be wrong to downplay the significance of the private sector in providing outdoor recreation opportunities, particularly in the areas of accommodation and winter sports, a much larger area of recreational land is owned and administered by public agencies. These include the national parks which are under federal jurisdiction; the provincial parks and other areas which provide outdoor recreational opportunities, such as crown lands and the Conservation Authority lands in Ontario; and municipal parks. A recent study of the structure of recreational responsibilities in federal and provincial governments showed that 66 agencies in the federal government were concerned with recreation and, although the parts played by the ten provincial governments varies markedly, 58 agencies in 19 different ministries were concerned with some aspect of recreation in Ontario alone.[70] Hall has suggested that this gives rise to a number of major problems of coordination:

1. The problem of the duplication of facilities;
2. The problem of underprovision, particularly on the edge of large cities like Toronto, where municipal governments have not been able to provide resources outside their boundaries, and rural municipalities have insufficient resources to provide extensive facilities;
3. Resources are not evenly divided between the various levels of government. For example, the federal government is capable of raising large sums of money, but the provincial governments, with their responsibility for crown lands, have large resources;
4. It has been claimed that the public has problems in understanding the roles of different agencies, and the absence of a unified approach probably leads to difficulty in accepting the different standards of behaviour required in recreation areas of different agencies.[71]

Burton and Kyllo added the following problems to those listed above: the existence of conflicts within and between federal and provincial governments, lack of a rational distribution of the services between them and the inadequacy of machinery for policy development, priority definition and general coordination within these levels of government.[72] Furthermore, the role of the private sector remains unspecified. Nevertheless, in spite of the above observations, Burton and Kyllo concluded that there is:

. . . little evidence of overlapping and duplication that has so often been feared; the primary problem has not been one of duplication but of services operating at cross purposes.[73]

There are also some signs of increased cooperation between the various levels of government as, for example, is illustrated by the establishment of the Federal-Provincial Parks Conference, the Agreements for Recreation and Conservation scheme (formerly called the Byways and Special Places Programme), and the joint funding of Harbourfront in Toronto.[74]

Various means of public participation have been employed to facilitate communication between planners and managers and their clienteles. Public participation has rapidly become part of the conventional wisdom but there is little agreement as to how best to proceed, and evaluations of public participation programs in the recreational field are in their infancy.

Some of those which exist have, themselves, generated controversy.[75] One can only applaud any attempt to solicit input from the public and to keep interested parties informed of developments. But one wonders how much can be achieved when set positions are taken with little prospect of compromise. In the case of Kouchibouguac National Park, for instance, consultation rapidly turned into confrontation.[76]

Conclusion

Canada is a large country with a small population. The large areas of forests and lakes, coupled with the low man-land ratio, give rise to a rich natural resource base for extensive forms of outdoor use. This use has been fostered by the creation of numerous parks. An image of recreational participation in the northern wilderness is close to the heart of many Canadians and attracts many visitors from south of the international border. Nevertheless, the vast majority of Canadians are urban dwellers and they are clustered in a small number of spots on the southern margin of the country. Most of their leisure is spent in the cities and not in the wilderness.

Recreational research in Canada has had a marked wilderness emphasis. There are numerous studies of recreation in national and provincial parks, but comparatively few investigations of urban recreation. The countryside as a recreational resource has received even less attention. Unlike in Britain, where the countryside is a major focus of outdoor recreation, in Canada the farmed landscape has often been seen as a barrier which has to be crossed to reach a wilderness goal. There are some signs that this emphasis may be changing slowly. A conference on the country-side in Ontario devoted considerable attention to outdoor recreation.[77] There is also evidence of increased interest in urban recreation and tourism as downtown areas are rehabilitated and major recreational and cultural facilities are constructed.[78] An increasingly tight energy situation may encourage people to recreate closer to home, placing further stress on near-urban areas but relieving some of the pressures on remote places. The designation of near-urban parks is one policy response to this possibility.[79] These trends suggest that Canadians may come to appreciate their man-modified and man-made landscapes to a greater extent, and that a more balanced selection of research themes is required with greater emphasis on near-urban and urban recreation.

Economic recession is likely to place limitations on budgets for development, operation and maintenance of recreation facilities, as well as for research. Tight finances are causing increasing attention to be turned to the economics of outdoor recreation. As cost-effectiveness becomes the slogan of the day and public facilities are expected to pay for themselves, the roles of the public and private sector will require clarification, and it is even possible that the distinctions between them could blur. On the other hand, it may mean that the public sector will be increasingly reluctant to spend money on capital improvements. Economic concerns may also increase pressures for resource exploitation in parks, with a resulting increase in the potential for conflict between recreation and other potential uses of scarce land and water resources. There will also be greater concern for the identification of who gains and who loses from the provision of recreational opportunities.

Canada has an enviable record in recreational research. Although their objectives have not always been achieved, and they have received extensive criticism from within the country, studies such as the Canada Land Inventory, the Canadian Outdoor Recreation Demand Study, and the Tourism and Outdoor Recreation Planning Study have received international acclaim. They have been bold and innovative in conception, and they have also resulted in the compilation of large volumes of information. The days are gone when it was possible to bemoan the lack of data. There is now a vast quantity of information on recreation and tourism in Canada, and considerable quantities of it are stored in data banks, such as the Leisure Studies Data Bank at the University of Waterloo, and are available for secondary analysis. Much of these data are on what activities people participate in and on their social characteristics. There is a paucity of information on why people do what they do. In consequence, existing data are good for describing recreational behaviour but they do not go very far in explaining it.

In spite of attempts at coordination and rationalization, a large number of agencies will continue to exercise some responsibility for recreation in Canada. This may lead to some duplication of services and some inefficiencies in their provision, but it should ensure variety in the types of opportunities available so that Canadians will be able to exercise that element of choice which is essential if outdoor activities are to be truly recreational.

Notes

1 Hugh Cunningham, *Leisure in the Industrial Revolution* (London: Croom Helm, 1980), p. 13.
2 B.L. Driver and S.R. Tocher, "Toward a behavioral interpretation of recreational engagements, with implications for planning," *Elements of Outdoor Recreation Planning*, ed. B.L. Driver (Ann Arbor: University of Michigan Press, 1974), pp. 9–31.
3 Robert Britton, "Some notes on the geography of tourism," *Canadian Geographer* 23 (Winter 1979), pp. 276–282.
4 Adrian Phillips, *Research into Planning for Recreation* (London: Countryside Commission, 1970), p. 4.
5 Resources for Tomorrow, *Conference Background Papers* (Ottawa: Queen's Printer, 1961), 3 vols.

6 R.B. Crowe, G.A. McKay and W.M. Baker, *The Tourist and Outdoor Recreation Climate of Ontario* (Toronto: Atmospheric Environment Service, Department of Fisheries and the Environment, 1977 and 1978), 3 vols; J.M. Masterton, R.B. Crowe and W.M. Baker, *The Tourism and Outdoor Recreation Climate of the Prairie Provinces* (Toronto: Atmospheric Environment Service, Environment Canada, 1976); A.D. Gates, *The Tourism and Outdoor Recreation Climate of the Maritime Provinces* (Toronto: Atmospheric Environment Service, Environment Canada, 1975); R.B. Crowe, *A Climatic Classification of the Northwest Territories for Recreation and Tourism,* Project Report No. 25 (Toronto: Atmospheric Environment Service, Environment Canada, 1976).

7 B.F. Findlay, *Climatography of Pukaskwa National Park, Ontario* (Toronto: Atmospheric Environment Service, Environment Canada, 1976).

8 J.M. Masterton and B.F. Findlay, *The Climate of Auyuittuq National Park, Baffin Island, Northwest Territories,* Project Report No. 22 (Toronto: Atmospheric Environment Service, Environment Canada, 1976); E.E.D. Day, R.J. McCalla, H.A. Millward and B.S. Robinson, *The Climate of Fundy National Park and Its Implications for Recreation and Development,* Atlantic Regional Geographical Studies (Halifax: Saint Mary's University, 1977); W.B. Watson, *The Climate of Kejimkujik National Park, Nova Scotia* (Toronto: Atmospheric Environment Service, Environment Canada, 1977); W.B. Watson, *The Climate of Kouchibouguac National Park, New Brunswick* (Toronto: Atmospheric Environment Service, Environment Canada, 1977); D.J. Bauer, *The Climate of Prince Albert National Park* (Toronto: Atmospheric Environment Service, Environment Canada, 1976); A.J. Keck, *The Climate of Riding Mountain National Park, Manitoba* (Toronto: Atmospheric Environment Service, Environment Canada, 1975).

9 W.D. Wyllie and L.A. Maguire, eds., *Workshop on the Application of Meteorological Information to Recreation and Tourism* (Toronto: Atmospheric Environment Service, Environment Canada, 1980); J.M. Powell, ed., *Socioeconomic Impacts of Climate: Proceedings of the Workshop and Annual Meeting of the Alberta Climatological Association, March 1979* (Edmonton: Northern Forestry Research Centre, Environment Canada, 1980).

10 W.M. Baker, "The utilization of climatic data and weather services in tourist planning and facility operation in Ontario," in *Workshop on the Application of Meteorological Information to Recreation and Tourism,* eds. W.D. Wyllie and L.A. Maguire (Toronto: Atmospheric Environment Service, Environment Canada, 1980), pp. 37–55.

11 Ontario, Tourism and Outdoor Recreation Planning Study Committee, *Ontario Recreation Supply Inventory Users Manual* (Toronto, 1975).

12 Canada, Department of Regional Economic Expansion, *The Canada Land Inventory Land Capability Classification for Outdoor Recreation* (Ottawa, 1970).

13 Louis Hamill, "Canadian approaches to the description and evaluation of the recreation resources and scenery of near-natural areas, 1961–1976," paper presented to the Annual Meeting of the Canadian Association of Geographers (London: University of Western Ontario, 1978).

14 Donald Smith, "Cottages and Land Capability: The Case of Prince Edward Island", unpublished M.A. thesis (Waterloo: University of Waterloo, 1976).

15 Bruce Mitchell, *Geography and Resource Analysis* (London: Longman, 1979), pp. 144–175.

16 Philip Deardon, "Landscape assessment: the last decade," *Canadian Geographer* 24 (Fall 1980), pp. 316–325.

17 R.A. Hooper, *Assessing the Recreational Potential of Waterways: A Description and Evaluation of Selected Systems* and *A System to Inventory and Evaluate Mountain Rivers for Canoeing and Kayaking: A Basis for the Determination of Recreational Potential*, Research Papers 77–1 and 77–3 (Edmonton: Natural History Research Division, Western Region, Parks Canada, 1977); George Priddle, "Measuring the view from the road," *Geographical Inter-University Resource Management Seminar*, Department of Geography, Wilfrid Laurier University, Waterloo 4 (1973–1974), pp. 67–81.

18 J.R. Wright, W.M. Braithwaite and R.R. Forster, *Planning for Urban Recreational Open Space: Towards Community-Specific Standards* (Toronto: Ontario Ministry of Housing, 1976).

19 A notable exception is Peter W. Williams, "A Case Study of Industrial Recreation in Kitchener-Waterloo and its Role in Urban Recreational Planning," unpublished M.A. thesis (Waterloo: University of Waterloo, 1971).

20 Adrian Phillips, *Research into Planning for Recreation* (London: Countryside Commission, 1970), p. 2.

21 Federal-Provincial Parks Conference, *Canadian Outdoor Recreation Demand Study* (Waterloo: Ontario Research Council on Leisure, 1976), 3 vols; Ontario, Tourism and Outdoor Recreation Planning Study Committee, *Ontario Recreation Survey, Tourism and Recreational Behaviour of Ontario Residents* (Toronto, 1977 to 1979), 8 reports.

22 Ontario, Ministry of Natural Resources, *Statistical Report* (Toronto, Various dates).

23 Ontario, Tourism and Outdoor Recreation Planning Study Committee, *Ontario Recreation Survey, Tourism and Recreational Behaviour of Ontario Residents 6, Special Groups* (Toronto, 1979).

24 Gerald Romsa, "A method of deriving outdoor recreational activity packages," *Journal of Leisure Research* 5 (Autumn 1973), pp. 34–46.

25 Recreational studies using or discussing statistical grouping procedures include the following: D.W. Bishop, "Stability of the factor structure of leisure behavior: analyses of four communities," *Journal of Leisure Research* 2 (Summer 1970), pp. 160–170; R.J. Burdge and D.R. Field, "Methodological perspectives for the study of outdoor recreation," *Journal of Leisure Research* 4 (Winter 1972), pp. 63–72; J.C. Hendee and R.J. Burdge, "The substitutability concept: implications for recreation research and management," *Journal of Leisure Research* 6 (Spring 1974), pp. 157–162; J.C. Hendee, R.P. Gale, and W.R. Catton Jr., "A typology of outdoor recreation activities," *Journal of Environmental Education* 3 (Fall 1971), pp. 28–34; G.F. McKechnie, "The psychological structure of leisure: past behavior," *Journal of Leisure Research* 6 (Winter 1974), pp. 27–45; R.L. Tatham and R.J. Dornoff, "Market segmentation for outdoor recreation," *Journal of Leisure Research* 3 (Winter 1971), pp. 5–16.

26 J. Beaman, "Statistical projections that go beyond projections of past trends," *Geographical Inter-University Resource Management Seminar*, Department of Geography, Wilfrid Laurier University, Waterloo 4 (1973–1974), pp. 131–144.

27 Leo Lehtiniemi, "Futures forecasting techniques," in *Park and Recreation Futures in Canada: Issues and Options*, Canadian Outdoor Recreation Research Commit-

258/Canadian Resource Policies

tee (Toronto: Ontario Research Council on Leisure, 1976), pp. 11–52.

28 Geoffrey Wall, *Recreational Land Use in Southern Ontario*, Department of Geography Publication Series No. 14 (Waterloo: University of Waterloo, 1979).

29 Tourism and Recreation Research Unit, University of Edinburgh, *Research Study into Provision for Recreation in the Highlands and Islands Phase 1—Areas Affected by Oil-related Development* (Edinburgh, 1976).

30 Hans Huth, *Nature and the American: Three Centuries of Changing Attitudes* (Berkeley: University of California Press, 1972); Roderick Nash, *Wilderness and the American Mind* (New Haven: Yale University Press, 1967).

31 Janet Foster, *Working for Wildlife: The Beginning of Preservation in Canada* (Toronto: University of Toronto Press, 1978).

32 See, for example, J.G. Nelson, *Canadian Parks in Perspective* (Montreal: Harvest House, 1969); J.G. Nelson and R.C. Scace, *The Canadian National Parks: Today and Tomorrow*, Studies in Land Use History and Landscape Change, National Park Series No. 3 (Calgary: The University, 1969); W.F. Lothian, *A History of Canada's National Parks* (Ottawa: Parks Canada, 1976 and 1977), 2 vols; R.D. Turner, "A Comparison of National Parks Policy in Canada and the United States", unpublished M.Sc. thesis (Vancouver: University of British Columbia, 1971); S.M. Van Kirk, "The Development of National Park Policy in Canada's Mountain National Parks 1885 to 1930", unpublished M.A. thesis (Edmonton: University of Alberta, 1968); R.C. Johnson, "The Effect of Contemporary Thought upon Park Policy and Landscape Change in Canada's National Parks, 1885–1911," unpublished Ph.D. thesis (Minneapolis: University of Minnesota, 1972).

33 Ken Youds, "A Park System as an Evolving Cultural Institution: A Case Study of the British Columbia Provincial Park System, 1911–1976," unpublished M.A. thesis (Waterloo: University of Waterloo, 1978).

34 E.H. Dale, "The Role of Successive Town and City Councils in the Evolution of Edmonton, Alberta, 1892–1966," unpublished Ph.D. thesis (Edmonton: University of Alberta, 1969); W.C. McKee, "The Vancouver park system, 1886–1929: a product of local businessmen," *Urban History Review* 3 (1978), pp. 33–49.

35 Jan Lundgren, "The development of tourist accommodation in the Montreal Laurentians," *Bulletin de l'Association des Géographes d'Amériques Française* II (1967), pp. 113–121.

36 Gerald Killan, "Mowat and a park policy for Niagara Falls, 1873–1887," *Ontario History* 70 (June 1978), pp. 115–135; Robert C. Scace, "Banff townsite: an historical-geographical view of urban development in a Canadian National Park," in *The Canadian National Parks: Today and Tomorrow*, eds. J.G. Nelson and R.C. Scace (Calgary: The University, 1969), pp. 770–793.

37 James Overton, "Tourism development, conservation and conflict: game laws for caribou protection in Newfoundland," *Canadian Geographer* 24 (Spring 1980, pp. 40–49.

38 Geoffrey Wall and John Marsh, *Recreational Land Use: Perspectives on Its Evolution in Canada* (in press).

39 Colin K. Campbell, "An Analysis of the Relationship between the Urban Based Skier and His Recreational Hinterland," unpublished M.A. thesis (Vancouver: University of British Columbia, 1967); Freda Rajotte, "The Quebec Recreational Hinterland", unpublished Ph.D. thesis (Montreal: McGill University, 1973); Tricia Greer and Geoffrey Wall, "Recreational hinterlands: a theoretical and

empirical analysis," in *Recreational Land Use in Southern Ontario,* Department of Geography Publication Series No. 14, ed. Geoffrey Wall (Waterloo: University of Waterloo, 1979), pp. 227–245.

40 Economist Intelligence Unit, "National Report No. 23: Ireland," *International Tourism Quarterly* No. 2 (June 1975), pp. 23–49.

41 J.B. Ellis and C.S. Van Doren, "A comparative evaluation of gravity and system theory models for state-wide recreational traffic flow," *Journal of Regional Science* 6 (Winter 1966), pp. 57–70.

42 J.H. Ross, *A Measure of Site Attraction,* Occasional Paper No. 2 (Ottawa: Lands Directorate, Environment Canada, 1973).

43 Gordon O. Ewing, "A multinational logit regression model of the distribution of multi-stop trips and hours," paper presented at the Annual Meeting of the Association of American Geographers, Philadelphia, April 1979.

44 J.T. Coppock and B.S. Duffield, *Recreation in the Countryside: A Spatial Analysis* (London: Macmillan, 1975).

45 D.W. Fischer, "Willingness to pay as a behavioral criterion for environmental decision making," *Journal of Environmental Mangement* 3 (January 1975), pp. 29–41.

46 T.L. Burton and M.N. Fulcher, "Measurement of recreation benefits—a survey", *Journal of Economic Studies* 3 (June 1968), pp. 35–48; O.L. Cary, "The economics of recreation: progress and problems," *Western Economic Journal* 3 (Spring 1965), pp. 172–181; J.L. Knetsch, "Outdoor recreation demands and benefits," *Land Economics* 39 (November 1963), pp. 387–396; A.H. Trice and S.E. Wood, "Measurement of recreation benefits," *Land Economics* 34 (August 1958), pp. 195–207.

47 B.H. Archer, *The Impact of Domestic Tourism,* Bangor Occasional Paper in Economics No. 2 (Cardiff: University of Wales Press, 1973), B.H. Archer, "Uses and abuses of multipliers," in *Planning for Tourism Development: Quantitative Approaches,* eds. G.E. Gearing, W.W. Swart and T. Var (New York: Praeger, 1976), pp. 115–132; B.H. Archer, *Tourism Multipliers: The State of the Art* (Bangor Occasional Paper in Economics No. 11, Cardiff: University of Wales Press, 1977); B.H. Archer and C.B. Owen "Towards a tourist regional multiplier," *Journal of Travel Research* II (Fall 1972), pp. 9–13.

48 K.M. Bohlin and R.G. Ironside, "Recreation expenditures and sales in the Pigeon Lake area of Alberta: a case of 'trickle-up'," *Journal of Leisure Research* 8 (Autumn 1976), pp. 275–288.

49 Alister Mathieson, "The Impacts of Tourism: A State of the Art Study," unpublished M.A. thesis (Waterloo: University of Waterloo, 1979).

50 Geoffrey Wall and Cynthia Wright, *The Environmental Impact of Outdoor Recreation,* Department of Geography Publication Series No. 11 (Waterloo: University of Waterloo, 1977).

51 M.J. Liddle, "A selective review of the ecological effects of human trampling on natural ecosystems," *Biological Conservation* 7 (January 1975), pp. 17–34.

52 Cameron Clark, "Prescribing carrying capacity standards for wildland areas: bridging the gap between policy and management," *Contact, Journal of Urban and Environmental Affairs* 10 (Spring 1978), pp 63–83.

53 Pat White, Geoffrey Wall and George Priddle, "Anti-social behaviour in Ontario Provincial Parks," *Recreation Research Review* 6 (May 1978), pp. 13–23.

54 R.C. Lucas, "Wilderness perception and use: the example of the Boundary

Waters Canoe Area," *Natural Resources Journal* 3 (January 1964), pp. 394-411.

55 George Priddle, "Recreational Use and 'Wilderness' Perception of the Algonquin Park Interior," unpublished M.A. thesis (Worcester, Mass.: Clark University, 1964); Cameron Clark, "The Algonquin Canoeist: A Preliminary Study of His Characteristics, Motivation, Use and Attitudes Regarding the Interior of Algonquin Park," unpublished M.A. thesis (Waterloo: University of Waterloo, 1975); Kenneth Morrison, "An Exploratory Study of Wilderness Use, Users and Management in Killarney Provincial Park," unpublished M.A. thesis (Waterloo: University of Waterloo, 1979).

56 Thomas Heberlein, "Density, crowding, and satisfaction: sociological studies for determining carrying capacities," in *Proceedings: River Recreation Management and Research Symposium* USDA Forest Service General Technical Report NC-28 (Minnesota: North Central Forest Experiment Station, 1977), pp. 67-76.

57 John Clarke, "War on wheels: the battle for Stanley Park," *The Globe and Mail* (May 31, 1980), p. 8.

58 Richard Butler, "Social implications of tourist development," *Annals of Tourism Research* 2 (November/December 1974), pp. 100-111.

59 George Doxey, "When enough's enough: the natives are restless in old Niagara," *Heritage Canada* 2 (Spring 1976), pp. 26-27; Richard MacFarlane, "Social Impact of Tourism: Resident Attitudes in Stratford," unpublished M.A. thesis (London: Unversity of Western Ontario, 1979); Jacqueline Cheng, "Tourism: how much is too much? Lessons for Canmore from Banff," *Canadian Geographer* 24 (Spring 1980), pp. 72-80.

60 Richard Butler, "The concept of a tourist area cycle of evolution: implications for management of resources," *Canadian Geographer* 24 (Spring 1980), pp. 5-12.

61 Abt Associates, *Tourism Impact Study for Prince Edward Island* (Cambridge, Mass., 1976).

62 Richard Butler, *The Development of Tourism in the North and Implications for the Inuit*, Renewable Resources Project Vol. 9 (Ottawa: Inuit Tapirisat of Canada, 1975).

63 Bruce Mitchell, *Geography and Resource Analysis* (London: Longman, 1979), pp. 176-200.

64 George Priddle, "The revised Ontario Provincial Park classification system," *Geographical Inter-University Resource Management Seminar*, Department of Geography, Wilfrid Laurier University, Waterloo 6 (1975-1976), pp. 48-78.

65 David Mercer, "The role of perception in the recreation experience: a review and discussion," *Journal of Leisure Research* 3 (Fall 1971), pp. 261-276.

66 J. Leslie Grant, "Recreational Behaviour, Perceptions and Characteristics of Summer Visitors to Point Pelee National Park, Ontario," unpublished M.A. thesis (Waterloo: University of Waterloo, 1976); Ronald Johnson, "Attitudes towards the use of designated versus non-designated urban recreation space," *Leisure Sciences* 1, 3 (1978), pp. 259-269.

67 Susan Phillips, "Recreation and Personality: A Systems Approach," unpublished M.A. thesis (Waterloo: University of Waterloo, 1978).

68 Prince Edward Island, Royal Commission on Land Ownership and Land Use, *Report* (Charlottetown, 1973).

69 Judith Cullington, "Attitudes to the promotion of private land for recreation," *Geographical Inter-University Resource Mangement Seminar*, Department of Geog-

raphy, Wilfrid Laurier University, Waterloo 10 (1979–1980), pp. 1–40.
70 T.L. Burton and L.T. Kyllo, *Federal-Provincial Responsibilities for Leisure Services in Alberta and Ontario* (Waterloo: Ontario Research Council on Leisure, 1974), 4 vols.
71 Robert K. Hall, *Outdoor Recreation Provision in Canada*, Discussion Papers in Geography No. 2 (Oxford: The Polytechnic, 1976).
72 T.L. Burton and L.T. Kyllo, *op. cit.*
73 *Ibid.*, ch. 7.
74 Robert K. Hall, *op. cit.*, p. 38.
75 Arthur Hoole, "Public participation in park planning: the Riding Mountain case," *Canadian Geographer* 22 (Spring 1978), pp. 41–50; H.G. Kariel, "Public participation in national park planning: comment no. 1," *Canadian Geographer* 23 (Summer 1979), pp. 172–173; Richard MacFarlane, "Comment No. 2 in public participation in national park planning," *Canadian Geographer* 23 (Summer 1979), pp. 173–176; A.T. Davidson, "Public participation in national park planning: reply," *Canadian Geographer* 23 (Summer 1979), pp. 176–179.
76 David Folster, "Refusing to take yes for an answer," in *The Globe and Mail* (May 31, 1980), p. 8.
77 M.J. Troughton, J.G. Nelson and S.I. Brown, *The Countryside in Ontario, Proceedings of the Countryside in Ontario Conference* (London: University of Western Ontario, 1974).
78 Peter Murphy, "Tourism management using land use planning and landscape design: the Victoria experience," *Canadian Geographer* 24 (Spring 1980), pp. 60–71; Geoffrey Wall and Jack Sinnott, "Urban recreational and cultural facilities as tourist attractions," *Canadian Geographer*, 24 (Spring 1980), pp. 50–59.
79 *Park News* 13 (November 1977) (Special issue on near-urban parks).

10/The Way Ahead

W.R. Derrick Sewell and Bruce Mitchell

Introduction

The Canadian scene is presently one of intense flux, economically, socially, and politically. In particular, although the country is experiencing a period of slower economic growth and higher than normal unemployment, some sectors of the economy and certain regions are experiencing boom conditions. While there have been cutbacks in employment in some industries, such as forestry and some branches of mining, there is buoyancy in others, notably those concerned with the production of energy. Similarly, while certain regions continue to experience economic difficulties, notably the Maritimes, others, particularly the western provinces, are witnessing a sustained period of growth.

It is also a period of considerable social change, characterized by a challenge to the conventional wisdom and a questioning of existing institutions.[1] Significant segments of the public at large are concerned about such matters as to what constitutes the good life and what is a desirable future for Canadians. They wonder about the relative emphasis that should be placed upon the pursuit of high levels of economic growth, the attainment of a more egalitarian society and the preservation of environmental quality. The traditional consumer society is now being challenged by a small but vociferous group which believes that a conserver society is superior.[2]

Both of these developments have played an important role in the political ferment that has heightened in the past decade. As things stand at the beginning of the 1980s, there is sharply divided opinion on the relative roles that the various levels of government should play in the management of Canada's economic and social affairs. In the past few years, relationships between Ottawa and the provinces have deteriorated considerably, and a move towards regionalism has gathered increasing momentum. The divergent viewpoints have been given concrete expression in the debate on the repatriation of the Canadian Constitution, and especially on matters concerned with the management of Canada's natural resources. Three issues in particular have been raised in this connection: namely, which level of administration should have the major powers relating to the management of economic affairs; how far does the ownership of resources imply complete control over their management; and what should be the respective roles of the federal and provincial authorities in the management of particular resources, notably petroleum, natural gas, fisheries, and various offshore resources, such as energy and minerals?

Two other matters have also been the subject of protracted discussion. The first concerns the high degree of control exerted by foreign interests over resources development in this country.[3] As noted in Chapter 1, a very considerable portion of the Canadian petroleum industry is owned by non-Canadians. The same is true of much of the mining, forest and fishing industries. Foreign investment in these activities has had many advantages, notably the acceleration of development and the provision of employment opportunities for Canadians. At the same time, however, it has meant that much of the decision making takes place outside Canada, particularly with respect to the location and the rate of development. Canadians have become increasingly resentful of the image of a branch plant economy controlled from elsewhere, and there is mounting criticism of the export of natural resource products, especially those which are likely to be in short supply by the end of the century, notably petroleum and natural gas. There is also apprehension of the likelihood that there will be increasing pressure from the United States for Canada to export water on a large scale.[4]

There have been several responses to such concerns by the federal authority and by various provincial governments. The federal government, for example, has tried to diminish foreign control of the Canadian petroleum industry, firstly by the establishment of Petro-Canada, and secondly by offering financial incentives to Canadian companies which embark upon programs of exploration and development. It has also offered encouragement for take-overs of foreign-owned petroleum companies. At the same time, several provincial governments have tried to deal with the problem of foreign ownership of land within their territories by passing restrictive legislation. Simultaneously, however, the governments have sought to attract investment into certain economic sectors and regions to provide jobs and economic development. The result has been tension between policy objectives which often are in conflict.

A second matter of continuing debate relates to the reconciliation of national and regional goals. For its part, the federal authority sees its role as a common denominator in a country of very diverse physical conditions, resource endowments and differing cultural heritages. It views its responsibilities as paramount in certain matters, notably in such functions as defence of the realm, management of the economy, relationships with other countries and the reconciliation of disputes among the provinces. It recognizes that as a confederation, Canada can only be governed effectively if there is cooperation among its constituent parts. At the same time, it feels that it has a major leadership role to play in matters of a common interest. Occasionally, however, the pursuit of the latter may confound the former. This seems to have been especially so in the attempt to deal with the energy crisis. The federal authority has announced a general goal of energy self-sufficiency, coupled with an objective of ensuring that the effects of differing energy endowments across the country shall be minimized. It has also stated that the country as a whole should benefit from revenues which are derived from the exploitation of oil and natural gas resources.

In contrast, a number or provinces, notably Alberta, have taken the view that the resources within their territory belong to them, and that the citizenry within their respective areas have a right to enjoy the wealth that results from their exploitation. They resent attempts to control the rate of exploitation, such as through the external imposition of taxes or royalties or regulations, or the control of prices at which oil or natural gas may be sold whether in Canada or to the United States. As a protest against federal initiatives in this connection, the Alberta government introduced restrictions of its own on the daily volume of oil production, thus forcing the federal government to seek alternative (and much more expensive) supplies elsewhere to fuel the economies of other provinces that would suffer from the shortfall. Alberta's apparent aim was to force the federal authority to raise the price of domestic crude to a level much closer to world prices, thus enabling the province to gather significantly higher revenues than it could at the lower, federally regulated price. Ottawa hesitates to allow this because such a move would undoubtedly have adverse effects in eastern Canada, both on the domestic scene and in the manufacturing industry.

There have been other major conflicts between the federal and provincial governments elsewhere in Canada, notably on the east and west coasts. New discoveries of offshore hydrocarbon resources, particularly in the Hibernian field, have prompted the Newfoundland government to claim primary (if not sole) jurisdiction over their exploitation. Other Maritime provinces are watching these developments with a keen interest, trying to determine what their own position would be should they also discover oil, natural gas, or mineral resources in offshore areas. At the same time, British Columbia has threatened to act as the collection agent for all taxes unless the federal authority rescinds its recently announced policy to increase levies on the export of natural gas. It has also become increasingly apprehensive of the use of federal powers with respect to fishery resources, notably in the case of a proposed addition to the Kemano project to provide additional hydroelectric power for an expansion of industry in the north of the province. A recent B.C. Supreme Court ruling endorsed the right of the federal authority to ban developments which would harm the fishery resource.[5]

Doubtless, the political manoeuvres between the federal and provincial authorities will continue and will heighten. There is likely to be an increasing number of cases submitted to the provincial and federal Supreme Courts for adjudication of disputes as to jurisdiction. Confrontation will grow and there may be threats to leave confederation. While a break up of the latter seems improbable, given the many advantages attached to its preservation, it is clear that the present turmoil will produce a new set of relationships between the federal and provincial authorities, giving each of them more clearly defined rights and responsibilities, especially in the resources management and development fields. It is also certain that resource exploitation will become a major issue in United States–Canadian relationships.[6] There are already major disputes with respect to fisheries and oil and natural gas. Others are emerging in connection with the management of water resources and the atmosphere. Resource problems, therefore, are likely to become key political issues in Canada in the 1980s.

Resource Issues of the 1980s

The exploitation of natural resources has provided the basis for Canada's ascent of the ladder of economic development to become one of the world's most wealthy nations. So vast has been the endowment that relatively few major conflicts or scarcities have occurred until recently. It seems, however, that confrontation will multiply rapidly in the present decade between competitors for the use of a given resource, and between developers of a particular resource and developers of other resources. These conflicts are expected to be especially acute in the case of five particular resources: energy, water, fisheries, the oceans and land. In addition, problems of maintaining environmental quality are likely to increase in scope and severity, particularly as a result of the spread of certain kinds of pollution, notably that resulting from the disposal of toxic wastes and those associated with the "new pollutions," such as acid rain and mercury poisoning.

Energy Resources

As Barker has demonstrated in Chapter 2, there is little doubt that the problem of energy scarcity will become a dominant political issue in Canada during the 1980s. Statistics show that, on a per capita basis, Canadians are the world's heaviest energy users, and that despite all the warning signs since the OPEC embargo of 1974, there has been little or no slowing down of the rate of increase in consumption. It could well be that unless really major shifts in policy are introduced in the next year or so, very severe shortages of energy supply may occur, resulting in substantial economic and social consequences.

As noted earlier, the search for a solution to these problems will be profoundly influenced by attitudes and decisions relating to the division of responsibilities between the federal and provincial levels of administration. As things presently stand, there is the prospect of a continuing battle over the rate at which such resources should be exploited, the price that should be charged, and the levies that can properly be made by the various levels of administration. There will also be debate as to the kinds of incentive that may be required to stimulate the development of renewable sources, such as solar energy, wind energy, tidal power or biomass.

The federal government has recently proclaimed its intention to encourage self-sufficiency in energy supplies, notably through accelerated programs of exploration and development in offshore areas, and by granting incentives for the adoption of new kinds of energy.[7] More funds are to be provided for research. As in the past, however, the focus remains dominantly on conventional sources and nuclear power.[8] The allocation of research funds emphasizes physical and natural science and technological aspects. Only a very limited amount of attention is given to non-technological dimensions, such as the environmental implications of developing different kinds of energy, or the relative effectiveness of various types of incentive programs. In general, a very conservative view is taken of the future, expecting that it will be rather similar to the present.[9]

Water Resources

Until about 30 years ago, water problems in Canada were of little more than local concern. Except when a major flood or drought occurred, such matters were considered to be beyond the interest of the federal authority. A dramatic change has taken place since the 1950s, particularly with the harnessing of some of the nation's rivers, such as the Columbia, the Saskatchewan-Nelson, and those involved in the James Bay scheme, and as a consequence of massive pollution of the Great Lakes. The federal government has responded with new legislation, aimed at raising the sophistication of water planning and at protecting and improving the quality of the nation's water bodies. An Inland Waters Directorate was established within Environment Canada to carry out a wide range of data collection, research and planning functions. Similar responses have occurred at the provincial level as well. This evolution of approaches and strategies is outlined clearly in Chapter 6 by Tate.

Despite all of this, however, a major water crisis is likely to occur in Canada by the end of the century.[10] A recent study by the Inland Waters Directorate shows that major water deficiencies will be experienced in at least six of Canada's river basins within the next twenty years, mostly in the Prairie Provinces,[11] both as a result of population growth, agricultural expansion and industrialization, and as a consequence of Canada's drive towards energy self-sufficiency. At the same time, unless there is a sustained and more vigorous attempt to reduce water pollution, particularly that associated with toxic materials, many of the nation's water bodies will have been damaged beyond the point of repair. Added to this, continued economic development in the arid West of the United States, and emerging scarcities elsewhere in that country, are likely to lead to rapidly mounting pressure for export. Studies undertaken by the United States Water Resources Council,[12] and other bodies,[13] have indicated that several regions of the United States already suffer from serious water scarcities and that by the end of the century many more will have been added to the list.

A basic problem in Canada is that insufficient is known about the extent of the nation's water resources or the demands that are likely to be put upon them in the next two or three decades. This makes it difficult to develop firm policies or to enter confidently into negotiations with the United States about possible transfers of water back and forth across the border.

Fisheries

Canada has long been one of the world's major seafaring nations, and has developed a substantial fishing industry on both the Atlantic and Pacific Coasts, as well as on freshwater lakes. This industry provides tens of thousands of jobs for those who man the fishing vessels and those on shore who process the catch. The annual produce of the industry exceeds $713 million.

As Draper has shown in Chapter 5, the fishing industry has witnessed changing fortunes in the past half century. It is threatened on the one side by growing competition from other nations, and on the other by the effects of industrial development in estuaries and on rivers, and the impacts of offshore exploration and development. Other concerns include rising and unstable fish prices, shifts in market patterns, technological changes, and expansion of capacity of fleets which already are too large. Nevertheless, many of the problems of the fishery can be attributed to overcapacity of the fishery fleets. The lot of the individual fisherman may well worsen unless measures are taken to reduce the amount of effort involved in obtaining the catch. Valiant efforts were made to accomplish this objective in the B.C. salmon fishery, but apparently with mixed success.[14]

Fishery management problems provide an array of challenges for geographic research. The common property nature of the resource creates many externalities, many of which have spatial manifestations. Thus, institutional arrangements often are inadequate since fish stocks do not respect political boundaries. "Natural" management regions also are hard to establish due to the variety and intermixing of fish stocks. Because those dependent on the fishery resource for their livelihood often have little economic mobility, the social and economic implications of proposed changes can be substantial, and therefore call for sensitive analysis of policy alternatives. The conflicts among different interests are numerous:

inshore versus offshore, angler versus commercial fisherman, seiner versus gillnetter. The scale of inquiry may range from the local to the international, and invites the expertise of those with understanding of biophysical and social systems.

Offshore Resources

In the eighteenth and nineteenth centuries, the Indian subcontinent, Africa and South America became the hunting ground of European powers seeking colonial empires. Attracted by sources of raw materials and by potential markets for their growing industrial economies, they divided up vast territories between them, and reaped rich rewards from their development. The continental shelves have become another hunting ground, initially for oil and natural gas, but eventually for minerals as well. The areas involved are enormous. Those relating to Canada are greater in extent than all the provinces combined.

As the discussions by Harrison and Kwamena and Draper in Chapters 4 and 5 show, the search for resources in the oceans' depths has come suddenly and has proceeded feverishly. The stakes are high. Multimillion dollar investments in exploration and development of such resources are now commonplace. But so are the potential rewards. At the same time, however, there is great uncertainty how such development can be controlled in such a way as to ensure that the public's interest is properly served. In the first place, there is confusion as to who owns the resources that are being sought. Not only do the provinces and the federal government lay claim to them, but in some cases there is dispute with the United States. Moreover, protracted discussions in the United Nations and in the Law of the Sea Conference have indicated a growing desire of land-locked nations and Third World countries to share the wealth that is in and below the oceans.

Experience in developing guidelines for the exploitation of these common property resources is very limited. It is clear, however, that a number of important issues are beginning to emerge. They are well illustrated in the debate that has surrounded the introduction of Bill C-48 in the House of Commons.[15] Its basic purpose is to put into practice the principles enunciated for the federal government's recent energy program, namely, to attain self-sufficiency. Towards this end, it specifies lead agencies in the search for hydrocarbons in offshore locations. The Department of Energy, Mines and Resources is indicated as the lead agency south of 60°N latitude, while the Department of Indian Affairs and Northern Development is named as the main agency to oversee development in the North. Statements before the Standing Committee on National Resources and Public Works which is currently reviewing Bill C-48, however, have revealed widely diverging views as to which of a number of possible agencies should be given lead status.[16] Differences in opinion were rooted in large part in the fact that offshore resource development brings into conflict several legitimate, but sometimes opposing, social goals, such as the improvement of the standard of living, redistribution of income and preservation of the environment. Such conflicts may be expected to multiply and to escalate in the next two decades. As they do, the need for modification of legislation, policies and administrative structures will become increasingly urgent.

Land Resources

Resource management problems associated with land-based resources are numerous. In the decades ahead, as Wonders has shown in Chapter 3, a major policy concern must be the Canadian North where numerous conflicting interests must be reconciled. The North appears on the verge of major resource development projects comparable to those on the scale of the James Bay power scheme in Quebec. In charting a path for the future, the needs of those who will live with the aftermath of the development must be balanced against the gains to Canadians in other regions who will gain through access to such resources as petroleum, natural gas and minerals. The question is not likely to be one of development or no development, but rather one which involves different trade-offs and compromises under which all participants share benefits and costs.

While the North has and should attract much attention, we should not forget that major resource allocation issues exist in and adjacent to cities and other settled areas. In Chapter 7, McLellan has outlined a classic dilemma. The public has created a demand for a product (building materials such as sand and gravel) but inevitably has objected whenever an aggregate producer proposes to open a new sand and gravel pit. Contributions from geomorphologists, economic geographers and social geographers could help in resolving such conflicts.

Wall also has reminded us in Chapter 9 that while recreation investigators have frequently focussed on nonurban environments, many recreation policy issues have an urban orientation and require more attention by geographers. With increasing energy costs, and the likelihood of people searching for recreational opportunities involving reduced travel, a growing opportunity is created for recreation geographers at the urban scale. One activity which might be given more attention is the assessment of sites for their recreational and tourism potential. This would draw upon the skills of the location analyst, and would demonstrate the utility of geographical research to the private as well as to the public sector. The opening of Canada's Wonderland, the 150 hectare fantasyland park just north of Toronto in May 1981 is likely to be only the first of similar ventures at different scales across the nation.[17]

Another important policy issue will continue to be agriculture. Geographers have worked in this area for many years, a necessary ongoing commitment. Perhaps a key research area in the next two decades will be the resource allocation decisions which must be made in the urban fringe areas across the country. Individuals such as Krueger have outlined how a sustained and long-term research program combined with a willingness to become involved in the policy process can contribute to the shaping of policy.[18] This mixing of research and advocacy activities is something that more geographers might consider.

New Pollutions

One of the most dramatic discoveries of the late 1970s was that emissions of sulphur dioxide and nitrogen oxides from plants in particular locations were causing serious environmental damage thousands of miles away.[19] This is because gases from the smelting of sulphur-rich ores, or the burning of coal or oil in power plants, mix with moisture in the atmosphere to produce nitric and sulphuric acids which then fall as "acid rain." A consequence has been that some parts of Canada are now receiving rainfall that is from 5 to 40 times more acidic than is natural in such locations.[20] The problem is caused only partly by Canadian plants. While it is true that the province of Ontario emits more than 2.4 million metric tons of sulphur dioxide per year, and that the International Nickel Company smelter in Sudbury has the dubious distinction of being the world's largest single source of that pollutant, [21] the major portion of acid rain falling in Canada originates in the United States. With accelerated programs of thermal power generation, much of it based on coal with a high sulphur content, it can be anticipated that the problem will escalate rapidly in the 1980s.

The environmental consequences will be serious. Although not all of the effects have yet been identified, it appears that acid rain results in major damages to fish populations, lower yields from forested areas, the leaching of nutrients and the disruption of soil balances, greater mobility of certain toxic metals such as lead and mercury, and the inactivation of certain significant microorganisms and disruptions of the food chain. It also accelerates building decay and automobile corrosion, and may adversely affect human health, particularly through the deposition of heavy metals in drinking water.[22]

At the beginning of 1981, the most severely affected areas in Canada were Ontario and Quebec. In Ontario alone, fish populations of tens of thousands of lakes have declined rapidly in the past few years as a result of increasing acidification.[23] The problem, however, is spreading to the Maritimes and to the Prairies. If no action is taken soon, few parts of the country will be unaffected by acid rain by the end of the 1980s.

Acid rain is an illustration of the classic problem of negative externalities resulting from the use of a common property resource, in this case, the atmosphere. The issue is further complicated by the fact that several jurisdictions are involved: provinces, states and the two federal governments. While there have been discussions between Canada and the United States, and a Memorandum of Intent on Transboundary Air Pollution was signed by the two countries in Washington, D.C. on August 5, 1980, there has been little concrete action to deal with the problem so far. Part of the difficulty lies in the fact that technology to deal with the problem effectively is not yet available: building higher smokestacks merely removes its incidence to a more distant location.[24] Another impediment is the cost. Experts in the field suggest that large-scale abatement of acid rain in the United States would add more than $7 billion each year to the cost of power generation, manufacturing and transportation. The bill would be more than $350 million annually in Canada. In a period of economic recession, such an increase in costs is certain to be vigorously resisted.

As with many other resources management issues, the primary focus of research in the acid rain problem has been on the physical origins and a few of the biological impacts. Studies of the broader ecological consequences and the economic and social impacts have been few in number and very modestly funded. Interestingly, although the problem has many spatial dimensions, it has stimulated very few geographers to devote any attention to it.

The acid rain issue is but one of several illustrations of "new pollutions" that are emerging in Canada and elsewhere. Others include mercury poisoning and chemicals used in attempts to control insects and other pests that damage forests and impair agricultural production.[25] Although they often differ considerably in nature, they have a number of common characteristics. One is that their impacts may be very difficult to detect until long after an emission of the pollutant. Another is that effects may be experienced hundreds and possibly thousands of kilometers away from the source. A third is that there is sometimes great uncertainty as to who should initiate action to deal with the problem. All of this emphasizes the need not only for a large research effort, but also for a refocussing of its emphases.

Refocussing Canadian Resources Research
The Level of Effort

Investment in scientific research and the development of technology (commonly referred to as R and D) is generally regarded as the key to economic and social progress. Certainly, those nations which allocate the highest proportion of their Gross National Product to such activities tend to enjoy the highest levels of material well-being, education, leisure, and social services. Currently, the United States, for example, is allocating some 2.5 percent of its GNP for this purpose, while the United Kingdom, Japan and West Germany are devoting about 2 percent towards this end.[26] The importance of maintaining a high level of effort in R and D is especially critical in those countries which have a high ratio of capital to labour, or in which natural resources play a dominant role in the nation's economic fortunes. Canada is one of those countries. It is not sufficient, however, to maintain a high level of R and D. Equally essential is the maintenance of flexibility in the topics which receive top priority, aiming to ensure that research is geared towards future problems as well as those encountered today.

While Canada has made major contributions to scientific research and the development of technology, the level of effort and the directions it has taken have not been commensurate with the problems the country now faces and will encounter in the next decade. Not only are expenditures on R and D in Canada now below one percent of GNP, but the percentage has tended to decline over the past decade. Moreover, undue reliance is placed on governments and, especially on the federal government, for funding and performance of R and D activities. As of 1978, the private sector in Canada accounted for only 34 percent of the R and D funds, and undertook slightly less than 43 percent of the effort. This contrasts considerably with the situation in other industrialized countries, such as Germany and Sweden, where between one-half and two-thirds of the R and D activity is funded and undertaken by the private sector.[27]

One implication of this imbalance may be that the R and D effort will be devoted mainly to aspects of direct interest to the government of the day, and much of it will be performed in-house, thus limiting the educational and training function of R and D. Another implication is that the R and D activities will tend to be conservative rather than innovative. If such implications do have foundation, the consequences could be very serious for the management and development of Canadian natural resources and the maintenance of environmental quality.

Needed Research on Resources and Environmental Management

One of the essential purposes of this volume has been to highlight the emerging problems in particular areas of resources management, to identify the kinds of research that would be especially useful in the search for solutions to such issues, and to suggest types of contributions which geographers might make in this connection. The foregoing chapters have detailed the types of research needs with respect to several of the nation's major natural resources and the Canadian environment. From the diverse inventory so compiled, one can discern several common threads. In a sense these might be regarded as major areas of emphasis in an agenda for research in the 1980s.

1. Assessment of Resource Availability

Canada is world-renowned as a vast storehouse of natural resources. Official documents, school textbooks and other literature refer to the country's enormous forests, abundant fisheries, huge water resources and its massive energy reserves. Yet, as the recent energy crisis has shown, some of the estimates of the nation's resources have been highly inaccurate. Most of them are based on physical availability and have little reference to cost. In many cases, the surveys on which the estimates are based have not been empirically verified, even on a sample basis. In the field of water resources, for example, there is only vague knowledge of the nation's ground water reserves. Again, while it is known that there are thousands of lakes, it is uncertain how much water they contain. Moreover, although it is clear that water pollution exisits in many parts of the country, there is no overall assessment of the problem. Similar deficiencies occur with respect to inventories of other resources, notably energy and minerals of various kinds.

It is clear that much more effort needs to be made to assess and update information about Canada's natural resources. While resource inventorying is a well-established practice in some countries, notably the United States,[28] it is done only irregularly in Canada, and generally focusses upon only a few resources. Experience has shown, however, the lack of basic data on resources reserves acts as a major impediment in the formulation of economic policies and in negotiations with foreign powers over trade in resource commodities.

2. Methodologies for Forecasting Future Demands

As the demand for the products of various natural resources continues to accelerate, as scarcities in some of these resources begin to appear, and as conflicts among alternative uses multiply, the need for much more sophisticated approaches to demand forecasting will become more urgent. While much progress has been made in some resource areas in this connection in Canada,[29] the methods used in many are still very crude, and in many instances they are little better than straight-line extrapolations of experience in the recent past. Little account is taken of the facts that improvements are made in technology, tastes alter, and new kinds of demand emerge over time.

Unfortunately, the subject of forecasting methodologies has been given relatively little attention in research programs in Canada. This contrasts considerably with the situation in the United States, where a great deal of effort has been devoted to the improvement of such approaches and techniques. A consequence has been that policy formulation in some fields has been impeded by the lack of reliable forecasts. This is especially so in the field of water resources management, but it has had adverse effects in planning with respect to other resources too, notably in energy resources development.

3. Expanding the Range of Choices

One of the greatest dangers faced by all societies is a narrowing of the range of options for future action.[30] This is especially so where a society is heavily dependent on a given resource, such as agricultural land or a mineral deposit. Once the resource becomes exhausted, the economic base may be severely damaged, and its political viability may be in jeopardy too. To avoid such a situation, a society needs to be searching constantly for alternatives—for new sources of supply and better ways of using existing ones.

Social scientists in general, and geographers in particular, could play a very useful role in helping to identify instances where the range of choice is narrowing, and offer suggestions as to ways in which it might be expanded. Specifically, in the case of energy, they might examine, for example, the potentialities and the consequences of various conservation measures (such as improvements in engine efficiency, recycling of waste heat, banning of cars from city centres and so on). They could also identify circumstances in which various renewable energy resources—such as solar power, wind power, biomass or geothermal energy—would have particularly appropriate applications. Beyond this, they could examine the various institutional inhibitions to the adoption of such innovations, and suggest necessary modifications to such institutions or new institutional forms.

4. Monitoring Shifts in Social Values

Among the most important challenges to be faced by planners and policy makers is the accurate assessment of public preferences. At one time politicians and their technical advisors were able to gauge such preferences fairly easily, especially where it could be assumed that what the public wanted was more of what they had at present. It seems that such an assumption can no longer be made. Value systems are changing and traditional goals are being questioned. Planners and politicians in North America and many western European countries are discovering that projects which they believed were in the public interest fail to obtain the necessary public support. Opposition to highway schemes, hydro-power projects, airport construction and nuclear power development illustrates this dilemma. The problem is especially significant, however, because the costs—economic, social, environmental and political—can be very high.

What is needed is a much greater understanding of the factors which condition public perceptions, and factors which stimulate changes in public views. Research is also required on ways in which such shifts can be detected and fed more effectively into the decision-making process.

5. Technology Assessment

Another major thrust for social science research in the resources management field is that of technology assessment. During the past few years, in North America in particular, there has been growing concern about the social desirability of certain technological innovations, such as supersonic transport planes, continental water transfer schemes, large-scale weather modification programs, or nuclear power development. While each of these innovations would bring certain benefits, they would also occasion adverse environmental and social consequences. Techniques are required for assessing the likely effects of such technologies before they are introduced. Social scientists could play a useful role not only in undertaking technology assessments, but in designing institutional arrangements to ensure that evaluations are both thorough and objective. Work undertaken through the U.S. National Academy of Sciences, the U.S. National Science Foundation, and the Science Council of Canada offers some helpful guidance in this connection.[31]

6. Environmental and Social Impact Assessment

Environmental impact assessment is another area of needed study. Stimulated by the environmental movement of the late 1960s, and given institutional support at the central government level particularly, environmental impact assessment is now an accepted aspect of resources policy making in many countries.[32] More recently, there has emerged a broader type of evaluation which embraces environmental effects, but also incorporates the human dimension. It is known as social impact assessment.[33]

In both instances, however, there remain many questions as to what should be considered, what weights should be attached to various factors, and who should undertake the assessment. Here indeed is an area of inquiry to which social scientists could make valuable contributions. Among the problems on which they might work are the development of techniques for assessing the impacts of resources development on local and regional economies, social interrelationships, and various elements of the physical environment, and means for weighing different sets of impacts against each other (such as economic impacts against effects on wildlife or native peoples). Even more important than the development of such techniques perhaps is the improvement of the process of assessment so that it can adequately reflect the perceptions and value systems of those who are likely to be affected. To the extent that present procedures rely to a considerable degree on the perceptions of professionals as to what the public wants or what it values most, there may be an incorrect evaluation of gains or losses from a given development.[34] One way of overcoming this potential difficulty would be to find more effective ways of involving the public in the evaluation process.

7. Ex-Post Evaluation

Ex-post or hindsight evaluation is a much-needed, but highly neglected, aspect of resources management. Thus far there have been relatively few attempts to assess the performance of resources projects or policies anywhere in the world. As a consequence, programs have often continued, even though it has been uncertain whether they have attained the desired objectives, or whether they have resulted in unpredicted adverse effects.

On the basis of some of the hindsight evaluations that have been done in the water resources field in Canada,[35] it seems that considerable economic, social and environmental losses might have been avoided through systematic *post hoc* assessments. Similar conclusions are arrived at in examining experience in the United States, and in various other parts of the world.[36]

Although the idea of ex-post evaluation has taken a long time to find acceptance, its value is gradually being recognized by various agencies in Canada and the United States, as well as by a number of international bodies, notably the World Bank. Drawing heavily upon the methodological skills and insights into causality testing that are found in the areas of sociology, psychology and economics,[37] a new discipline known as program evaluation (or evaluation research) has emerged. A number of universities in the United States now offer advanced degrees in the subject.

8. Risk Assessment

Experience over the the past two or three decades has shown that Canadians are being subjected to an increasing range of risks, many of which are caused by others, but some of which they are able to respond to and reduce.[38] Some of these risks are economic in nature, such as the purchase of assets like houses or land. Others, illustrated by Foster in Chapter 8, are rooted more in nature, as in the incidence of floods, earthquakes or windstorms. Yet others stem from technological innovation, such as the possibility of contamination from an accident in transportation of chemicals, or in a nuclear power station.

The subject of risk assessment has become a popular area of research, beginning initially in the field of natural hazards, and moving on to consider those which are more man-made in origin.[39] The importance of this field of inquiry is underlined by a number of recent events, notably the Mississauga train disaster and the impact of Mount St. Helens eruption. Risk assessment also will be a valuable analytical perspective to bring to bear when deciding where to locate such noxious facilities as oil terminals and refineries, nuclear power plants and toxic waste disposal sites.[40]

9. Contemplating the Future

The future has generally received very little attention in planning and policy-making processes in Canada. An underlying assumption in most decisions seems to have been that present trends will continue, so that the world of tomorrow will be rather like that of today. Experience shows, however, that things do change over time, sometimes very radically.[41]

There is a growing tendency in several other countries for resource management and development plans to include a consideration of several alternative scenarios of the future. One might consist, for example, of a society which is devoted to the maintenance of a high level of economic growth regardless of the social or ecological costs it might occasion.

Another might be a society in which the attainment of the highest possible level of material well-being is not the most important goal, but rather a state of existence in which economic growth, racial equality and environmental preservation are brought into harmony. Obviously, the resource requirements of these two alternative societies would be vastly different.

Since it must be anticipated that there will be important shifts in social values, innovations in ideas and technology, and alterations in government policies, a critical area of research in resources management should be that of outlining different scenarios of the future. Such investigations will need to draw upon concepts derived from several disciplines and experience in different parts of the world. Geographers should have an important role to play in both connections.

Contributions to the Policy-Making Process

There are many possible ways in which geographers might contribute to the policy-making and implementation processes in resources management. As Figure 1.10 suggests, there are four major phases in these processes, beginning with problem identification and strategy specification, and continuing progressively through policy formulation, implementation and evaluation. Inputs can be made at several levels within each of these phases, ranging from the provision of information or the registering of an opinion, to the actual making of a decision or the implementation of a policy. Figure 1.10 indicates that such inputs may range from continuous and highly important contributions to those which are only occasional and not especially significant in determining the course of events.

A review of roles played by geographers in a number of countries, and especially the United Kingdom, the United States, and Canada, suggests that they have been mainly concerned with the first and third stages of policy evolution, and have been involved more as uninvolved observers, critics or technical advisors, than as policy makers or other politicians.[42] This, of course, is similar to the situation with respect to other professionals. Interestingly, however, some important changes have been taking place in the past decade or so, especially in Canada. One is that there has been an expanding demand for geographers interested in the resources and environmental fields, and especially those with training in various aspects of policy analysis. A major stimulus in this connection has come from the recognition of environmental quality and the need to involve the public more effectively in planning and policy making. Thus, an increasing number of geographers have found employment not only in government agencies dealing with various aspects of environmental management and conservation, but also in the private sector. They have acted in many instances as key persons in the development of environmental protection policies and programs, and in the preparation of environmental impact assessments. They have also often played a leading role in the development of programs for public participation in planning. While much of the work undertaken has emphasized the economic and social dimensions of resources and environmental management, the demand for geographers who have competence in the physical aspects continues to grow as well.

Another development has been the appointment of an increasing number of geographers as technical advisors to government agencies or as members of Advisory Boards, notably those concerned with environmental matters. As this has occurred, the geographical profession has

Table 1.10
Old and New Experts in Planning

Old Expert	New Expert
Solution-oriented (defines a problem in terms of a solution)	*Problem-Oriented* (explores a situation to define the problem)
Bounded	Unbounded
Emphasis on primary effects	Secondary and tertiary effects
Simplifying	Complexifying
Assumption accepting	Assumption challenging
Question-Answering Expertise	*Question-Asking Expertise*
Professional	Extra professional
Error denying	Error embracing
Surprise free	Surprise embracing
System Closing	*System Opening*
Elitist	Democratic
Technocratic	Public
Comforting	Threatening
Conflict masking	Conflict exposing
Produce oriented	Process oriented
Organization Captive	*Boundary Spanning*
Protected	Exposed
"Hired Gun"	Free floating
Institutional	Personal
Client oriented	Issue opportunistic
Politically Explicit	*Politically Ambiguous*
Late in political process	Early in political process
Choice related	Issue formulating
Well-defined expectations	Uncertain expectations

Source: Michael, 1973.

Figure 1.10

STAGES AND LEVELS OF POLICY INVOLVEMENT

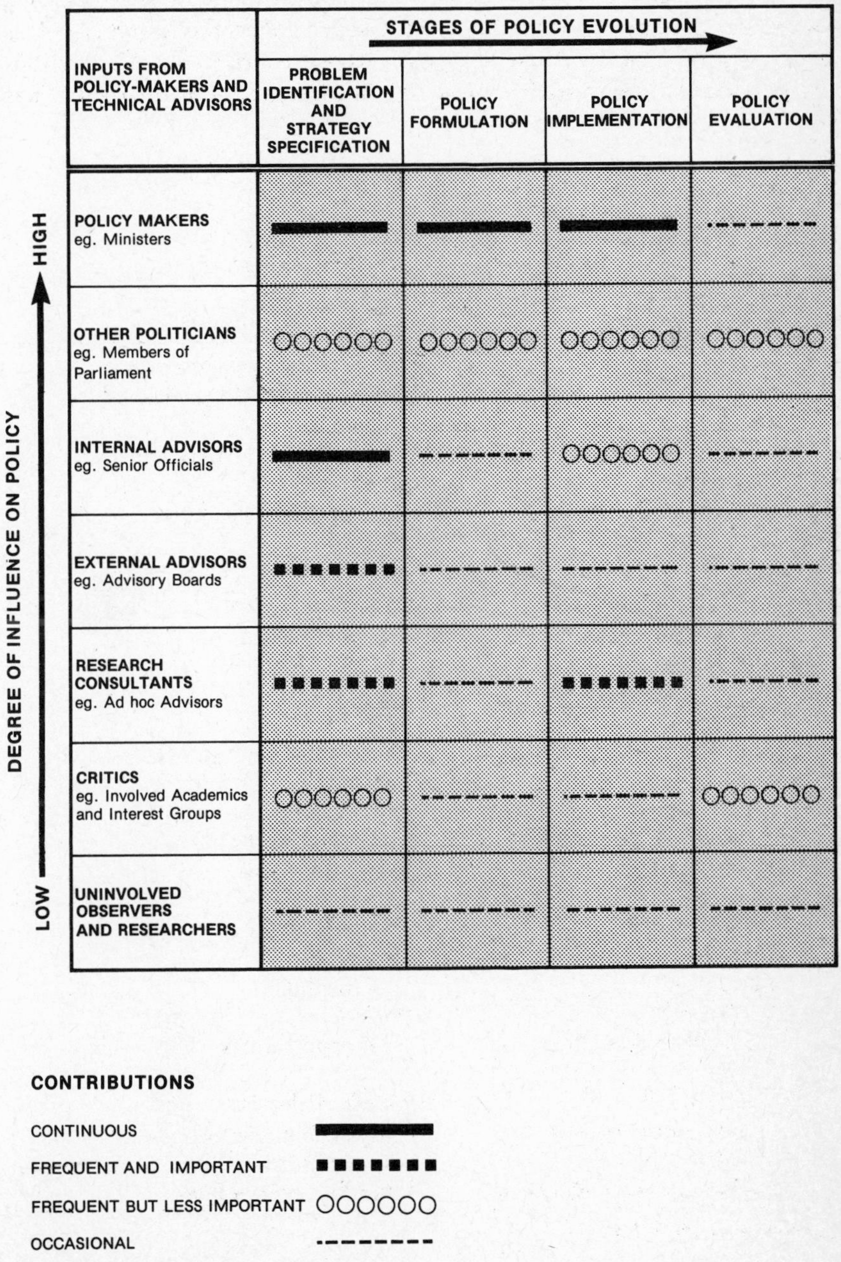

INPUTS FROM POLICY-MAKERS AND TECHNICAL ADVISORS	STAGES OF POLICY EVOLUTION →			
	PROBLEM IDENTIFICATION AND STRATEGY SPECIFICATION	POLICY FORMULATION	POLICY IMPLEMENTATION	POLICY EVALUATION
POLICY MAKERS eg. Ministers	▬▬▬▬	▬▬▬▬	▬▬▬▬	-------
OTHER POLITICIANS eg. Members of Parliament	OOOOOO	OOOOOO	OOOOOO	OOOOOO
INTERNAL ADVISORS eg. Senior Officials	▬▬▬▬	-------	OOOOOO	-------
EXTERNAL ADVISORS eg. Advisory Boards	■■■■■■	-------	-------	-------
RESEARCH CONSULTANTS eg. Ad hoc Advisors	■■■■■■	-------	■■■■■■	-------
CRITICS eg. Involved Academics and Interest Groups	OOOOOO	-------	-------	OOOOOO
UNINVOLVED OBSERVERS AND RESEARCHERS	-------	-------	-------	-------

DEGREE OF INFLUENCE ON POLICY — HIGH ↑ LOW

CONTRIBUTIONS

CONTINUOUS ▬▬▬▬

FREQUENT AND IMPORTANT ■■■■■■

FREQUENT BUT LESS IMPORTANT OOOOOO

OCCASIONAL -------

become more and more influential in the planning and policy process. In many instances, this may have been a recognition of the kind of training geographers receive and the types of problems in which they now interest themselves. It may also be an indication of the tendency to break out of the classical mold of the scientist who isolates himself from the forefront of policy formulation and implementation, preferring instead to work on topics not directly concerned with politics. In contrast, a desire to make their work "socially relevant" doubtless accounts for the fact that many geographers have chosen to work on applied topics of immediate concern to policy makers.

To an important degree, geographers met many of the challenges of the 1970s both in research and in other contributions to planning and policy making. The issues of the 1980s will be even tougher. One thing is very clear. A new breed of experts will be needed. The characteristics of such a breed have been outlined by Donald Michael, in his essay, "On Learning to Plan and Planning to Learn,"[43] and they are summarized in Table 1.10. Developing such a breed will not be easy since many of the attributes are quite opposite to those of the existing experts. Their introduction would certainly shake the present system, but it would also provide an even more exciting and useful role for the scientist (including the geographer) than he enjoys today.

Notes

[1] W.R. Derrick Sewell and Harold D. Foster, *Images of Canadian Futures: The Role of Conservation and Renewable Energy* (Ottawa: Minister of Supply and Services Canada, 1978).

[2] For a discussion of the underlying concepts of the Conserver Society see, Science Council of Canada, *Canada as a Conserver Society: Resource Uncertainties and the Need for New Technologies*, Science Council of Canada Report No. 27 (Ottawa: Minister of Supply and Services, 1977). For an assessment of its differential social impacts, see *Alternatives*, Special Issue on the Conserver Society and Low Income People, Vol. 9, No. 3, Summer/Fall, 1980.

[3] For a view of the implications of the problems of foreign investment in Canada, see A.E. Safarian, *Foreign Ownership of Canadian Industry* (Toronto: McGraw-Hill, 1966); Task Force on the Structure of Canadian Industry, *Foreign Ownership and the Structure of Canadian Industry* (Ottawa: Queen's Printer, 1970); J. Phillip Mathias, *Forced Growth* (Toronto: James Lewis and Samuel, 1971); Government of Canada, *Foreign Direct Investment in Canada* (Ottawa: Information Canada, 1972); A.E. Safarian, "Issues raised by foreign direct investment in Canada," in L.H. Ottice and L.B. Smith, *Issues in Canadian Economics* (Toronto: McGraw-Hill Ryerson, 1974), pp. 80–94; John N.H. Britton, "Industrial impacts of foreign enterprise: a Canadian technological perspective," *Professional Geographer*, Vol. 33, No. 1, 1981, pp. 36–47.

[4] Harold D. Foster and W.R. Derrick Sewell, *Water: The Emerging Crisis in Canada* (Toronto: James Lorimer and Co., 1981).

5 See, "A Push Too Far," *The Vancouver Sun*, August 6, 1980, p. A4.

6 For an excellent discussion of the problems of Canadian–United States relations in resource management policy, see Carl. E. Beigie and Alfred O. Hero, Jr., *Natural Resources in U.S.-Canadian Relations* (Boulder, Colorado: Westview Press, 1980).

7 Canada, Energy, Mines and Resources Canada, *The National Energy Program, 1980* (Ottawa: Minister of Supply and Services, 1980).

8 As an illustration, in 1979–1980 the Department of Energy, Mines and Resources was allocated some $156 million to support research in the energy field. Of this, about $147 million was spent on natural science research and $9 million on human science studies. Over $86 million was allocated to research on nuclear power.

9 The adoption of a conservative view contrasts vividly with the recommendations of several reviews of Canadian energy policy, notably, James E. Gander and Fred W. Belaire, *Energy Futures for Canadians*, Report of a study prepared for Energy, Mines and Resources Canada (Ottawa: Minister of Supply and Services Canada, 1978), and Science Council of Canada, *Roads to Energy Self-Reliance: the Necessary National Demonstrations* (Ottawa: Minister of Supply and Services, 1979).

10 See Sewell and Foster, *op. cit.*

11 Canada, Environment Canada, Inland Waters Directorate, *Water and the Canadian Economy*, Working Paper, Ottawa, April, 1980.

12 See U.S. Water Resources Council, *The Nation's Water Resources* (Washington, D.C.: U.S. Government Printing Office, 1968); and U.S. Water Resources Council, *The Second National Water Assessment* (Washington, D.C.: U.S. Government Printing Office, 1978).

13 See, for example, U.S. National Water Commission, *Water Policies for the Future* (Washington, D.C.: U.S. Government Printing Office, June, 1973).

14 For a review of the licensing program introduced as part of the attempt to rationalize the B.C. salmon fishery, see Bruce Mitchell, "Hindsight Reviews: the British Columbia Licence Programme," in D.V. Ellis, ed., *Pacific Salmon Management for People*, University of Victoria, Department of Geography, Western Geographical Series, Volume 13, Victoria, B.C., 1977, pp. 148–186. See also a recent assessment by Sol Sinclair, on the findings of whose report the original licensing program was based; Sol Sinclair, *A Licensing and Fee System for the Coastal Fisheries of British Columbia*, a report prepared for Canadian Department of Fisheries and Oceans (Vancouver, B.C.: December 1978, 2 vols). Substantial policy changes are described in Government of Canada, Fisheries and Oceans, *Fishermen's Newsletter*, Vol. 3, No. 3, November 1980 (Vancouver, B.C.: Fisheries and Oceans).

15 Bill C-48 is intended to introduce an Act to regulate oil and gas interests in Canada lands and to amend the Oil and Gas Production and Conservation Act.

16 See Canada, Standing Committee on National Resources and Public Works, *Minutes and Proceedings of Evidence*, First Session of the Twenty-second Parliament, 1980–1981 (Ottawa: Canadian Government Publishing Centre 1980–1981).

17 Dorothy Sangster, "Canada's first Disney-style fantasyland," *Canadian Geographic*, Vol. 101, No. 2, 1981, pp. 44–51.

[18] Ralph R. Krueger, "Unity out of diversity: the ruminations of a traditional geographer," *Canadian Geographer*, Vol. 24 (Winter 1980), pp. 341–42.

[19] See A.P. Altschuller and G.A. McBean, *The LRTAP Problem in North America: A Preliminary Overview*, report prepared by the United States–Canada Research Consultation Group on Long Range Transportation of Air Pollutants, Canada, Environment Canada, Atmospheric Environment Service, Downsview, Ontario, October 1979.

[20] See Roy MacGregor, "Acid Rain: Who will Save Our Lakes?" *Maclean's*, Vol. 93, No. 26, 1980, pp. 40–44.

[21] See Lydia Dotto, "What Acid Rain Does to Our Land and Water," *Canadian Geographic*, Vol, 99, No. 3, 1979–1980, pp. 36–41.

[22] See Harvey Babich, Debra Lee Davis and Guenther Stotsky, "Acid Precipitation: Causes and Consequences," *Environment*, Vol. 22, No. 4, 1980, pp. 6–13, and 40–41.

[23] See Phil Weller and the Waterloo Public Interest Research Group, *Acid Rain: the Silent Crisis* (Kitchener, Ontario: Between the Lines and the Waterloo Public Interest Research Group, 1980).

[24] See George S. Wetstone, "The Need for a New Regulatory Approach," *Environment*, Vol. 22, No. 5, 1980, pp. 9–14.

[25] For a stimulating examination of a number of cases involving such new pollutions, see Ross Howard, *Poisons in Public: Case Studies of Environmental Pollution in Canada* (Toronto: James Lorimer and Co., 1980). Mercury pollution is discussed in Fikret Berkes, "The mercury problem: an examination of the scientific basis for policy-making," in *Resources and the Environment: Policy Perspectives for Canada*, ed. O.P. Dwivedi (Toronto: McClelland and Stewart, 1980), pp. 288–305.

[26] Colin Norman, "The World's Research and Development Budget," *Environment*, Vol. 21, No. 10, December 1979, pp. 6–11.

[27] Canada, Ministry of State for Science and Technology, *Federal Science Activities, 1979–1980* (Ottawa: Minister of Supply and Services, Canada, 1979).

[28] Inventories in the United States have been undertaken both by government agencies and by private foundations. Among these have been broad assessments of the resource picture as a whole, such as that undertaken by the U.S. President's Materials Policy Commission, *Resources for Freedom* (Washington, D.C.: U.S. Government Printing Office, 1952). Resource for the Future Inc., *The Nation Looks at its Resources* (Washington, D.C., 1954), and Hans Landsberg et al., *Resources in America's Future: Patterns of Requirements and Availabilities, 1960–2000* (Baltimore, Md: Johns Hopkins Press, 1963).

Other assessments have focussed on particular resources, such as water or energy. See, for example, U.S. Water Resources Council, *op. cit.*; U.S. National Water Commission, *op. cit.*; the Ford Foundation, *A Time to Choose: America's Energy Future* (Cambridge, Mass.: Ballinger Publishing Co., 1974).

[29] Pioneering attempts were made in the 1960s and early 1970s in Canada to improve the sophistication of water demand forecasting techniques. Illustrations of these efforts appear in W.R. Derrick Sewell, Blair T. Bower, et al., *Forecasting the Demands for Water* (Ottawa: Queen's Printer, 1968). The federal

government played an important role in encouraging and in supporting research in this connection, both in universities and in-house. For reviews of these efforts, see Donald M. Tate, *Water Use and Demand Forecasting*, International Institute for Applied Systems Analysis Working Paper, Vienna, December 1977; and W.R. Derrick Sewell and Stephen B. McLellan, *Refinement of Techniques for Water Demand Forecasting: a Review of Some Canadian Contributions*, International Institute for Applied Systems Analysis Working Paper, December 1977.

30 Sewell and Foster, *op. cit.*

31 See, for example, M. Gibbons and R. Voyer, *A Technology Assessment System: A Case Study of East Coast Offshore Petroleum Exploration* (Ottawa: Minister of Supply and Services Canada, 1974); Robert F. Keith et al., *Northern Development and Technology Assessment Systems: a Study of Petroleum Development Programs in the MacKenzie Delta-Beaufort Sea Region and the Arctic Islands* (Ottawa: Minister of Supply and Services, 1976).

32 See Timothy O'Riordan and W.R. Derrick Sewell, eds., *Project Appraisal and Policy Review* (London: John Wiley and Sons Ltd., 1981).

33 See, for example, Kurt Finsterbusch and C.P. Wolf, eds., *Methodology of Social Impact Assessment* (New York: McGraw-Hill Book Co., 1977).

34 See, for example, W.R. Derrick Sewell and B.R. Little, "Specialists, laymen, and the process of environmental appraisal," *Regional Studies*, Vol. 7, July 1973, pp. 161-71.

35 See, for example Helen Buckley and Eva Tihanyi, *Canadian Policies for Rural Adjustment: a Study of the Economic Impact of ARDA, PFRA, and MMRA*, Economic Council of Canada Special Study, No. 7 (Ottawa: Information Canada, 1967); and J.C. Day, "Benefit-Cost Analysis and Multiple Purpose Reservoirs: A Re-assessment of the Conservation Authorities' Branch Deer Creek Project, Ontario," in F.M. Leversedge, ed., *Priorities in Water Management* (Victoria: University of Victoria, Department of Geography, Western Geographical Series, Vol. 8, 1974), pp. 23-26, and Mitchell, *op. cit.*

36 See, for example, Charles Goldman et al., *Environmental Quality and Water Development* (San Francisco: W.H. Freeman and Co., 1973); and John R. King, Jr., *Economic Development Projects and their Appraisal* (Baltimore, Md.: Johns Hopkins Press, 1967).

37 N. Caplan et. al., *The Use of Social Science Knowledge in Policy Decisions at the National Level* (Ann Arbor, Mich.: Institute for Social Research, 1975).

38 For an excellent discussion of decision making in one area of risks, see U.S. National Academy of Sciences, *Decision-Making for Regulating Chemicals in the Environment* (Washington, D.C., 1975).

39 Robert W. Kates, *Risk Assessment of Environmental Hazard*, Scope 8 (Chichester: John Wiley, 1978); Anne Whyte and Ian Burton, *Environmental Risk Assessment*, Scope 15 (New York: Wiley Interscience, 1980).

40 C. Starr, "General philosophy of risk-benefit analysis," in *Energy and the Environment: A Risk Benefit Approach*, ed., H. Ashley, R.L. Rudman and C. Whipple (New York, Pergamon Press, 1976), pp. 1-30.

41 For a discussion of the relevance of the study of the future in policy making in

the resources field, see W.R. Derrick Sewell, "The Changing Context of Water Resources Planning: the Next 25 Years," *Natural Resources Journal*, Vol. 16, No. 4, October 1976, pp. 791-805.

[42] See J.T. Coppock and W.R.D. Sewell, eds., *Spatial Dimensions of Public Policy* (Oxford: Pergamon Press, 1976). For detailed discussions of the role of geographers in public policy in Canada, see especially C.I. Jackson, "Policy Planning in the Government of Canada," in Coppock and Sewell, *op. cit.*, pp. 20-41; and F.K. Hare, "Geography and Public Policy Issues in Canada," in Coppock and Sewell, *op. cit.*, pp. 42-49.

[43] See Donald N. Michael, *On Learning to Plan and Planning to Learn* (San Francisco: Jossey-Bass, Inc., 1973).

Index